Elizabeth and the English Reformation

*The struggle for a
stable settlement of religion*

ELIZABETH AND THE ENGLISH REFORMATION

THE STRUGGLE FOR
A STABLE SETTLEMENT OF
RELIGION

BY

WILLIAM P. HAUGAARD

CAMBRIDGE
AT THE UNIVERSITY PRESS
1968

Published by the Syndics of the Cambridge University Press
Bentley House, 200 Euston Road, London, N.W. 1
American Branch: 32 East 57th Street, New York, N.Y. 10022

Library of Congress Catalogue Card Number: 68-23179

Standard Book Number: 521 07245 X

Printed in Great Britain
at the University Printing House, Cambridge
(Brooke Crutchley, University Printer)

Contents

Preface   *page* vii

1 The Convocation men of 1563   1

    Ecclesiastical independence 4
    Triumph of reform 12
    Return to Rome 20
    Protestant havens abroad 26
    The primacy 32
    The Marian bishops 36
    The episcopal bench in 1563 43
    The variegated Lower House 50

2 The course of Convocation   52

    Convocation gets under way 53
    The accomplishments of the Convocation 62
    The ruin of the reformers' programme 67
    Religious affairs in Parliament 73

3 The liturgy: compromise and constancy   79

    Parliamentary frustration 81
    Easter: Elizabeth's change of tactics 92
    The Prayer Book of 1559 104
    The queen's liturgical modifications 112
    The Prayer Book in the Convocation of 1563 119

4 The Supreme Governor: administration and finance   128

    The statutory Ecclesiastical Commission 130
    The royal visitation and the Injunctions 135
    The Elizabethan Primer 144
    Church buildings: care and conservation 147
    The Crown and church finances 151
    The bishops: visitations and 'interpretations' 162
    The Supreme Governor and the Convocation of 1563 166

Contents

5 The queen and her bishops: images, vestments, and apparel   *page* 183

Crosses and copes 185
Married clerics and an angry queen 200
Vestments and images in the Convocation of 1563 205
The 1565 campaign for conformity 211
The queen and her bishops in the campaign of 1566 224

6 Doctrine: definition and discipline   233

Tentative doctrinal declarations 234
'Apologia Ecclesiae Anglicanae' 242
Adoption of the Thirty-nine Articles 247
An evaluation of the English Articles 258
The new book of homilies 273
Nowell's catechism and doctrinal discipline 277

7 Roman Catholic recusants: diplomacy and forbearance   291

Two papal nuncios 292
Lingering Roman Catholic hopes 302
Early government policy towards Roman Catholics 309
Legislative severity and administrative moderation 317
The queen's policy 324

Epilogue   333

Appendix I The records of the Convocation   342

Appendix II The members of the Lower House and their careers in the reign of Queen Mary   357

List of works cited   360

Index   373

Preface

WAS the age of Elizabeth 'a secular period between two outbreaks of protestantism, a period in which religious enthusiasm was sufficiently dormant' to allow the new humanism to come to the fore? So Professor Tillyard describes a popular assessment of Elizabethan England, an assessment which he judges to be a misleading representation of a period dominated by a 'still solidly theocratic' world picture.[1] This present study of the Elizabethan ecclesiastical settlement is written in the conviction that Professor Tillyard and other contemporary scholars are right in assigning to religion a position of central significance in an understanding of the people of Elizabethan England.

The 'Elizabethan Settlement of Religion' is a descriptive label known to generations of students of history and theology. I should not have the temerity to travel once again such a well-worn road were it not that recent historical studies have suggested that the paving blocks of ecclesiastical history demand not only repair, but some rearrangement as well. Above all, the magisterial work of the constitutional historian John E. Neale on the Elizabethan parliaments (especially the first Parliament of 1559) has made necessary a thorough reassessment of the decisive events which shaped the Church of England during the first decade of Elizabeth's reign. Works which have appeared in the succeeding fifteen years by such men as J. E. Booty, V. J. K. Brook, P. Collinson, P. M. Dawley, A. G. Dickens, C. W. Dugmore, C. Meyer, and W. M. Southgate have clarified various facets of the reassessment, and my intention is that this book should be a further contribution to that historical endeavour.

I have chosen to view the Elizabethan settlement from the vantage-point of the 1563 Convocation partly because the incomplete but informative documents from that synod have seemed to me to tell a story that has not yet been told, and partly because the major

[1] E[ustace] M[andeville] W[etenhall] Tillyard, *The Elizabethan World Picture* (New York), pp. 3-4.

vii

issues and conflicts of the definitive early years of the settlement were largely drawn into the proposals and debates of the Convocation. The negative decisions of this synod were more important than its positive results: what the Convocation rejected is more important than what it adopted. I have chosen to call the nascent puritans by the slightly anachronistic term 'precisians', and it is one of my conclusions, as will appear, that in these clerical meetings they launched a major attack on the shape of the Elizabethan church as it was developing under the guidance of Elizabeth and her chosen bishops. Their proposals would have altered the doctrine, liturgy, and discipline of the Church of England in a manner that could not help but have myriad effects on the immediate course of England's social and political life. In religion, to be sure, the success of the precisians' programme would have drastically altered, if it did not entirely prevent, the development of that variety of Christian faith and practice known today as 'anglicanism'.

The reader may soon perceive that my own sympathies lie with the 'anglican' opponents of the precisians, but at the same time I confess to a certain respect for the tenacity and consistency with which many of these 'precise men' pursued their aims. Their view of the world and of the church was narrow, but it was clear-cut and unquestionably conscientious.

Much of the research for this book was done as a part of the preparation for my doctoral dissertation presented in 1962 at the General Theological Seminary in New York City and entitled: '*Elizabeth I and the Church of England: A study of the Religious Convictions of Elizabeth Tudor and their Influence on the Settlement of the Church of England.*' The studies in preparation for the thesis not only brought me under the spell of that extraordinary woman; they also convinced me of the error of that popular historical judgment, that Elizabeth 'knew much about Christianity, but probably had little religious conviction'. Here again the work of Professor Neale had called attention to evidence that simply was not compatible with the picture of the opportunistic monarch, ready to jettison religious principle for the sake of political advantage. Christianity, as it is known and practised by most anglicans today, resembles in its forms and attitudes the religion of Queen Elizabeth far more closely than it does that of many of her leading clerics in the opening years of her reign. Had she been of a different persuasion, the subsequent development of the English Church would possibly have been quite different. Sixteenth-century Roman Catholics and puritans knew this. The one sought to brand her a machiavellian Jezebel, while the other accused her of being 'neither hot nor cold', and of caring more for the 'trifles' than for the substance of sincere religion. Those judgments were to be expected; more surprising is the way in which many historians have accepted without question the judgment of those who had every motive for impugning Elizabeth's sincerity. Inevitably my conclusions about Elizabeth's convictions have influenced the writing of this present book, and she is probably its most important single figure throughout. Yet, here for the most part, I only ask the reader to consider the queen's consistency in her religious policies; rarely do I glimpse at the motivations which might underlie that consistency. I have focused not on any one person or group of persons, but upon the English *leaders*, queen, clerics, and laymen, whose common work, conflicts, and struggles were to confer on the national church a character which has distinguished it from any other body in Christendom.

II

Historians have used the documents of the 1563 Convocation as they have been printed by John Strype, Gilbert Burnet, and others after them. The manuscripts in the libraries of the Inner Temple and Corpus Christi College, Cambridge have lain largely unused. Although I came to many of my conclusions about the relationship of the documents to one another before examining the originals, I discovered that Strype erred in important details and that the pattern of Convocation becomes clearer when these are taken into consideration. I feel that these documents will prove of value to others and, therefore, I have included in Appendix I a description of each manuscript which, with one exception, includes all the significant errors and omissions of Strype's reproductions. The exception is the manuscript 'Articles for government'. The length of the document would have required a section twice as long as the entire appendix as it is, and so I have regretfully left it out. One important document, the Acts of the Upper House, is only known through the transcription which Edmund Gibson made of it two hundred and fifty years ago. It gives every appearance of being accurate, but I am sure that the manuscript volume of Parker's, for which I have vainly searched, would have more to tell us should it ever be discovered.

I have referred to other original manuscripts which seemed to me to be of particular significance, but the bulk of the rest of my research has been in printed sources comprising both Elizabethan publications and copies of Elizabethan manuscripts. Any revision of historical judgment in a period as thoroughly studied as Elizabethan England requires the student to bring a new set of questions to sixteenth-century sources combed many times before. Fortunately, these sources are available in large numbers.

A close study of the Calendars of State Papers proved most fruitful. The entries in the Domestic Calendar provide little more than descriptive titles, but the Foreign, Spanish, Venetian, and Roman Calendars contain much more complete précis, and they have a larger amount of information to yield to church historians than has previously been noted. The reports of de Quadra, de Silva, and Il Schifanoya, the correspondence between Elizabeth, her government officials, and their representatives abroad, the garnerings of Vatican diplomatic intelligence all provide important contemporary reflections on the events taking place in England, and these help to provide much of the new perspective.

Another reservoir of letters and papers, largely undigested, is found in the works of seventeenth- and eighteenth-century antiquaries. Some of these must be used with caution; for example, Strype used the dubious documents collected by Robert Ware. None the less, Strype and others, such as Bishop Gilbert Burnet, reprinted great quantities of documents that endow their works with a value quite apart from their historical or biographical narrative. Innumerable manuscripts are incorporated in the miscellaneous collections of Hardwicke, Haynes, Lodge, and Peck, and also in the more specialized collections of Forbes and Clifford. The monumental documentary collections of Rymer and Wilkins are still useful for this period together with Cardwell's various collections made in the nineteenth century. Although I have generally followed Neale through the parliamentary records, I have found it helpful to use the printed journals of both houses and D'Ewes' summary.

Such learned and antiquarian associations as the Parker and Camden Societies have made it easy to consult large quantities of sixteenth-century printed works and manuscripts. The county historical societies, the Alcuin Club, and the Surtees Society have similarly made valuable contributions to the work of students, as a glance at *Texts and Calendars* will show. These printed sources sometimes reproduce Elizabethan spelling and other times modernize it; my citations reflect their variations.

I am, of course, indebted to historians from William Camden, through W. H. Frere, to Conyers Read, Christopher Hill, G. R. Elton, and A. L. Rowse, but it is fair to say that the conclusions reached are based on a fresh examination and use of the evidence.

III

Since the focal point of the study is the Convocation of 1563, the first chapter reviews the English Reformation up to 1558 with special reference to the men who later sat in the synod, and then follows the selection of church leaders in the first years of Elizabeth's reign. This sets the stage for the meetings of Convocation, the course of which occupies the second chapter. Then each of the successive chapters considers one particular aspect of the ecclesiastical settlement: Prayer Book; church administration, finances, and discipline; controversy over images, apparel, and vestments; doctrine; and, finally, the policy towards Roman Catholics. With each of these topics, it has been necessary to turn back to the opening months of Elizabeth's reign, then to carry the subject through the 1563 Convocation and to continue the narrative as far as necessary for the establishment of the definitive policy of the Elizabethan church. In the case of the Prayer Book, for example, it was possible to stop the narrative with the 1563 Convocation, whereas the chapter on doctrine required some consideration of events through the Convocation and Parliament of 1571. Since the study deals only with a relatively short period of time, I trust that this topical division will not prove too confusing for the reader. Cross-references are frequently provided in the notes.

IV

The human polarity of the individual and the community is nowhere more plainly evident than in the world of scholarship, and as I come to the end of this study I am acutely aware of those who have contributed to it. My references to published works in the earlier part of this preface and in the footnotes of the succeeding chapters suggest the scope of my debt to others whom I have known only through their books and articles, but I have other less obvious acknowledgments to make.

My own doctoral studies provided the basic background for my work, and these would not have been possible without my appointment as a Fellow and Tutor at the General Theological Seminary. I must express my gratitude not only to the Faculty and Board of Trustees in general, but in particular to the Very Reverend Lawrence Rose who, as Dean, was not only personally a constant source of encouragement, but whose deep concern for serious study played no little part in my decision to leave a satisfying parochial ministry for teaching and historical research. A Rockefeller Doctoral Fellowship in Religion allowed me to devote full time to my studies during the last half of my four years at General. More recently, a grant from the Episcopal Church Foundation allowed me to spend a sabbatical term in England, both commencing the initial searches for a study of Nicholas Heath and examining the manuscript sources of this present book. I am also grateful, of course, to the Dean and Board of Trustees of El Seminario Episcopal del Caribe for their policy of faculty sabbatical leaves.

Dr Niels Henry Sonne and his staff at the St Mark's Library of General Seminary have given me invaluable assistance over the years, and Miss Alison Smith, librarian at the seminary here in

Preface

Puerto Rico, has arranged for innumerable inter-library loans. I wish also to record my thanks to the more anonymous staffs of the New York Public, Union Theological Seminary, Columbia University, the J. Pierpont Morgan, the British Museum, and the University of London libraries, all of which I consulted at various stages of this study. I owe special thanks to Mr W. W. S. Breem, librarian, and to Mr. F. B. Barringer, sub-librarian, of the Inner Temple, and to Professor Bruce Dickins, acting librarian, and Mrs J. Rolfe, assistant librarian, of Corpus Christi College, Cambridge for their courtesies while I was examining at length the documents described in Appendix I. Although my studies in the marvellous working historians' library at the Institute for Historical Research and in the archives of the Public Record Office, Lambeth Palace Library, and the Worcestershire Record Office were primarily directed towards Nicholas Heath, I did discover information relevant to this book, and I am in debt to their staffs.

My colleague, the Rev. James E. Griffiss, read and offered suggestions in an early draft of chapter 6. Dr J. Conway Davis of the Public Record Office identified a letter in the Inner Temple. Dr H. C. Porter of Selwyn College, Cambridge read the entire manuscript, and his critical comments on its form aided me in making the final revision. I join a large company of authors grateful to the staff of the Cambridge University Press for their careful concern in matters textual and stylistic.

My largest expressions of appreciation must be reserved for those two men who, as teachers and exemplars, have held up for me an ideal of rigorous integrity in historical studies: the Rev. Powel M. Dawley and the Rev. Robert S. Bosher. Their patient criticisms of drafts of my doctoral thesis helped more than anything else to instil in me whatever historical sense I may possess. In my subsequent work on this book, Dr Dawley, who had led me to share his own enthusiasm for Elizabethan studies, has repeatedly given me both helpful criticism and timely encouragement. To him I owe a debt that can be understood only by someone fortunate enough to have had the benefit of the same kind of wise guidance.

W. P. H.

List of Abbreviations

Note. Full details of sources cited in the footnotes will be found in the List of works cited on pp. 360–72. The works given below are listed there under the initial letter of the abbreviation.

CPR   *Calendar of the Patent Rolls preserved in the Public Record Office*

CSP, Dom., 1547–80   *Calendar of State Papers, Domestic Series, of the Reigns of Edward VI, Mary, Elizabeth, 1547–80 . . .*

CSP, Dom. Add., 1566–79   *Calendar of State Papers, Domestic Series, of the Reign of Elizabeth, Addenda, 1566–79*

CSP, For.   *Calendar of State Papers, Foreign Series, of the Reign of Elizabeth . . .*

CSP, Rome   *Calendar of State Papers, relating to English Affairs, preserved principally at Rome, in the Vatican Archives and Library*

CSP, Sp.   *Calendar of Letters and State Papers relating to English Affairs, preserved principally in the Archives of Simancas*

CSP, Ven.   *Calendar of State Papers and Manuscripts, relating to English Affairs, existing in the Archives and Collections of Venice and in other Libraries of Northern Italy*

Calvin, CR   John Calvin, *Corpus Reformatorum . . .*

CRS   Catholic Record Society

De Maisse   *A Journal of All that was Accomplished by Monsieur de Maisse Ambassador in England from Henri IV to Queen Elizabeth Anno Domini 1597*

DNB   *The Dictionary of National Biography*

Homilies   *Certain Sermons or Homilies Appointed to be read in Churches in the Time of the Late Queen Elizabeth of Famous Memory and Now Thought to be reprinted . . .*

JHC   *Journals of the House of Commons*

JHL   *Journals of the House of Lords*

OL   *Original Letters relative to the English Reformation . . .*

Prayer Books   *The First and Second Prayer Books of Edward VI*

List of Abbreviations

STC   *A Short Title Catalogue of Books Printed in England, Scotland, and Ireland, and of English Books Printed Abroad, 1475–1640*

Troubles at Frankfort   *A Brief Discourse of the Troubles Begun at Frankfort in the Year 1554, About the Book of Common Prayer and Ceremonies*

ZL   *The Zurich Letters, Comprising the Correspondence of Several English Bishops and others with some of the Helvetian Reformers, during...the Reign of Queen Elizabeth*

1. The Convocation men of 1563

AT about eight o'clock Wednesday morning, 13 January 1563, Archbishop Matthew Parker of Canterbury, accompanied by Bishop Nicholas Bullingham of Lincoln, stepped off his barge at Paul's Wharf on the Thames. Joined by the group of officials who had come to meet him, he walked the short distance to the south entrance of St Paul's where the surpliced cathedral choir waited to lead him through the church to the vestry. After the primate had put on his Convocation robes, he was conducted to the dean's stall in the choir. The other diocesan bishops of the provinces were already in stalls on both sides of the choir, and the clergy of the Lower House of Convocation were in their places near by.[1]

These men were about to begin a struggle—a struggle largely obscured by the formal procedures of a Convocation of Canterbury, but a struggle, none the less, whose outcome determined the direction of the future course of the Church of England. Many of the clergy who stood for the archbishop's entrance that winter morning earnestly prayed and confidently expected that this synod would complete the reforms which had been initiated by Parliament and Queen Elizabeth in 1559. Nine months earlier one of the bishops, John Parkhurst of Norwich, had written to Bullinger in Zurich: 'Religion is in the same state among us as heretofore; a state, I say, not altogether to be thought lightly of. But I hope for an improvement at the approaching convocation. There are in England many good and zealous men; there are many too cold, and not a few lukewarm, whom the Lord will spue out of his mouth.'[2]

[1] Edward Cardwell, *Synodalia, A Collection of Articles of Religion, Canons, and Proceedings of Convocations in the Province of Canterbury from the Year 1547 to the Year 1717*, 2 vols. (Oxford, 1842), II, 497 f. All nineteen living bishops of the Province were present, except for the ailing Kitchin of Llandaff who was to die about 31 October 1563 (William Stubbs, *Registrum Sacrum Anglicanum* [Oxford, 1897], under Llandaff).

[2] *The Zurich Letters, Comprising the Correspondence of Several English Bishops and others with some of the Helvetian Reformers, during...the Reign of Queen Elizabeth*, 2 vols., ed. Hastings Robinson (Cambridge, 1842 and 1845; hereafter called ZL), I, 108. Parkhurst to Bullinger, 28 April 1562.

I

I

HET

We may well imagine that Bishop Parkhurst and other Convocation men who shared his hopes looked about the cathedral to estimate the strength of the 'good and zealous' men against those whom they judged to be cold or lukewarm.

Four years later two zealous Englishmen expressed their dismay at the results of the 1563 Convocation in another letter to Zurich reformers. Complaining of the popish remains in their church, they cited this synod which had adopted 'many things of the greatest advantage to the church' that were subsequently 'suppressed and never saw the light'. They went on to describe a scene in the last session of Convocation in which a 'certain most learned man', connected with Bishop Parkhurst, had proposed what they termed 'our case'. Another of the bishops 'interrupted him saying, "What are these things to you? We begun this matter, and we will make an end of it." [The learned man] made answer, "We thought the queen was the author of this business, but we now perceive that you yourselves are", and so they would not suffer the matter to be brought forward.'[1] According to these militant reformers, the bishops in Convocation had suppressed the godly reforms which many of its other members sought to introduce into the English Church.

To return to St Paul's as the Convocation awaited the opening words of the English litany, whatever mixtures of hope and fearfulness, zeal and conviction, concern and indifference may have filled the members' minds, surely few of them could have failed to realize the potential significance of this first Convocation in the reformed Elizabethan church. As usual in England, it was to be this southern Convocation, comprising four-fifths of the English dioceses, which determined matters for the entire church.[2] Inevitably most of the major and minor issues concerning the recent ecclesiastical settlement were to find their way into the proposals and discussions of the ensuing sessions. For us today, the Convocation of

[1] *ZL*, II, 150, George Withers and John Barthelot to Bullinger and Gualter, February 1567 (see p. x). The translator introduced an ambiguity which suggests that this incident might have occurred at the 1566 Convocation, but the Latin seems to refer to 1563 (see p. 89 of the Latin section).

[2] E. W. Kemp, *Counsel and Consent* (London, 1961), p. 118.

1563 provides a convenient vantage-point from which to view the settlement of religion in these early determinative years of Elizabeth's reign.

Who were these men gathered in St Paul's for the opening of Convocation? Knowledge of the past experiences and convictions of these leaders provides one of the keys to an understanding of the Elizabethan settlement. Legislation and liturgies do not stand by themselves; men minister and administer and interpret them, and the mass of common people respond in ways which inevitably influence the actions of their leaders.

The Elizabethan settlement did not arise out of a vacuum. The English Church passed through the most turbulent period of its life in the thirty years before Elizabeth began to rule. Her reign brought a stability solidly based upon a unique combination of elements drawn from that church's recent and more distant past. Two generations after Elizabeth's death, the civil war would reveal the uncertain underpinnings of a stability resting upon imposed religious uniformity, but, by that time, the terms of the Elizabethan settlement had become embedded in a self-conscious and distinct Christian tradition. The peculiar ways of the Church of England were then secured even if all Englishmen could not be persuaded of their superiority to other traditions. Not in 1558! Elizabeth inherited thirty years of religious change and counter-change, and only a rash historian would claim that the Elizabethan church was the inevitable—or even the logical—outgrowth of events earlier in the century.

The men in the 1563 Convocation did not read their knowledge of England's recent past out of a history book. They were themselves a part of that history. If we are to understand a little of their plans and hopes, we need to recall some of the events which had helped to shape their lives, their hopes, and their conflicts. We can also learn from others, absent in 1563, who had shared in the leadership of the English Church in earlier years. Six of the bishops of Queen Mary's reign were in the Tower, just a mile away from St Paul's; one was just across London Bridge in the Marshalsea prison; another, within a few blocks, locked up in the Fleet; another enjoyed a restricted freedom at large; and a tenth had fled to safety abroad. The distribution of the Convocation men between the two houses also merits our reflection, for some whose reputation and abilities might have marked them out for the highest ecclesiastical responsibilities were sitting not in the choir with the bishops, but near by in lower echelons of leadership. In trying to recall some of the common past experiences of these men, we shall grasp more of the character of their problems and the heritage of the church which they helped to mould at a critical moment in her life. In the reigns of Henry, Edward, and Mary Tudor, the church and the men who served her had known moments of profound agony, and, from their several standpoints, moments of spiritual triumph.

ECCLESIASTICAL INDEPENDENCE

Although the religious life of most Englishmen remained substantially unchanged during the reign of Henry VIII, the foundations for more thorough-going reforms were laid during the last fifteen years of his rule.[1] Then it was that the English Church repudiated the bonds of obedience to the see of Rome, dissolved her monastic communities, promulgated the English Bible, and took the first tentative steps in the reform of her doctrine and liturgy.

With the encouragement and prodding of Henry and his ministers, Parliament freed the English Church from Rome in a remarkable series of acts which began with the tentative conditional restraint of papal taxes in 1532 and culminated in the supremacy act of 1534 which declared Henry ' *supremum caput*' of the Church of England. The Convocations acquiesced by acknowledging royal supremacy, including the king's right to license their meetings and to veto their

[1] Among the many studies of the English Reformation, none is more up-to-date, convincing, and readable than A. G. Dickens, *The English Reformation* (New York, 1964). Biographical information about the 1563 ecclesiastics is largely drawn from standard studies and in particular from the *DNB* and Foster's and Venn's accounts of university graduates: *The Dictionary of National Biography*, ed. Leslie Stephen and Sidney Lee (London, 1885–1900); Joseph Foster, *Alumni Oxonienses: The Members of the University of Oxford, 1500–1715*, 4 vols. (Oxford, 1891); and John and J. A. Venn, *Alumni Cantabrigienses: A Biographical List of...the University of Cambridge ...to 1900*, Part I (to 1751), 4 vols. (Cambridge, 1927).

canonical legislation, and by declaring that neither pope nor any other foreign bishop had rightful authority over the English Church. Although most of the Convocation men of 1563 had been in childhood or at too early a stage in their clerical careers to have taken much part in these official affairs, many had been vitally interested onlookers.

Inextricably bound up with the repudiation of Rome was Henry's divorce, motivated jointly by his passion for Anne Boleyn, by the country's need for a male heir to the throne, and by his own rationalized, but probably sincere conviction that his twenty-year marriage to Catherine of Aragon contravened divine law. Several of the Marian bishops imprisoned in 1563 had taken an active part in the divorce proceedings. Bishop Bonner, in the Marshalsea in 1563, had risen in the service of Cardinal Wolsey, and after his master's fall from royal grace he had continued futile threats and pleas at the papal court on behalf of Henry until 1533. As a loyal supporter of royal supremacy, Bonner contributed a preface to the second edition of Stephen Gardiner's *De Vera Obedientia*, the most significant theological treatise in defence of that supremacy. Two of the deprived bishops in the Tower in 1563 had also willingly justified Henry's proceedings abroad: Thomas Thirlby at the court of Charles V, and Nicholas Heath on embassies to Luther and to the princes of the Augsburg Confession.

Only a very few Englishmen had openly opposed English ecclesiastical independence under Henry. Thomas Goldwell, who in 1563 attended not Convocation but the Council of Trent, had, in the early thirties, settled down in Padua with Reginald Pole. Both were attainted for high treason in 1539. Richard Pate, in the Tower during the 1563 Convocation, had sought refuge at the court of Charles V in 1540 where he was serving as Henry's ambassador.[1] A few years later the pope had named and consecrated him titular bishop of Worcester. At home in England other clerics silently nurtured convictions of papal loyalty similar to those of these men who defied English law from the safety of continental havens.

---

[1] *State Papers Published under the Authority of His Majesty's Commission, Henry VIII,* 11 vols. (1830–52), VIII, 490 and 507. Pate to Gardiner and Knevet and Charles V to Henry VIII, 1 and 27 December 1540.

Some men in 1563 could remember the events surrounding Henry's divorce and remarriage as the occasions for their own change in fortunes. Both Nicholas Heath, in the Tower, and William Barlow, in the choir of St Paul's, probably owed important preferments to the goodwill of the family of Anne Boleyn.[1] Archbishop Matthew Parker had an even closer tie to the mother of Elizabeth, for it was she that brought him to court as her chaplain and then preferred him to his first academic administrative post as dean of the college of Stoke Clare. Parker handsomely survived his patroness's downfall, for Henry made him his own chaplain in 1537 and commended him to the fellows of Corpus Christi College, Cambridge, to be their master in 1544. In 1559 Parker wrote with warm affection of 'what words her grace's mother said to me of her, not six days before her apprehension'. We may doubt the spiritual benefits that Elizabeth received at the tender ages of two and seven from Parker's sermons, but we cannot question their importance to the preacher, who made due record of them in his sparse autobiographical notes.[2]

The divorce had also brought to the primacy Thomas Cranmer, the most important clerical figure in the English Reformation. Firmly, even dogmatically dedicated to royal supremacy, Cranmer faithfully served Henry, but at the same time he exerted a steady, if tempered, pressure on behalf of religious reform. Nicholas Heath, Owen Oglethorpe, and David Pole among the Marian bishops, and John Scory, Nicholas Bullingham, and Richard Cox among the Elizabethans in Convocation had all at one time or another been protégés of Cranmer.

If an Englishman had been asked at the end of Henry's reign to name the biggest change in church life, he might well have pointed to the loss of the monasteries. Henry's able minister, Thomas Cromwell, saw in the monastic properties an opportunity to re-

---

[1] For the confusing facts of the various clerical Barlows, see E. Gordon Rupp, *Studies in the Making of the English Protestant Tradition* (Cambridge, 1949), pp. 62–72.

[2] John Strype, *The Life and Acts of Matthew Parker*, 3 vols. (Oxford, 1821), III, 269–307, the 'Matthaeus'; *Correspondence of Matthew Parker*, ed. John Bruce (Cambridge, 1853), pp. vi–x and 481–4, autobiographical memoranda; p. 59, Parker to Bacon, 1 March 1559.

plenish an ever-dwindling national treasury, and applying his administrative skill to the task in 1535, he had the houses investigated, the appropriate legislation passed, and the communities themselves dissolved within five years. John Salisbury, a former abbot who came to the 1563 Convocation as dean of Norwich, had been initially put in that post in 1539 as the first head of the newly secularized cathedral chapter. Thomas Thirlby, in the Tower in 1563, had been named bishop of Westminster, one of six new dioceses founded on monastic funds.

The English religious houses contributed only a small number of leaders to the church. Of the deprived Marian bishops, only Thomas Goldwell had belonged to a religious order, and he not to an English house, but to the Italian Theatines whose recent foundation marked one of the first stirrings of the Counter-Reformation. The deprived bishops' companion in the Tower, John Feckenham, Mary's Benedictine abbot of Westminster, was the only distinguished Marian leader to emerge from monastic origins. Among the Elizabethan bishops, John Scory had begun his vocation as a Dominican friar, and William Barlow and Anthony Kitchin were both former Benedictine abbots whom Henry moved into the episcopate. In the Lower House of the 1563 Convocation, scarcely more than a half-dozen men, including the zealous reformer John Bale, left records of earlier monastic profession.[1] Outside Convocation, one eminent ex-Augustinian, Miles Coverdale, remained unbeneficed in 1563. Neither papal adherents, zealous reformers, nor the moderates in 1563 drew much strength from men who had once made vows of religion.

Both the repudiation of papal authority and the suppression of the monasteries aligned England with continental protestants, but Henry had been given the title 'Defender of the Faith' for his book against Luther, and he had no intention of allowing foreign 'heresies' in England. Early English protestantism was most intensively

---

[1] In addition to the former Carmelite John Bale and the former Benedictine John Salisbury, Gregory Dodds and possibly Thomas Bolt had been Dominicans, James Procter had been a Cistercian, and Thomas Huet and possibly John Lawrence had also been Benedictines.

concentrated in that group of Englishmen who lived and worked abroad during parts of Henry's reign. William Tyndale, John Frith, Miles Coverdale, and others prepared vernacular versions of the Bible, translated writings of the continental reformers, and produced their own polemical works. Some of these men, including Tyndale and Frith, died in fires lit by Roman Catholics abroad or by fellow-Englishmen when they ventured home. Coverdale missed the flames of martyrdom, but his writings were condemned at the end of Henry's reign. The same list of heretical works included writings of John Bale, the ex-Carmelite who had fled England in 1540 and who sat in Convocation in 1563. Two others in the Elizabethan Convocation had also seen their writings committed to the flames during the last years of Henry's reign, although they had not left English shores: Thomas Becon and Robert Wisdom.[1]

The writings and examples of such men inspired many of their fellow-countrymen with zeal for religious reform, but most of the actual substance of reform in the Henrician church itself was achieved through the patient efforts of men of a milder stamp. Like Archbishop Cranmer himself, these men tended to evolve and mature their theological reforms even while they shouldered responsibilities within the largely unreformed church. They accepted the limits which Henry imposed on reform, even while they continually strove to extend them. Matthew Parker, William Barlow, and Richard Cox of the 1563 Convocation had all been sufficiently advanced in their clerical careers to share responsibilities in this work.

The symbol of the continental Reformation, the vernacular scriptures, secured its place in the English Church under Henry. The official Great Bible of 1539 was based on the translations of the voluntary exiles, and Miles Coverdale was himself entrusted with the revision. Two of the Marian bishops alive at Elizabeth's accession,

---

[1] For the theology and relationships of the early reformers, see William A. Clebsch, *England's Earliest Protestants* (New Haven, 1964); for lists of heretical books, see John Foxe, *Acts and Monuments*, ed. Stephen Reed Cattley, 8 vols. (London, 1839), v, 563; on Wisdom and Becon, see Foxe, v, 448 and 696; Charles Wriothesley, *A Chronicle of England...from A.D. 1435 to 1559*, ed. W. D. Hamilton, 2 vols., Camden Society, 2nd series, nos. xi and xxvi (London, 1875–7), I, 142; Becon, *Works*, ed. John Eyre, 2 vols. (Cambridge, 1844), pp. 422–3.

Heath and Cuthbert Tunstall, had shared with Cranmer the oversight of the Great Bible.

The royal injunctions promulgated by Henry not only established the English Bible, but also ordered more regular preaching, mildly curbed excesses of the cult of the saints, and insisted that pastors teach the vernacular Creed, the Our Father, and the Ten Commandments.

One of the minor Henrician innovations, the official Primer of 1545, may have had more influence than has commonly been recognized on the generation which supplied the leaders in Elizabeth's reign. The Primers, both in Latin and the vernacular, were laymen's devotional books. Built around the liturgical hours of Our Lady, they usually also included the seven penitential psalms, the fifteen gradual psalms, the litany of the saints, the *dirige* or office for the dead, and a variety of occasional prayers. Although the Primers traditionally reflected a popular taste for florid and even superstitious devotions, in the late thirties several Primers appeared under the influence of the movement for reform.[1]

The title of Henry's 1545 Primer ordered that it 'be taught, learned, and read, and none other to be used'. Although it contained almost all the medieval constituents, the book bore signs of reform. Its litany was Cranmer's reformed English litany, the calendar was drastically pruned, and the *dirige* had lost so much of its penitential material that a modern commentator terms it 'the most triumphant and cheerful *Dirige* on record'. The book accurately expressed, on the devotional level, the spirit of Henry's national traditional catholicism.[2]

Parliament also accurately expressed Henry's convictions when they declared in 1534 that they did not intend 'to decline or vary... in any things concerning the very articles of the catholic faith'. As

---

[1] Rouen Primers, the Bydell-Marshall Primers, and Bishop Hilsey's Primer; Edgar Hoskyns, *Horae Beatae Mariae Virginis, or, Sarum and York Primers with Kindred Books and Primers of the Reformed Roman Use* (London, 1901), pp. x–xiv, 159–75, and 195–234; Helen C. White, *The Tudor Books of Private Devotion* (University of Wisconsin, 1951), pp. 56, 72–80, and 100–1.

[2] *The Primer...set forth by the King's Majesty, and his clergy: to be taught, learned, and read, and none other to be used throughout all his dominions* (Grafton, 1545), *STC* no. 16034; for summary and comment, see Hoskyns, pp. 237–44 and White, pp. 108–13.

long as men agreed as to the contents of the 'catholic faith', no problem would arise. But theology in the sixteenth century raised that very problem with an intensity unknown since the great Christological controversies of the first centuries of the church. Gradually the clerics who advised the king tended to gravitate either to the conservative group, most consistently led by Bishop Stephen Gardiner, or to the reformers around Archbishop Cranmer. By and large, conservatives had sufficient support from Henry to keep the official doctrinal statements of the church free from those teachings which they thought heretical, but signs of the struggle left their mark on a succession of formulae in the last decade of the reign.

Henry's diplomatic negotiations with the German Lutheran princes influenced these formulae, and the king's embassy, which included Heath, sought doctrinal accommodations with Luther and Melanchthon. 'Ten Articles' of 1536, which were susceptible of a mildly Lutheran interpretation, bore the approval of Convocation and king. Among the signatures appear the names of David Pole and Edmund Bonner, deprived Marian bishops in 1563; William Barlow and Anthony Kitchin, Elizabethan diocesan bishops; and George Carew, dean of Elizabeth's chapel and a perennial Convocation man. The commission which issued the more conservative Bishops' Book a year later included Heath and Bonner in addition to three Convocation men of 1563, Barlow, Richard Cox, and Nicholas Wotton. A theological delegation from Germany came to London in 1538, and their discussions with their English counterparts produced an unofficial and unpublished set of Thirteen Articles.[1] When

[1] The best account of the historical development of the various sets of articles of religion remains the out-of-date book by Charles Hardwick, with its useful appended documents: *A History of the Articles of Religion* (London, 1895). Two recent accounts of the German negotiations: Edwin Doernburg, *Henry VIII and Luther* (Stanford, 1961) and Neelak Serawlook Tjernagel, *Henry VIII and the Lutherans* (St Louis, 1965). The signatures to the Ten Articles (BM, Cotton MSS, Cleopatra E 5, fos. 72a–74b) are reproduced by Gilbert Burnet, *The History of the Reformation of the Church of England*, 7 vols., ed. Nicholas Pocock (Oxford, 1865), IV, 286–9. The signatures to the letter accompanying the Bishops' Book are in David Wilkins, *Concilia Magnae Britanniae et Hiberniae...*, 4 vols. (London, 1737), III, 830.

Convocation obediently approved the six conservative articles enforced in a parliamentary act of 1539, three of the deprived Marian bishops favoured the measure: Heath, Pate, and David Pole.[1]

Doctrine in the Henrician church reached a resting point in the King's Book of 1543, which carried the full authority of Convocation, Parliament, and king. Heath, Barlow, and Cox had all participated in the framing of the book. Although unquestionably conservative in its theological orientation, more than one passage in the book shows the balancing influence of the reforming party.

Men in and out of the Convocation in 1563 had either watched or actively participated in the shaping of the independent national church under Henry VIII. Five Henrician bishops were still alive in 1563: Barlow and Kitchin on the Elizabethan bench, and Heath, Bonner, and Thirlby in prison. Other men such as Parker, Cox, Carew, Salisbury, and David Pole had only slightly less important posts during Henry's reign. A large proportion of the Elizabethans had been theologically nurtured within the Henrician church. All of the Elizabethan bishops had at least gone as far as their first university degree during Henry's reign, and so had more than two-thirds of the Lower House members with identifiable degrees.[2] Ten of the bishops and over twenty Lower House members had been elected fellows of their colleges in Henry's reign and must have participated in many theological discussions of current church policies. Almost one-half of the bishops and one-third of the Lower House had received at least one benefice before Henry's death and so were already launched in their clerical careers.

These men intimately knew the controversies and the achievements of the Henrician church. They knew that repudiation of papal authority did not automatically require the adoption of the teaching and practices of continental reformers. They knew that ecclesiastical independence did not preclude substantial continuity with the past. They had been schooled in the habit of appeal to historical precedent

[1] *Letters and Papers, Foreign and Domestic, of the Reign of Henry VIII*, xiv, ed. James Gairdner (London, 1895), part i, no. 1065.

[2] For convenience I include the Elizabethan bishops of both provinces, but only the Lower House members of the southern province; we know nothing of Barlow's degrees.

and the church fathers in opposing Roman claims. They had also tasted those initial reforms which had whetted the appetites of many for more ample reforming fare. The traditional catholicism of the Henrician church was very much a part of the living memory of the 1563 Convocation.

TRIUMPH OF REFORM

All the men sitting in the 1563 Convocation could remember the changes of direction taken when the boy King Edward sat on the throne of England. Religious reform began within six months of the beginning of the reign, and new reforms were still being introduced six years later when the king's death brought them all to a sudden halt. The central place of the Prayer Book in the Church of England gives the succession of liturgical reforms a peculiar interest, but changes in the exercise of royal supremacy and changes in doctrine were no less a part of men's memory in 1563.

In the first year the Privy Council, ruling in the name of the king, altered the ordinary liturgical and devotional life of Englishmen more than Henry had ever done or permitted. Injunctions, largely brand new, accompanied a royal visitation of the kingdom. These introduced a series of reforms which prescribed a greater use of English scripture in church services and ordered the destruction of images which gave occasion to 'idolatry'. The following year the Council used the difficulty of determining such images as an excuse for ordering wholesale iconoclasm. A number of the bishops may have disliked the new rules, but only Bonner and Gardiner whole-heartedly opposed them. Both were sent to the Fleet prison, until Bonner, at least, agreed to enforce the injunctions.

At the behest of the government, Parliament passed a bill ordering holy communion to be given in two kinds. In implementing the act, the Council took the opportunity to introduce into the Latin Mass the 1548 'Order of Communion', a series of vernacular devotions which later became an integral part of the Prayer Book Eucharist. In the House of Lords, Barlow favoured the act, whereas Bonner and Heath recorded their opposition.

Triumph of reform

The first Prayer Book of 1549 reformed the traditional services by replacing Latin with English, by eliminating many old ceremonies, and by changing certain theological emphases of the rites. In the debates in the Lords, Barlow actively supported the book, but Bonner, Heath, and Thirlby all defended transubstantiation in the debates and recorded their dissent from the first Act of Uniformity. Kitchin tacitly went along with the reformed liturgy.[1] The Elizabethan bishop Richard Cox had been one of Cranmer's assistants in drafting the book.

Bonner resisted the introduction of the Prayer Book and was once again arrested. Although he finally agreed to use the new liturgy, he failed to satisfy the government, and so was left in the Marshalsea where he again lodged in 1563. Heath, Thirlby, and Kitchin all enforced the new liturgy in their dioceses. Two other Marian bishops, Pole and Bourne, as archdeacons, were presumably responsible for its use on their circuits. Thirlby was even put on a commission in 1551 for the enforcement of the Prayer Book along with a number of men who in 1563 held seats in Convocation: John Scory, Matthew Parker, Nicholas Bullingham, Richard Cox, and Nicholas Wotton.

Nicholas Heath, named to the committee for drawing up a new Ordinal, refused to subscribe to the reformed rite drawn up by other committee members. The government sent him to the Fleet in 1550 for his first experience of imprisonment and deprived him of his see a year later.[2] Heath's successor at Worcester, John Hooper, required a period of imprisonment himself before he would consent to be consecrated in the traditional episcopal vestments. Thomas Sampson, who sat in Convocation in 1563, had indeed been ordained priest in 1549 without the rubrical vestments, but Cranmer would not brook such outright vestiarian defiance in a bishop. Hooper had been a close friend of John Parkhurst, the Elizabethan bishop, who hoped for reform in the 1563 Convocation.

[1] For votes on the Order of Communion, and on the 1549 and 1552 Prayer Books, see *Journals of the House of Lords: Beginning Anno Primo Henrici Octavo* (hereafter called *JHL*), I, 306, 331, and 421.

[2] John Roche Dasent, ed., *Acts of the Privy Council of England*, n.s. vols. II–VII (1547–70; London, 1890–3), III, 361, 22 September 1551.

13

The first major revision of the king's Primer appeared in 1551—a publication that has been largely unnoticed in Reformation histories. A response to a parliamentary act for reform of devotional books, the 1551 Primer was infused with the spirit of the first Prayer Book. Englishmen might pray that 'light perpetual' might shine upon the departed, but not that God might 'purge them all their sins'. The seven liturgical hours retained their traditional structure, but minor alterations changed the emphasis to praise of Christ rather than of his mother. The 1551 Primer was a reformed book, but any casual observer would recognize its ancestry in the medieval book of hours.[1]

Less than nine months before Edward VI died, Englishmen heard a new revision of their vernacular liturgy read in their churches. To the 1549 rites, Cranmer added didactic exhortations, simplified ceremonies and vestments, and rearranged the Eucharist to move the English Lord's Supper a further step away from the Latin Mass. Scory and Kitchin were absent from the House of Lords in the division on the new Prayer Book, but Barlow supported it. Heath and Bonner were in prison, but Thirlby attended the Lords to register his dissent once again. Cranmer stubbornly refused a last-minute Council request to eliminate kneeling to receive communion, but he did agree to an added rubric in black print which declared that kneeling implied no 'real or essential presence' of Christ in the eucharistic elements.

A new devotional manual appeared at the very end of Edward's reign entitled *A Primer or Book of Private Prayer*. In spite of the title, the book does not belong to the genre of earlier Primers. Lacking almost all the major traditional elements, the new book was actually the 1552 Prayer Book itself adapted for private use. Devotions based on Morning and Evening Prayer replaced the liturgical hours. The editor followed the Prayer Book so slavishly that even the priest's absolution followed the general confession with personal pronouns changed from 'you' and 'your' to 'my' and 'me'. Whereas the 1545 Primer and its 1551 revision had largely drawn on ancient and medieval sources for occasional prayers, the 1553 book had a wide

[1] *Statutes of the Realm*, IV (London, 1819), pp. 110–11, 3° and 4° Edward VI, c. 10; 1551 revised Primer, *STC* no. 16053 (also nos. 16054 and 16057).

selection of Reformation composition. The publication marked the high point of protestant influence on official devotional books in sixteenth-century England.[1]

The liturgical and devotional reforms of Edward's reign were largely enacted and enforced by the Privy Council, who exercised the royal supremacy on behalf of the king. One measure of the Council's control of ecclesiastical affairs can be found in their cavalier treatment of the episcopate. By the time that Barlow, Scory, and Coverdale were named to various bishoprics, Edward's Council was appointing them by simple letters patent from the king in place of the traditional election of the king's nominee by the cathedral chapter. Two members of the Lower House of the 1563 Convocation, John Bale and Thomas Lancaster, had been similarly named to Irish dioceses. The Council deprived five bishops, including Bonner and Heath, of their dioceses.

The wealth of the church aroused the acquisitive instincts of the Council. Edward's government needed funds, and the personal cupidity of councillors has seldom been exceeded. After the government exhausted the funds seized in 1547 from chantries and other religious corporations, they turned elsewhere. After Bonner's deprivation, Ridley took over the diocese of London at a substantially reduced income. The wealthy diocese of Winchester was yet more severely treated when John Poynet accepted a modest yearly stipend after the deprivation of Gardiner. The Council suppressed two of Henry's new dioceses, reuniting Westminster with London and attaching Gloucester again to Worcester. To facilitate the former move, Thomas Thirlby obligingly accepted his translation from Westminster to Norwich. After the Council deprived Bishop Tunstall of Durham, they secured legislation to divide the wealthy diocese, to seize its income, and to grant moderate stipends to its new bishops. One Elizabethan bishop, Robert Horn, earned Dudley's ire for refusing a mitre on such terms.

The Council's treatment of bishops and financial depredations

[1] *STC* no. 20373; conveniently reprinted in the Parker Society edition by Joseph Ketley, *The Two Liturgies...of King Edward VI* (Cambridge, 1844), pp. 357–484; Hoskyns, *Horae*, pp. 290–5; White, *Tudor Books*, pp. 121–2.

illustrate the fundamental opportunism of their church policies, an opportunism far more pronounced in the régime of Northumberland than in that of Somerset. Convocation was entirely ineffective during Edward's reign, and it was not even formally consulted on most of the vital religious decisions made. Henry had bullied, coerced, and dominated Convocation. For a period he had used his lay vicar-general for the purpose, yet Henry had kept the traditional ecclesiastical machinery intact. Cranmer's role, indeed even his leadership, in the ecclesiastical decisions of Edward's Council could not assure the church any measure of consistent integrity. The day-to-day policies of the church became matters not only for Council discussions, but for immediate Council decision and action. Inevitably current political expediencies dictated religious policies to a degree quite unknown in the previous reign. Edward's Council attempted to reduce the church, as an institution, to the level of a governmental ministry of religion.

English reformers had long favoured clerical marriage in principle and in practice. Many of the men sitting in the 1563 Convocation had married in Edward's reign. Archbishop Parker himself took his wife just as soon as Parliament had repealed the penalties in the Six Articles Act. When in 1549 Parliament enacted a measure putting England on statutory record against the western canonical requirement of clerical celibacy, Bonner, Heath, and Tunstall opposed it; favouring it were Thirlby, in the Tower in 1563, and Barlow, who sat in Convocation.[1]

The 1547 Parliament cleared the deck of doctrinal formularies by setting aside not only the Six Articles, but the King's Book as well. Among their new injunctions, the Privy Council ordered all clerics with insufficient ability and education for preaching to read each Sunday from the newly issued Book of Homilies. These instructional sermons expressed a theological orientation far closer to that of the continental reformers than the teaching of any book previously authorized in England.

Most eminent among the foreign theologians whom Cranmer brought to England were Martin Bucer of Strasbourg, and Peter

[1] JHL, I, 343.

Martyr Vermigli, the itinerant Italian reformer who spent his last years teaching in Zurich. John Jewel studied under Peter Martyr at Oxford and wrote him confidential letters up to Martyr's death two months before the 1563 Convocation convened. Parker became a close enough friend of Bucer at Cambridge for Bucer to dun him for a ten-crown loan and make him an executor of his estate. The moderate irenic theology of Bucer provides an important clue to Parker's own convictions.[1]

On the eve of its collapse in 1553, the Edwardian government published the Forty-two Articles of Religion and, in most Latin and English editions, an appended catechism of substantial length. The Articles claimed the authority of Convocation as well as of king, but the church's legislative body had never considered them. Partly based on the Lutheran-inspired Thirteen Articles of 1538, they veered close to Swiss doctrine on the sacraments, and they vigorously repudiated views thought to be held by Roman Catholics and Anabaptists. Six royal chaplains who reviewed and approved an early version of the Articles included Robert Horn and Edmund Grindal, Elizabethan bishops, and Andrew Perne, who sat in the Lower House as dean of Ely.[2]

The attached Catechism bore only the king's commendation 'for the better instruction of youth, to be taught in English schools'. Written by John Poynet, discursive, unbalanced in the proportion of its content, the Catechism expounded a near-Zwinglian interpretation of the sacraments.[3]

Henry had never acted on the proposal in a 1534 parliamentary act

---

[1] *Parker Corr.*, pp. 42 and 46–8; V. J. K. Brook, *A Life of Archbishop Parker* (Oxford, 1962), p. 42; William Paul McClure Kennedy, *Archbishop Parker* (London, 1908), p. 67.

[2] Hardwick, *Articles*, pp. 279–88. Richard Watson Dixon convincingly argued against Convocation's action on the Articles in his *History of the Church of England from the Abolition of the Roman Jurisdiction*, 6 vols. (Oxford, 1887–1902), III, 512–13; see also Edgar C. S. Gibson, *The Thirty-nine Articles of the Church of England* (London, 1910), pp. 12–20; cf. Hardwick, *Articles*, pp. 105–12.

[3] Ketley, *Two Liturgies*, pp. 485–582; for the author's name, see Cheke's letter of 7 June 1553 to Bullinger in *Original Letters Relative to the English Reformation . . . Chiefly from the Archives of Zurich*, tr. and ed. Hastings Robinson, 2 vols. (Cambridge, 1846–7; hereafter called *OL*), I, 142.

17

which authorized him to appoint a commission of thirty-two men to revise canon law in the light of England's ecclesiastical independence. Many English reformers, especially those influenced by Geneva and Strasbourg, desired 'godly discipline' to educate the church in the 'school of Christ'. Eventually, in 1551, a working committee of eight men, including Richard Cox, were appointed to draw up a new canonical code.[1] Their work, the *Reformatio Legum Ecclesiasticarum*, remained unpublished in Edward's reign.

Historians have sometimes overlooked the comprehensiveness of the reforms which were in hand at the very end of Edward's reign. In four books the reformers presented a complete programme for the religious life of the nation: a public liturgy in the second Prayer Book, a devotional guide in the 1553 Primer, a doctrinal standard in the Forty-two Articles and the accompanying Catechism, and a new body of canon law in the unpublished *Reformatio*. The programme died with the king. Within seven weeks of the publication of the Articles, Queen Mary reversed the course of the English Church in order to lead it back not only to more conservative teachings and rites but to the very papal fold itself.

The careers of the Marian bishops alive in 1563 show some curious patterns in the Edwardian years. Of the Henrician holdovers, Kitchin and Thirlby managed to hang on to their sees to the end. Heath had opposed changes and was eventually deprived, but like Tunstall, who died in 1559, he conformed through the introduction of the first Prayer Book. Bonner had been in trouble with the government almost from the start. Bonner's protégé, Gilbert Bourne, was presented to an archdeaconry during Edward's reign, and he and David Pole remained archdeacons to the end of the reign. Thomas Watson ran afoul of the Privy Council for suspected resistance to reform, and tasted imprisonment for the first time. Cuthbert Scot was beneficed and unmolested, and James Turberville also presumably continued his ministry throughout the reign. Needless to say, Goldwell and Pate remained in their safe papal havens abroad.

A number of the Elizabethan bishops had held administrative

---

[1] Dasent, *Privy Council*, II, 410, 9 November 1551.

posts in their dioceses or universities during Edward's reign, and in these positions they had enforced the new regulations. Barlow and Scory had both been bishops favoured by the government. Jewel, Nicholas Bullingham, and Richard Cheyney had all become arch-deacons in the Edwardian church. By one of those curious quirks of these years, Cheyney had risen partly by favour of Nicholas Heath. Cox became dean of Westminster, Horn of Durham, and Thomas Young held the comparable post of precentor at St David's. Thomas Davies held on to his chancellorship of Bangor, and Rowland Merrick was named chancellor successively of Wells and of St David's. Parker, Edwin Sandys, and James Pilkington all held major posts in their colleges, and Thomas Bentham, Edmund Guest, and Edmund Grindal also shared academic administrative respon-sibilities. The other Elizabethan bishops, with the possible exception of Edmund Scambler, had at least been beneficed during Edward's reign.[1]

The Lower House of the 1563 Convocation also contained a large proportion of men who had held responsible positions in the Edwardian church. Others, younger men, first entered their minis-tries during these years of change. Seventeen members of the Lower House had received their first university degrees; thirteen had been elected fellows of their colleges while Edward reigned. Eighteen Convocation men had received their first benefices in this time of reform. In their maturity, such men had experienced only the suc-cession of reforms under Edward and their vigorous suppression under the subsequent rule of Mary. In 1563 the culmination of the reformers' programme lay only ten years in the past.

[1] Standard biographical works assign benefices to all the Elizabethan bishops in Edward's reign except Scambler and John Best. Foster lists a prebend for Best in 1553 which could have been assigned in either reign. However, Cranmer's Register lists Best's collation to the vicarage of Wrotham on 1 November 1544 and his resignation on 23 December 1549—presumably for another, unknown, benefice (Lambeth Palace Library, fos. 393b and 410a). Heath collated Cheyney to two of the relatively few parishes in his patronage, both overlooked in the *DNB* biography: to St Helen's, Worcester on 27 December 1545 and to Halford on 22 July 1547 (Heath's register in Diocesan Archives kept in St Helen's Church, B.A. 2648, parcel 9 (iv), fos. 10a and 12a).

RETURN TO ROME

The Convocation men of 1563 had watched Mary's accession to the throne with a variety of reactions. Conservatives had looked forward to the expected return to the old ways in religion. Some reformers had been torn between their dismay at this prospect and their inclination to join their fellow-Englishmen in rejoicing that the hated rule of Northumberland was at an end. The more single-minded reformers had viewed the change of sovereigns as God's visitation on England for her sins. A few had joined Archbishop Cranmer in giving their support to the short-lived reign of Queen Jane. Probably John Aylmer, her chaplain, archdeacon of Lincoln in 1563, had been among them, and the Elizabethan bishops Richard Cox and Edwin Sandys had been briefly imprisoned for their support of Northumberland's scheme.

Mary, wholeheartedly loyal to the papacy, could not avoid using the machinery of royal supremacy in order to undo it. She quickly released and restored to their dioceses Tunstall, Bonner, and Heath, along with Gardiner, whom she made Lord Chancellor. Bonner's release occasioned a sermon by Gilbert Bourne at Paul's Cross which offended the reforming sympathies of many Londoners; little did Bourne suspect that in ten years both Bonner *and he* would be in near-by prisons. By the end of 1553 Mary had undone the Edwardian reforms and had restored traditional catholicism, but not papal authority.

The restoration of clerical celibacy meant that many who later sat in the 1563 Convocation were deprived for canonically unchaste marriages. The Edwardian bishop Barlow resigned his see before he could be deprived, but Scory, after his deprivation from Chichester, put away his wife and was restored to priestly functions.[1] Other Elizabethan bishops deprived for marriage under Mary included Parker, Bullingham, Horn, Davies, Merrick, and Berkeley.

Before the end of 1554 Mary celebrated her marriage to her Spanish Hapsburg cousin, Philip, and Cardinal Pole returned from exile to absolve England of her schism from Rome. Parliament forced

---

[1] Burnet, *Reformation*, v, 389–90, extract from Bonner's Register.

the cardinal to delay his arrival until the pope had reassured them that monastic and other former religious properties might remain in the hands of those who now held them. Only a half-dozen religious houses reappeared in Mary's reign, including the monastery at Westminster Abbey, whose abbot, John Feckenham, lodged in the Tower in 1563 with the deprived bishops.

Interwoven with papal religion and the Spanish presence in the popular mind were the heresy trials which followed on Parliament's revival of the old penal laws. Beginning in 1555, almost three hundred heretics were burned in three and a half years. Although these numbers were small by continental standards, the consequences were disastrous for the cause closest to Mary's heart. The horror of the public scenes was etched into the memory of future generations of Englishmen by John Foxe, who published the first English edition of his massive martyrology on 20 March 1563 when Convocation was in session. We may imagine that not a few Convocation men found their way to John Day's shop in Aldersgate to examine a copy. Popular opinion in Elizabeth's reign identified the brusque Bonner as the 'bloody butcher', for the largest number of *autos-da-fé* took place in his metropolitan diocese. The mild David Pole, the only deprived bishop at liberty in England in 1563, served on heresy commissions in the active persecutions in the diocese of Canterbury, and he also was a commissioner for the degradation of Ridley, Latimer, and Cranmer before their executions. Earlier, Cuthbert Scot had disputed with the three bishops who had been brought out of prison for the formal theological debate. Men sitting in the 1563 Convocation had personally known the victims of persecution, and many believed that it was only by the grace of God that they had escaped the same fate.

The Convocation men of 1563 can be roughly divided into groups based on their responses to Mary's policies. The neatest division lies between the men who remained in England and those who chose exile rather than live under the Roman Catholic Mary. Few generalizations can be made about the men who remained in England. These included eleven out of the twenty-five Elizabethan bishops and a large majority of the Lower House of Canterbury. They can be

roughly divided into convinced papalists, willing or reluctant conformists, and clerics who retired rather than exercise their ministries
under the conditions of papal obedience.

Englishmen who fled Henry's independence and Edward's reforms returned eager to restore the Roman obedience. Mary knew
where the men stood, and with papal acquiescence she put Reginald
Pole in the primatial see to succeed Cranmer, gave Richard Pate
possession of Worcester, whose title he had long enjoyed, and sent
Thomas Goldwell to the see of St Asaph. The reign of Edward
persuaded many conservative clerics of the folly of ecclesiastical
independence. Although under Henry the *supremum caput* had provided a workable structure of authority, these men had seen Edward's
Privy Council use this same authority to undermine the traditional
faith and practice of the church. However bitter a pill papal obedience
may have been for them, the bishops deprived under Edward
accepted it as necessary medicine. Mary returned Tunstall to Durham
and Bonner to London. She translated Heath to the northern
primacy at York to make way for Pate at Worcester, and in 1556
Heath became her Lord Chancellor. She accepted the compliant
conformity of Kitchin, and she favoured Thirlby by promoting him
to the diocese of Ely.

Other priests were equally convinced of the righteousness of the
Roman cause. Early in Mary's reign Thomas Watson replaced
Pilkington as Master of St John's College, Cambridge, and Robert
Horn as dean of Durham. Mary soon promoted him to the see of
Lincoln. Cuthbert Scot, who had been named master of Christ's
College, Cambridge in 1553, was named to the see of Chester in
1556. Even though Gilbert Bourne and David Pole had retained
their archdeaconries to the end of Edward's reign, their conservative
convictions soon won Mary's favour. In 1554 she named Bourne to
Bath and Wells. David Pole, who served Reginald Pole as vicar-
general of Canterbury as he had once served Cranmer, became
second bishop of Peterborough in 1557. In 1555, James Turberville
emerged from a quiet parish ministry to receive the see of Exeter.
Thomas Stanley was consecrated to the northern island diocese of
Sodor and Man in 1556, presumably by nomination of the Earl of

Derby.[1] All these Marian bishops, except Kitchin and the little-known Stanley, were deprived early in Elizabeth's reign.

By no stretch of the imagination could we include any of the new bishops sitting in the choir of St Paul's in 1563 in such a group of enthusiastic and convinced papalists, but some of the Lower House had once shown such convictions. Francis Mallet, for example, may not have attended any sessions of Convocation in 1563, but he held a seat by virtue of his deanery of Lincoln, a post Mary had given him in 1554, and he gave his proxy to an attending member of the house. Mallet had been Mary's chaplain from the time of her father's reign, and he had been imprisoned for saying the Latin Mass under Northumberland's rule. Mary's death robbed him of the see for which she had designated him, but he remained dean of Lincoln until his death in 1570. Stephen Cheston had received a Cambridge law degree in 1542, but only in 1554 did he receive ecclesiastical preferment. The following year he became archdeacon of Winchester, and in this capacity he attended Convocation in 1563. Thomas White, warden of New College, Oxford, from 1553 to 1573, had been a fellow of the college for over twenty years before becoming head. In short order, he added one more parish, two prebends, and an archdeaconry to his livings, and in 1557 he served as vice-chancellor of the university. However such men as Mallet, Cheston, and White may have justified their later conformity under Elizabeth, there seems little doubt but that they were convinced supporters of the Roman Catholic restoration in Mary's reign.

At least three Elizabethan diocesan bishops had conformed as priests in the Marian church. William Downham, sometime chaplain to Princess Elizabeth, received one living in 1548, but two in 1555. Thomas Davies held preferments through the years of both Edward and Mary, and when Bishop Glynn of Bangor died, Cardinal Pole appointed Davies to take custody of the spiritualities of the see.[2] At the first Convocation of Mary's reign, Richard

[1] George T. O. Bridgeman, *The History of the Church and Manor of Wigan in the County of Lancaster*, Part I, Chetham Society, xv (Manchester, 1888), 131–3; A. W. Moore, *Sodor and Man* (London, 1893), p. 138.
[2] Arthur Ivor Pryce, ed., *The Diocese of Bangor in the Sixteenth Century: being a Digest of the Registers of the Bishops A.D. 1512–1646* (Bangor, 1923), pp. 11, 15–17; cf. Venn,

Cheyney, as archdeacon of Hereford, was among five or six who refused to subscribe to transubstantiation, insisting, however, that the natural body and blood of Christ are 'actually present' in the sacrament. Cheyney retained his archdeaconry until 1557, and three days before Elizabeth's accession he was made a canon at Gloucester.[1]

Thirty-one out of the one hundred and four known members of the Lower House of 1563 had actively conformed in the Marian church to the extent of accepting benefices or ordination, and eight more had received university degrees at a time when adherents of Roman Catholic religion were in firm control.[2] These thirty-nine included both enthusiastic papal supporters, such as Mallet and Cheston, and more reluctant conformists, such as John Salisbury, William Latimer, and Nicholas Robinson. The former monk Salisbury, suffragan bishop of Thetford, archdeacon of Anglesey, and first dean of the secularized Norwich, had married in Edward's reign. In 1554 he was deprived of his deanery and archdeaconry, but he was reconciled and proceeded to serve as chancellor of the diocese of Lincoln for the remainder of Mary's reign. Latimer lost three livings presumably for marriage, but in 1556 he was renamed to one of them. The Welshman Nicholas Robinson signed a series of Roman Catholic articles in 1555 and was ordained by Bishop Glynn in 1557, but he received no living until the reign of Elizabeth.

In between the convinced papalists and reluctant conformists stand such men as the pliable Andrew Perne, who served as vice-chancellor of Cambridge at various times under Edward, Mary, and Elizabeth. John Cotterell came to the 1563 Convocation as archdeacon of Dorset, an office to which he had been appointed under Edward, and also as archdeacon of Wells, an office picked up

Alumni, II, 17. Davies' *DNB* biographer points out a BM MS. which establishes Cardinal Pole's appointment, and Pryce's digest of the episcopal register confirms the appointment by entries on 20 and 27 July and 15 December.

[1] Cardwell, *Synodalia*, II, 426; Valerand Pollanus, *Vera Exposita Disputationis Institutae Mandato D. Mariae...in Synodo...1553* (1554); Darwell Stone, *A History of the Doctrine of the Holy Eucharist*, 2 vols. (London, 1909), II, 162.

[2] See Appendix II for a discussion of the members of the 1563 Lower House and their careers under Mary (p. 360, below).

while Mary reigned. George Carew, dean of Elizabeth's chapel royal, had steadily amassed pluralities during the reigns of four Tudors.

What are we to make of these men who were willing to conform to such conflicting ecclesiastical conditions? Were they not inevitably vicars of Bray devoted not to religion but to their comfortable benefices? As historians we are all inclined to judge the religious integrity of such clerics from the clear-cut standpoints of easily defined ecclesiastical positions. We forget that choices which men faced were infinitely more complex. Undoubtedly opportunism, fear, and expediency did induce men to change their ecclesiastical loyalties. Yet sincere men could feel an obligation to their vocation in the church in which God had placed them. Roman Catholic and zealous reformer alike insisted that clergy choose between God and Baal. Others who could not see the issues in such clear-cut categories might have agreed with Queen Elizabeth who once told a French ambassador that 'there was only one Jesus Christ and one faith, and all the rest they disputed about were trifles'.[1] We ought not assume too quickly that religious indifference motivates such attitudes. Even in that age of theological controversy, some men might grasp the fundamental unity underlying the divisions of Western Christendom. Making allowances for those whose Marian records are obscure, half of the men eligible for the Elizabethan Lower House in 1563 had, for various reasons of expediency and conviction, probably conformed to Marian Roman Catholicism.

A number of reform-minded clerics retired from an active ministry although they remained in England. Some did so because they could not conscientiously return to the unreformed doctrines and rites; others, perhaps, because they refused to abandon their families. Mathew Parker, deprived of all his preferments, chose the '*dulcissimum otium literarium*', as he himself described his life in retirement with his wife and two children.[2] His fellow Elizabethan bishops, Rowland Merrick, Edmund Guest, John Best, and William

[1] *A Journal of. . .Monsieur de Maisse Ambassador in England*, tr. and ed. G. B. Harrison and R. A. Jones (Bloomsbury, 1931), p. 58.
[2] *Parker Corr.*, pp. viii and 483, autobiographical memoranda.

Alley, probably followed a similar course in Mary's reign.[1] Two other Elizabethan bishops, Edmund Scambler, who did not leave Britain, and Thomas Bentham, who spent part of the reign abroad, are known to have ministered to the secret Prayer Book congregation in London at the risk of their lives. Sitting in the Lower House in 1563 were ten clerics whose records suggest that they too had either retired from the active ministry under Mary or held up their ordinations until Elizabeth's accession. Such men did not share with the émigrés the immediate experience and influences of the various continental protestant churches, but it would be misleading to assume on this account alone that any one of them fell behind their brethren abroad in their zeal for reform.

PROTESTANT HAVENS ABROAD

English reformers in Henry's day had found haven in protestant communities on the continent, and when Mary undid the Edwardian reforms it was natural for such Englishmen to look again to foreign ports of safety. Some reformers made a show of conformity before leaving. Scory received his licence to minister as a priest, and John Jewel signed a set of doctrinal articles. According to the count of C. H. Garrett, the émigrés included one hundred and eighty-six clerics and 'theological students'.[2] These men all shared a mutual antipathy to the Romish religion restored by Mary and a corresponding sympathy for the direction of Edwardian reform, but beyond this, they exhibited important and even violent disagreements. An exile's experience of reformed church life depended upon the character of his chosen English enclave abroad. Emden, partly a way station for émigrés in transit, sheltered a congregation which, as

---

[1] For Merrick, see Pryce, *Bangor*, p. 13; and John Strype, *Ecclesiastical Memorials...*
under King Henry VIII, King Edward VI, and Queen Mary I, 3 vols. (Oxford, 1822),
III, part II, 355–63; for Guest, see *'Matthaeus'* in Strype, *Parker*, III, 233 (Bullingham
also included as one who stayed in England; see p. 27, n. 2); for Best, see only
Strype's undocumented statement in *Memorials*, III, part II, 149; for Alley, both
Venn and the *DNB* refer to John Vowell, alias Hooker, *Catalog of the Bishops of
Excester* (1584), no. 46.

[2] Christina Hallowell Garrett, *The Marian Exiles* (Cambridge, 1938).

recent evidence reveals, maintained John Scory as pastor for the entire reign.[1] Less confidently, we can speculate that three of Scory's fellow bishops in Elizabeth's reign stayed in Emden for what may have been no more than brief visits to the continent: Nicholas Bullingham, Thomas Young, and Gilbert Berkeley.[2]

Most of the remaining former émigrés among the Elizabethan bishops spent all or part of their exile in the moderate communities of Strasburg and Zurich, where men sought to reproduce religion as close as their new conditions permitted to what they had known in England in 1553. Grindal and Sandys made Strasburg their chief residence, and Parkhurst lived in Zurich. Jewel followed Peter Martyr first to Strasburg and then to Zurich. Cox passed most of his exile in these two cities. Horn and Bentham began their exiles in Zurich, and Pilkington remained there about two years. The 1563 Lower House of Convocation contained twenty-seven former émigrés, but Strasburg and Zurich could claim only two of these men as residents for the duration. Another, Thomas Sampson, who flitted about from one exile community to another, made such a nuisance of himself in Zurich that Bullinger was later to warn Beza in Geneva that Sampson had shown himself a man of 'captious and unquiet disposition'.[3]

With John Knox as pastor, the militant community at Geneva rejected the Prayer Book and adopted an English liturgy and discipline modelled after the order which Calvin had established in the city. The Elizabethan bishops Scory, Bentham, and Pilkington

---

[1] Stanford E. Lehinberg, 'Archbishop Grindal and the Prophesyings', *The Historical Magazine of the Protestant Episcopal Church*, XXXIX (1965), 116; from the Laud–Seldon–Fairhurst MSS. in Lambeth Palace Library (no. 2003, fol. 10, 18 July 1576, Scory to Grindal). Scory was enrolled some time in 1556 in the Genevan congregation, but his stay was undoubtedly very brief ('Livre des Anglois', in Charles Martin, *Les Protestants Anglais Réfugiés à Génève* [Geneva, 1915], p. 332; see also p. 7 and Garrett, *Marian Exiles*, p. 286).

[2] Bullingham and Young: see 'Emden list' prefaced to a contemporary edition of Cranmer's *Defensio*, *Works*, 2 vols. (Cambridge, 1844), ed. J. E. Cox, p. 9 of *Defensio*; for Berkeley, see contemporary reference mentioned by F. O. White in *Lives of the Elizabethan Bishops of the Anglican Church* (London, 1898), p. 136; see comment on Bullingham in note 1, p. 26.

[3] *ZL*, II, 152, Bullinger to Beza, 15 March 1567; the Marian careers of the émigrés in the Lower House are discussed in Appendix II (see below, p. 358).

all visited Geneva, but none for more than a few months.[1] The Edwardian bishop Miles Coverdale settled in Geneva towards the end of Mary's reign, was elected a senior of the congregation, and stood as godfather to Knox's son. Of the 1563 Lower House, Thomas Lever spent at least nine months attending 'all the sermons and lectures of Calvin'. John Pullan served as deacon in the congregation, and three other Lower House members made Geneva their abode abroad. Thomas Sampson briefly visited the city. The spirit of Geneva penetrated men's hearts and it remained for many that place where, in the words of one émigré, 'Gods worde is truly preached, manners best reformed, and in earthe the chiefest place off true comforte'.[2]

The English communities at Arau and Basle were closer in spirit to Geneva than to Strasburg and Zurich. The Arau community had first lived in Wesel with Miles Coverdale and then Thomas Lever as pastors. Lutheran suspicions of English theology forced their move to Arau, where Lever remained in charge of the congregation. Englishmen came to Basle registered as students. Bentham visited Basle, and Pilkington and Horn probably stayed there for more than a year. The Irish bishop John Bale settled in Basle for the whole latter half of Queen Mary's rule.[3]

[1] For Scory, see above, p. 27, n. 1; for Bentham, see 'Livre des Anglois'; received on 20 November 1557 and married before end of year, Martin, *Protestants anglais*, pp. 333 and 337; back in England with secret London congregation, Strype, *Memorials*, III, part II, 133–5; Foxe, *Acts*, VIII, 558–60, 445–7, and 457–8; for Pilkington registered in early 1556, left by June, see Martin, p. 332, 'Livre des Anglois'; *OL*, I, 134–6 and 136–7, Pilkington to Gualter and to Bullinger, 7 April and 27 June 1556. Horn was said to have left Frankfort in 1557 for Arau and Geneva, but his name appears neither in Genevan nor Arau records, and he turns up as a student in Basle in 1558; see *A Brief Discourse of the Troubles Begun at Frankfort in the Year 1554, About the Book of Common Prayer and Ceremonies*, ed. J. P., from ed. of 1575 (London, 1846), p. 186 (hereafter called *Troubles at Frankfort*); Garrett, *Marian Exiles*, p. 357, Basle student list.

[2] Martin, *Protestants anglais*, pp. 332–6, 'Livre des Anglois'; *Troubles at Frankfort*, p. 49; *OL*, I, 153–9, Lever to Bullinger, 11 and 23 April 1554, 28 June, and 17 January 1555.

[3] Garrett, *Marian Exiles*, pp. 357–8; *The Remains of Edmund Grindal*, ed. William Nicholson (Cambridge, 1843), pp. 222–4, 228, and 234, Grindal to Foxe, 1 August 1556, 18 June 1557 and 28 December; *OL*, I, 160, 162, and 167, Lever to Bullinger, 4 January 1556, 12 May (or 1557?), to Gualter, 11 August 1557.

Some of the 1563 Convocation men had taken part in two serious disputes which rent the English congregation in Frankfort. The first controversy arose after the congregation, including John Bale and Thomas Cole, invited John Knox to become their pastor. Under his leadership, they drastically revised the English liturgy, explaining in a letter to fellow-countrymen in Strasburg that they intended to use the Prayer Book only 'so farre as gods words doth assure it and the state of this countrie permit'.[1] Cole and Bale were the only members of the anti-Prayer Book party to sit in the 1563 Convocation, and even Bale had reversed his position before the dispute was over.[2] Five Elizabethan bishops and eight members of the 1563 Lower House were among those signing letters from Strasburg and Zurich urging their fellow-countrymen to maintain their 'good conformitie' to that 'godly order sett forthe and receaved in England'.[3] Early in 1555 Cox and his future episcopal colleagues Grindal, Sandys, Jewel, and Horn converged on Frankfort to strengthen Prayer Book supporters. After a bitter struggle, Cox led the Prayer Book forces to victory, and Knox and most of his supporters departed to Geneva. The Frankfort congregation chose David Whitehead to be their pastor, a reformer whom Cranmer had once recommended for the archiepiscopal see of Armagh in Ireland. Cox and his followers wrote two letters to Calvin justifying their actions, and among those 1563 Convocation men to sign them were Grindal, Sandys, and Horn, along with Lever, Sampson, Becon and, curiously, Bale. With minor emendations the 1552 Prayer Book became the liturgical guide of the Frankforters, as it was for most of the other exile congregations.[4]

At the beginning of 1557 some members of the turbulent Frankfort congregation attempted to unseat Robert Horn, who had replaced Whitehead as pastor, and to establish a 'New Discipline', an order of doctrine and polity which provided for the use of Calvin's catechism and, more controversially, for congregational election

[1] *Troubles at Frankfort*, pp. 20 and 76.
[2] *OL*, II, 755; Strype, *Memorials*, III, part II, 313–15.
[3] *Troubles at Frankfort*, pp. 16 and 22–3.
[4] *Ibid. passim*; *OL*, II, 755 and 763; John Strype, *Memorials of . . . Thomas Cranmer*, 3 vols. (Oxford, 1840), II, 405–6, Cranmer to Cecil, 25 August 1552.

and ordination of ministers. Thomas Bentham won puritan commendation for his unsuccessful attempt to arbitrate, but he joined the
group who refused to accept office under the New Discipline.[1]
Another Elizabethan bishop, Richard Davies, who had settled in
Frankfort, joined Horn in protesting the congregational order.[2] Ten
members of the Lower House in 1463, including Alexander Nowell
and John Pedder, subscribed the New Discipline; they were joined
by their former pastor Whitehead and a majority of the congregation. A hard core, including Whitehead and Pedder, described
efforts to heal the breach, 'contrary to godds worde and good
reason'.[3] The New Discipline remained, and Robert Horn left the
city. A large block of men in the Lower House in 1563 had supported
the New Discipline in Frankfort, but all three Elizabethan bishops
who declared themselves in the controversy had stood out against it.

France and Italy drew some English travellers including three who
sat in the Lower House in 1563. Attached to the entourage of the
duchess of Suffolk in Germany and Poland was Bishop Barlow, who
won two Lutheran recommendations to Elizabeth: Melanchthon
commended him as a 'learned man, one who rightly worships God',
and the elector of Brandenburg described him as 'attached to the
Confession of Augsburg'.[4]

Writing occupied the time of some of the exiles. John Foxe collected material for his martyrology while in Basle, and Coverdale and
other émigrés in Geneva prepared a new English Bible. John Poynet
in Strasburg and John Knox and Christopher Goodman in Geneva
urged the duty of subjects to rise up against ungodly rulers. Sampson
warned his former parishioners of the spiritual dangers of partici-

[1] *Troubles at Frankfort*, pp. 76–7 and 97.
[2] *Ibid.* p. 168; for a discussion of the possibility of Davies' residence at Geneva, see
Glanmore Williams, 'The Deprivation and Exile of Bishop Richard Davies',
Journal of the Historical Society of the Church in Wales, I (1947), 81–90.
[3] *Troubles at Frankfort*, p. 174.
[4] John Brett, 'The English Refugees in Germany', *Transactions of the Royal Historical
Society*, n.s. XI (London, 1897), ed. I. S. Leadham, pp. 125–8; *Calendar of State
Papers, Foreign Series, of the Reign of Elizabeth*, vols. I–VII, ed. Joseph Stevenson,
vols. VIII–IX, ed. Alan Jones Crosby (London, 1863–74; hereafter called *CSP, For.*),
I, 109, Albert of Brandenburg to Elizabeth, 31 January 1559; I, 155, Melanchthon,
1 March; I, 354, Elizabeth to Albert, 2 July.

pating in the 'horrible profanation' of the Latin Mass.[1] Thomas Becon wrote even more violently against the 'abominable masses full of superstition, idolatry, blasphemy, spiritual whoredom, and of all that displeaseth God, and is horrible in the judgment and sight of all good men'. Forgetting perhaps that the reformers' political hopes centred on Mary's sister, he lamented publicly to God: 'Thou hast set to rule over us a woman, whom nature hath formed to be in subjection unto man, and whom thou by thine holy apostle commandest to keep silence....Ah, Lord! to take away the empire from a man, and to give it unto a woman, seemeth to be an evident token of thine anger toward us Englishmen.'[2] The real mystery is how Becon had the temerity to publish these words in 1563!

The joyous news of Elizabeth's accession brought the émigrés flocking back home. A group of exiles at Geneva, including Pullan and Coverdale, proposed to the other exiles that they form a common front on their return that 'religion best proceade and florishe'. Only the congregation at Arau, led by their pastor Lever, replied favourably to Geneva's 'most godly requeste'. Frankfort, including Pilkington, Alexander Nowell, and two other Convocation men of 1563, tartly retorted: 'We purpos to submit oure selues to such orders as shall be established by authoritie, beinge not of themselves wicked, so we would wishe you willingly to do the same.'[3]

What a variety of experiences the clerics brought with them to St Paul's in 1563! The bishops represented a much narrower portion of the ecclesiastical spectrum than the Lower House, whose potential membership ranged all the way from the former personal chaplain of Princess Mary to Thomas Cole, who had opposed the Prayer Book at Frankfort.

In the reigns of Edward and Mary some Henrician conservatives had become convinced Roman Catholics; some reformers found their zeal fired and their resolution tempered in adversity; the serviceable loyalty of most English clerics to their national church

[1] Strype, *Memorials*, III, part II, 238.
[2] Becon, *Works*, III, 207 and 228; see also III, 247 and 253–86.
[3] *Troubles at Frankfort*, pp. 187–91.

remained unimpaired. Whether men conformed for reasons of expediency or conscience through the changes of the English Reformation, their example bespoke a Christianity whose doctrines could not be completely confined in the formulae of theological disputation and whose worship might be honestly, even if not ideally, expressed in a variety of liturgical forms. By and large such men had not risen, and would not rise, to the higher positions of leadership in their church, but their attitude influenced and rubbed off on many of the men who did rise to such leadership.

THE PRIMACY

On 11 November 1562 Queen Elizabeth sent Archbishop Matthew Parker her brief which licensed him to assemble Convocation in January.[1] How their lives had changed since 11 November 1558 when Parker was still living quietly with his books and Elizabeth was awaiting news of her sister's health in the relative seclusion of Hatfield! How too had religion changed in England! In the intervening four years the Church of England was already becoming established in that framework of liturgy, discipline, and doctrine which we call the Elizabethan settlement. Before turning to the details of that framework, we must trace in the remaining pages of this chapter Elizabeth's choice of leadership up to the opening of the Convocation. No ruler better understood the importance of the right choice of men than the queen who had placed the bishops and many of the lower clergy in the positions which they occupied in Convocation. Other men could well have sat in their places, and their relative positions could have been rearranged. But partly because these men occupied their seats in St Paul's, the shape of the Elizabethan church developed as it did.

The primatial see of Canterbury had loomed large in the history of the English Church. Cardinal Pole's death coincided with that of Mary Tudor—a providential stroke of luck for the new reign. Not only was the chair of St Augustine vacant for Elizabeth to fill with her own choice, but also prelates loyal to Rome were left without

---

[1] Strype, *Parker*, I, 236, writ.

their distinguished and uncompromising leader. Both the political and religious consequences made the choice of a primate of all England one of the most important decisions facing Elizabeth at the beginning of her reign.

Within a month of Elizabeth's accession to the throne, Bacon and Cecil began a course of correspondence with Matthew Parker which reveals the queen's inclination to place him in the see of Canterbury. In spite of the judgment of Strype and others that these letters were not of Elizabeth's doing, it is inconceivable that the queen would have left such a decision to the hands of even her most trusted advisers, or that they would have embarked upon such negotiations without her approval.[1] She had every reason not to become openly and directly involved in the conversations with Parker. If it became general knowledge that she had already selected a man of Parker's known reforming convictions for the primacy, she would have tipped her hand too early and thereby have forfeited all chances of achieving an orderly peaceful transition in Parliament.

Parker reluctantly came to London and after pleading his insufficiency for the primacy and preaching two sermons at court, he returned home. In mid-May Parker was officially summoned back to London, and by 6 June Il Schifanoya, an Italian living in London, had heard of the new appointment to Canterbury.[2] Parker presided over the 1563 Convocation because the queen had chosen him in the first weeks of her reign.

The names of three other clerics have been mentioned as serious contenders for the primacy in 1559: David Whitehead, John Feckenham, and Nicholas Wotton. David Whitehead's candidature goes back to a remark by Strype that Parker had been chosen after the

[1] *Parker Corr.*, pp. 49–53; Strype, *Parker*, III, 278, the *Matthaeus*; I, 71; Conyers Read, *Mr. Secretary Cecil and Queen Elizabeth* (London, 1955), the first of a two-volume biography, I, 261.
[2] *Parker Corr.*, pp. 57–63, 68, and 68–89; see below, p. 89; *Calendar of State Papers and Manuscripts, relating to English Affairs, existing in...Venice and in other Libraries of Northern Italy* (hereafter called *CSP, Ven.*), vols. v and vi, ed. Rawdon Brown, vol. VII, ed. Rawdon Brown and G. Cavendish Bentinck, vol. VIII, ed. Horatio F. Brown (London, 1873–94), VII, 96; see also *CSP, For.* I, 287, Nowell [?] to Abel, 28 May 1559.

elimination of Wotton, Whitehead, 'and some other [who] are said
by *some* to have been under consideration'.[1] Unfortunately Strype
did not identify the 'some' who thought Whitehead a likely primate.
Whitehead preached at court in February 1559, but if his return to
England was like that of other Marian émigrés, he was still abroad
in religious exile when Elizabeth began to take steps to appoint
Matthew Parker. Some of Whitehead's fellow-exiles may have
wished that he were a candidate for the primacy, but there is little
reason to think that the queen considered him as such.[2]

Dom David Knowles has given credence to the claim that Nicholas
Sander reported Abbot Feckenham's candidature for Canterbury. The
Elizabethan Roman Catholic Sander reported nothing of the kind,
but in 1722 a John Stevens, referring to Sander's account, implied that
Elizabeth had offered the primacy to Feckenham. The offer originated
in the ambiguous hyperbole of the eighteenth-century writer.[3]

Nicholas Wotton has a better claim to have been a real candidate
for Canterbury, for three contemporary witnesses, all foreigners,
wrote late in 1558 that Wotton, dean of both Canterbury and York,

[1] Strype, *Parker*, I, 71, italics mine; see *DNB*, under David Whitehead.

[2] The 'Device for the Alteration of Religion' had proposed Whitehead as one of
seven revisers of the Prayer Book; see Henry Gee, *The Elizabethan Prayer Book and
Ornaments* (London, 1902), p. 200. The last reference to him in exile records is on
30 September 1557; see *Troubles at Frankfort*, p. 174. He preached at court on 15
February 1559; see Henry Machyn, *The Diary of Henry Machyn*, ed. John Gough
Nichols, Camden Society, o.s. no. xlii (London, 1848), p. 189.

[3] David Knowles, *The Religious Orders in England*, III (Cambridge, 1959), 433; *DNB*,
under John Feckenham. Both Knowles and the *DNB* refer not to Sander, but to
John Stevens' additions to Dugdale's *Monasticon Anglicanum* (*The History of the
Antient Abbeys, Monasteries, Hospitals, Cathedral and Collegiate Churches, being the
Additional Volumes to Sir William Dugdale's Monasticon Anglicanum*, I [London, 1722],
289): 'Sander says, the Queen did heartily wish to have a new sort of Monks in
her Innovation in Religious Affairs. But it was in vain, for the holy man could not
be drawn from the receiv'd Faith of the Church by any Allurements or Threats,
tho' the queen offer'd him the Archbishoprick of Canterbury upon that condition, as
Sander writes' (italics mine). Nicholas Sander, in his history of the 'schism', does
state everything in this passage except the crucial clause which I have italicized;
neither is there a parallel to it in his report to Cardinal Moroni; see Sander, *Rise
and Growth of the Anglican Schism*, tr. and ed. David Lewis (London, 1877), p. 271;
Sander, *De Origine ac Progressa Schismatis Anglicani*, ed. Edward Rishton (Ingolstadt,
1587), p. 295; Catholic Record Society, *Miscellanea*, I (London, 1905), I f.).

might become archbishop. The able clerical diplomat was, however, engaged in France until April in peace negotiations, and it seems unlikely that Elizabeth would have offered the post through intermediaries crossing the Channel.[1]

No contemporary evidence suggests that Queen Elizabeth herself ever considered Whitehead or Feckenham for the primacy, and only court rumours in the opening days of the reign point to the diplomatic dean of Canterbury and York. In 1563 not one of the three men attended Convocation although Wotton was entitled to a seat and was attending Privy Council meetings at the time. In spite of Whitehead's yeoman service on behalf of the Prayer Book in Frankfort, he never was able to adjust to the Elizabethan church—either as one of its pillars or as an effective critic. The deprived Feckenham was in the Tower. Whitehead the zealous reformer, Feckenham the staunch traditionalist, and Wotton the experienced ecclesiastical statesman, provide illuminating foils to Matthew Parker. Had Elizabeth been of a different mind, these men and others like them had been available, but it was Matthew Parker who presided over Convocation in 1563.

When Il Schifanoya reported Parker's appointment, he could describe him only as 'a married priest...who was chaplain to Queen Anne Boleyn'.[2] Elizabeth knew considerably more. A scholar of moderate reforming convictions, Parker was also a man of proven administrative ability. Although Parker's experience had been in the University rather than national or diocesan life, we are well reminded that he had a 'high reputation as a man of affairs and practical efficiency', and that he was made archbishop on more recommendation than the fact that he had never left English shores.[3] Elizabeth entrusted the highest position of leadership in the English Church to

[1] *Calendar of Letters and State Papers relating to English Affairs, preserved principally in the Archives of Simancas*, vol. I, ed. Martin A. S. Hume (London, 1892, hereafter called *CSP, Sp.*), p. 3, Feria to Philip, 21 November 1558; *CSP, Ven.* VI, Part III, 1559, Priuli to Giberti, 27 November; VII, I, Il Schifanoya, 17 December. The *DNB* suggests that Wotton refused the proffered primacy. He did not return from the negotiations until after mid-April (Machyn, p. 194).
[2] *CSP, Ven.* VII, 96, 6 June 1559.
[3] Brook, *Parker*, pp. 37–42 (quotation on p. 42).

the hands of a scholarly, temperate, and committed reformer. Parker was to become, not the chief designer of the Elizabethan ecclesiastical ship, but its steady helmsman for more than fifteen years.

THE MARIAN BISHOPS

The contrast between the bishops in the choir of St Paul's in 1563 and some of their predecessors in near-by prisons illustrates the change in the episcopate from the reign of Mary to that of Elizabeth. Only the aged Anthony Kitchin of Llandaff, who did not attend Convocation and died before the year was out, and Thomas Stanley of Sodor and Man, in the north, continued in their episcopal posts.[1] Yet if Elizabeth had had her way, the situation might have been quite different.

The Marian bishops had undoubtedly anticipated trouble when the daughter of Anne Boleyn ascended the throne. Her actions in the first two months of her reign so confirmed their fears that only the junior bishop, Owen Oglethorpe, would perform the episcopal ministries in the coronation rites. To a man, the bishops present in the 1559 Parliament opposed all the proposed changes in religious affairs. Bishop Scot speaking in mid-March pointed out that just as a nation finds its unity in its monarch, 'Evin so it is the churche of Christe', which maintains its unity by a hierarchy culminating in the pope, 'whose auctoritie beinge taken away, the shepe, as the scripture sayethe, be scattred abrode'. Archbishop Heath spoke equally resolute words about the danger that by 'leapinge out of Peter's shippe', England would be 'overwhelmed and drowned in the waters of schisme, sects, and divisions'.[2]

It might be expected that whatever Elizabeth's original intentions

---

[1] For various references to the non-resident bishop of Sodor in the early years of Elizabeth, see Bridgeman, *Wigan*, p. 133, 138n.; Henry Gee, *The Elizabethan Clergy and the Settlement of Religion, 1558–1564* (Oxford, 1898), p. 88; *Parker Corr.*, p. 222. He was not completely overlooked in the ecclesiastical politics of 1559, for Il Schifanoya in June included him in a list of 'bishops living and not yet deprived' (*CSP, Ven.* VII, 105).

[2] John Strype, *Annals of the Reformation and Establishment of Religion...during Queen Elizabeth's Happy Reign*, 4 vols. with two parts of each in I, II, and III (Oxford, 1824), I, part II, 409 and 400.

towards the Marian bishops had been, their obduracy towards her religious policies would have made deprivation inevitable. The queen kept her intentions largely hidden as usual. Two days after Parliament rose, Bishop de Quadra, the ambassador of Philip II, predicted in a letter that the Marian bishops would 'be all deprived at one blow, and new bishops put in their seats'. 'One blow' would have been the appropriate action if Elizabeth had wanted to rid herself of the old episcopate. John Parkhurst wrote to Bullinger at this time that the bishops were 'worthy of being suspended not only from their office, but from a halter'. The failure to employ the obvious method of 'one blow' suggests that other plans were afoot.[1]

An extant work sheet of Cecil's allows us to glimpse into early planning for the queen's episcopal nominations. He first listed sixteen dioceses and, to their right, twenty-three potential candidates. The Marian bishops of eight of these sees were still living. Then he added a second set of ten dioceses, including eight more with living bishops: Heath of York, Thirlby of Ely, Turberville of Exeter, Morgan of St David's, Tunstall of Durham, Bourne of Bath and Wells, David Pole of Peterborough, and Kitchin of Llandaff. The arrangement suggests that Cecil did not intend to propose men for these sees.[2]

On 23 May the queen commissioned Privy Council members to receive the oath of supremacy from the bishops. Bonner the 'bloody butcher' of London was the first to be deprived in legal course for refusing the oath. Before June was out, the commission began action against Bishop Bayne of Lichfield, Oglethorpe of Carlisle, Scot of Chester, Pate of Worcester, White of Winchester, Watson of Lincoln and, surprisingly, Kitchin of Llandaff.[3] Thomas Goldwell of

---

[1] *CSP, Sp.* I, 69, 10 May 1559; *ZL,* I, 30, 21 May.

[2] P.R.O., S.P. 12 (Eliz. IV, 39), fo. 133. H. N. Birt believed that, in addition to four candidates clearly attached to specific sees, the other column of nineteen names also corresponded with specific dioceses; P. Collinson is probably correct to deny this (*The Elizabethan Religious Settlement* [London, 1907], p. 230; *The Elizabethan Puritan Movement* [London, 1967], p. 474, n. 6). Strype reproduced the paper, but he misread 'l'v' as 'deprived' rather than 'living' (*Annals,* I, part I, 227). See also below, pp. 46–7.

[3] Thomas Rymer, *Foedera, Conventiones, Literae, et cuiuscunque Generis,* 3rd ed., vol. VI (The Hague, 1741), part IV, 76, writ for oath; *Calendar of the Patent Rolls pre-*

St Asaph's had fled to the continent for the second time in his life, and was deprived *in absentia* before 15 July.[1]

These 'deprivations' were not final, for the commissioners gave further opportunities to these prelates to subscribe to the supremacy oath. They succeeded in winning Kitchin's conformity. By 12 July, de Quadra reported the 'greedy old man...wavering', and six days later Kitchin signed a pledge 'to set forthe in mine own person and cause...other...to accept and obey the whole course of religion now approved in the state of her Grace's Realme'.[2] Apparently Cecil had judged aright when he had proposed no candidate to replace Kitchin at Llandaff. By the end of June, the commissioners had been well advanced in the deprivation proceedings against the eight bishops for whom replacements were proposed on Cecil's list.

Except for Tunstall of Durham, the two most eminent bishops left on the bench were Nicholas Heath and Thomas Thirlby. Not until the first week in July was legal action begun to deprive them. Il Schifanoya explained that the delay was deliberate, for York and Ely 'remain for the last to be summoned in hope of gaining them, all possible temptations not wanting, being such rare men as they are, and necessary in affairs [of state]; but there is no doubt of their faith

served in the P.R.O., Elizabeth, vols. I–IV (London, 1939–64; hereafter called *CPR*), I, 80, London *congé d'élire*; Machyn, *Diary*, pp. 200–1, 29 May and 21 June; *CSP, Ven.* VII, 94–5 and 104–5, Il Schifanoya, 30 May and 6 and 27 June; *CSP. Sp.* I, 76 and 79, de Quadra, 19 and 27 June. Gee stated that Machyn was 'clearly in error' for including Kitchin (*Elizabethan Clergy*, p. 35); he overlooked the corroborating testimony of Il Schifanoya and the frequently inexact use of the word 'deprivation'.

[1] P.R.O., S.P. 12 (Eliz. IV, 71–2), fo. 218; John Le Neve, *Fasti Ecclesiae Anglicanae*, ed. T. Duffus Hardy, 3 vols. (Oxford, 1854), under St Asaph's; see also Thomas Edward Bridgett and Thomas Francis Knox, *The True Story of the Catholic Hierarchy Deposed by Queen Elizabeth* (New York, 1889), pp. 230–2.

[2] *CSP, Sp.* I, 86, de Quadra to Philip, 12 July 1559; John Lamb, *An Historical Account of the Thirty-Nine Articles from...MDLIII to MDLXXI* (Cambridge, 1829), p. 11. R. W. Dixon followed Lamb in judging that the curious wording of the submission provided Kitchin with a means to conform without taking the oath (*History*, V, 122). I think not. The signed statement was not a substitute for the supremacy oath, but the 'whole course of religion' implies that oath as well as the Prayer Book and Injunctions. The references to deferring of the oath may apply to the commissioners' delay *before* 18 July.

and constancy'. Sander reported that when Bishop Tunstall later reproved Elizabeth for depriving his fellow bishops, she confessed that she was 'grieved for York and Ely'.[1]

Elizabeth had earlier hoped to keep Nicholas Heath in at least some of his duties in affairs of state. It was he who as Lord Chancellor on 17 November 1558 proclaimed Elizabeth queen. A few days earlier he had asked William Cecil to intercede with the future queen that he 'might be utterly disburdened' of his office. On 21 November, the Council members with the queen at Hatfield authorized Heath and two others to transact necessary business in London. Although the last Council meeting which Heath attended was on 5 January 1559, the official account of the Westminster disputation in April still described him as 'one of the...privie counsayle'. Elizabeth apparently also tried to keep his services in the church. In mid-June, de Quadra reported that the government had even promised Heath that they would refrain from administering him the supremacy oath and allow him his revenues if he would appoint a 'heretic vicar-general' to perform those episcopal functions he would not in conscience do.[2]

John Mason wrote to Cecil in March that he 'assuredly' thought Thomas Thirlby would conform. In April the bishop returned from France where he had been an English representative in the peace negotiations. Count Feria was relieved to report to Philip that Thirlby spoke in the Lords 'like a good Catholic', and that in spite of the efforts of the 'heretics...to gain him over by presents', he had remained firm. Although Elizabeth had assigned Richard Cox the diocese of Norwich, by mid-July, she switched him to Thirlby's

---

[1] Machyn, *Diary*, p. 203; *CSP, Sp.* I, 85, de Quadra, 12 July 1559. They disagree on the exact date of their appearance: 5 or 7 July. *CSP, Ven.* VII, 104, Il Schifanoya, 27 June 1559; CRS, *Miscellanea*, I, 35–6, Sander's report to Cardinal Moroni.

[2] John Hayward, *Annals of the First Four Years of the Reign of Queen Elizabeth*, ed. John Bruce, Camden Society, o.s. vii (London, 1840), p. 2; BM, Cotton MSS, Vespasian F xiii, fo. 287, Heath to Cecil, 26 September 1573; Edmund Lodge, *Illustrations of British History, Biography, and Manners in the Reigns of Henry VIII, Edward VI, Mary, Elizabeth, and James I* (London, 1791), pp. 301–2; Raphael Holinshed, *The Laste Volume of the Chronicles of England, Scotland, and Irelande* (London, 1577), p. 1799 ('1776'); Dasent, *Privy Council*, VII, 5–38; see also Strype, *Annals*, II, part II, 707; *CSP, Sp.* I, 77, de Quadra to Philip, 19 June 1559.

diocese of Ely. Apparently Thirlby's unexpected intransigence had thwarted Elizabeth's plans.[1]

The bishops of Exeter and St David's were deprived in the second week of August. The delay in the case of Turberville of Exeter was clearly deliberate, for Turberville had been in London to stand with his fellow bishops against the religious legislation and could have been deprived with the others. Morgan of St David's, on the other hand, had been absent from Parliament.[2]

On 20 July Cuthbert Tunstall of Durham arrived at court, according to de Quadra, in order 'to tell the Queen what he thought' about religious affairs, and to urge her 'at least, to respect the will of her father'. After he saw the iconoclasm of the queen's visitation in London, he indignantly wrote to Cecil that he could not consent to a similar visitation in Durham nor allow 'any doctrine in my diocese other than Catholic'. On 9 September Elizabeth issued a mandate to him and other bishops to consecrate Parker. No such consecration ensued, and Tunstall was deprived on 28 September.[3] Elizabeth still did not give up. She entrusted Parker with the task of winning Tunstall's conformity. In reply to initial encouraging reports from the archbishop-elect, Cecil wrote: 'It is meant, if he will conform

[1] *CSP, For.* I, 178, Mason to Cecil, 18 March 1559; *CSP, Sp.* I, 64 and 66, Feria to Philip, 29 April and 10 May; *JHL*, I, 574; Machyn, *Diary*, pp. 194 and 201; *ZL*, I, 23, Jewel to Peter Martyr; *CPR*, I, 80, *congés d'élire* for Norwich and for Ely, 5 June and 18 July; *Registrum Matthei Parker, Diocensis Cantuariensis, A.D. 1559–1575*, Register I, ed. E. Margaret Thompson and W. H. Frere (Oxford, 1928), I, 53–6, certificate of election for Ely; see also *ZL*, I, 40, Jewel to P.M., 1 August.

[2] *CSP, Sp.* I, 89, de Quadra to Philip, 3 August 1559; Gee, *Elizabethan Clergy*, p. 37, 10 August; *CSP, For.* I, 471, Marquess of Winchester to Cecil, 14 August; Le Neve, see under 'Exeter', spiritualities seized, 16 November.

[3] *Calendar of State Papers, Domestic Series, of the Reigns of Edward VI, Mary, Elizabeth, 1547–80*, ed. Robert Lemon (London, 1856; hereafter called *CSP, Dom., 1547–80*), p. 127 (I, 37), Elizabeth to Tunstall, 19 December 1558; *CSP, For.* I, 250–1 and 258, 12 and 16 May, Tunstall to Elizabeth and reply; II, 4, Cecil to Throckmorton, 1 October; *CSP, Sp.* I, 89, de Quadra to Philip, 13 August 1559; Machyn, *Diary*, pp. 204 and 214; *Calendar of State Papers, relating to English Affairs, preserved principally at Rome, in the Vatican Archives and Library*, vols. I and II, ed. J. M. Rigg (London, 1916–26; hereafter called *CSP, Rome*), I, 61, Sander to Cardinal Moroni; see also *CSP, For.* I, 346 and 381, 30 June and 13 July, Tunstall to Elizabeth and to Shrewsbury; Charles Sturge, *Cuthbert Tunstall* (London, 1938), p. 323 (from P.R.O. MS, 19 August 1559); Rymer, *Foedera*, VI, part IV, 84.

himself, that both he shall remain bishop and in good favour and credit; otherwise he must needs receive the common order of those who refuse to obey laws.' The hopes were premature, for a few days later, Cecil wrote of the queen's disappointment, since 'the recovery of such a man would have furthered the common affairs of this realm very much'.[1]

Elizabeth had included two other Marian bishops along with Tunstall in her first mandate for Parker's consecration: Bourne of Bath and Wells and David Pole of Peterborough. On 18 October, Elizabeth authorized four local justices to receive Bourne's oath. He refused, for, some time before early January 1560, he was deprived. David Pole was also deprived before the end of 1559.[2] The government retained gleams of hope for Pole and Bourne longer than for any of the other recalcitrant Marian bishops.

The evidence points to one clear conclusion: Elizabeth hoped to win the conformity of eight of Mary's bishops. The second set of dioceses on Cecil's working list of May 1559 correspond exactly to those whose bishops were deprived later than their more obdurate colleagues. Four of the eight had been Henrician bishops, former supporters of royal supremacy who had gone along with Edward's reforms far enough to enforce the first Prayer Book; two others had remained archdeacons to the end of Edward's reign. Morgan had acquired a long string of preferments during the reigns of both Henry and Edward. Although Turberville's record is obscure, he was of an age with older Henrician bishops and had followed Henry as a mature priest into independence. The records of the past ministries of these men could have led the government to expect that they might conform again to a moderate course of reform in an independent church.

In contrast stand the records of Bonner, White, and Watson, to say nothing of the Henrician exiles, Pate, Goldwell, and Bayne who had taught Hebrew in Paris from 1544 until Mary's accession. Bonner had

---

[1] *Parker Corr.*, pp. 77–8, Parker to Cecil, 27 September 1559 and reply, 2 and 5 October; *CSP, For.* II, 4, Cecil to Throckmorton, 1 October.

[2] Rymer, *Foedera*, VI, part IV, 86; *CPR*, I, 447, *congé d'élire* for Bath, 11 January 1560; *Registrum Matthei Parker*, I, 198, *sede vacante* entry for Peterborough, 30 December 1559.

resisted reform earlier and more vigorously than either Heath or Tunstall. Heath and Tunstall had later been imprisoned because, as bishops, a greater degree of conformity to the Edwardian reforms was asked than they were prepared to give. White, just like Watson, had held no such position, and yet he and Watson had been jailed for religion.

Scot, a somewhat younger man like Watson and White, left few traces of his earlier career. On Oglethorpe's record alone, he would be grouped with the more moderate Marians, and he did, after all, anoint and crown the queen. However, by May the government had apparently lost hope of his conformity and expected to replace him as one of the more obdurate papists.

Even with the meagre information available to us today, we can generally distinguish between the two groups of Marian bishops. With infinitely greater knowledge of the men, Elizabeth and her advisers could assess the possibility—and the desirability—of convincing several prelates to retain their sees in the reformed church. Yet, of the eight bishops whom they hoped to win, Kitchin was their sole catch.

How could the queen and her advisers have judged so wrongly? Elizabeth thought that because these men had once left Rome, they would do so again. She misjudged the effects of the reigns of her brother and sister on the religious temper of these conservatives. Their past experiences, on which Elizabeth counted, had, on the contrary, sensitized them to the dangerous consequences of departing from the apostolic see. If some of them were wavering, the protestant efforts in the Commons in early 1559 must have confirmed their fears. They fought the repudiation of Rome with all the legal weapons at their command. Only the aged bishop of Llandaff and the distant bishop of Sodor and Man conformed to the settlement. How different the 1563 Convocation might have been if some of the deprived bishops in prison had, instead, been sitting in the choir of St Paul's!

THE EPISCOPAL BENCH IN 1563

The bishops sitting in the Upper House of Convocation, along with their counterparts of York, shared the major responsibility for the leadership of the Church of England. Elizabeth and her advisers had faced serious difficulties in choosing these men. The failure to win a solid half of the Marian episcopate increased their problem quantitatively and deepened it strategically. If Elizabeth were to pursue a moderate religious policy without the counterbalance of the Marian bishops, she had to pick new prelates with the utmost care in order to keep the church from the domination of the more extreme reformers. Three decades of religious turmoil had seriously disturbed the normal routes of ecclesiastical advancement. The old system of personal recommendation and influence persisted, but after such wholesale changes of leadership it was difficult for the queen to know whose advice to accept.

The problem would have been simple had Elizabeth been content to put clerics on the episcopal bench who were distinguished only for their willingness to comply with the 'king's religion'. To find men of learning, commitment, and leadership who might commend the national church to the people was far more difficult. The experience of Mary's reign had tended to drive such priests either back into the arms of Rome or into exile to learn of continental protestants. Elizabeth could only turn to the returned émigrés for a large proportion of the men of devotion and ability who were to occupy English dioceses during the first years of her reign.

In June and July of 1559 Elizabeth made known her choice of five bishops in addition to Parker: two Edwardian bishops, Barlow for Chichester and Scory for Hereford, and three other moderate exiles, Cox for Ely, Grindal for London, and Jewel for Salisbury.[1] Elizabeth never reinstated the Edwardian practice of naming bishops by

---

[1] Cox was originally named to Norwich, and Edmund Allen, who died in August, to Rochester. *CSP, For.* I, 287, Nowel [?] to Abel, 28 May 1559; Machyn, *Diary*, pp. 200, 201, and 208, 29 May, 23 June, and August; *CSP, Ven.* VII, 94, Il Schifanoya, 5 June; *ZL*, I, 23, 40, and 46, Jewel to Peter Martyr, undated, 1 August, and 2 November; *CPR*, I, 80, *congés d'élire* for Norwich (5 June), Hereford, London, and Chichester (22 June), Ely (18 July), Rochester and Salisbury (27 July).

letters patent, but sent her nominations to cathedral chapters for their elections by the traditional formalities.

Five more bishops were named in November: Sandys to Worcester, Bullingham to Lincoln, Merrick to Bangor, Richard Davies to St Asaph's, and Young to St David's.[1] Parker as archbishop leaned on Bullingham's legal skills, and it was not wholly fortuitous that he arrived for the opening of Convocation in 1563 accompanied by Bullingham. The appointments to the three Welsh dioceses point up a frequently unrecognized side of Elizabeth's policy: they were themselves Welshmen. Of the sixteen bishops she placed in the four Welsh sees, twelve were natives and one a Welsh-speaking Englishman—a proportion which has seldom been greater, before or since.[2]

In December and January Elizabeth nominated four bishops: Pilkington to Winchester, Bentham to Coventry and Lichfield, Berkeley to Bath and Wells, and Guest to Rochester. In the meantime, after Parker was consecrated early in December, the other bishops-elect were gradually consecrated and put in possession of their sees.[3]

In March and April, Elizabeth issued *congés d'élire* for Norwich and Exeter, nominating Parkhurst and Alley.[4] Thus in the first year after the parliamentary settlement, Elizabeth had nominated bishops for all but the four new Henrician sees of the southern province and the four sees in the north.[5] In July 1560 she nominated William May for the archiepiscopal see of York, but he died within two weeks of his

[1] *CPR*, I, 80 and 449, *congés d'élire* for Lincoln (25 November) and Worcester (13 November); *Registrum Matthei Parker*, I, 66–75 and 82–5, election to Bangor (1 December), to St David's (6 December), and to St Asaph's (4 December); see also *ZL*, I, 73, Sandys to Peter Martyr, 1 April 1560.
[2] William Jones, unpublished S.T.B. thesis at General Theological Seminary, New York, 'The Elizabethan Church Settlement in Wales' (1956); see also A. L. Rowse, *The Expansion of Elizabethan England* (London, 1955), p. 178.
[3] *CPR*, I, 408, 447, and 449, *congés d'élire* for Winchester and Coventry (18 and 27 December 1559), and for Bath and Rochester (11 and 22 January 1560); *ZL*, I, 63, Sampson to Peter Martyr, 6 January; Machyn, *Diary*, p. 127, 8 March; *CSP, For.* II, 138, to Challoner, 25 November 1559.
[4] *CPR*, I, 252 and 449, *congés d'élire* for Norwich (27 March 1560) and Exeter (27 April).
[5] On 27 March 1560 Elizabeth also issued a *congé d'élire* for Carlisle, concurrently naming Bernard Gilpin who demurred; see Christopher Wordsworth, *Ecclesiastical Biography...*, 3rd ed. (London, 1839), III, 369–432, especially pp. 395–6 and 411–12; *CPR*, I, 447; *ZL*, I, 73, Sandys to Peter Martyr, 1 April 1560.

nomination. May's career as a moderate reformer was strikingly similar to that of Parker, except that May was more prominent under Edward as dean of St Paul's, and he may have accepted a living under the Marian restoration of Roman obedience.[1]

Archbishop Parker wrote to Cecil on 16 October proposing that Young be translated to York and Guest to Durham.[2] Parker's argument reveals the difficulties which the queen encountered in finding qualified candidates, for he suggested that she play chess with her present bishops if she could not immediately find additional priests suitable to be introduced to the episcopal board. Parker reported that it was 'commonly judged' that the queen delayed 'for money's sake' and pointed to the long-range expense of badly managed dioceses. However, he went on to point out that vacancies in Rochester and St David's would be less damaging than in York and Durham. Since neither southern diocese had sufficient income to substitute for the wealthy northern sees, Parker's argument only applied to a shortage of suitable clerics.

Elizabeth took Parker's advice of moving Young to York, but by the end of December she nominated, not Guest, but Pilkington to Durham.[3] Elizabeth had already reassigned Winchester to Robert Horn, a simple matter since Pilkington seems to have refused it.[4]

[1] *CPR*, I, 449, 25 July 1560; *CSP, For.* II, 138, to Challoner, 25 November 1559; Samuel Haynes, *A Collection of State Papers...from the Year 1542 to 1570...Left by William Cecil*, 2 vols. (London, 1740), I, 323, Cecil to Petre, 4 June; *CSP, For.* III, 100, Petre to Cecil, 6 June; Thomas Wright, ed., *Queen Elizabeth and her Times*, 2 vols. (London, 1838), I, 39, Honning to Sussex, 25 July; Machyn, *Diary*, p. 241. May's *DNB* biographer wrote that May lived 'quietly and unmolested' under Mary; Venn explicitly reported that he became rector of Pulham in Norfolk and 'perhaps' of Longstanton in Cambridgeshire in 1557—could his wife have died in the meantime? (III, 167). For May's restoration in 1559, see *Parker Corr.*, p. 67; H. C. Porter, *Reformation and Reaction in Tudor Cambridge* (Cambridge, 1958), p. 102; Machyn, *Diary*, p. 200; and *CSP, Sp.* I, 76.

[2] *Parker Corr.*, p. 123; see also p. 114.

[3] *Parker Corr.*, p. 134, mandate for Young's translation, 22 January 1561; *CPR*, II, 120, *congé d'élire* for Durham, 26 December 1560; Challoner's correspondent of 25 November 1559 noted that Winchester had been offered to Pilkington 'but refused' (*CSP, For.* II, 138); see above, note 3, p. 44.

[4] *CSP, Dom.*, *1547–80*, p. 163 (XIV, 47), Elizabeth's nomination for Winchester, 24 November 1560; *ZL*, I, 93, Jewel to Peter Martyr, 6 November; *CSP, For.* III, 642, Jones to Throckmorton, 2 or 5 December; *Registrum Matthei Parker*, I, 103–5.

By May 1561 she had translated Richard Davies to take Young's place at St David's and nominated another Welshman, Thomas Davies, to take his namesake's place at St Asaph's.[1]

Just before the beginning of 1561 the queen named Scambler to Peterborough and, a little later, Best to Carlisle and Downham to Chester.[2] Two years after the 1559 Parliament rose, all the English dioceses had been filled except for Gloucester, Bristol and Oxford.

Not until February 1562 did Elizabeth issue the *congé d'élire* for Cheyney to Gloucester and arrange for him to hold Bristol *in commendam*. At the 1563 Convocation, he held the spiritual jurisdiction over both sees, but later in the year complaints from Bristol clerics induced Parker to withdraw the spiritualities of Bristol from Cheyney's charge.[3]

With the appointment of Cheyney, only Oxford lacked direct episcopal supervision, and that was to be the normal state of its affairs. The translation of the infirm Archbishop of Dublin to Oxford in 1567 was merely an accommodation, not a serious attempt to supply the vacancy.[4] Its income, like that of Bristol, was very small. When Cecil drew up his list of dioceses with their values and possible candidates in 1559, he included these two with the sees for which he proposed no candidates, implying that it might be best to make other provision for their care.[5] The arrangement was not as inconvenient to the church as it appears at first glance. Parker

---

[1] *CPR*, II, 147, *congé d'élire* for St David's, 20 February 1561; *Registrum Matthei Parker*, I, 111–14, election to St Asaph's, 5 May 1561.

[2] *CSP, Dom.*, *1547–80*, p. 164 (XIV, 62), election process for Peterborough, 21 December 1560; no preliminary papers for Best's nomination have turned up, but he is listed as consecrated with Pilkington on 2 March 1561 in Parker's *De Antiquitate Britannicae Ecclesiae* (Hanoviae, 1603), p. 37 (second page so numbered); see also Machyn, *Diary*, p. 252, 2 March and *CPR*, II, 2; II, 148, royal assent for Downham, 1 May; *CSP, For.* III, 462, Cecil to Throckmorton, 2 or 5 December 1560.

[3] *CPR*, II, 364, *congé d'élire*, 27 February 1562; *Registrum Matthei Parker*, I, 117–19 and III, 952–6; Henry Ellis, *Original Letters, Illustrative of English History*, 3rd series (London, 1846), 4 vols., III, 354–5, Cheyney to Cecil, 17 September [1563].

[4] *Registrum Matthei Parker*, I, 124 f.; Evelyn Philip Shirley, ed., *Original Letters and Papers...of the Church of Ireland* (London, 1851), pp. 94, 125, and 238; Sussex to Cecil, 2 November 1560; Elizabeth to Sussex, 15 October 1563; and Sidney to Cecil, 23 April 1566; *Parker Corr.*, p. 305, 5 October 1567. Elizabeth also put a bishop in Oxford in 1589 who remained until his death in 1592.

[5] See above, p. 37, n. 2.

delegated administrative responsibilities to the archdeacon of Oxford
—by chance, the same priest who had held the post when the diocese
had been one archdeaconry in the diocese of Lincoln.[1] Neighbouring
bishops or a suffragan might provide episcopal sacramental ministries.
It was hardly an ideal situation from the standpoint of theology, polity,
or pastoral concern, but the alternative of the times for a small impecunious diocese was to allow the bishop to retain parish or cathedral
livings to augment his inadequate episcopal revenues.[2]

The Elizabethan bench of bishops in 1563 comprised a varied
group of men, but given the religious upheavals of the preceding
years, their qualifications were not unimpressive. The proportion of
scholarly attainments among them is striking. Six of the twenty-
three newly preferred bishops in both provinces had held major
university or college posts. Thirteen of them had been fellows of
their colleges, and of the remaining ten, three had bachelor degrees in
theology and three had doctorates in law.

Three of the Elizabethan bishops had similarly served in Edward's
reign, four had been deans, and three archdeacons. In all, fourteen
of the twenty-four had carried out important academic or diocesan
administrative responsibilities during the Edwardian reforms,
giving them some experience in the initiation and enforcement of
important changes in church life. Thomas Davies, and of course
Kitchin, had had similar diocesan administrative experience under
the Marian restoration.

The deprived Marian bishops were not the only 'might-have-
beens' of the Upper House of Convocation in 1563. Nine members
of the Lower House and four other clerics had had in 1559 a serious
claim on an episcopal appointment. Three former Edwardian
bishops[3] were available: Miles Coverdale, John Bale, and Thomas

[1] Edward Marshall, *Oxford* (London, 1882), pp. 106–9.
[2] For example, Elizabeth licensed the following Welsh bishops to hold other livings
in commendam: Young, 22 December 1559; R. Davies, St Asaph's, 4 January 1560;
Merrick, Bangor, 20 December 1559 (Rymer, *Foedera*, VI, part IV, 89–92). Parker
once observed that 'the inconvenience may be thought less than that the order of
godly ministers in that function should be brought to contempt for lack of reasonable
necessaries' (*Parker Corr.*, 18 March 1564).
[3] I am omitting here one aged deprived Edwardian bishop, Edward Staples, formerly
of Meath; see Shirley, *Original Letters*, pp. 87–9. I also omit all suffragan bishops

47

Lancaster. Cecil's work sheet listed ten men for possible bishoprics who did not subsequently receive them: William Bill, David White-head, Thomas Sampson, Alexander Nowell, Thomas Becon, John Pullan, John Aylmer, Robert Wisdom, John Peddar, and Thomas Lever. These thirteen were clearly viable candidates for the newly independent national church. They illuminate, by contrast, the character of the men who actually sat in the Upper House in 1563.

Two-and-a-half centuries ago Bishop Burnet wrote that Thomas Sampson refused the see of Norwich, and ever since historians have given the troublesome former exile plaudits he does not deserve. Careful reading of the evidence suggests that he was considered for the post, but that Elizabeth never offered it to him—much to his feigned relief and deep chagrin.[1]

Of the thirteen unsuccessful candidates, Bill and Lancaster were the only two who had not gone abroad in Mary's reign. Bill, who died before the 1563 Convocation met, had been Elizabeth's chaplain and almoner, and it may be that after Abbot Feckenham's refusal to conform she decided to employ him as dean of Westminster rather than as a bishop.[2] Elizabeth preferred Lancaster to the minor post of treasurer of Salisbury Cathedral, in which capacity he attended the 1563 Convocation, and in 1568, at the request of the Lord Deputy of Ireland, she was to appoint him to the see of Armagh where he earned the reputation of a zealous reformer.[3]

---

such as John Hodgekin and John Salisbury since the qualifications for a suffragan are not necessarily those for a diocesan.

[1] I have set out the evidence in *Historical Magazine of the Protestant Episcopal Church*, xxxvi (1967), 383–6. My statement there that Peter Martyr 'consistently' advised Sampson to accept a proffered bishopric ought to be qualified by the observation that by November 1559 Bullinger had momentarily persuaded Martyr to advise that vestments ought never be worn; by February both men had changed their minds (*ZL*, ii, 32–3 and 38–41).

[2] Machyn, *Diary*, p. 201; *CSP, For.* i, 287; Rymer, *Foedera*, vi, part iv, 66 and 103–4, almoner, 20 December 1558, establishment of collegiate church, 21 June 1560; *CSP, Sp.* i, 18, Feria to Philip, 29 December; Machyn, *Diary*, p. 204, 4 July 1559; *CSP, Ven.* vii, 95, Il Schifanoya, 6 June.

[3] Rymer, *Foedera*, vi, part iv, 85; G. V. Jourdan, *History of the Church of Ireland...*, ii, 169–579, ed. W. A. Phillips (London, 1934), p. 361; for the manœuvres before Lancaster's appointment see Shirley, *Original Letters*, pp. 307 and 322–3.

John Aylmer did eventually become bishop of London, but not until 1577. Elizabeth may have objected to his services to the usurper Lady Jane Grey, or she may have disliked the condescending tone of his defence of the rule of women. In any case, for eighteen years, as he once described his life, he 'studied to be forgotten and bury [him]self in the country' as archdeacon of Lincoln.[1]

Except for Aylmer, the exiles among these potential bishops had records of reforming zeal well to the ecclesiastical left of the men whom Elizabeth actually named. Coverdale, Bale, Wisdom, and Becon had all been in trouble in Henry's reign for heretical writings or activities—a nonconforming disobedience not likely to appeal to Elizabeth. Sampson had been one of the first to refuse the usual priestly vestments. During the exile, Coverdale and Pullan had held office in the Genevan congregation. Lever had left Geneva to take Coverdale's pastorate with the Wesel–Arau congregation. These three had all subscribed to the proposal for an exiles' common front at the beginning of Elizabeth's reign. Nowell, Peddar, and White-head had supported the congregational New Discipline at Frankfort. The controversial writings of Becon and Sampson had been ex-cessively violent, as had Bale's in earlier years. After Pullan returned to England, he was arrested in April 1559 for preaching in violation of Elizabeth's proclamation banning sermons.[2]

The Convocation of 1563 might have taken a drastically different course had a large proportion of these militant reformers been sitting in the Upper House in the place of some of their more moderate brethren. Elizabeth had not been successful in persuading a signi-ficant portion of the Marian bishops to remain, but she had kept potential candidates on the opposite end of the English religious spectrum out of the first ranks of leadership. Fourteen of the Eliza-bethan bishops had been drawn from the Marian exiles with con-servative records abroad; six from the clerics who retired in England

---

[1] John Aylmer, *An Harborowe for Faithful and Trewe Subjectes Agaynst the Late Blowne Blaste, Concerning the Gouernmēt of Women* (Strasburg [but probably London], 1559), fos. B2, I1; see also *Parker Corr.*, p. 350, to Cecil, 3 June 1569; *Calendar of State Papers, Domestic Series…Addenda, 1547–1565*, ed. M. A. E. Green (London, 1870), p. 563 (XII, 54), Aylmer to Throckmorton, 14 April 1565.

[2] Dasent, *Privy Council*, VII, 87–8 and 92, 17 and 24 April 1559.

while Mary was on the throne; and three from those who continued their priestly work during the Marian reaction; finally, one from each province remained bishop from Mary's reign, ineffective leaders, but symbols of episcopal continuity.

Shortly after Convocation, Parker wrote to Cecil of his fellow bishops: 'the Queen Majesty may have good cause to be well contented with her choice of the most of them, very few excepted'.[1] Puritans and Roman Catholics judged quite differently from Parker, and their judgments have been perpetuated in succeeding centuries, tarring the Elizabethan episcopate with one brush. Considering the achievement of the Elizabethan church in establishing a distinct and enduring Christian tradition, Parker's judgment deserves more serious consideration than it has received.

THE VARIEGATED LOWER HOUSE

The Lower House of the 1563 Convocation, as we have seen, represented a far wider variety of ecclesiastical loyalties and theological convictions than the upper body. Not only were some former convinced Roman Catholics and many Marian conformists in the house, but also included were a far wider range of militant reformers. All the potential bishops of 1559 among the militants except for Coverdale and Whitehead found seats in the Lower House. Twelve more former émigrés in the house had had records abroad as militant as those of the rejected episcopal candidates.[2] These twenty Convocation men, about one-fifth of the membership present, constituted a formidable legislative minority if they were prepared to work together. Drawing to them the considerable number of other reform-minded clerics, they could serve as the nucleus of a group determined to bring the English Church to greater spiritual perfection —a group who cannot yet be called 'puritans', but may, after Archbishop Parker's slightly later use, be termed 'precisians'.

[1] *Parker Corr.*, p. 173.
[2] Besely, Crowley, Mullins, Rogers, Saul, Sorby, Watts, Wilson, Beaumont, Spencer, Wiburn, and Thomas Cole are all to be grouped with Bale, Lever, Becon, Nowell, Peddar, Pullan, Sampson, and Wisdom.

How did these men so quickly achieve positions of leadership in the Elizabethan church so that they were indeed eligible for Convocation? For one thing, they held many of the posts which had, under Mary, been given to strong Roman Catholic supporters; understandably, a higher proportion than the average among English clerics refused to conform to the Elizabethan church and so left their livings vacant. Correspondingly, clerical exiles returned looking for jobs. Elizabeth probably favoured about seventy of these men herself with preferments to Crown livings between 1559 and 1561.[1]

The attitude of the queen is instructive. Although she slightly tended to favour the more conservative exiles in these presentations, she erected none of the barriers which had kept the more militant reformers from episcopal office.[2] She and her advisers well knew that, as a group, the returned exiles were well above the average of the parish clergy in learning and in devotion to their calling. She was content that they should exercise their ministry in England, provided they were willing to conform. Some of these men could not conscientiously conform to Prayer Book discipline and were later deprived, but Elizabeth presumed their conformity until they publicly paraded their scruples.

When the whole Convocation assembled in the cathedral to ask God's blessings on their common deliberations, its members harboured quite diverse hopes and plans. The Lower and Upper Houses were to follow distinct courses of action partly because of the different mixtures of convictions represented in the two parts of the Synod. More distinguished bodies of British clerics have on occasion gathered in St Paul's to open a Convocation of Canterbury, but seldom, if ever, were Convocation men to engage in so bitter a struggle over so wide a range of issues concerning the church's liturgy, discipline, and doctrine.

[1] Henry Gee reported that the Lansdowne MSS include 583 royal presentations in Elizabeth's reign up to 25 March 1561 (*Elizabethan Clergy*, pp. 238 and 143). Rymer lists 246 for this same period (*Foedera*, VI, part IV, 69–115, *passim*). Twenty-nine of these names, or 12 per cent, can be probably identified as exiles. If the proportion holds good for all 583 men, about 70 would have been exiles.

[2] Fifteen of her presentees (excluding the fifteen episcopal nominations) belonged to the more moderate body of exiles; thirteen had revealed more militant convictions abroad. By these same rough standards, the whole group of clerics and students abroad divide into seventy-nine 'moderates' and ninety-nine 'militants'.

4-2

2. The course of Convocation

THE Convocation of 1563 was the first synod of the English Church to meet under the conditions of the Elizabethan settlement. Too often historians have treated that settlement either as the uncreative dénouement to the events in earlier years, or as a compromise forced on the English Church by a politically minded queen determined to please as many of her subjects as possible. The settlement was both a dénouement and a compromise, but such minimizing terms do not do justice to the historical record. If in these pages I seem to give inordinate attention to the ecclesiastical details of the first decade of Elizabeth's reign, it is because I hope, in some small measure, to redress the balance. I am convinced that the unique character of the Church of England has always lain precisely in the peculiar combination and use which it has made of elements bequeathed to it in 1558 from earlier years. The shape which the English Church assumed in the opening years of Elizabeth's reign determined much of its future life as an heir of the church catholic with a distinctive life and thought of its own.

The ecclesiastical possibilities open to Elizabeth in 1558 were much wider than historians have usually recognized. Indeed, had she been so minded, a continuation of the Roman obedience is not so far-fetched as it is often assumed. Free of Mary's Spanish marriage and her unnecessarily harsh scourging of heresy, a papal church need not have been onerous to the vast majority of Englishmen. The pope had every reason to overlook Elizabeth's technical illegitimacy in order to retain England's spiritual allegiance. Elizabeth was not so minded, and in the first weeks of the reign signs appeared to indicate that she was preparing to assert once again the ecclesiastical independence of her nation.

Rejection of Rome settled very little about the particular form of the Church of England. The course of the independent church from 1534 to 1553 and the lives of the exile communities abroad showed some of the various moulds to which the independent church might be shaped. It remained to be seen whether the church would travel farther along the road taken in Edward's reign, or return to the final Edwardian settlement, or look for guidance in earlier and milder reforming measures.

The reigns of Edward and Mary had made convinced papists out of the most resolute of the conservatives and, consequently, their refusal to take the supremacy oath eliminated them as an influence within the English Church. Other conservatives were now finally prepared to come to terms with the English Reformation. The struggle for the leadership of the church was rapidly shifting from the old polarization between conservatives and a somewhat amorphous body of reformers to a new alignment, which drew together the heirs of Henrician conservatism with the moderate reformers in opposition to more militant reformers who were determined to press for more drastic changes. The word puritan had not yet come into currency, but the Convocation was the first major battleground of those groups which we call today puritan and anglican. Their struggles had been foreshadowed by many disagreements in the reigns of Henry, Edward, and Mary, but these skirmishes had seldom been fought centre-stage. Now, in the reign of Elizabeth, with the independence of the national church finally assured, they battled to establish their respective ideals in the forms and policies of the Church of England, and in the hearts and minds of her sons.

CONVOCATION GETS UNDER WAY

The legislative struggle between the precisians and the more moderate reformers in the Convocation of 1563 has left only a few marks on the records available to us today. The full Convocation acts have not survived, and so we have no account of the crucial course of events in the Lower House other than the report of one voting division. Bishop Edmund Gibson fortunately included an account of the acts of the Upper House in his *Synodus Anglicana* of 1702. Some of the working papers have survived in the Petyt collection of the Inner Temple and in the Synodalia manuscripts which Archbishop Parker left to Corpus Christi College, Cambridge.

John Strype and others have called attention to these documents by reprinting parts of them, but no real attempt has been made to go beyond the very imprecise generalities offered by Strype concerning their use in Convocation. I hope that the ensuing reconstruction of the course of this synod may serve as the beginning of a re-evaluation of these documents.[1]

The Convocation bore two fruits: the Thirty-nine Articles of Religion with their attached second book of Homilies and the clerical subsidy for the Queen. The passage of these two successful bits of legislation can be traced with some fair accuracy through Convocation. The other proposals considered in these meetings have left more ambiguous traces in our records. Yet we can discern at least the shadow of some of these proposals as they made their uncertain and, in the end, unsuccessful passages through the clerical legislative meetings.

After Archbishop Parker received Elizabeth's brief of 11 November licensing him to summon the province of Canterbury in Convocation on 12 January 1563, he ordered Bishop Grindal of London, as *ex officio* dean of the province, to pass his summons along to the other bishops.[2] Since Parliament, scheduled to open on 11 January, was postponed one day, Convocation could not begin until Wednesday, 13 January. In the meantime, on Tuesday, at parliamentary formalities, Alexander Nowell, dean of St Paul's, preached in the Abbey.[3] This zealous Marian exile was to become one of the main actors in the drama of Convocation.

On the following morning, as we have seen, Archbishop Parker arrived at St Paul's Cathedral for the opening of Convocation. After the Prayer Book litany and the *Veni Creator* had been sung in English, William Day, the provost of Eton College, preached in

---

[1] Appendix 1 discusses the manuscripts in detail, and the following reconstruction assumes the information and conclusions of that discussion (see below pp. 342 f.).

[2] Strype, *Parker*, 1, 236; quotations and references to the meetings of Convocation, unless otherwise indicated, are all taken from the transcript of the acts of the Upper House in Cardwell's *Synodalia* (see below, Appendix 1, p. 342).

[3] *Journals of the House of Commons from...1547...to 1628*, vol. 1 (1803) (hereafter called *JHC*), p. 62; *A Catechism Written in Latin by Alexander Nowell*, ed. G. E. Corrie (Cambridge, 1853), pp. 223–9, Nowell's sermon.

Latin on the text 'Feed the flock of God which is among you'. A psalm was sung, and Bishop Grindal began the Holy Communion. If the order proposed in a preliminary treatise prepared for Parker was actually followed, the archbishop and his suffragans went forward at the time of the offertory to 'offer an oblation'. They presumably would have followed the manner of the 1549 Prayer Book which directed 'as many as are disposed' to come forward to the 'poor men's box' which was placed near the altar. The bishops, and perhaps others as well, all received the 'sacrament of the body and blood of the Lord'.[1]

Reassembling in the chapter house with the bishops seated and the other clergy standing, the archbishop presided over the opening formalities.[2] He then made a 'brief speech full of eloquence' to the Convocation setting forth its purposes. He announced that, among other things, the synod provided an opportunity to 'reform things in the Church of England'. No unusual significance ought to be read into this proposal, for Gibson has collected a whole series of comments from opening primatial addresses back to 1400 which declared the *reformanda* to be among the reasons for the summons of Convocation.[3] The archbishop ended by asking the clergy of the Lower House to elect a prolocutor and to present him on the coming Saturday; he commended to them the name of Alexander Nowell. The archbishop was not obliged to nominate a man for the office, but, in earlier years, the prolocutor had often been one of the archbishop's own officials, and, in subsequent years, other primates occasionally followed Parker's example in explicitly naming a candidate.[4] Parker then ordered his officials to examine the certificates of the bishops and to inspect the proxies of those absent and their reasons. Finally, he prorogued the Convocation until Saturday the sixteenth.

At the next session the archbishop led the whole congregation in the litany in Latin with collects and a special prayer, newly edited for

[1] Edmund Gibson, *Synodus Anglicana*, ed. Edward Cardwell (Oxford, 1854), p. 164; *The First and Second Prayer Books of Edward VI*, Everyman ed. (London, 1949), p. 219.
[2] The standing of the lower clergy is explicitly mentioned in Parker's preliminary treatise (Gibson, *Synodus*, pp. 164–6).
[3] Gibson, *Synodus*, pp. 118 f.   [4] *Ibid.* pp. 53–4.

the provincial synod. The Lower House departed and soon sent Nowell back as their choice for prolocutor, escorted by his fellow exile Thomas Sampson, dean of Oxford, and by the Marian conformist Gabriel Goodman, dean of Westminster.[1] Not unexpectedly, once the formal procedures had been observed, Parker 'approved and confirmed' the election of the man whom he himself had nominated. He then dismissed the clerics of the Lower House and instructed his episcopal brethren to be ready at the next session to present those things needing reform in their dioceses. The session was prorogued, but not before the bishops had held one of their many 'certain secret discussions'. How frustrating are these episcopal executive sessions to the historian! He cannot help but think that during them the most interesting and revealing conversations took place. It was probably such conversations as these that Parker described to Cecil in the letter following the end of the synod:

Calling to remembrance [what] the qualities of all my brethren be in experience of our convocation societies, I see some of them to be *pleni rimarum, hac atque illac effluunt* [i.e. unable to keep anything to themselves], although indeed the Queen's Majesty may have good cause to be well contended with her choice of most of them, very few excepted, amongst whom I count my self. And furthermore, though we have done amongst ourselves little in our own cause, yet I assure you our mutual conferences have taught us such experiences, that I trust we shall all be the better in governance for hereafter.[2]

The conferences held in secret certainly did not bring all of the bishops to one mind, but they apparently understood better both one another and their common responsibilities.

Among the working papers are two proposals of Bishop Sandys of Worcester and one of Bishop Alley of Exeter.[3] These bishops may well have presented their proposals at the next session on Tuesday, 19 January as Parker had requested. In the first of these papers, Sandys proposed minor changes in the Prayer Book and called for the reconstitution of the committee on canon law revision provided

[1] 'Exon.' after Sampson's name is an obvious error for 'Oxon.' (*Synodalia*, II, 504).
[2] *Parker Corr.*, p. 173, Parker to Cecil.
[3] See Appendix I, pp. 343–4.

for in legislation of the reigns of both Henry and Edward. Bishop Grindal noted in the margin that the liturgical changes could be done in synod. Such notes by Grindal, which appear on several papers, ought not to be misinterpreted. They may indicate that he contributed to and supported the proposals in the papers, but this is not necessarily the case. As dean of the province, Grindal was an officer of Convocation and a means of communication between the metropolitan and his suffragans. He could well have made such personal comments as an aid to the archbishop before he passed the papers on to him.

The second paper of the bishop of Worcester listed eight various items 'to be observed by the bishops and other ecclesiastical persons, by their consents and subscriptions in this present synod'. No subscription was forthcoming, and the proposals must have died in the executive sessions of the Upper House. Bishop Parkhurst, in his hope for reform, must have heard Sandys' proposals with joy.

Bishop Alley's paper, in the form of a speech to the house, touched on matters of doctrine and discipline. His concern for some definition of the credal clause about Christ's descent into hell must have provided substance for the ensuing discussions over the Articles of Religion. In Alley's practical requests for ending controversies and establishing better discipline, we hear the voice of a pastoral bishop, exasperated by foolish arguments about vestments and frustrated by his inability to enforce good order in his diocese.

The session of 19 January took place in Westminster Abbey and marked the beginning of the real work of Convocation. The proceedings illustrate the relationship between the houses and their respective powers. The bishops first talked of 'certain articles being made in relation to the Christian faith'—undoubtedly the opening formal discussions on the Articles of Religion. Then the archbishop turned his attention to the work of the Lower House, and the formal report of the meeting continued:

At length the said most reverend commanded the prolocutor of the Lower House to be summoned to him: wherewith, indeed, the prolocutor, being present before the fathers together with six other clerics from the Lower House, reported and claimed that certain of the said Lower House had exhibited papers of things to be reformed, these having been devised by them and rendered in writing. Which papers were indeed by common consent handed over to certain grave and learned men selected for this purpose from the meeting of the said Lower House to be looked over and considered. It was assigned to these selected men (as [Nowell] asserted) that by this means they might reduce the papers into chapters and exhibit them in the next session before the same prolocutor. And [Nowell] further reported that the articles published (as he asserted) in the Synod of London in the time of the late King Edward VI were handed over to certain other men selected for that purpose also out of the said Lower House that they might diligently look over, examine, and consider them, and, just as it will be seen by them, that they may correct, reform, and also exhibit them at the next session. And then the most reverend willed and commanded them to proceed in these things towards the next session according to their determination.

It is clear, first of all, that the prolocutor served not only the legislative house which elected him, but also the metropolitan who approved and confirmed his election. In this session, Parker commanded Nowell to appear before the bishops, heard a full account of the proceedings of the Lower House to date and, approving them, ordered Nowell to have the clergy proceed as they had determined. The Convocation controversy at the opening of the eighteenth century stimulated Bishop Gibson to search out the development of these Convocation procedures. He established that in its medieval origin the prolocutor had been both a spokesman for the lower clergy when the two houses met in one body and also the presiding officer at the occasional sessions of the clergy when the archbishop ordered them to withdraw and to consider particular assigned topics. As Gibson noted, Parker's 1563 pre-Convocation description of the proceedings had specifically described the prolocutor's office in these terms.[1] Since by custom Convocation had come to meet more frequently in separate houses than as one body, the prolocutor's responsibilities were naturally extended so that he also carried back the advice and directions of the bishops to the lower clergy.

The subordination of the prolocutor to the archbishop suggests

[1] Gibson, *Synodus*, pp. 50–1 and 165.

the more important subordination of the Lower House to the bishops. Again, as Gibson so convincingly insisted, the position of the Lower House in Convocation was not at all comparable to the position of the House of Commons in Parliament. Rather 'the constitution and proceedings of an English convocation, to the glory of it, are exactly modelled according to the primitive distinction between bishops and their presbyters in point of order and authority'. In more recent studies, both Canon E. W. Kemp and the late Dr Norman Sykes have substantially confirmed Bishop Gibson's conclusions.[1]

The actual powers of the Lower House were summarized by Gibson in four parts:

To present their own and the church's grievances to the president and bishops.

To offer to their lordships their petitions of any other kind.

To be with them as a part of the judicature upon persons convened and examined in convocation.

To dissent finally from any matter, so as to hinder its passing into a synodical act.[2]

The Lower House had a veto over synodical action, but otherwise their legislative initiative was limited to their offering advice and proposals to the bishops for their consideration.

Bishops Grindal and Horn were somewhat less than completely frank when in 1567 they defended themselves in a letter to Zurich against puritan charges that the bishops dominated the church government:

That railing accusation...is false, that the whole management of church government is in the hands of the bishops; although we do not deny but that a precedence is allowed them. For ecclesiastical matters...are usually deliberated upon in convocation....The bishops are present, and also certain of the more learned of the clergy of the whole province, whose number is three times as great as that of the bishops. These deliberate by

---

[1] *Ibid.* pp. 15 f. and 75; Kemp, *Counsel and Consent*, pp. 166–9; Norman Sykes, *From Sheldon to Secker* (Cambridge, 1959), chapter 2, 'The eclipse of Convocation', especially pp. 45–52.

[2] Gibson, *Synodus*, p. 112.

themselves upon ecclesiastical matters apart from the bishops, and nothing is determined or decided in convocation without the common consent and approbation of both parties, or at least of a majority. So far are we from not allowing the clergy to give their opinion in ecclesiastical matters of this kind.

The puritans who replied in turn to this defence filled in the other side of the picture: 'They may discuss and determine, but in such a way as that nothing is held to be binding and ratified without the consent of the queen and the archbishop.' The lower clergy might propose, but in Convocation it was indeed the bishops who disposed as they deemed best.[1]

Nowell reported to the bishops that some members of the Lower House had exhibited lists of 'things to be reformed'. This was in accordance with traditional Convocation procedures. As Gibson summarized the evidence from both pre-Reformation and post-Reformation synods, the clergy in the Lower House, 'who are supposed to be eyewitnesses of many things which do not ordinarily reach the notice of their diocesan', may either by voice or by schedules place such *reformanda* before the bishops.[2]

These *reformanda* before the Lower House probably included two of the extant working papers: 'Certain articles' and 'General notes'.[3] Both papers had been prepared prior to the opening of Convocation. Strype suggested that the 'Certain articles' originated in the immediate circle of Parker and Grindal, and a host of succeeding writers, including the archbishop's recent biographer, have echoed the suggestion. The evidence, as discussed in the appendix, indicates only that Grindal took a warm enough interest in the paper to propose changes in it and that Parker more sparingly commented upon it. The participation of the metropolitan and dean of the province in the conception of the paper remains an open question. I rather suspect that the paper was submitted, either voluntarily or by request, for Parker's perusal and that then Grindal and Parker added their comments. Such a submission to the presiding officer of

[1] *ZL*, I, 179, Grindal and Horn to Bullinger and Gualter, 6 February 1567; II, 150, Withers and Barthelot to Bullinger and Gualter, February 1567.
[2] Gibson, *Synodus*, p. 123. [3] See appendix I, pp. 345–52.

the Upper House would have been highly irregular had the Lower House been a body with a status equal to that of the bishops, but given its position as a subordinate part of Convocation under the presidency of the archbishop, this procedure would have been natural and orderly.

In the absence of more evidence, the place of 'Certain articles' must remain conjectural, but certainly the paper represented the concern of some members of Convocation to use the meetings to introduce a programme of wide doctrinal, liturgical, and disciplinary reforms in the Church of England. The full title read, 'Certain articles in substance desired to be granted by the queen's majesty'. The authors realized that Convocation was only the first step, for they would eventually have to persuade the queen to approve their reforms.

'General notes' was unquestionably the most important and influential of these preliminary papers. Many of its specific proposals were taken up word for word in two of the later papers produced by the Lower House. Divided into four main sections on doctrine, liturgy, clerical and lay discipline, and ministerial finances, the paper treated of topics from the position of the holy table in churches to the penalties for stealing a 'maid from her parents'. The omissions and faulty arrangement in Strype's transcription have obscured its careful organization.

A series of occasional marginal comments appear on the manuscript, two of them in Parker's hand, and another suggesting that he may have dictated others. The archbishop probably made such comments in his normal role as president of the Convocation rather than as an advocate of all the reforms contained in it. Seven of the many articles have a marginal note like '*deliberatur*', indicating that the commentator selected some items which he judged appropriate for discussion in synod.

If it can be maintained that the militant reformers of the Lower House of the 1563 Convocation formed a coherent party, then 'General notes' served as its most complete official prospectus. It proposed a carefully articulated programme of reform in almost all aspects of church life.

Nowell also reported to the Upper House that a committee of lower clergy were at work to reduce the *reformanda* into chapters. Presumably they wished to lay before the bishops not only the ills of the church, but also specific medicines which might be taken to cure them. The Lower House normally framed such proposals in the form of petitions subscribed by its members.[1]

Nowell told the bishops that the lower clergy were also considering the Forty-two Articles of Edward VI. The initiative taken by members of the Lower House in doctrinal matters was perhaps somewhat unusual, but they did have the immediate precedent of the strongly Roman Catholic Convocation of 1559 in which the lower clergy had petitioned the bishops to maintain five articles which they had drawn up to buttress traditional medieval doctrines of the Eucharist and of the papacy.[2]

By Tuesday 19 January the Convocation had been launched into its work. The formalities were over. At the recommendation of the primate, the Lower House had chosen the zealous Nowell as its chief officer. Proposals of reform had been introduced into both houses. The bishops had begun talking about the Articles of Religion, while their subordinate clerical brethren were discussing both doctrine and more general plans of reform.

THE ACCOMPLISHMENTS OF THE CONVOCATION

During the fifteen sessions between 20 January and 22 February, Convocation completed both the Articles of Religion and the clerical subsidy. The bishops held only four 'secret discussions' before they subscribed the Thirty-nine Articles of Religion on 29 January. The manuscript which the bishops signed was originally prepared with forty-two articles like the 1553 set, but the bishops introduced further changes in the course of their discussions, reducing the articles to thirty-nine.[3] Although the bishops knew that the nether house was also considering the doctrinal articles they probably

[1] Gibson, *Synodus*, p. 125.
[2] Cardwell, *Synodalia*, II, 492–3; see below, pp. 86–8.
[3] See appendix I, p. 352.

had sufficient difficulty in resolving their own disagreements without compounding the problem by adding the opinions of their
presbyteral brethren. Three bishops from the province of York also
signed the manuscript of the Articles, and these northern prelates, in
London to attend the House of Lords, may have been invited to
sit in on some of the discussions of the Upper House of Canterbury.

Subscription was normal Convocation procedure, for Gibson
concluded that at least from 1536 more important legislation such
as 'articles, canons, and constitutions' had been passed by subscription of both bishops and lower clergy.[1] The metropolitan sent
the Articles of Religion on to the Lower House for their approval,
and on 5 February, in answer to the Bishops' summons, prolocutor
Nowell and six fellow-members of the nether house appeared with
the 'little book of doctrine'. Nowell reported that some of the lower
clergy had already subscribed and asked that others might still have
opportunity to do so. The bishops granted the extension of time,
but specified that they wanted the names of the non-subscribers at
the next meeting.

At the next session on 10 February, Nowell again appeared with
eight others before the bishops and showed them the book of articles
with more, but still not all, of the subscriptions of the members of
the Lower House. The manuscript attached to the bishops' signed
copy of the Articles bears ninety-one signatures and is headed by the
statement that the men who signed below had subscribed to the
book of articles on 5 February. We do not know whether the list
contains the names of any who signed after that date.

Apparently the bishops received the book with its incomplete
signatures and ordered Nowell to have the list of non-subscribers at
the next session. No entry in the acts indicates whether such a list
was ever presented, but five months later Grindal believed that all
the clergy present at Convocation had signed.[2]

In the subscriptions to the Articles, the members of the Lower

[1] Gibson, *Synodus*, pp. 135–7.
[2] *The Remains of Edmund Grindal*, ed. William Nicholson, Parker Society (Cambridge, 1843), p. 257, Grindal to Cecil, 17 July 1563; on the MS, 87 Lower House members signed in person and 4 more through prolocutors.

House had exercised their right to approve or disapprove the action of the bishops. This right of the lower clergy to the veto grew out of the final fusion of two separate clerical bodies in the latter part of the fourteenth century: Convocation and the provincial council. From that time in England, the synodical titles were virtually interchangeable, and since the English clergy had a veto over the subsidies of Convocation, they assumed a similar veto in the ecclesiastical concerns of the council.[1] And so the approval of the Lower House was required for the Articles of Religion; after some hesitation, the clergy subscribed.

Doctrinal matters did not absorb the entire attention of the lower clergy, for the militant party were busy rallying support for the liturgical reforms which they proposed in their 'Seven articles' and 'Six articles'.[2] A third of the Lower House signed the 'Seven articles' which called for reform of Prayer Book ceremonies and of clerical garb. Led by Prolocutor Nowell himself, the subscribers included six cathedral deans, thirteen archdeacons and fifteen others. Twenty out of the twenty-seven Marian exiles in the house subscribed, accounting for well over half of the thirty-four signatures. 'General notes' had proposed about half of the reforms demanded in the 'Seven articles'. Even though the authors did not win the support of a majority of the house, the number of subscribers was impressive.

Probably the failure of the precisians to win majority support for the 'Seven articles' led to the preparation of the 'Six articles', which were slightly more moderate in their demands for reform. The one extant scrap of the acts of the Lower House describes the debate and division which took place over the 'Six articles' on Saturday 13 February. Some of the lower clergy declared themselves in favour of or against the articles; others simply wanted to refer the reforms to the bishops without recommendation; still others also gave no opinion on the merits of the articles, but objected to any proposal which contravened the Prayer Book authorized by Parliament. Debate was especially fierce over the proposal to modify the rubric for kneeling at holy communion. All the eight speakers who

[1] Gibson, *Synodus*, pp. 130–1; Kemp, *Counsel and Consent*, pp. 106–12.
[2] See appendix 1, pp. 353–4.

supported the reforms had subscribed the earlier 'Seven articles', and they included the prolocutor's brother Lawrence, Lever, Pullan, and Pedder. Among the four opposing the reforms in debate were Andrew Perne, the conforming dean of Ely, Archdeacon John Cottrell, and Thomas Byckley, one of the archbishop's chaplains.[1]

When the division was finally taken, forty-three members present favoured the liturgical reforms and only thirty-five opposed them. But when the proxies were totalled up, the precisians discovered that they had been defeated by one vote, fifty-nine to fifty-eight. The prolocutor could not present even the 'Six articles' to the bishops as the mind of the Lower House. The militant reformers had won considerable support for their programme of liturgical reform, but this was clearly an issue which divided the members of the Lower House into two groups of approximately equal strength.

Popular church history has magnified this vote beyond all proportion. Had the vote gone in favour of the 'Six articles', they would have still had difficult hurdles to jump before they could have affected church life. A favourable vote would have assured a formal petition to the Upper House—and nothing more. The bishops disposed in Convocation, and the queen's assent would have presented an even more formidable barrier to liturgical changes.

The subsidy from the clergy to the queen was a minor issue from our standpoint, but of immediate concern to the clergy who would pay it and to the government which had to meet expenses incurred in its recent military adventures in Scotland and France. The acts report that the Upper House discussed the subsidy on 5 February, and when Nowell returned the subscriptions to the Articles of Religion on 10 February, he also brought with him a book of the subsidy and 'gave it up to the authority of the bishops'. The bishops were discussing the subsidy during the debate and division of the lower clergy on 13 February, and they discussed it again two days later.

[1] The other four speakers in favour of the articles were Crowley, another Marian exile, Calfhill and Nevinson, two men who had delayed their ordinations until Elizabeth's reign, and John Walker. The other speaker against the articles was Thomas Hewit.

On 19 February the archbishop called Nowell, who came with six others to the Upper House. The archbishop presented them with six articles in English, and asked them to return the opinions of the Lower House in writing. Four of the articles asked about the financial conditions of benefices, one asked for the number of vacancies in each diocese, and the initial article inquired whether a new financial survey of the English Church, presumably with new valuations of each living, would 'turn to the queen's commodity'. It seems likely that the discussions about the royal subsidy had broadened into a larger discussion on the financial structure of the English Church, a topic of considerable concern in some of the preliminary papers. The bishops were at least considering the possibility of asking the queen to order a new survey to replace the Henrician schedules contained in the *Valor Ecclesiasticus*. Unfortunately, the acts contain no further information of the use which may have been made of the answers to these synodical articles of inquiry. Certainly Convocation promulgated no financial reforms.

On this same day, 19 February, Thomas Yale, Parker's vicar-general, appeared in the Lower House on behalf of the archbishop to warn the members not to leave London without licence before the end of Convocation. Gibson cites this example together with several other later instances to illustrate the authority of the arch-bishop to require attendance of the members of the Lower House.[1] It may be that the archbishop had reason at this point to fear that some members of the Lower House would leave before the subsidy was approved.

The subsidy was rapidly concluded. On 22 February, the bishops unanimously agreed to its form and conditions, and at the nine-teenth session on 24 February, the surrogate of the prolocutor (Nowell being absent) together with the whole Lower House were called to the bishop's presence. The book of the subsidy was read through and 'the said clergy of the Lower House unanimously joined their consent and assent'. The ephemeral second and final accomplishment of the 1563 Convocation took its place alongside the durable and far-reaching Articles of Religion.

[1] Gibson, *Synodus*, pp. 29–31.

A few signs of other Convocation activities appear in the records during this month of productive accomplishment. No sooner had the bishops signed the Articles than the archbishop appointed Grindal, Horn, Bullingham, and Scory to a committee 'to devise certain chapters in discipline in the church'. The acts record nothing further of the committee. Either they did not function or, more likely, they reported back during a secret session, and the bishops decided not to propose any Convocation action on discipline.

On 5 February, a book entitled '*The Catechism*' was assigned to Jewel, Richard Davies, and Alley for their examination. Nowell had prepared a lengthy Latin catechism for the synod, but this English title in the midst of the Latin acts precludes its identification with Nowell's Latin work. '*The Catechism*' may be related to the slightly expanded version of the Prayer Book catechism which appeared in later years, but its identity cannot be established with any certainty.[1]

The meeting on 5 February was the first at which the metropolitan did not preside in person. He had commissioned Grindal, Horn, Sandys, or Bullingham to take his place, and so the ranking prelate, Grindal, dean of the province, took the chair. Parker presided again on 13 February.

The accomplishments of the 1563 Convocation were completed by 22 February with the approval of the Articles and the subsidy. The precisians had lost a close battle in the Lower House, but little did they realize that their bitterest defeat lay in the weeks ahead.

THE RUIN OF THE REFORMERS' PROGRAMME

The militant reformers won an important victory in the Lower House some time after their defeat over the liturgical 'Six articles', for on 26 February a delegation of the lower clergy formally presented a proposal of their house to the bishops. The acts of the Upper House tell us that after the bishops had held their own secret discussions

---

[1] This English book first turns up in 1571 in Horn's injunctions for Winchester College as 'the little English Catechism with the right use of the Sacraments lately set forth' (Walter Howard Frere, *Visitation Articles and Injunctions of the Period of the Reformation*, 3 vols., Alcuin Club Collections xv and xvi [London, 1910], iii, 328).

'for a time', the prolocutor together with five cathedral deans and five archdeacons appeared to present 'both in behalf of their own names and also in the place of and in the name of all the meeting' of the Lower House 'a certain book of discipline'. The secretary of the Upper House judged the occasion sufficiently important to record all the names of the delegation. The delegation asserted that the book had received the unanimous consent of the lower clergy. This claim could mean that the book had the approval of all the members or, more probably, that the opposition did not insist that a division be taken to record the dissenters. The archbishop entrusted the book to a committee of leading bishops including himself, Grindal, Horn, Barlow, Scory, and Cox. Three of these prelates had been on the committee of bishops appointed on 29 January to devise chapters of discipline. It was obvious that both houses treated the proposal of the lower clergy as a matter of considerable significance.

On 1 March, after about two hours of secret episcopal discussions, prolocutor Nowell appeared and reported that the Lower House had devised some additional chapters for the book of discipline. He requested that the book be returned to them so that they might make their additions. The archbishop consented and ordered the book to be returned to the bishops at the next session.

The book of discipline was not returned as ordered, but the prolocutor appeared with Dean Sampson of Oxford and Provost William Day of Eton. They presented the bishops with the *Catechismus Puerorum* 'to which (as they claimed) all of the meeting of the [Lower] House unanimously consented'. This book is Prolocutor Nowell's *Catechism* which both 'Certain articles' and 'General notes' had expressly mentioned and endorsed. The acts record no further action on the book, but the archbishop continued secret discussions with Horn, Scory, Bullingham, and Bentham for more than two hours.

What was this heralded 'book of discipline'? Two extant documents qualify as candidates: 'Articles for government' and 'Twenty-one articles'.[1] Slightly more than half of the items in each of these papers are closely related to 'General notes', and the wording of

---

[1] See appendix 1, pp. 354–6.

many follows so closely that their parentage cannot be seriously questioned. The result is exactly what we would expect from a legislative committee which took 'General notes', modified it, reorganized it, introduced material from other proposals, and reduced it all 'into chapters'. Nowell had informed the bishops on 19 January that a Lower House committee was at work on preliminary proposals. 'Articles for government' includes from 'General notes' three-quarters of the items concerning both clergy and laity in part III on 'ecclesiastical laws and discipline', three liturgical items from part II, and two financial items from part IV. Three other items in 'Articles for government' could have been suggested by the preliminary paper 'Certain articles', which may also have provided grist for the committee's mill. 'Twenty-one articles' takes over all but one of the items in part I of 'General notes', designed to enforce 'a certain form of doctrine', and it also reproduces two liturgical proposals from part II. In their use of 'General notes', 'Articles for government' and 'Twenty-one articles' complement each other, one concentrating on general clerical and lay discipline and the other on the enforcement of doctrinal standards. This complementary relationship of the working papers has been overlooked, partly because Strype reprinted only a summary of 'Articles for government' and partly because he omitted important sections of 'General notes'.

The 'Articles for government' add to this material taken from 'General notes' a few liturgical regulations, a number of rules for the better operation of ecclesiastical courts, several laws for ensuring the collection of church income, and other miscellanea. Although none of the articles would have altered the Prayer Book, three of them contradicted specific liturgical orders of Queen Elizabeth.[1]

'Twenty-one articles' would have established the strict doctrinal standards envisaged in 'General notes', and it would have enforced them even more vigorously than the preliminary paper proposed. They would also have modified the Prayer Book order of baptism as 'General notes' had recommended. Three other provisions have no parallel in other Convocation documents. One called for the

---

[1] Articles 25, 26, and 27 (see below, p. 120).

destruction of remaining images which had been 'superstitiously abused'. The other two would have changed the Prayer Book communion office by requiring those not receiving holy communion to leave church before the general confession and by adding a specific denunciation of 'the idolatrous mass' to that confession. This polemical denunciation of the traditional Latin rite strikes most modern readers as the most extreme provision of the document, but in 1563 it would have been a relatively minor matter compared with the imposition of the paper's strict doctrinal discipline on the clergy and laity of the English Church.

The wide range of regulations in these two papers, had they been adopted, would have provided the Church of England with a good beginning of a body of reformed canon law, not greatly different in spirit from that of the *Reformatio* drawn up at the end of the reign of King Edward.

Which of these two documents is to be identified with the 'book of discipline' that Nowell presented to the bishops on 26 February? Bishop Frere, followed more recently by Dr Brook, tentatively identified the 'Articles for government' with the Lower House proposal.[1] I am convinced that the evidence points definitely to the 'Twenty-one articles'. Superficially, the description 'book of discipline' seems better to fit the 'Articles for government' which drew a large section of its items from the proposals of 'General notes' for 'ecclesiastical laws and discipline'. But the word discipline applies also to the 'Twenty-one articles' which are intended to enforce doctrinal standards by penalties. 'Discipline for doctrine' is one of the marginal subtitles for a section of these articles in the manuscript. When Wilkins transcribed the document from Strype

---

[1] W. H. Frere, *The English Church in the Reigns of Elizabeth and James I* (London, 1924), p. 99; Brook, *Parker*, p. 139. The former stated that 'It seems possible indeed, ...' and the latter wrote, 'it seems likely (though not certain)...'. For a description of the Convocation as a whole, Dixon's account is the most detailed of modern reconstructions, but he compounds some of Strype's misleading statements and, in at least one case, confounds 'Articles for government' with 'Certain articles' (*History*, v, 382–411; on the MSS, see pp. 384n. and 387). Frere is more accurate, but very brief (pp. 96–101). Brook's account is the most satisfactory to date (pp. 129–41). J. C. Barry has recently contributed a thoughtful discussion which sets the Convocation against its background (*History Today*, XIII [1963], 490–501).

in his *Concilia*, he added the words 'for discipline' as a natural description. This is not 'discipline' in the sense of the division of religion into 'doctrine, sacraments, and discipline', but the word had sufficiently wide a connotation to make it thoroughly appropriate in this instance.

The titles of the two papers are significant. Parker wrote in his own hand the vague title over the 'Articles for government': 'Articles drawn out by some certain, and were exhibited to be admitted by authority; but not so allowed.' In contrast, the title of 'Twenty-one articles' expressly states that they are 'the requests and petitions of the clergy in the Lower House of Convocation'. Taken at face value, this means that this paper constituted a formal proposal of the Lower House to the bishops presented in the normal manner of subscription.

The sixty-three signatures to 'Twenty-one articles' further confirm this interpretation. Historians have strangely overlooked their significance, Canon Dixon blandly reporting that the 'Twenty-one articles' received 'only' sixty-three subscriptions.[1] Only sixty-three! This clear majority of the members attending the Lower House represented seventy-five votes if the known multiple offices and permanent proxies held by the subscribers are counted, and it represented ninety-two votes if the proxies which they exercised in the division over the 'Six articles' are included. A majority of those moderates in the Lower House who voted against the 'Six articles' subscribed to these 'Twenty-one articles'. The precisians won the overwhelming support of the Lower House of Convocation for their programme of doctrinal reform.

The title and the wide clerical support for 'Twenty-one articles' establish it as a proposal of the Lower House and also make it the more likely candidate for the 'book of discipline'. Furthermore, two sessions after Nowell presented these articles, he formally brought the bishops his *Catechismus Puerorum* which was one of the key provisions of the paper.

[1] Dixon, *History*, v, 388. Frere ignored the doctrinal provisions of the 'Twenty-one Articles' (*History*, pp. 98–9). Dr Brook merely reported the document (*Parker*, p. 137).

The ten clerics from the Lower House who accompanied Nowell in the presentation of the 'book of discipline' to the bishops included only two men who, like Nowell, could be called precisians: Peddar and Lever. Six of the delegation had voted against the 'Six articles', and two had taken no part in the division. Three of the ten, Dean Carew of the chapel royal, Archdeacon Cottrell of Dorset and Wells, and Archdeacon Walker of Stafford and Derby, had not even sub-scribed the 'Twenty-one articles', but, for that matter, neither had Nowell. The presence of such conservatives meant that they were willing to go along with the measure supported by so many of their fellow-members of the house. By choosing a moderate delegation, the legislative tacticians seem to have been bent on impressing the bishops with the wide range of support for their proposals.

The Lower House, which had taken the 'book of discipline' back for alteration, returned it to the bishops on 5 March. The acts of the Upper House note that it now included 'certain additional chapters, namely of adultery, etc.'. Since no such items are attached to 'Articles for government' nor to 'Twenty-one articles', this added schedule may have been lost. Both papers contain articles which are extraneous to their main content, and so such an addition could have been con-ceivably appended to either document.

The precisians had won a major victory by carrying the Lower House along in their programme for doctrinal reform, but the triumph soon turned to ashes. Neither the acts of Convocation nor the pages of church history record anything more about the 'book of discipline'. The bishops received the book and sat on it. Con-vocation continued formally for another six weeks, but the only working sessions were three more episcopal executive discussions. The 'Twenty-one articles' were destined for ecclesiastical oblivion.

The complementary 'Articles for government' never even enjoyed a brief triumph. We do not know whether these articles ever received the full approval of the Lower House, but in any case they were not formally presented to the bishops. The Lower House committee-men may have been the 'some certain' who 'exhibited' the proposed regulations to the archbishop. Certainly both of these working papers form part of those 'things of the greatest advantage' which the puritans in 1567 accused the bishops of suppressing in Convocation four years earlier.

The bishops had framed the Articles of Religion and determined the queen's subsidy, and they had secured the consent of the Lower House to both. In the final unproductive weeks of the synod, the bishops disposed of the accomplishments of the precisians in the Lower House by the simple expedient of doing nothing about the 'book of discipline' and the *Catechismus puerorum*. We may doubt that the more militant members of Convocation would have agreed with Bishop Jewel's approving judgment which he wrote in a letter to Bullinger on 5 March: 'We are now assembling the great council of the nation and are going on successfully both as to the affairs of religion and of state.'[1]

On 10 April, Convocation heard the queen's brief and the archbishop's mandate proroguing the synod; four days later, they were officially adjourned until October. The 1563 Convocation became part of the history of the English Church.

RELIGIOUS AFFAIRS IN PARLIAMENT

The concurrent session of the Parliament of England took up several matters of importance to the church. At the opening of Parliament on 12 January, the queen, Lords, and Commons went first to Westminster Abbey to hear Dean Nowell's sermon, and then they moved to the Parliamentary chambers where they heard Lord Keeper Bacon declare that the purposes of these meetings were 'Religion, Discipline, and Aid to the State, in Defence of Enemies'.[2] The first matter of major religious importance came up a month later on 13 February, the day that the Lower House of Convocation voted on the 'Six articles'. The government introduced in the Commons 'the bill against those that extol the Power of the Bishop of Rome'.[3] Two days later the bill was assigned to a committee headed by the one privy councillor who wholeheartedly belonged

[1] *ZL*, I, 124.   [2] *JHC*, I, 62.
[3] *JHC*, I, 65. John E. Neale discusses the passage of the bill in detail: *Elizabeth I and her Parliaments*, 2 vols. (London, 1953–7), I, 116–21.

to the group of militant reformers, Vice-Chamberlain Francis Knollys, a subscriber to the New Discipline in Frankfort. The bill emerged the next day as a new bill which was brought to a division and passed by a vote of 186 to 83 on 20 February.[1] By 3 March the Lords had amended and concluded the bill; after further amendment in the Commons, the bill was finally approved in its ultimate form on 16 March.[2] The bill provided for more severe penalties for the refusal of the oath of supremacy than the law of 1559, and it required the oath of a whole additional group of clerical and lay officials.[3]

Parliament also passed a bill providing for the Prayer Book and Bible to be rendered in Welsh. Introduced into the Commons on 22 February, the bill was concluded almost five weeks later and sent to the Lords. The Upper House rapidly approved the bill, which called for the translation of both books before 1 March 1567, under the supervision of the four Welsh bishops and the bishop of Hereford. The authors of the bill were not content to wait until the work was done, for they ordered that, in the meantime, Welsh be used for epistles and gospels at Communion and that certain parts of the service appointed by the bishop be read weekly in the vernacular in Welsh-speaking parishes. The Lords added a note of nationalism in their requirement that an *English* Bible and Prayer Book be also made available in all Welsh parish churches 'that suche as understande them may resorte at all convenient times to reade and to use the same, and also suche as doo not understande the sayd Language maye by conferring bothe Tongues together, the sooner attayne to the knowledge of the Englyshe tongue'.[4]

The clerical subsidy which had been completed in Convocation on 24 February appeared in the Lords on 2 March, and was concluded in the Commons nine days later.[5] Finally, one bill, which

---

[1] *JHC*, I, 65–6 (15, 16, 17 and 20 February).
[2] *JHL*, I, 593–604 (20 and 25 February; 1, 3, 11, and 16 March); *JHC*, I, 67–8 (4 and 11 March).
[3] *Statutes of the Realm*, IV, 400–5; 5° Eliz., c. 1.
[4] *Statutes of the Realm*, IV, 457; 5° Eliz., c. 28; *JHC*, I, 66–72 (22 February, 4 and 27 March, and 5 April); *JHL*, I, 611–14 (30 and 31 March, and 5 and 6 April).
[5] *Statutes of the Realm*, IV, 458–61; 5° Eliz., c. 29; *JHL*, I, 597–602 (2, 3, 6, and 11 March); *JHC*, I, 67–8 (6, 8, 9, and 11 March).

was inspired by the proposals for reform presented in Convocation, was approved to enable bishops to secure the support of sheriffs in returning ecclesiastical offenders who had been served with the writ *De excommunicato capiendo*. Some of the bishops themselves may have introduced the bill, for it appeared in the Lords on 18 March, long after Convocation had completed its significant deliberations. After some slight signs of hesitation in the Commons, the bill was completed on 9 April.[1]

Some unsuccessful religious legislation was introduced during this session in a pattern which was to become quite usual in Elizabethan parliaments. A bill, which again may have had its origins with the bishops, appeared in the Lords on 9 March to provide for the 'uniting and annexing of Churches'. The bill was committed to Justice Southcote, '*ut in duos libros redigatur*' and bills introduced on 13 and 27 March may correspond to two parts of the bill in its original form. The second of these, 'touching decayed Cures, in Cities, Boroughs, and Towns Corporate', never got beyond one reading, but the first, 'for the Uniting of Churches in Cities, Boroughs, and Towns Corporate', was concluded in the Lords on 16 March. This bill, however, ran foul of the Commons, who let it drop after its second reading on 20 March. The Commons clerk tells us a little more about the bill by pointing out in his title that the uniting was to be done 'by the Bishop, so that the Value be not above twenty-four Pounds of the Churches united'. Two alternative bills, both apparently intended to improve parish livings, were introduced in the Commons on 30 March and 9 April, but neither of these got further than a single reading.[2]

The House of Commons concluded a bill on 26 March requiring the officials of ecclesiastical courts to be university graduates, but the bill died in the Lords.[3] A bill was introduced in the Commons for the consecration of bishops 'with such ceremonies as the time of' King Edward, but its title never appears after the order for

---

[1] *Statutes of the Realm*, IV, 451–3; 5° Eliz., c. 23; *JHL*, I, 605–17 (18, 27, and 29 March and 9 April); *JHC*, I, 71–2 (29 and 30 March; 7, 8, and 9 April).

[2] *JHL*, I, 600–10 (9, 13, 16, and 27 March); *JHC*, I, 69–72 (17, 18, 20 and 30 March, and 9 April).

[3] *JHC*, I, 68–71 (6, 13, 26, and 27 March); *JHL*, I, 611 (30 March).

engrossing.[1] Some M.P. also must have felt that parish clergy were negligent in keeping the parish registers, for a bill was introduced 'for an Office of a Register, to keep the Church Books for Wedding, Christening and Burying'.[2]

A bill appeared in the Lords early in the session concerning the 'Assurance of Certain Lands' taken by the queen during episcopal vacancies. It was read for the second time on 19 January and eleven days later entrusted to a committee headed by both archbishops, the duke of Norfolk, the Lord Treasurer, six earls, five leading bishops, and eight other lords.[3] The bill never reappeared after its consideration by that august and distinguished company. Whatever was in the bill must have mattered to someone! Finally, a bill to end peculiar jurisdictions in the various dioceses was twice read in mid-March before being handed over to a less distinguished committee which, none the less, dispatched it to a similar oblivion.[4]

All in all, the religious proposals made in the 1563 Parliament were limited and modest. In view of the failure of the militant reformers to implement their proposals in Convocation, they were increasingly in future years to turn to Parliament. They well remembered that in 1559 the great religious battlefield had been Parliament, not Convocation, and there they had gained substantial ground. In 1563, however, religion was a *major* parliamentary issue only in respect of the bill against Roman Catholics.

The 1563 Convocation showed that Elizabeth had chosen her bishops with discernment. The top leaders of the church were prepared to support the settlement without serious modification.

Leadership just below the episcopate ranged from those who had enthusiastically supported Mary's Roman Catholic policies all the way to those who militantly worked to change the patterns of liturgy, discipline, and doctrine of the English Church to conform to the best reformed churches abroad. The latter, the precisians, as the most determined, cohesive, and zealous group, carried the day in the Lower House of Convocation in 1563. They reached a peak of strength in the organized political life of the English Church which

[1] *JHC*, 1, 68–9 (8 and 12 March).　　[2] *JHC*, 1, 68 (9 March).
[3] *JHL*, 1, 583–7 (19 and 30 January).　　[4] *JHL*, 1, 605–6 (18 and 20 March).

they were not to surpass until they stormed the church by force in the civil wars of the next century.

How were the precisians able to dominate the Lower House when they lacked an outright majority? J. E. Neale has described the strength of a militant reforming minority in the 1559 House of Commons:

In a large assembly a resolute minority, knowing its own mind and how to lead, can carry the day.... If our evidence suggests that the House went full-cry after its radical leaders, sweeping aside any feeble Catholic opposition or the cautious promptings of moderate or official opinion, there seems nothing inherently impossible or even improbable in that.[1]

The Lower House of Convocation in 1563 in many ways resembled the Commons of four years past. A resolute core of militant reformers, drawn from the exiles, drew to it a significant number of like-minded men and dominated the house. By and large, the majority of Convocation men had no programme, no plan; they were prepared to follow the lead of their brethren who had a programme and a plan. Only when the ceremonial and vestiarian articles were proposed did the moderates rise in protest. Otherwise, they rallied to the precisians' proposals for doctrinal discipline, and they may also have been ready to support the reforms of more general clerical and lay discipline.

The comparison between the Lower House in 1563 and the Commons in 1559 breaks down seriously at one point. The militants in the Commons in 1559 had not achieved all that they desired but, as we shall see in the next chapter, they won a considerable victory which influenced the future course of the English Church. The Lower House of Convocation in 1563 forgot that its status was not that of the Commons. The House of Commons was one-half of a legislative body and well on its way to equality with the Upper House. The Lower House of Convocation remained essentially an advisory body to the bishops. The unidentified bishop spoke truly, if not tactfully, when he interrupted a member of the Lower House with the words, 'What are these things to you? We begun this

[1] Neale, *Parliaments*, I, 58.

business, and we will make an end of it.' The eventual frustration of the precisians arose not out of any lack of ability to control the diverse members of the Lower House, but rather out of the impotence of the house in the face of the bishops' willingness to maintain the substance of the 1559 settlement.

The results of the first synod of the reformed Elizabethan church could please only the moderate reformers. The bishops had produced the Articles of Religion and the queen's subsidy. Their refusal to act on other reforms proposed in the 1563 Convocation guaranteed the substantial continuation of the terms of the settlement as they had been determined in the opening year of Elizabeth's reign. Bishop Parkhurst did not secure the 'improvement at the approaching convocation' for which he had hoped and prayed. No wonder Lawrence Humphrey lamented to Bullinger in the summer of 1563 that 'the affairs of religion have made so little progress'.[1] The die had indeed been cast, and partly because of the defeat of the reformers in this Convocation, the Church of England was to gain a distinctive character of its own—neither Lutheran, Roman Catholic, nor Reformed. The issues raised in the Convocation of 1563 delineated not only the major ecclesiastical controversies in the opening years of Queen Elizabeth, but something of the distinctive character of future anglicanism as well. It now remains for us to look at one group of issues at a time, and this we shall do in the succeeding chapters. Anglicanism has no 'normative period', but few periods in its history have been as decisive for its future development as the first decade of the reign of Elizabeth Tudor.

[1] *ZL*, I, 133 (no. 60), 16 August 1563.

3. The liturgy: compromise and constancy

THE Book of Common Prayer had already established itself in the Elizabethan church by the time of the Convocation. No one in 1563 seriously proposed a major revision. Even Thomas Cole kept silence—and he had supported Knox's attempt at Frankfort to supplant the second Edwardian book with the precursor of the Genevan service book. Although the liturgy of the English Church retained far too much of traditional catholic rites and ceremonies for the liking of the militant reformers, and although even the more moderate would have liked to revise it here and there, the precisians did not press for thorough liturgical reform. They concentrated on proposals which would win the support of as wide a range of reformers as possible. The preparatory 'Certain articles' proposed that 'some few imperfections escaped in the book of service, as well in choice of the chapters as of the Psalms, with other such things concerning the rites and ceremonies in the church may be reduced to edification, as nigh as may be, to the godly purity and simplicity used in the primitive church'.[1] The ornaments rubric, with its authorization of many traditional vestments, irritated the precisians more than any other single part of the book. It touched off the first great protracted struggle between them and the bishops, and consequently it merits separate consideration in a succeeding chapter. But the precisians found other irritants which also chafed their conscientious sensibilities and kept the English Church some further distance from the 'godly purity and simplicity' which they desired. These objections, raised in 1563, formed the core of the list which was to be repeated again and again through the succeeding hundred years by their spiritual descendants.

How had it come to pass that the Prayer Book in 1563 seemed so unassailable? Why did the reformers not succeed even in amending those 'few imperfections' which many of the bishops would have

---

[1] No references are given for documents of the 1563 Convocation; see below, pp. 342–56.

gladly corrected? The reasons for the inviolable position of the liturgy are rooted in the struggle which took place during the Parliament of the first months of Elizabeth's reign.

The Elizabethan Prayer Book is fundamentally the story of the 1559 Parliament. Historians from William Camden up to those of the present century have assumed that the legislative acts of Supremacy and Uniformity embodied the determined policy of Queen Elizabeth and her advisers. The assumption rested on two tenuous but largely unexamined assumptions: first, that the members of Parliament, except for some obstinate Roman Catholics, were subservient to their young queen; and second, that the manuscript entitled 'Device for the Alteration of Religion' was not only a proposed plan of procedure for the queen's consideration, but the actual programme which she adopted and followed. This hypothesis presumed that Roman Catholic opposition forced the government to fight a long parliamentary battle to restore the independence of the English Church and to secure adoption of the Prayer Book liturgy. John E. Neale, in his brilliant reconstruction of the 1559 session of Parliament, has shattered this time-honoured reconstruction of the events. Neale has demonstrated that the bitter opposition to the government programme came from protestants dissatisfied with its too conservative proposals.[1]

Neale's studies not only make sense out of the legislative evidence which he so thoroughly mastered; they also make it possible for us to arrange the remnants of ecclesiastical events in those early months in much clearer order and perspective. Ecclesiastical historians have been far too content to accept Neale's work on Parliament without an equally searching examination of these associated incidents. Such is our task in the next few pages. The struggle in the 1559 Parliament, together with a few subsequent liturgical orders of the queen, illuminate the dynamics of the 1563 Convocation.

[1] William Camden, *Annales*, tr. R[obert] N[aunton], 3rd ed. (London, 1635), p. 6. The 'Device' was reprinted by Henry Gee, *Elizabethan Prayer Book*, pp. 195–202; Neale, *Parliaments*, I, 33–84; *idem*, 'The Elizabethan Acts of Supremacy and Uniformity', *EHR*, LXV (1950), 304–32.

The liturgy: compromise and constancy

The 1559 Parliament opened in an atmosphere of uncertainty and expectation. The queen and her advisers kept their plans for the English Church to themselves. Elizabeth had declared in a proclamation of 27 December 1558, in which she permitted the use of the English litany and certain other English intrusions into the Latin liturgy, that she and Parliament would subsequently consult 'in matters and ceremonies of religion'. A few days earlier the Privy Council had appointed a committee to frame the government's proposed legislation, and included, along with various legal officials, were Thomas Smith and Richard Goodrich, two laymen who had conformed under Mary, but were known to have assisted in Edwardian reforms.[1]

When the Lords and lay members of Parliament gathered on 25 January to attend the traditional opening Votive Mass of the Holy Ghost, they were surprised to discover that it had already been sung 'at an early hour in Westminster Abbey, without elevating the Sacrament, as is done in the Chapel Royal'.[2] Elizabeth apparently wanted the official liturgical prayer for the legislature to follow the ceremonial which she had ordered observed in her own chapel since Christmas, when she had left Mass early because Bishop Oglethorpe refused to omit the elevations.[3] The early hour may have been chosen in order to avoid an initial jarring note in a session bound to be difficult. The bishops would have found the omission of the elevations offensive; the former exiles would have balked at the Latin Mass.

Il Schifanoya described Elizabeth's arrival at Westminster Abbey:

The Abbot, robed pontifically, with all his monks in procession, each of them having a lighted torch in his hand, received her as usual, giving her

---

[1] Strype, *Annals*, I, part II, 392; Dasent, *Privy Council*, VII, 28; Neale, *Parliaments*, I, 38; see below, pp. 132–3.

[2] *CSP, Ven.* VII, 22, Il Schifanoya, 30 January 1559.

[3] C. G. Bayne, *EHR*, XXII (1907), 662, taken from *Annales Ecclesiastices*, XXIV (Rome, 1737); *CSP, Sp.* I, 17, Feria to Philip, 29 December 1558; *CSP, Ven.* VII, 2, Il Schifanoya, 31 December; *CSP, Rome*, I, 61, Sander to Moroni; Thomas Wright, *Queen Elizabeth and Her Times...*, 2 vols. (London, 1838), I, 4, Fitzwilliam to More, 6 December.

first of all incense and holy water, and when her Majesty saw the monks who accompanied her with the torches, she said, 'Away with those torches for we see very well'; and her choristers singing the litany in English, she was accompanied to the high altar under her canopy.

This incident has led commentators astray; they have attributed it to her supposed dislike of ancient ceremonial. But Il Schifanoya did not suggest that Elizabeth refused the formal ceremonial welcome with incense and holy water. She balked at the *processional* lights. The mention of the litany and choristers provides a clue to Elizabeth's motivation: if she had wanted to continue her current chapel usage and enter the abbey to the measured cadences of the vulgar litany, she would have wanted to be accompanied not by the monks of Westminster but by the dependable singers of the Chapel Royal.[1]

Richard Cox, just back from his exile abroad, ascended the very abbey pulpit from which Mary had ousted him six years before. To the Roman Catholic ears of Il Schifanoya, the lengthy sermon seemed to attack the essential foundations of true religion.[2] Reports of sermons are notoriously inaccurate, but the very choice of Cox to preach to the newly assembled Parliament must have greatly encouraged those who hoped for religious reform.

Lord Keeper Nicholas Bacon opened Parliament on behalf of the queen. Professor Neale points out that such speeches must not be taken to be literal outlines of the government's proposed legislative programme, yet Bacon did speak of the need to unite 'these people of the Realm into an uniform order of Religion'. Roman Catholics thought that Mary had already established such an order, and both Feria and Il Schifanoya feared that the words boded ill for the papal establishment in England.[3]

On the first working day of Parliament, 30 January, the House of Lords listened to the reading of a bill to transfer papal taxes to the Crown. At the same time in the Commons some members claimed

[1] *CSP, Ven.* VII, 23, Il Schifanoya, 30 January 1559; *CSP, Sp.* I, 25, Feria to Philip, 21 January 1559.   [2] *CSP, Ven.* VII, 23, 30 January 1559.
[3] Simonds D'Ewes, *The Journals of All the Parliaments during the Reign of Queen Elizabeth...* (London, 1682), pp. 11–14; Neale, *Parliaments*, I, 42; *CSP, Sp.* I, 25, Feria to Philip, 31 January 1559; *CSP, Ven.* VII, 23, Il Schifanoya, 30 January.

that the session was illegal because Elizabeth had not used the title 'Supreme Head' in her writ of summons. These two items fore-shadowed the character of the religious disputes which were to dominate the session: anti-papal legislation and the unexpected aggressive strength of the reformers in the Commons.

The bill which the government introduced in the Lords was primarily concerned with income which Henry VIII had appropriated for the Crown and which Mary, in conscience, had returned to the pope. Although royal appropriation of papal income was not in itself a formal repudiation of papal authority, similar legislation had begun the series of parliamentary acts by which Henry had established England's ecclesiastical independence. The Lords concluded the bill within the week with only the nine bishops present dissenting; even Lord Montague, who subsequently became the only lay peer to stand with the bishops, did not vote against it. The bill was not finally concluded until March because of successive amendments in the two houses, but its initial swift passage through the Lords impressively illustrated for Il Schifanoya the strength of the movement for the repudiation of Roman obedience.[1]

The challenge to the queen's writ gave an initial intimation of the protestant zeal of the House of Commons. F. W. Maitland pointed out that in Cecil's memorandum of 18 November for the new queen he had included an item, 'a commission to make out wryttes for ye Parlement touchyng &c in ye style of wryttes'. Elizabeth, in her list of titles in the writs, had added the '&c' to substitute for the 'Supreme Head' which Mary had dropped. The deliberate addition did not satisfy the militant reformers in the Commons, who gave public notice of their zeal by protesting that Elizabeth ought to have resumed the full title of her father and brother.[2]

The government's initial ecclesiastical programme pleased neither the Marian bishops nor the reformers in the Commons. Although on 9 February the government introduced in the Lower House 'the Bill

[1] *JHL*, I, 544, 552, and 563 (30 and 31 January; 4, 21, and 22 February; 13, 15, and 22 March); *JHC*, I, 54–5, 58 (6, 17, 20, and 21 February; 16, 20, and 22 March).
[2] Frederick William Maitland, *The Collected Papers of...*, ed. H. A. L. Fisher (Cambridge, 1911), III, 164–5; memorandum listed in *CSP, Dom., 1547–80*, p. 115 (I, 3); *JHC*, I, 53–4; *CSP, Ven.* VII, 26, Il Schifanoya, 6 February 1559.

to restore the Supremacy of the Church of England &c. to the Crown of the Realm', the opposition was so strong that not until 29 April did a Supremacy bill finally emerge from its tortuous route through committee and plenary sessions of both houses.[1]

One provision embedded in this bill suggested to Professor Neale that Elizabeth and her advisers never intended to introduce a 'Uniformity bill' into her first Parliament: the strange authorization for holy communion to be administered in two kinds. If the government intended to pass liturgical legislation in a separate bill, this provision was superfluous; if, on the other hand, the government had *not* contemplated such a bill, the provision was eminently appropriate as a step of mild reform. C. W. Dugmore has challenged Neale's interpretation and has alternatively suggested that the clause might have been introduced by 'the prayer book men of the Coxian party'. I doubt that the 'Coxian party'—if such could be identified in the tumultuous 1559 Commons—would have found the continuation of the Latin Mass much more acceptable than the 'Knoxian'.[2]

Neale estimates that at least one hundred M.P.s were in sympathy with the returned Marian exiles. Furthermore, returned clerical exiles were in London, unemployed and with time to spare for planning and encouraging their lay allies in the Commons. The reform-minded nucleus actually in the House of Commons included the father-in-law of Cecil and Bacon, Anthony Cooke, and Privy Councillor Francis Knollys, both returned émigrés. Less militant sympathizers, such as Richard Hills, could be counted on to go along with the reforming cause.[3] Three days after the Supremacy

[1] *JHC*, I, 54–5, 58–9, 61 (9, 13, 14, 15, 21, 22, 25 February; 18, 20, 21, 22 March; 10, 12, 27 April); *JHL*, I, 555, 563, 564, 568, and 574 (27, 28 February; 13, 15, 17, 18, 22 March; 17 April); E. J. Davis, 'An Unpublished Manuscript of the Lords' Journal for April and May 1559', *EHR*, XXVIII (1913), pp. 536–7 and 539 (14, 15, 17, 25, 26, 28, 29 April); *CSP, Sp.* I, 38, 19 March, Feria to Philip; Neale, *Parliaments,* I, 52.
[2] C. W. Dugmore, *The Mass and the English Reformers* (London, 1958), pp. 210–11; see *ZL*, I, 17–18, Jewel to Peter Martyr, 14 April 1559; see below, note 1, p. 93.
[3] Neale, *Parliaments*, I, 57–8; for Hills, see Browne Willis, *Notitia Parliamentaria...* (London, 1750), III, 65; Neale, *EHR*, LXV, 317; although an old acquaintance of Bullinger, Hills had conformed under Mary and could write with equanimity on both the Augsburg and second Helvetic confessions (*ZL*, II, 14–17 and I, 171–4, Hills to Bullinger, 28 February 1559 and 20 December 1566).

bill had been first read in the Commons, Sir Anthony Cooke wrote to Peter Martyr in Zurich that 'we are moving far too slowly,... but the result of...Parliament will, as far as I can judge, confirm my hope'.[1] The 'slow movement' could hardly refer to the resistance of papal M.P.s to the royal supremacy, for the bill had just been introduced, but it aptly applied to the Crown's intention to repudiate the pope without reforming the Latin rites. After lengthy debate on the Act of Supremacy, on Wednesday, 15 February, the House of Commons committed the bill to the two exiles, Knollys and Cooke. This commitment is itself an indication of the sentiment of the house, a sentiment which may have provided the grounds of Cooke's hope of good results in Parliament.

On Wednesday and Thursday two bills proposing an English liturgy were introduced. Neale is confident that the government did not sponsor them. Twenty-seven years later, a puritan wrote of a concerted effort at the beginning of Elizabeth's reign to provide 'a booke and such order for the discipline of the Church, as thei had seene in the best reformed Churches abroad'. Possibly the Commons Journal entry on 15 February is the only other remains of that abortive attempt.[2]

The mysterious disappearance of the two bills suggests that they were also assigned to the committee of Cooke and Knollys, for when they reported the Supremacy bill back on Tuesday, 21 February, it included liturgical provision for an English Prayer Book: a Supremacy and Uniformity bill rolled up in one.[3] No wonder the

---

[1] *ZL*, II, 13–14, 12 February 1559.

[2] 'The Bill for the Order of Service and Ministers in the Church' and 'The Book for Common Prayer and Ministration of the Sacraments', *JHC*, I, 54; Neale, *Parliaments*, I, 59–60; *EHR*, LXV, 312–14; 'A Generall Supplication made to the Parliament in Anno 1586 November', Albert Peel, ed., *The Seconde Parte of a Register...* (Cambridge, 1915), p. 84. Neale thinks that the two entries referred to a single bill establishing either the 1552 Prayer Book or the modification used at Frankfort. However, each of the entries has the numeral '1', indicating a first reading. Perhaps the angry protestants first introduced a more radical liturgy, either the Genevan service book or one of their own devising. The first title mentions not only a service book but 'ministers', matching the word 'discipline' mentioned in the puritan manifesto. By the next day, cooler heads gained sway, and they proposed a milder alternative—the 1552 book or something like it.

[3] *JHC*, I, 55; Strype, *Annals*, I, part II, 408, Scot's speech; *CSP, Ven.* VII, 52, Il Schifanoya, 21 March; *CSP, Sp.* I, 38, Feria to Philip, 19 March.

Commons clerk put the word '*nova*' next to the entry! No wonder the conservatively minded Paget wrote urgently to Parry and Cecil on the eve of the bill's reintroduction:

For God's sake move that good Quene to put her Sword into her Hand. She shall the better make her Bargayne with her dowtfull Frends and Enemys. Move her to cause those Things, that she will haue done by Parliament, to be shortly done; and to provide for the rest.[1]

The experienced Paget had caught wind of the Commons' proceeding and entreated Elizabeth's advisers to urge her to act before her 'dowtfull Frends' were completely out of hand.

The Commons concluded the revised and expanded Supremacy bill on Saturday, 25 February. On Monday, the House of Lords received the bill and after three days of debate the entire bill dropped out of sight for two weeks. The silence provided an opportunity for the government, who were able to control this Upper House, to debate their conservative policies in the face of the unexpected pressure for liturgical reform.[2] It was during this period of silence that an angry letter was crossing Europe to Cecil from the militant duchess of Suffolk in Poland, who had heard that Elizabeth's advisers were actually

impeding a godly reformation; such as should...be spurs, holdeth her Majesty from her own inclination running most back, among which you are especially named....I am forced to say with the prophet Eli, 'How long halt ye between two opinions?' If the mass be good, tarry not to follow it....You know there is no part of it good.

Both the Marian hierarchy and the militant reformers in the Commons would have agreed with the invocation of Elijah. Those who wanted to halt between two opinions faced increasing pressure from both sides.[3]

The tumultuous course of religion in Parliament in February 1559

[1] Haynes, *Collection*, I, 209.
[2] *JHL*, I, 555–63; *CSP, Sp.* I, 32, Feria to Philip, 20 February 1559; *CSP, Ven.* VII, 48, Tiepolo, 14 March 1559; VII, 46, Il Schifanoya, 14 March; *CSP, Rome*, I, 8, Canobio to Paul IV, 19 March 1559 from Brussels.
[3] *CSP, For.* I, 160, 4 March 1559 from Crossen, Poland; Read, *Cecil*, I, 134.

was accompanied by two other ecclesiastical activities in London, Convocation and court sermons. Two days after Elizabeth opened Parliament at Westminster, Bishop Bonner celebrated the opening Mass for the Convocation of Canterbury at St Paul's, rather as his successor Grindal was to celebrate the reformed rite four years later. The legislative drama of Convocation ran for a few weeks alongside the main show in the Houses of Parliament, and I am convinced that the clerical body acted in response to the course of religion in the Commons. On Friday, 3 February, the Lower House elected Archdeacon Nicholas Harpsfield, a strong supporter of the Marian restoration, for its prolocutor, and before a week was out the Privy Council had accused the archdeacon of stirring people to sedition and of having said that 'religion could not nor should not be altered'. After the election, the Convocation adjourned for another week— perhaps to see what Parliament would do.[1]

On Friday, 10 February, the day after the Supremacy bill had been introduced in the Commons, the clerics reconvened, and the Lower House asked the bishops '*quo modo religio posset conservari*'. The bishops answered that it seemed to them that the clergy might make a request of the queen that Parliament should not put a burden on them. Convocation was adjourned to Friday, 17 February and thence to Saturday, 25 February. On that day the Commons concluded the radically altered Supremacy bill, and Convocation considered certain written articles 'for the discharge of their consciences and the protestation of their faith'. Their action appears to be a deliberate response to Commons legislation to reform the church.[2]

The articles were quickly reported back on Tuesday, 28 February, and, approved by the Lower House, they were passed on to the bishops, who promised to present them the next day to the Lords. In almost direct reference to the Commons, the Lower House declared that they set forth these articles because the church's teaching had been called in doubt 'by public rumour'. The five articles asserted the traditional doctrines of the Mass and the authority of

---

[1] Cardwell, *Synodalia*, II, 490–1; Dasent, *Privy Council*, VII, 53–4, 9 and 11 February 1559.

[2] Cardwell, *Synodalia*, II, 491–2.

the pope; in what was patently a slap at the M.P.s who had just passed the altered Supremacy bill, and perhaps indirectly at the queen as well, they insisted that authority in faith, sacraments, and discipline belonged to the clergy '*et non ad laicos*'.[1]

The next Friday, 3 March, the bishop of London reported to the Lower House that he had delivered the articles to the Lord Keeper, who 'gladly' received them, but gave no response. In the midst of the tense debates over the revised Supremacy bill from the Commons, the bishop of London perhaps realized that he would only lose support if he displayed the provocative articles on the floor of the House of Lords.[2]

The zeal of the militant reformers in the Commons must have added fuel to the fire of the opposition of the Convocation men to religious change, confirming their conservative fears that royal supremacy would once again bring with it an irresistible wave of heresy and innovation. Their articles of protest, however, could accomplish little but stiffen the resistance of the bishops in the Lords, and they could only watch on the sidelines to see whether the militant reformers or the supporters of the queen's more moderate policies would win the day.[3]

The court sermons provided a public religious exercise which, I feel certain, also reflected the course of parliamentary events. In her proclamation of 27 December, Elizabeth had called a moratorium on all preaching in order to avoid inflaming religious passions. The Privy Council enforced the regulation, for between 3 January and 25 March they ordered the arrest of at least fifteen clerics who were variously accused of 'lewde words', 'unsemely talk', 'lewde preaching', or simply preaching 'notwithstandinge the Quenes Majesties Proclamacion'.[4]

---

[1] *Ibid.* II, 492–3; and see below p. 238.   [2] *Ibid.* II, 494.

[3] On Friday 10 March, Bonner told the Lower House that the Universities had accepted all the articles except for the last one denying lay authority. The next session was called for the following Friday, but sessions continued to be postponed until early May. Cardwell omits these details, but they are in an MS volume in the Bodleian Library (Add. MSS, 85a, fos. 204a–207b).

[4] Strype, *Annals*, I, part II, 391–2; Dasent, *Privy Council*, VII, 36, 47, 52, 59, 62, 63, 64, 65, 67, 71, and 72.

Against this background of homiletic silence, the Lenten sermons at court resounded throughout the city. On Ash Wednesday, 8 February, just the day before the Supremacy bill was introduced in the Commons, the first of a series of reform-minded preachers was heard in the court pulpit, presumably by order of the queen. Machyn's diary provides the names of the clerics for seven out of the nine sermons known to have been given: Cox (twice), Parker, Scory, Whitehead, Grindal, and Sandys. Five Marian exiles, a priest who had been in retirement, and two other unidentified preachers were allowed openly to express their convictions in a place where the legislators might hear them.[1]

Il Schifanoya, who attended Scory's sermon, was shocked that he

said so much evil of the Pope, of the Bishops, of the prelates, of the regulars, of the Church, of the mass and finally of our entire faith, in the presence of the Queen and of her Council, the rest of the congregation consisting of more than 5,000 persons, that I was scandalized, and I promise never to go there again after hearing the outrageous and extravagent things which they say, and yet more was I surprised at the concourse of people who madly flocked to hear such vain things.

On 28 February Richard Hills delightedly wrote to Bullinger:

Silence has been imposed upon the catholic preachers (as they are called) by a royal proclamation, and sufficient liberty is allowed to the gospellers, to preach three times a week during this Lent before the queen.

Hills' appreciative words are matched by the outrage not only of Il Schifanoya but also of Count Feria, who warned Elizabeth that 'the poltroons who preached to her were Lutherans and Zwinglians such as her father had burnt'.[2]

Machyn listed no court preachers after Sunday, 26 February. His subsequent silence, together with the silence of other possible witnesses, strongly suggests that the Lenten series abruptly terminated on the third Sunday in Lent. The coincidence with the Commons' conclusion of the drastically revised Supremacy bill is almost too

[1] Machyn, *Diary*, pp. 189–90.
[2] *CSP, Ven.* VII, 30–1, 13 February 1559; *ZL*, II, 16–17; *CSP, Sp.* I, 44, Feria to Philip, 24 March 1559.

close to be fortuitous. The legislative events in February revealed to Elizabeth that instead of the spurs of the preachers to hasten Parliament to adopt the government's proposals for reform, restraining reins were the order of the day. We hear no more of sermons for the remainder of Lent.[1]

With Convocation inactive and the court preachers silent, activity on the ecclesiastical measures slipped out of sight. The parliamentary journals show almost two weeks with no visible action or talk on the church bills. This legislative silence was broken on Monday 13 March when the Supremacy bill reappeared in the Lords and was committed to a conservative committee including three privy councillors and two bishops.[2] The committee sheared off the liturgical additions of the Commons, modified it by 'certain provisoes', and returned it to the Lords substantially as the government had originally presented it in the Commons.[3] The queen with her advisers had apparently decided to resist the pressure of the Commons and to return to her original policies. The Lords quickly concluded the bill on 18 March over the dissents of all the bishops, of Montague, and of Shrewsbury. Even with liturgical changes removed once more, Bishop Scot insisted that the Supremacy bill introduced a new religion in place of the old.

Thers is not yet fyftye yeres olde, and ours above fifteen hundrethe yeres olde. They have for auctoritie and commendation of their religion Luther and his schoolmaster [the Devil]...We have for ours St. Peter and his master Christ.[4]

Il Schifanoya vividly described the Commons' frustrated reaction to the work of the Upper House:

[1] Machyn lists the final three sermons: one on 23 February, one on 25 February, and the final sermon by Cox on an unspecified day (*Diary*, p. 190). Perhaps the dates should have been 22 and 24 February, the normal Wednesday and Friday for Lenten sermons, but in any case, the set of three for the week would close with the sermon on Sunday, if Machyn made his notes as usual.

[2] *JHL*, I, 563.

[3] *JHL*, I, 564; *CSP, Sp.* I, 38, Feria to Philip, 19 March 1559.

[4] Strype, *Annals*, I, part II, 422. The timing of Scot's speech is clear from its opening: the Supremacy bill had been read twice already in the Lords.

The members of the Lower House, seeing that the Lords passed this article of the Queen's supremacy of the Church, but not as Commons drew it up...grew angry, and would consent to nothing, but are in very great controversy, as they must of necessity ratify what the Lords have done in the Upper House.[1]

Since a negative vote would have left the pope in England, the M.P.s bowed to necessity and passed the bill on 22 March.[2] They expressed their anger, however, in a flurry of protestant legislation which Neale describes as the propaganda tactics of revolution.[3] The most extreme of these measures would have allowed the optional use of the 1552 Prayer Book alongside the Latin Mass.[4] Short of outright disobedience, the reformers in the Commons displayed in every possible way their opposition to the government's programme of royal supremacy without liturgical reformation.

Elizabeth and her conservative advisers had forced their policy through Parliament: the Church would be independent, the queen would be free to urge the minor reforms which she had introduced into her chapel, and, in good time, further reforms could be calmly and leisurely adopted. Yet ominous clouds cast sombre shadows on Elizabeth's success. The higher Marian clergy had shown themselves unyieldingly obdurate in opposition to the Crown's renewed supremacy, and the more militant reformers in the Commons had shown themselves dangerously disaffected by reason of the government's conservative programme. In the eyes of both, the government was indeed halting between two opinions.

[1] *CSP, Ven.* VII, 52, 21 March 1559.
[2] *JHC*, I, 58; note new proviso, see *JHL*, I, 568.
[3] *Parliaments*, I, 67; 'Bill for Thirty-two persons to make Ecclesiastical Laws', 'to make lawful the Deprivation of Bishops...in the time of King Edward', for punishing the bishop of Winchester for alleged cancellation of records, and for bishops to be appointed by royal collation, *JHC*, I, 55–8.
[4] 'Bill that no Persons shall be punished for using the Religion used in King Edward's last Year', *JHC*, I, 58.

The liturgy: compromise and constancy

Holy Week of 1559 turned out to be one of the most important weeks in the religious history of England. Everyone expected Parliament to conclude its working sessions on Wednesday, 22 March. The parliamentary journals show that the two houses carefully wound up necessary business that day and Feria and Il Schifanoya both confirmed the expectation.[1]

Elizabeth had a proclamation prepared, to be issued that same Wednesday, permitting Englishmen to make their Easter communions in both kinds 'according to the first institution and to the common use both of the Apostles and the Primitive Church'. The proclamation assumed that Parliament would have completed its legislation:

The foresaid statute now made in this last Parliament, being of great length, cannot be printed and published abroad, nor any other manner of divine service for the communion of the said holy Sacrament (than that which is now used in the Church) can presently be established by any law until further time therefor may be had.

The Queen's Majesty hath in the present last session of Parliament... made amongst others one statute to repeal sundry acts of Parliament made in the time of the late Queen...and to revive...other necessary and godly laws used in the times of...King Henry...and King Edward,...amongst the which one godly Act there revived entitled an Act against such persons as shall unreverently speak against the Sacrament...and for the receiving thereof under both kinds.

The preparation of the proclamation signalled the success of the government's legislative programme, not its failure, as the Roman Catholic H. N. Birt supposed.[2]

Included in the prepared proclamation stood the curious reference to a forthcoming publication. A full Prayer Book is not indicated by the words, 'other manner of divine service for the communion

---

[1] *JHC*, I, 59; *JHL*, I, 568; *CSP, Sp.* I, 38, 44, 50, Feria to Philip, 19 and 24 March and 11 April 1559; *CSP, Ven.* VII, 55, Il Schifanoya, 21 March; see also *CSP, Rome*, I, 8, 26 March.

[2] Gee, *Elizabethan Prayer Book*, pp. 255–7; Birt, *Elizabethan Settlement*, p. 77.

of the said holy sacrament'. In the light of the revival of the Edwardian act, Elizabeth's words suggest that she intended to promulgate
the 1548 Order of Communion, or something like it. The Order had,
after all, been issued on the authority of King Edward in order to
implement the parliamentary act for communion in both kinds, and
to provide an interim measure of reform while they prepared the
1549 Prayer Book.

Innovations in the Chapel Royal on Easter Day substantiate this
interpretation. Il Schifanoya's report of the queen's Easter Mass has
always proved difficult to its interpreters, but the difficulties almost
vanish if we only assume that the English devotions of the 1548
Order were interpolated into the Latin liturgy:

They had ordered and printed a proclamation for every one to take
Communion in both kinds. Some other reforms of theirs had also been
ordered for publication, but subsequently nothing else was done, except
that on Easter Day her Majesty appeared in Chapel where mass was sung
in English, according to use of her brother, King Edward, and the Communion was received in both kinds, kneeling, *facendoli il sacerdote la
credenza del corpo et sangue prima*, nor did he wear anything but the mere
surplice, having divested himself of the vestments in which he had sung
mass; and thus her Majesty was followed by many Lords both of the
Council and others.[1]

The 'other reforms' ordered for publication and later rescinded
sound like a reference to a new version of the Order of Communion.

Occasionally it has been supposed that Elizabeth introduced the
Edwardian Prayer Book Eucharist on Easter Day. She would have
drastically departed from her consistent policy if she had ordered the
full Prayer Book liturgy to be used, for it would have denied all her
notions of legality. Furthermore, according to the Italian, the priest
quickly changed from Mass vestments to a surplice, and made for
them the belief in the body and blood before they received. These
statements are thoroughly bewildering in the context of the 1552
liturgy. But if the 1548 Order had been used, the priest would have

---

[1] *CSP, Ven.* VII, 57; Il Schifanoya to Vivaldine, 28 March 1559; *CSP, Rome,* I, 8.
Dr Dugmore believed that Neale's reconstruction implied the 1548 Order, but
he assumed this to be a *reductio ad absurdum* (*Mass,* pp. 210–11).

celebrated the chapel's Latin rite, inserting the English communion devotions of the Order between his own communion and the communions of the congregation. Although the rubrics of the 1548 Order did not call for a change of vestments, the break which the Order introduced into the Mass would have allowed an opportunity for such a change. To one unfamiliar with the Prayer Book liturgies, such as Il Schifanoya or his informer, the communion devotions might well be described as 'the priest making for them the belief in the body and blood'.[1] The Italian did report that the Mass itself was sung in English. However, it would have been precisely the litany (if used), epistle, gospel, and communion devotions which would have been said in a loud voice. The use of these in English would have impressed auditors unfamiliar with the queen's chapel use, and the inaccurate extension of English to the entire rite is not at all improbable.

Elizabeth never hesitated to assert her authority in chapel liturgics, but all her innovations had been carefully based on some legal foundation. She could not have so justified the use of either Prayer Book, but, for the 1548 Order, she had the Edwardian precedent for the implementation of the parliamentary act for communion in two kinds.[2] At the last moment she had continued Parliament so that the Act was not yet statutory, but it had passed both houses of Parliament.

The Easter use of a version of the 1548 Order in the Chapel Royal would have prepared the way for its wider use, just as the queen's introduction of the English litany in early December had prepared the way for its subsequent use in parish churches.[3] Although Elizabeth had already abandoned the interim, this remnant of former plans may have been carried through at the Easter Mass in the Chapel Royal.

We can now attempt to reconstruct the interim settlement as

[1] Il Schifanoya had written on 13 February that he would never attend the chapel again, but perhaps his curiosity got the better of his piety (*CSP, Ven.* VII, 31).

[2] A few weeks later John Jewel complained to Peter Martyr of the Mass in the Chapel Royal (*ZL*, I, 18, 14 April 1559).

[3] *CSP, Ven.* VII, 1, Il Schifanoya, 17 December 1558; Proclamation of 27 December 1558, Strype, *Annals*, I, part II, 391–2.

Elizabeth and her advisers may have originally planned it. An independent national church would have continued to use the Latin liturgy modified by the elimination of the elevations, by the use of English in the litany and the eucharistic lections, by communion in both kinds, and by the interpolation of communion devotions similar to those of the 1548 Order. It had much in its favour. These interim arrangements would have provided a resting-point while the permanent settlement was being prepared. The resting-point would have been a little in advance of the arrangements in the reign of Henry VIII, but not so much so that they would have offended her more traditionally minded councillors, such as the earls of Shrewsbury and Arundel. Without the militancy of reformers in the Commons, more of the Marian prelates might have been expected to accept such an interim, and the oath of supremacy would have eliminated the more obstinate Romanists. On the other hand, only those more conservative reformers willing to accept the interim would have been given positions of leadership in the church. The church could have moved ahead through its own moderate composite leadership to arrive at a final settlement.

Elizabeth had believed that many reformers would be content with a temporary arrangement drawn out of the early years of Edward's reign. Of course, she was wrong. Hardened by years of exile, deprivation, or persecution, the more reform-minded clergy had no patience with such legal dilly-dallying. Count Feria, to whose Spanish piety the measures appeared outlandishly heretical, was clearly bewildered when he reported on Good Friday that he saw 'the heretics...very downcast in the last few days'.[1]

On the basis of Feria's testimony, Neale has pinned down the time of Elizabeth's decision to continue Parliament, and so to abandon the interim policy, to the hours between Maundy Thursday evening and Good Friday morning. She permitted Bill, Cox, Horn, and Sampson to preach at St Mary's Spital and Paul's Cross during Easter week. These sermons constituted the first authorized preaching outside the Royal Chapel since the end of December. Although these sermons were probably scheduled while the queen still intended to push

---

[1] *CSP, Sp.* I, 44, Feria to Philip, 24 March 1559.

through the interim arrangements, their delivery revealed that she judged it no longer necessary to silence public discussion of religious affairs.[1] She had decided to allow further reform.

There are important straws of evidence that even before the queen determined to continue Parliament, she had already decided to push on with deliberate speed to a genuine vernacular liturgy. On Monday she asked Count Feria whether Philip would be angry 'at the mass being said in English'. Elizabeth's diplomatic parries have to be interpreted cautiously, but this statement tallies with a letter written on the same day by John Jewel to Peter Martyr. The recent exile gave full details of a coming disputation between the bishops and 'our side'. In spite of Neale's opinion that the government only began to arrange the debate on Saturday or Sunday, this detailed information in Jewel's hands on Monday suggests that the government had been planning it for more than one or two days.[2]

The disputation was designed to provide the foundation for liturgical reforms. The Privy Council chose three articles of debate: the necessity of the liturgical use of the vernacular, the right of a national church to determine its own liturgy, and the denial of a propitiatory sacrifice in the Mass.[3] The reformers' successful defence was to prepare the way for the introduction of a reformed national liturgy in English. Neale assumes that such reforms and the continuation of Parliament went hand-in-hand. This is not necessarily so. The

---

[1] *Parliaments*, I, 69; *EHR*, LXV, 325; *CSP*, *Sp.* I, 44, Feria to Philip, 24 March 1559; Machyn, *Diary*, p. 192; Wriothesley, *Chronicle*, II, 144.

[2] *CSP*, *Sp.* I, 43, Feria to Philip, 24 March 1559; *ZL*, I, 10–14, 20 March 1559; Neale, *Parliaments*, I, 70–2; *EHR*, LXV, 325. Sander did write that the bishops had only six days to prepare for the debate, but he wrote two years later (Birt, *Elizabethan Settlement*, p. 104). Since the official account specifically states that the bishops chose their own representatives, whom Jewel was able to name in his letter, they must already have received news of the coming event.

[3] '1. It is against the worde of God, and the custome of the auncient Church, to use a tongue unknowne to the people, in common prayer and the administration of the Sacraments.

2. Euerie Church hath authoritie to appoynt take awaye and chaunge Ceremonies and Ecclesiasticall rytes, so the same bee to edification.

3. It cannot be proued by the worde of God that ther is in the Masse offred up a sacrifice propiciatorie for the quicke and the dead'

(Holinshed, *Chronicles*, p. 1800).

initiation of liturgical reforms did not require Parliament. The first steps could be taken and then ratified by a later session of Parliament. It would have been thoroughly consistent with Elizabeth's later ecclesiastical policies—as Neale's own two volumes on her parliaments eloquently testify—for her to have had the liturgical reforms drawn up by a group of responsible clerics, submitted to Convocation for amendment and approval, and then submitted to Parliament for statutory authorization in an accompanying Uniformity bill. Had the interim policy been carried through, this would have been the order of events, an order which Neale endorses as Elizabeth's original plan.[1] The plan for the disputation meant that Elizabeth was now prepared to *initiate* the process of liturgical reform. Parliament did not need to reconvene immediately.

One of the details in the Westminster disputation, actually held on 31 March and 3 April, suggests that the initial plans were prepared with the understanding that the audience would be largely clerical rather than lay. Elizabeth had originally ordered the dispute to be in Latin and written—appropriate arrangements if clergy rather than the predominantly lay membership of Parliament were to hear the arguments.[2]

Just one week before Jewel wrote to Peter Martyr about the disputation, the long moratorium on the Supremacy bill in the Lords had been broken. The government's plans for the disputation, like the plans for the Lords' editing of the bill, may have been laid during that feverish silence if, indeed, the disputation had not been planned from the beginning. Jewel claimed that the purpose of the debate was that 'our bishops may have no ground of complaint that they are put down by power and authority of law'.[3]

Elizabeth may have intended a clerical committee to begin immediate work on Prayer Book revision. Philip Melanchthon, whom she had read in her youth, advised her in a letter at this time to establish the definite forms of doctrine and rites 'at once'. An undated letter, usually identified as Edmund Guest's, suggests that the author had

---

[1] *Parliaments*, I, 54.
[2] *CSP, Sp.* I, 45–6, Feria to Philip, 30 March 1559; Foxe, *Acts*, VIII, 688–9; Birt, *Elizabethan Settlement*, pp. 98–119.   [3] *ZL*, I, 10.

prepared the draft of a new liturgy which he expected to receive serious consideration. Guest was to be the only member of the panel of reformers in the disputation who had not been in exile, and this curious fact is more easily understood if he had already been authorized by the queen to prepare a revision of the Prayer Book.[1]

Whether or not Elizabeth had designated Guest to draft a liturgical proposal, the disputation with its Latin written theological arguments would have laid the ground for clerics considering such revisions for presentation to Convocation and Parliament. The articles of debate seem to assume the independence of the English Church as an accomplished fact.

The Good Friday decision to continue Parliament meant not so much a change of the queen's policy as a severe foreshortening of its timetable. The foreshortening, with its elimination of the interim, had two important long-range consequences for the settlement. First, it ruled out the possibility that Convocation might consider the reforming proposals before they were presented to Parliament; second, it gave the controlling party of reformers in the Commons far greater sway in the determination of the settlement than they would otherwise have had.

Any reconstruction of these events is conjectural, to be sure. In so far as the outline which I present differs from that of Neale, it avoids the two weakest points in his argument: his explanation of Elizabeth's 'ambiguous' policy during Holy Week and his stress on the importance of the news of peace from Cateau-Cambrésis.

Neale argues that the plans for the disputation early in Holy Week indicate that Elizabeth was following a double policy—an anomaly explained by the character of government inherent in a personal monarchy.[2] She was still uncertain what she would do and, therefore, she inconsistently granted to the reformers the disputation before she was willing to give up the interim arrangement as well. This explanation ought not be pressed unless the disputation made the continuation of Parliament inevitable. As we have seen, the disputation was not necessarily designed to influence an audience of legislators.

[1] See below, p. 109, n. 3; *CSP, For.* I, 154, Melanchthon to Elizabeth, 1 March 1559.
[2] *Parliaments*, I, 70; *EHR*, LXV, 325.

Neale also argues that the news of peace with France gave Elizabeth sufficient security 'to take the second step in her religious settlement'. Does this not imply that Elizabeth was grateful for the opportunity to move for immediate reform? Such a characterization oddly conflicts with Neale's own dominant picture of a queen reluctantly compromising in the face of the onslaught of the militant reformers in the Commons.[1] The preliminary agreements for the peace were reached on Sunday, 12 March, and news reached London either Saturday, 18 March or Palm Sunday.[2] Why would the news have thrown Elizabeth into the arms of the eager reformers? After all, she had known this news would be forthcoming: Calais had been the great sticking-point, and in a letter of 19 February, she had authorized her commissioners to 'permitt Callays to remayn in the hands of the Frenche' for up to eight years if it proved necessary to gain peace.[3] And Elizabeth herself did not regard this preliminary treaty of 12 March as final, for she wrote to her commissioners on 22 March to try to hold out for slightly better conditions in two minor issues.[4] The preliminary treaty was merely one step towards the end of the drawn-out negotiations to settle the conflict which Mary had bequeathed to her sister. It is difficult to see why this news would have led Elizabeth to capitulate to the timetables of the reformers in the Commons.

Grindal did write descriptively to Conrad Hubert that Parliament had delayed the reformation 'until a peace had been concluded', but this vague observation about Parliament hardly illuminates the delicate matter of the queen's motivation. The reformers knew their cause depended in large measure on the queen, and dared not expose their differences with her too openly in letters to their foreign friends.[5]

We do not need to search far for the reason for Elizabeth's Good

[1] *Parliaments*, I, 70 (cf. I, 79); *EHR*, LXV, 325 (cf. LXV, 324).
[2] *CSP, For.* I, 170, preliminary treaty, 12 March 1559; *CSP, Ven.* VII, 53, Il Schifanoya, 21 March; *CSP, Sp.* I, 38 and 42, Feria to Philip, 19 and 24 March.
[3] P. Forbes, *A Full View of the Public Transactions in the Reign of Q. Elizabeth*, 2 vols. (London, 1740–1), I, 61.   [4] *CSP, For.* I, 184.
[5] *ZL*, II, 19; Jewel came closest in a letter to Peter Martyr of 14 April to admitting the split (I, 17–19; see below, pp. 107–8).

Friday decision. Although she had coolly manipulated a reluctant Parliament to preserve the substance of her original ecclesiastical policies, religious issues had hardened during her sister's reign to a degree which she had not accurately assessed. Even though she may have had the sympathy and approval of many of her conservative lay counsellors and the support of a large portion of the House of Lords, leading ecclesiastics on both sides of the religious spectrum had registered resolute disapproval of the interim settlement. If she dismissed Parliament only to discover that few important clerical leaders from either side would support her ecclesiastical policies, she could lose all possibility of religious stability. She might brave the policy through and trust that a sufficient nucleus of clerical leadership would rally to her cause. The risk was too great. She decided that she could not face the prospect of a leaderless church and, at the last possible moment, she determined to continue Parliament after Easter. The last-minute display of reforming zeal in the Commons had proved decisive. The Good Friday decision to foreshorten the interim plans required more of a sacrifice to demands of the reformers than Elizabeth had intended to grant, but the alternative, as she may have seen it, was religious chaos. And perhaps she was right.

The Westminster disputation ended in a fiasco, but it still played its role in the drama that determined the legislation of the religious settlement. The debate provides an instance of what has become a typical anglican priority for the *lex orandi* over the *lex credendi*; rightly or wrongly, anglicans assume that doctrine grows out of patterns of worship. All three articles of debate bore directly on the immediate issue of liturgical reform. No sixteenth-century reformer of any stripe would have hesitated to support them, although many would have found them to touch only a small portion of the important issues of contemporary theological debate.

After the queen's Good Friday decision to allow Parliament to assume immediate responsibility for liturgical reform, the context of the debate was altered; to the anger of Roman Catholic commentators from Feria to modern times, it was now to be in English, spoken, and 'in Parliament'.[1] Latin theological treatises would have enlightened few of the members of the houses of Parliament. The bishops had cause for complaint in the change of conditions, but the new circumstances dictated the changes rather than a policy of deliberate deceit.

Feria's description of the disputation as 'in Parliament' is a bit misleading, and the parallel between it and the parliamentary debate of December 1548 is not nearly as striking as Professor Neale has argued. In its revised form, the disputation seems to have been designed to create a climate of opinion favourable to reform in both houses of Parliament. The Privy Council sent letters to county sheriffs to warn all M.P.s 'in no wise...to fayle to be here on Monday nexte, being the iiide of Aprill, as they wyll aunswer for the contrary'. It seems no accident that this was the day scheduled for the debate on the second proposition which asserted the right of 'euerie Church' to order its own rites and ceremonies.[2]

In the public eye, the dispute was between the 'bysshopes and nuw prychers'. Not only the Lords, M.P.s, and Privy Councillors, but also a 'great number of people of all sorts' attended the disputation in Westminster Abbey.[3] The bishops chose their own disputants,

---

[1] *CSP, Sp.* I, 45, Feria to Philip, 30 March 1559.

[2] Neale, *EHR*, LXV, 324; record of debate, printed in Francis Aidan Gasquet and Edmund Bishop, *Edward VI and the Book of Common Prayer* (London, 1891), appendix V, pp. 397–443; Dasent, *Privy Council*, VII, 74. The 1548 debate was in the Lords; that of 1559, in the Abbey. In 1548, all the participants were members of parliament; in 1559, the participating bishops were in the Lords, but neither the Roman Catholic doctors nor any of the reforming clerics belonged to either house. In 1548, discussion followed the impromptu order of parliamentary debate; in 1559, the arguments were formally presented with rebuttals. In 1548, the proposed Prayer Book had already been introduced into Parliament, and the debate frequently discussed its specific provisions; in 1559, there was no such proposal before either house.

[3] Machyn, *Diary*, p. 192; *CSP, Sp.* I, 46, Feria to Philip, 4 April 1559; *JHC*, I, 58. The major sources for our knowledge of the disputation are: (1) the official account printed as a pamphlet and included in Holinshed, *Chronicles*, pp. 1799–1800 (p. 1799 is wrongly paginated as p. 1776); (2) Feria's letters to Philip, *CSP, Sp.* I: 45–6, 30 March; 46–8, 4 April; (3) Foxe's account, *Acts*, VIII, 688–92; (4) Jewel's letters to Peter Martyr, *ZL*, I, 10–11 (no. 4), 20 March; 15–16 (no. 5), 6 April; (5) Il Schifanoya's report, *CSP, Ven.* VII, 64–5, 11 April; (6) Cox's letter to W. Weidner, *ZL*, I, 27–8 (no. 11), 20 May; and (7) Sander in his report to Cardinal Moroni, *CRS*, I, *Miscellanea*: I, 3–7 and 26–31. Copies of speeches prepared for the disputation have been reprinted by Foxe, *Acts*, VIII, 679–92; Strype,

four or five among themselves and four 'doctors'.[1] The bishops were
White, Bayne, Scot, and possibly Oglethorpe and Watson, all of
whom were later among those whom the government did not try to
win to conformity to the settlement; the doctors included the
prolocutor of the Lower House of Convocation, Nicholas Harpsfield, along with three other prominent Marian clerics. The reformers numbered Edmund Guest and eight Marian exiles, Scory,
Cox, Whitehead, Grindal, Horn, Sandys, Aylmer, and Jewel; as we
have seen, all but Whitehead and Aylmer were immediately
destined for the Elizabethan episcopate.

At the first session on Friday, 31 March, Dean Cole of St Paul's,
the initial spokesman for the bishops, had no prepared paper, and so
he argued the case against a vernacular liturgy squarely on the
grounds that such change would divide England from 'the catholike
church of God'. Although he did not specifically defend papal
authority, he left no doubt of his meaning: 'In *alteration* of the
service into our mother-tongue, we condemn the church of God,
which hath been heretofore, we condemn the church that is present,
and namely, the church of Rome.'[2] Cole must have dampened any
remaining hopes that the bishops' party might reluctantly accept
Parliament's decision to repudiate the pope.

Robert Horn, who delivered a learned and restrained paper on
behalf of the reformers, cited the scriptural, ancient, and Eastern
precedents for the use of the vernacular, and concluded with mock
amazement that his opponents were 'so loth to return to the first
original of St. Paul's doctrine, and the practice of the Primitive
Catholick Church of Christ'.[3]

The second day of the disputation on 3 April never got beyond
procedural wrangling. The bishops refused to follow the order
prescribed by the moderator Lord Keeper Bacon. The assembly

Annals, I, part II, 465–87; Dugdale, Henry Geast, *The Life and Character of Edmund
Geste* (London, 1839), pp. 149–76; and Edward Cardwell, *A History of Conferences
and Other Proceedings, Connected with the Revision of the Book of Common Prayer...*
(Oxford, 1849), pp. 55–92.

[1] There is disagreement over the exact number of disputants (Holinshed, *Chronicles*,
pp. 1799–1800; *ZL*, I, 11; *CSP, Dom., 1547–50*, p. 127 [I, 51]).
[2] Cardwell, *Prayer Book Conferences*, pp. 66, 70, and 72.
[3] Dugdale, *Geste*, p. 156.

broke up, and later in the day the Privy Council arrested all the papal participants.[1] Consequently neither the second nor the third debate was ever held.

The usual reason given for the bishops' refusal is one which they themselves offered: they would not permit their opponents to speak last again and, thereby, leave '*cum applausu populi*'.[2] It is an advantage in any debate to be able to have the last word, yet it hardly seems so compelling an advantage that the bishops would have been willing to risk royal displeasure and the punishment which they might have anticipated. Actually, a close examination of the course of the shifting arguments over procedure during the session reveals that the bishops' party used every bit of ingenuity at their command to avoid initiating the argument on the second proposition. This proposition, affirming the right of 'euerie church' to determine rites and ceremonies, could be attacked only by a *direct appeal* to papal authority. Such an attack would have been an explicit affront to the assembled Parliament, for it denied their very right to enact the Supremacy bill which they had so recently adopted. The bishops had, indeed, so argued against the bill in the Lords, but to continue the argument after the bill's passage could only antagonize.

The second proposition placed the bishops in a dilemma: if they compromised their previous opposition to the royal supremacy, they denied their conscientious convictions and became the queen's reluctant allies; if they maintained papal supremacy openly and forcefully, they alienated Parliament from what remained of their cause. Were they to treat of the second article as Bacon insisted, they could not merely imply papal authority as Cole had done on the first day; now they must confront the issue squarely, just as the reformers intended to do in the speech which they never delivered.[3] Bacon warned the bishops that the queen herself desired them to pass to the second article.[4] They still refused, convinced that defiance in procedural matters would damage their cause less than open defiance of the yet unsigned Supremacy act. They disliked the offer of Abbot

[1] Dasent, *Privy Council*, VII, 78; Cardwell, *Prayer Book Conferences*, p. 29.
[2] Foxe, *Acts*, VIII, 691.   [3] Cardwell, *Prayer Book Conferences*, p. 92.
[4] Il Schifanoya and Feria both assert this (*CSP, Ven.* VII, 65; *CSP, Sp.* I 47).

Feckenham to debate the issue on their behalf, for that would have forced the very issue they wished to avoid.[1] A few years later James Pilkington, answering a Roman Catholic polemic, implied that the bishops had preferred silence to a damaging defence of their position: 'Was there not a disputation for religion appointed by the queen's majesty, wherein your clergy was afraid to utter their foolishness in defending their superstition, lest they had taken more shame in answering than they did in holding their peace, which well they could not?'[2]

The bishops successfully avoided either horn of the dilemma which Elizabeth and her advisers sought to force upon them. Their outright disobedience served to warn the government that their opposition to royal supremacy in the Lords had been more than a gesture to discharge their consciences. In turn, the government's swift reprisal served notice on clerics of papal allegiance that royal supremacy would be enforced.

The bishops' party did not debate papal supremacy in the disputation, but neither did they compromise on the issue; they would not be drawn into a discussion of liturgical reforms which implied that they by-passed the issue. Elizabeth and her advisers now knew, if they had retained any doubts, that reform could not come as a compromise between the bishops and the reformers. It was even clearer than it had been on Good Friday that the government would have to rely on the reformers' support to secure the settlement of religion, and that, therefore, they must be prepared to give even greater consideration to their demands.

THE PRAYER BOOK OF 1559

Parliament authorized the new Elizabethan Prayer Book in its Uniformity bill before it adjourned, and the other legislative pillar of the Elizabethan settlement, the Supremacy bill, was also a product of the post-Easter deliberations. The new Supremacy bill, introduced

[1] *CSP, Sp.* I, 47; *ZL*, I, 16.
[2] James Pilkington, *Works*, ed. James Schoenfield, Parker Society (Cambridge, 1842), pp. 626–7.

in the Commons on 10 April, was completed by the 29th.[1] Changes
were few. Whereas the bill which had been passed in March seems to
have offered Elizabeth the choice of accepting or rejecting the title
'Supreme Head', the new bill specifically assigned the monarch the
title 'Supreme Governor'. The new designation avoided some of
the theological implications of the title of Henry and Edward.[2]
Both papists and the more militant reformers had objected to the
title, and both the Spanish Feria and the Marian exile Thomas Lever
were credited with persuading the queen to drop it. More likely is
John Jewel's opinion that Elizabeth herself 'seriously maintains that
this honour is due to Christ alone, and cannot belong to any human
being soever'.[3] The intense parliamentary debates must have caused
Elizabeth to reconsider the *supremum caput* and to decide it was not
an appropriate title to express the royal supremacy. She was not
slavishly tied to the precedents of the reigns of her father or brother.
The only other significant modification in the Supremacy bill was
the addition of the proviso limiting penal action against heretics
to those convicted of having contravened doctrine in Scriptures or
the first four general councils.[4]

The Uniformity bill establishing the 1559 Book of Common Prayer
was first read in the Commons on Tuesday, 18 April, and concluded
in the Lords on Friday, ten days later. Its swift passage would seem
to indicate that its terms had been well agreed upon by the government and by the reformers in the Commons before its introduction.
Only in the Lords did a strong group of conservatives including
the bishops, two privy councillors, and seven lay peers, dissent.[5]

[1] *JHC*, I, 59 ('nova'), 61; *JHL*, I, 574; Davis, *EHR*, xxviii (1913), 536, 537, and
539; F. W. Maitland, *Collected Papers*, III, 197–8; Neale, *EHR*, LXV, 330–1n.
[2] *CSP, Sp.* I, 37–8, 43, and 52; Feria to Philip; 19 and 24 March and 11 April, 1559;
CSP, Ven. VII, 58, Il Schifanoya, 28 March; VII, 64, Tiepolo to Doge and Senate,
9 April; *CSP, Rome*, I, 9; Intelligence from London, 28 March.
[3] *CSP, Ven.* VII, 58, Il Schifanoya, 28 March 1559; VII, 82, Tiepolo to Doge and Senate,
4 May; *Parker Corr.*, p. 66, Sandys to Parker, 30 April; *ZL*, I, 33, Jewel to Bullinger,
22 May 1559; see also I, 24, Jewel to Peter Martyr, no date; *CSP, Sp.* I, 43 and 55,
Feria to Philip, 24 March and 18 April; *CSP, Ven.* VII, 73, Il Schifanoya, 5 April.
[4] See below, pp. 236–7. Maitland, *Collected Papers*, III, 197–8.
[5] *JHC*, I, 60 (18, 19 and 20 April); Davis, *EHR*, xxviii, pp. 537–41 (25, 26, 27, 28
and 29 April); Neale, *EHR*, LXV, 332; *CSP, Sp.* I, 67, Feria to Philip, 10 May 1559.

The book attached to the bill was the Prayer Book of 1552

withe one Alteracōn or Addition of certayne Lessons to bee used on every Sundaye in the Yere, and the fourme of the Letanie altered and corrected, and twoo Sentences onelye added in the delyverye of the Sacrament to the Cōmunicantes, and none other or otherwise.

The act also provided that until the queen took other order, the 'ornaments of the church and of the ministers thereof' should be those of King Edward's second year. The rubrics in the Prayer Book were changed accordingly. Of the other alterations which appeared when the book was published, the only significant ones were the change in the rubric specifying the position of the officiant at Morning and Evening Prayer, and the omission of the 'Black Rubric' added by the Privy Council in 1552.[1]

The provision of special Sunday lections was a sensible pastoral accommodation for the normal weekly congregations. The correction of the litany merely continued the version currently in use; it was based on the form introduced in the Chapel Royal in the first weeks of Elizabeth's reign. Among other alterations it omitted the deprecation of 'the bishop of Rome and all his detestable enormities'.[2]

The other changes modified the Prayer Book in a conservative direction. The celebrated ornaments rubric meant that at the Eucharist the celebrant would wear either a cope or the traditional Mass vestments instead of the surplice ordered by the 1552 Book. The officiant at the daily offices was to stand 'in the accustomed place' rather than wherever 'the people may best hear'.

The two remaining alterations touched on that most sensitive of sixteenth-century theological issues: the doctrine of the presence of Christ in Holy Communion. The communion sentences of the 1549 book had implied the presence of Christ in a manner which would

---

[1] *Statutes of the Realm*, IV, 355–8; 1° Eliz., c. 2. The oath at ordinations was also changed to conform with the Supremacy Act. The 1559 Prayer Book is most conveniently available in the Parker Society edition edited by William Keatinge Clay, *Liturgies and Occasional Forms of Prayer Set Forth in the Reign of Queen Elizabeth* (Cambridge, 1847), pp. 23–298.
[2] Clay, *Liturgies*, pp. 9–22.

have been acceptable to Roman Catholics, to Lutherans, or to such men as Bucer and Calvin among the Reformed; those of 1552 emphasized only the commemorative signification which had been the centre of Zwingli's teaching. It is an error to think that their combination was a mere compromise; it clearly vindicated a doctrine unequivocally asserting the presence of Christ. The second sentence adds a devotional emphasis to the first, but does not in the least negate its positive assertion. This change, together with the omission of the Black Rubric, reopened the whole question of the eucharistic presence.[1]

How were these changes in the Prayer Book introduced? Who insisted on conservative modifications of the 1552 liturgy? Signs of a struggle between the queen and her advisers, on the one hand, and the émigré party with its strength in the Commons, on the other, appear in the rare glimpses into the behind-the-scenes negotiations from the time of the Westminster disputation to the introduction of the Uniformity bill. John Jewel wrote to Peter Martyr on 14 April:

O Mary and the Marian times! With how much greater tenderness and moderation is truth now contended for, than falsehood was defended some time since! Our adversaries acted always with precipitancy, without precedent, without authority, without law; while we manage everything with so much deliberation, and prudence, and wariness, and circumspection, as if God himself could scarce maintain his authority without our ordinances and precautions; so that it is idly and scurrilously said by way of joke that as heretofore Christ was *cast out* by his enemies, so he is now *kept out* by his friends. This dilatoriness has grievously dampened the spirits of our brethren, while it has wonderfully encouraged the rage and fury of our opponents.

The tone of Jewel's letter leaves little doubt but that he himself agreed with the jokes of the idle and scurrilous. A few sentences later, Jewel pointed to the queen herself:

If [she] would but banish [the Mass] from her private chapel, the whole thing might be easily got rid of.... This woman, excellent as she is, and earnest in the cause of true religion, notwithstanding she desires a thorough

[1] See below, pp. 265–9.

change as early as possible, cannot however be induced to effect such change without the sanction of law.... Meanwhile, many alterations in religion are effected in parliament, in spite of the opposition and gain-saying and disturbance of the bishops. These however I will not mention, as they are not yet publicly known, and are often brought on the anvil to be hammered over again.[1]

The government authorities representing the queen were far too conservative for the émigré tastes of Jewel. Elizabeth graciously allowed the reforming party to think that she sympathized with their aims—as she did, up to a point—but the reformers mired in the delays and precautions by which she sought to temper their demands.

Writing at the beginning of March, the time of the moratorium on discussion in religion in Parliament, the M.P. Richard Hills had anticipated a liturgical Reformation which would follow either the 1552 Prayer Book or the Augsburg confession, which he and other Englishmen apparently identified with the 1549 Book.[2] The possibility of a Lutheran England deeply disturbed the reformers of Zurich, for they realized that England could throw the balance of protestantism against them in favour of the Lutheranism dominant in the empire. Bullinger wrote that the possibility of English adoption of the Augsburg confession 'gives vexation to all the purer churches and would infect them all with its leaven'.[3] Englishmen recently returned from the tutelage of the Swiss reformed churches shared the concern of the danger of Lutheran infection. In these terms posed by Richard Hills of a 'Lutheran' 1549 Book and a 'reformed' 1552 Book, the émigrés would have fought vigorously for the 1552 Book. Even that reform was far too conservative for some of the Marian exiles, but in the rebellious bill of Holy Week, the reformers in the Commons seem to have agreed upon toleration of the second Prayer Book as their minimal demand. The modification of the vestiarian requirements and the eucharistic doctrine in the

[1] *ZL*, I, 17–18.
[2] *ZL*, II, 16 and 17, Hills to Bullinger in a postscript to a letter dated 28 February; the postscript was written after Parliament had been sitting almost six weeks—the first week of March; *OL*, I, 266, 5 June 1549.
[3] Strype, *Annals*, I, part I, 259. See also *ZL*, II, 5, Gualter to Elizabeth, 16 January 1559; II, 8–11, to Bedford; II, 11–12 to Masters; II, 56, Masters to Gualter, 16 June 1561.

Elizabethan Prayer Book were both further retrogressions towards the 1549 Book and Lutheranism.[1] To accept them, the reformers in the Commons and their émigré clerical advisers in London must have been convinced that there would be no reformed liturgy unless they made these concessions.

Queen Elizabeth herself probably championed these modifications of the 1552 Prayer Book. Her later insistence on the retention of vestments leads us to suppose that she favoured their use when she came to the throne. Since the Black Rubric had been introduced by the Privy Council in 1552, it was presumably Elizabeth who assumed the authority to omit it in 1559. On the very day that the Lords concluded the Uniformity bill, Elizabeth talked at length with Feria about religion. She told him that she would uphold something like the 'Augustanean' confession and that 'she differed very little from [Roman Catholics], as she believed that God was in the sacrament of the Eucharist, and only dissented from two or three things in the Mass'. Neale aptly terms this Elizabeth's *cri de cœur*. She could affirm the real presence because she believed that she had preserved its expression in the simple modifications introduced into the 1552 Prayer Book.[2]

If Elizabeth ordered Edmund Guest to prepare a revision of the Prayer Book, she seems to have expected him to base it on the first rather than the second Edwardian liturgy, for Guest's curious letter to Cecil appears to outline the substance of such a proposed revision.[3] If this interpretation is correct, then Elizabeth did intend her liturgical settlement to resemble more closely that of the 1549 Prayer Book than that of the 1552 Book. When she realized that any revision of 1549 would fail to win the support of any large section of the reforming

[1] Certainly some of the militants of Calvinist convictions would not have objected to the words of administration, but they would have been less pleased with the omission of the Black Rubric and its careful assertion of the local presence of Christ's body in heaven.

[2] *CSP, Sp.* 1, 61–2, Feria to Philip, 29 April 1559: Neale, *Parliaments*, 1, 79.

[3] In spite of E. C. Ratcliffe's judgment that the revision was not prepared by Guest, I have elsewhere argued Guest's probable authorship (Neale, *Parliaments*, 1, 77n., *Anglican Theological Review*, XLVI (1964), 177–89). The manuscript has been reprinted by Gee (*Elizabethan Prayer Book*, pp. 215–44); Cardwell (*Prayer Book Conferences*, pp. 48–54); and Dugdale (*Geste*, pp. 142–9).

party, she compromised on the 1552 liturgy with a few modifications. Having failed in making the 1549 Book slightly more protestant, she settled for making the 1552 Book slightly more catholic.

A provision in the Uniformity bill authorized the queen to promulgate 'further ceremonies and rites' if there were any contempt shown to the prescribed liturgy. Elizabeth later told Parker that without this provision she 'would not have agreed to divers orders of the book'.[1] This remark reveals the queen's personal concern for the details of the liturgy at the time of its adoption and her hesitancy to accept certain features of the 1552 Prayer Book. She *agreed* to it—after she had been assured of authority to maintain at least a minimum of ceremonial discipline. Elizabeth herself seems to have regarded the bill and its attached liturgy as a compromise between herself and the reformers.

In 1564 Canon de Silva reported to Philip a conversation with Elizabeth:

This Queen, referring no doubt to the beginning of her reign, told me that *she had to conceal her real feelings to prevail with her subjects in matters of religion*, but that God knew her heart, which was true to His service. She said other things to give me to understand that she was right in spirit, but not so clearly as I could have wished.[2]

This is as much of an admission of Elizabeth's concessions to the militant reformers as anyone could expect to come from her lips.

One other strand of evidence suggests that Elizabeth conceded far more in a protestant direction than she had intended. About ten days before the end of Parliament, the conservative marquess of Winchester attempted to persuade Elizabeth to veto the Uniformity bill. Neale suggests that this incident explains the vote of two privy councillors against the bill in the Lords; they knew that the queen sympathized with some of their objections and they hoped that their votes might encourage her to veto it.[3] Some men in a position

---

[1] *Statutes of the Realm*, IV, 358; 1° Eliz., c. 2, paragraph 13; *Parker Corr.*, p. 375, Parker to Cecil, 18 January 1571.
[2] *CSP, Sp.* I, 387; 9 October 1564; italics mine.
[3] *Parker Corr.*, pp. 65–6, Sandys to Parker, 30 April 1559; *CSP, Sp.* I, 63, Feria to Philip, 29 April; Neale, *Parliaments*, I, 80.

to know Elizabeth's attitude thought that the reformers had pressed their demands so rigorously that she might reject them *in toto*.

We shall undoubtedly remain ignorant of the course of events behind the scenes through which the compromise agreement was reached. William Cecil as the queen's most influential adviser would be expected to have played a significant role, and we have one explicit hint that his contribution may even have been decisive. In 1574 Thomas Sampson wrote to Cecil urging him to promote a better Reformation of the church; he began his plea:

Remember what you did, and could do, in the beginning of the reign of the Q's. Majesty, in the repairing of religion; what your authorite, credit, and doing then was, you know, God knoweth, and there are many witnesses of the same. Since then my Lord, remember how God hath advanced you.[1]

Sampson suggests that 'many' reformers of his own religious convictions acknowledged Cecil to have been a major force in the 'repairing of religion' at the opening of the reign. Since the settlement of religion determined at that time was just barely tolerable to men such as Sampson, he hints that Cecil saved England from a far worse religious fate. Sampson and his fellow militant reformers may have been convinced that it was Cecil who persuaded the queen to abandon her interim policies and to accept the 1552 Prayer Book.

Compromise produced the Uniformity bill of 1559 and its Prayer Book. Both the queen and the reformers drove hard bargains, and the concessions were painful to both parties. Yet the reformers needed the queen and, since the obduracy of the Marian bishops had been revealed, she herself depended upon the reformers for moral and spiritual leadership of the English Church. They compromised on a liturgical reform which was ideal to neither, but tolerable to both. Yet there was more here than compromise, for the Elizabethan Prayer Book proved to be remarkably durable. Anglicanism owes much of its subsequent character to the liturgical agreement between the queen and the reformers in the spring of 1559.

---

[1] Strype, *Parker*, III, 317, Sampson to Cecil; for date, see I, part II, 325.

The liturgy: compromise and constancy

Undoubtedly in 1559 many reformers hoped that they might chip away at the new Prayer Book, removing its 'imperfections' as occasion offered opportunity. Instead, in the years between 1559 and 1563, they saw the queen making minor changes in the statutory liturgy that removed it yet further from the 'godly purity and simplicity' which they so fervently desired. As Supreme Governor, she ordered rubrical glosses in her Injunctions in 1559, a Latin Prayer Book in 1560, and the new calendar in 1561.

Within a month of the end of Parliament, Elizabeth had had a set of Injunctions prepared to accompany a royal visitation and these remained a permanent part of the religious settlement.[1] Appended to them were two liturgical provisions which, in effect, modified rubrical provisions of the Book of Common Prayer. After the stone altar was removed from the churches under proper supervision, the new wooden holy table was to be placed in the chancel for Holy Communion services as the Prayer Book rubrics required. However, at all other times, the table was to stand 'in the place where the altar stood' at the east end and 'there commonly covered'. Except during the Communion itself, churches were to look much as they had of old.

In addition, the queen ordered the bread at communion to be unfigured but 'of the same fineness and fashion round, though somewhat bigger in compass and thickness, as the usual bread and water, heretofore named singing cakes'. The Prayer Book rubric called for bread which 'is usual to be eaten at Table with other meats but the best and purest wheat bread, that conveniently may be gotten'. Despite Parker's strained explanation that the rubric said only that such bread would 'suffice' for communion, the injunction clearly contradicted the spirit of the Prayer Book order.[2] Elizabeth's order for bread was almost a duplication of the rubric in the 1549 Prayer Book. In both of these royal orders the queen pressed for a more conservative reform than that represented in the 1552 book.

[1] See below, pp. 135–44; for the Injunctions, Frere, *Articles*, III, 17–18.
[2] *Parker Corr.*, p. 376; Parker to Cecil, 8 January 1571.

The *Liber Precum Publicarum*, authorized by letters patent of 6
April 1560, differed in many details from its 1559 English companion.
Elizabeth specified two purposes for the Latin book: that college
chapels might use the offices publicly and that 'all other ministers'
might privately read the choir offices in Latin when they were not
publicly officiating. The Edwardian Prayer Books had suggested
that ministers might say the daily offices privately 'in any language
that they themselves do understand', but Elizabeth established a new
policy by permitting the *public* recitation of the choir office, the Holy
Communion, and other Prayer Book services in Latin. The book,
which was not authorized for parish churches, appropriately omits
the occasional offices of Baptism, Confirmation, Marriage, Churching
of Women, and the commination service.[1]

The Latin Prayer Book frequently reverts to forms of the 1549
Book. Many such instances seem best explained by the 1549 editor's
use of the only Latin Prayer Book available, a translation of the 1549
Book prepared in 1551 by Alexander Aless.[2] But Aless' model does
not explain all the similarities to the 1549 Book.

The 1560 editor introduced deliberate rubrical variations from the
Elizabethan book in the Holy Communion. The rubrics before the
Holy Communion omit the directions for the holy table to stand in
the body or chancel of the church and those after the service omit
the order for plain ordinary bread—omissions which conform to the
queen's injunctions.[3] The rubrics for the Epistle and Gospel deliberately suggest that other ministers besides the celebrant might read

[1] *Liber Precum Publicarum, seu Ministerij Ecclesiasticae Administrationis Sacramentorum
Aliorumque Rituũ & Ceremoniarum in Ecclesia Anglicana cum privilegio.* For convenience,
page references will refer to Clay's reprint (*Liturgies*, pp. 299–434). Another version
of this Latin edition included all but the commination service of the occasional
offices omitted in the other edition. From the fact that these appear *after* the burial
office, they would seem to have been added later—perhaps for parish use in
Ireland, where Parliament had authorized the use of a Latin Prayer Book in places
where people did not speak English. See Clay, *Liturgies*, p. xxiii; Francis Procter
and Walter Howard Frere, *A New History of the Book of Common Prayer* (London,
1905), pp. 123–4; Frank Streatfeild, *Latin Versions of the Book of Common Prayer*,
Alcuin Club Pamphlet XIX (London, 1964), pp. 2–4.
[2] *Ordinatio Ecclesiae seu Ministerii Ecclesiastica, in Florentissimo Regno Angliae*, Alexandre
Alesio Scoto (1551).
[3] Clay, *Liturgies*, pp. 383 and 399.

them.[1] The offertory rubric proposes that the sentences might be sung rather than spoken.[2] The rubric which required 'three at the least' to be present to communicate with the priest is omitted, leaving only the vague stipulation that 'a convenient number' be present. In all of these rubrical variations, the editor designedly chose the practices of 1549 in preference to those of 1552 and 1559. These irritants to the militant reformers are hardly significant but, as anyone who has lived in a theological faculty knows, such liturgical minutiae can assume amazingly disproportionate stature in professional clerical minds.

The 1549 Prayer Book had provided for holy communion to be reserved for the sick on the day of the celebration, but the second book had omitted this provision. The Elizabethan Latin book reproduced the 1549 rubrics for the reservation. It is not likely that the 1560 editor borrowed carelessly in this case from Aless, for he partially corrected the 1551 translation so that it would better conform to the 1549 English wording of the rubrics. The Latin book deliberately authorizes a practice which probably had continued without specific rubrical direction, a practice suspect to many reformers, and still debated by twentieth-century Prayer Book revisers.[3]

The calendar of the Latin Prayer Book harks back to its medieval predecessors, for although it omits a few doctrinally dubious observances, it hardly leaves a day open throughout the year.[4] To this day, it is the fullest calendar ever to be set forth in an official anglican Prayer Book.

The militant reformers were reminded of the abuses of Masses for the dead when Elizabeth appended a section to the Latin book. An innocuous service for the commemoration of benefactors was an appropriate addition for a book to be used in college chapels. But

---

[1] Aless, *Ordinatio*, fo. 37; Clay, *Liturgies*, p. 385.

[2] Clay, *Liturgies*, p. 386.

[3] *Ibid.* pp. xxvi and 404; Aless, *Ordinatio*, fo. 59; Procter and Frere, *Prayer Book*, pp. 120–1; W. K. Lowther Clarke and Charles Harris, ed. *Liturgy and Worship* (London, 1950), p. 562.

[4] Clay, *Liturgies*, pp. 312–22. Assumption, All Souls and St Thomas à Becket are among those missing; popes are listed as '*episco. Ro*'.

attached to the commemoration were propers for a requiem celebration of the Holy Communion. These propers had been included in the 1549 Book and dropped in 1552. The collect, following Aless, mentions 'this our brother'—too specific an intercession for the 1552 revisers, who dropped the phrase when they adapted this particular collect for the regular burial office. The Latin book explained that the propers were provided 'if the friends and neighbours of the departed wish to communicate'. In her letters patent, Queen Elizabeth singled out for special authorization these additions in the Latin Prayer Book: 'We have commanded to be appended certain special things fit to be repeated at the funerals and obsequies of Christians, the aforesaid Statute of the rite of public prayer...promulgated in the first year of our reign, to the contrary notwithstanding'.[1]

No matter how it was described, the requiem Eucharist offended many of the reformers. Before the Latin book appeared, notable public obsequies had been held with accompanying celebrations of the Holy Communion: for Henry II of France and at the actual funeral of Frances, duchess of Suffolk.[2] Machyn also described two other funerals with communions in December 1559 and January 1560.[3] Before 1560 was out, the earl of Shrewsbury had been buried with a Eucharist.[4] Presumably the seasonal propers were used at these services. An unidentified set of visitation articles reveals reformers' opposition to the custom; the articles, assigned by Strype to 1559 and by Frere to 1560, asked 'whether they kepe any communion for the deade, the morrow after the burial, as they were wonte to kepe their requiem masse, or no'.[5] Elizabeth's order

---

[1] Clay, *Liturgies*, pp. 431–4, and 301 (translation mine).
[2] Strype, *Annals*, I, part I, 189–91 and 292–3; *CSP, For.* I, 472 and 546, marquess of Winchester to Cecil, 14 August 1559 and list of expenses; Grindal in a sermon at the service held on 3 October 1564 for Emperor Ferdinand pointed out that in the ceremonies, which included Ante-Communion *only*, 'here is no invocation or massing for the dead' (*Remains*, p. 27; see 'Stowe's Memoranda', *Three Fifteenth Century Chronicles*, ed. James Gairdner, Camden Society, o.s. 28 [Westminster, 1880], pp. 129–30).
[3] Machyn, *Diary*, pp. 221 and 222; 31 December 1559 and 8 January 1560.
[4] Francis Peck, *Desiderata Curiosa...* (new edition, London, 1779), II, 254–5.
[5] Strype, *Annals*, I, part II, 495; Frere, *Visitation Articles*, III, 88.

8-2

restored the official encouragement for requiems which had been rejected by the 1552 revisers. The commemoration with the requiem propers was also published as a separate volume.[1]

The Latin Prayer Book had been in preparation from an early stage of the settlement, for in August 1559 Sir John Mason had written to Cecil that 'the Book of Service in Latin is now in perfection'.[2] Walter Haddon is usually named as editor of the book, but although the Latin scholar was certainly equipped for the work, the evidence identifying him is far from conclusive.[3] Elizabeth followed up the Latin Prayer Book with direction to her ecclesiastical commissioners in January 1561 to prepare 'some good orders to the collegiate churches' for the use of the Latin book 'so that our good purpose in the said translation be not frustrated, nor be corruptly abused'.[4]

The general deviations of the Latin Prayer Book in favour of the 1549 book were undoubtedly offensive to many reformers, and the provision for the reservation of the sacrament for the sick and the propers for a requiem Eucharist would have been especially objectionable. In 1568 Archbishop Parker sought to enforce the book at Corpus Christi College and Gonville Hall in Cambridge, where students complained of the Latin service as 'the Pope's dregs'.[5] The irritant over the Latin book seems to have been removed when, in 1571, a more accurate translation of the Elizabethan Prayer Book appeared which avoided most of the distinctive features of the 1560 version.[6] Although the earlier book and the royal authorization were not revoked, no sign of its continued use remains; Elizabeth was probably persuaded of the futility of maintaining a Latin Prayer Book which did not conform to the statutory English book.

The 1560 Latin Prayer Book is an instance of the queen's attempt

---

[1] Streatfeild, *Latin Versions*, pp. 3–4.   [2] *CSP, For.* I, 468, 12 August 1559.

[3] Evidence goes back no further than an uncertain identification by Peter Heylen: 'The Queen had caused the English Liturgy to be translated into Latin, using therein the pen and diligence of Walter Haddon (as some suppose).' (*Ecclesia Restaurata...* [London, 1661], p. 131; see also Jeremy Collier, *An Ecclesiastical History of Great Britain*, ed. Thomas Lathbury [London, 1852], VI, 298–9).

[4] *Parker Corr.*, pp. 133–4; Elizabeth to Parker and other commissioners, 22 January 1561.

[5] Strype, *Parker*, 534–6.   [6] Procter and Frere, *Prayer Book*, p. 125.

to secure a settlement more traditional, and closer to the 1549 Prayer Book, than that implied by the parliamentary legislation. The attempt had limited success at best, but the book remains with its rubrical deviations, provision for reservation, full calendar and, above all, its requiem propers, as a reflection of the Queen's convictions and tastes in religion. She had abandoned neither her convictions nor her intention to translate those convictions into ecclesiastical policy.

Finally, Elizabeth attempted to modify the liturgical settlement in a minor way with her new calendar of 1561. She ordered a revision of the daily scriptural lectionary for Morning and Evening Prayer in her letter to the ecclesiastical commissioners of January 1561:

Understanding that there be in the [Prayer Book] certain chapters for lessons...which might be supplied with other...parcels of scripture, tending in the hearing of the unlearned or lay people more to their edification,...[we] have thought good to require you...to peruse the order of the said lessons throughout the whole year, and to cause some new calendars to be imprinted whereby such chapters or parcels of less edification may be removed, and other more profitable may supply their rooms.

In less than four weeks the commissioners prepared the new calendar and Parker ordered it to be published throughout his province. The calendar became a permanent part of subsequent editions of the Prayer Book.[1]

The commissioners made only one major change in the lections: they rearranged the Old Testament lessons so that on Prayer Book holy days, special first lessons, proper to the day, would be read. According to the 1559 lections, the minister apparently had to choose between reading the proper first lesson or the lesson listed in the daily calendar according to the day of the month. The commissioners eliminated this inconsistency by inserting the proper first lessons into the daily calendar. They made room by rearranging the daily readings and by eliminating a few Old Testament genealogies and ceremonial directions—certainly 'parcels of less edification'.

[1] *Parker Corr.*, pp. 132–6; Elizabeth to Parker and other commissioners, 22 January 1561; Parker to Grindal, 15 February 1561; Clay, *Liturgies*, pp. 435–55.

The main result of the lectionary changes was to ensure that the English Church would observe its official red-letter holy days in the biblical lections read at its daily offices.[1]

The new calendar also added fifty-nine black-letter holy days to the four which had been carried over into the 1559 Prayer Book from the 1552 Book. The selection of feasts bears no apparent relation to any of the official or semi-official calendars of earlier years. The commissioners chose freely from among the traditional calendars, and they assigned from three to nine black-letter holy days to each month. The newly added saints are an oddly mixed lot, and no one has yet discovered the precise criteria by which the commissioners made their choice. The new calendar also recognized the vigils of some red-letter feasts by labelling their eves as 'fasts'.

What was the purpose of the commissioners in adding the black-letter days? They made no liturgical provision for observing the feasts. It has been argued that they were added for secular convenience.[2] Whitgift insisted against a puritan opponent that the 'popish saints' were included not 'to nourish any superstition,... but to express the usuall tymes of payments, and the tymes of the courts and their returnes in both lawes'.[3] Whitgift's argument does not close the issue. First, the new calendar, unlike other less official calendars of Elizabeth's reign, is nowhere near full enough to be of more than limited value for secular affairs; second, the commissioners certainly did consider religion, for all doctrinally offensive days have been eliminated from it.[4] Secular convenience does not entirely

---

[1] The Elizabethan Uniformity bill had called for certain new lessons 'to be used on every Sunday of the year'. The 1559 Prayer Book calendar went beyond this provision by providing special Old Testament lessons not only for Sundays but for red-letter holy days as well, but, as mentioned, they neglected to insert these new readings into the daily calendars. Proper second lessons were not assigned to all the holy days, but where they were, they were inserted into the daily calendar in the 1559 book.

[2] Clay, *Liturgies*, p. xxxiii; Clarke and Harris, *Liturgy and Worship*, p. 216.

[3] Peel, *The Seconde Parte of a Register*, I, 212.

[4] For examples of full calendars expressly for legal purposes, see 'Preces Privatae', in William Keatinge Clay, ed. *Private Prayers Put Forth by Authority during the Reign of Queen Elizabeth*, Parker Society (Cambridge, 1851), p. 428; or *A Brief Treatise Conteyning Many Proper Tables and Easie Rules...Newly sette foorth and alowed, according to the Queenes Majesties Injunctions* (London, 1582).

explain the new calendar; as the puritans insisted, the inclusion of the names of the feasts in the Prayer Book could not be devoid of *all* religious significance.

One hundred years later the English bishops defended the black-letter days on the twofold ground that 'they are useful for the preservation of [the saints'] memories, and for other reasons, as for leases, law days, etc.'.[1] 'Preservation of their memories' may be as close as we can come to the religious purposes of those who restored the days to the official church calendar. Perhaps the editors thought that a priest saying the office might make a devotional thanksgiving; perhaps it was a means of reminding English churchmen of their continuity with their ancient and medieval forebears. In a highly diluted form, it was the reassertion of a traditional catholic element in the Elizabethan church. In the twentieth century, the rich liturgical provisions for black-letter days in many modern anglican Prayer Books testify to the effectiveness of the 1561 calendar as one means of 'preserving the saints' memories'.

Elizabeth had not mentioned the additional days in her mandate for the new calendar, but neither had she mentioned the holy-day lections. These were the chief innovations of the calendar, and it may be assumed that both she and the commissioners were agreed upon them.

The position of the tables, wafer bread, the conservative elements of the Latin Prayer Book, and the new calendar were very minor modifications of the parliamentary liturgical settlement. Yet they must have discouraged the precisians who had trusted to see a fuller reformation in the English Church; the modifications were in the wrong direction.

THE PRAYER BOOK IN THE CONVOCATION OF 1563

The precisians came to Convocation in 1563 determined that some of the most glaring 'imperfections' in the Book of Common Prayer would be removed; then might the Church of England move a little closer to the 'godly purity and simplicity used in the primitive

[1] Cardwell, *Prayer Book Conferences*, p. 341.

church'. The various proposals for liturgical changes reflect the offence which the book gave to their consciences.

The preliminary papers for the Convocation looked to the synod to correct Prayer Book imperfections.[1] The 'Certain articles', in addition to referring indirectly to the imperfections of 'certain rules and rubrics', also specified consideration of the 'choice of the chapters'. Perhaps it was the apocryphal lessons to which they objected, but the authors made no further details, and this particular proposal was not taken up by any of the other Convocation documents.

The eastward position of the holy table out of service and wafer bread for communion offended the precisians. The bishops, in a set of 'Interpretations' of 1561, had explained these orders of Elizabeth with only minor glosses. Since some chancels were far too small to hold a congregation for Holy Communion, they agreed that, in such cases, the table might be moved 'into the body of the church before the chancel door'. They carefully specified that the table was to be returned to the east wall 'according to the injunction'. The bread, as Elizabeth had directed, was to be 'thicker and broader than it is now commonly used.'[2]

The precisians were unhappy with both of these royal regulations, which subtly emphasized the continuity of the English Church with its unreformed medieval past. 'General notes' directly contradicted the queen's injunction by proposing that the tables 'stand no more altarwise' and 'Articles for government' repeated this direction, and also insisted that the communion bread was not to be the wafers ordered by the injunction, but 'as is appointed in the book of common prayer'.

Many reformers objected to the prescribed Prayer Book holy days. The 'General notes' asked that 'the number of fasting-days and holy days to be by name expressed in the said book; and the open observers of abrogated days to be punished'. This sounds as if the authors wanted the Prayer Book to designate some of its specified holy days to be observed by a real holiday from work and devotion to religious exercises.

[1] For Convocation documents, see appendix I, pp. 342–56.
[2] Frere, *Visitation Articles*, III, 70–1; see below, pp. 163–5.

The signers of the 'Seven articles' set forth, as their ideal, the abrogation of 'all saints' feasts and holy-days, bearing the name of any creature', but they were willing to settle for regulations which would allow a commemoration of such days 'by sermons, homilies, or common prayers for the better instructing of the people in histories', and which would allow men afterwards to 'occupy themselves in any bodily labour, as of any other working-day'. We can see in this proposal the incipient puritan desire to distinguish as absolutely as possible between the sabbath and other days as well as their suspicion that leisure hours encourage sin. The 'Six articles' which nearly passed the Lower House flatly called for all holy days to be abrogated except Sundays and the 'principal feasts of Christ'. 'Articles for government' would have established four new fasts a year complete with prayers and sermons. Half of the membership of the Lower House were prepared to jettison a major portion of the traditional Christian year, in direct contrast to the queen and her commissioners who had strengthened the observance of the occasional holy days.

The precisians objected to the Prayer Book office of baptism on several counts. 'General notes' proposed that in baptism the god-parents ought to declare their own faith in the Apostles' Creed, and not answer questions on the infants' behalf. The 'Twenty-one articles' which gained the support of the Lower House picked up this proposal and added the hope that the actual father of the infant might be present and join the godparents in their profession of the Christian faith. The traditional Catholic custom of sponsors answering on behalf of a child seemed to militant reformers to reduce faith to something less than evangelical centrality in the Christian's life.

Another objection to the Prayer Book baptismal rite was made by both 'General notes' and one of the papers Sandys prepared.[1] Both wanted baptisms to be performed only by ordained ministers, and not by midwives or other laymen in emergencies. The petition of the 'Seven articles' and the 'Twenty-one articles' similarly demanded the prohibition of lay baptisms. The motivation seems to have been twofold. St Paul had told women to keep silence, and the Calvinists

---

[1] Grindal commented in the margin of Sandys' paper, 'It can be done in synod.'

abhorred their performing any function in the church. An emergency baptism performed by a lay person somehow tended to make baptism a magical rite instead of the official act of the church acting through its designated minister. A vigorous clericalism was never far beneath the surface of Calvinistic circles. Significantly, in contrast, the bishops in their 1561 'Interpretations' had agreed that emergency baptisms ought to be ministered by the 'curate, deacon, or reader, or some other grave and sober person if the time will suffer'.[1]

Bishop Sandys wanted also to eliminate the crossing of the child's forehead in baptism, 'as it seems very superstitious'. This simple ceremony continued for many years to be a favourite target for puritans attacking the popery of the English Church. Both the 'Seven articles' and the 'Six articles' of the Lower House would have abolished it.

The 'Six articles' would have required that 'in all parish churches the minister in common prayer turn his face towards the people; and there distinctly read the divine service appointed, where all the people assembled may hear and be edified'. This would have been an explicit interpretation of the rubric in the 1552 Prayer Book, dropped in 1559, which had ordered the officiant at the office to be in such place and 'so turn him as the people may best hear'. A little more vaguely, the 'Seven articles' directed the minister to stand 'in such convenient place of the church, as all may hear and be edified'. The Elizabethan Book had rather directed the minister to be in the 'accustomed place', unless the bishop ordered otherwise. The characteristic Reformation stress on edification underlay the request —a stress that was often insensitive to the advantage of an architectural setting that suggested the mutual participation of officiant and congregation in an act of praise directed toward God. To many of the precisians, any focusing of congregational attention on the holy table was suspect because it recalled the idolatry which they believed had been practised before images and the reserved sacrament.

The authors of 'Certain articles' would have incidentally introduced this reform in churches whose chancels were 'decayed'. The

---

[1] Frere, *Visitation Articles*, III, 69.

paper pointed out that since impropriated tithes were often not applied properly to the repair of chancels, such chancels might be torn down, and the materials used for repairing the rest of the church. The minister would have had to lead the services from a position in the repaired nave—a by-product which would certainly not have displeased the reform-minded authors.

Another set of proposed alterations in the Prayer Book are found only in the documents prepared during the course of Convocation itself. Kneeling at communion had been unpopular with the more militant reformers ever since John Knox had preached against it before the king in 1553. Both the 'Seven articles' and the more widely supported 'Six articles' would have left kneeling at communion to the discretion of the ordinary. Although the 'Six articles' mentioned 'age, sickness, and sundry other infirmities' as the reasons for introducing an option to receive without kneeling, it was obviously horror at those who 'superstitiously both kneel and knock' which led them to make the demands. As if any priest with the slightest sense of his pastoral responsibilities has ever refused to communicate a parishioner physically incapable of kneeling! The discretion left to the ordinaries would have probably meant that the majority of bishops would have gladly granted the option and that the others would have been under importunate pressure from zealous reformers in their dioceses to do likewise. The precisians knew that it would not take too long to turn the option into a prohibition of kneeling. It would be interesting to know how Bishop Guest responded to these requests, for he preferred standing to kneeling, but solely on the ground of patristic precedent.[1]

The 'Twenty-one articles' contained two proposed changes in the Prayer Book related to the Communion service which did not continue on the lists of later puritan demands. One of these would have added to the general confession a statement that 'the communicants do detest and renounce the idolatrous mass'. Congregations would have declared with each celebration of the Prayer Book rite that no matter how their ceremonies and words may have resembled the former Latin rite, Mass and Lord's Supper were not

---

[1] *Anglican Theological Review*, XLVI, 177–89.

the same. Matters of similarity and contrast depend largely on the perspective of the observer. To reformers in the 1560s whose friends had been burned for refusal to adopt doctrines associated with the Latin Mass, and who had themselves been in personal jeopardy for similar reasons, the contrast impressed them much more vividly than the similarities. Provided the renunciation of the Mass had been suitably worded, most of the clerics, including those who had conformed under Mary, could have conscientiously taken it. Its appropriateness is another affair. Like the happily excised deprecation of the bishops of Rome in the litany, each celebration of the sacrament of unity would have rubbed salt into old wounds. Thankfully the proposal died a-borning.

The second distinctive proposal of the 'Twenty-one articles' would have required all those who did not intend to receive communion to leave the church before the general confession. By not permitting non-communicating attendance at the Supper itself, the proposal stressed the importance of full participation in the sacramental rite—a stress shared by all sixteenth-century reformers, but not expressed by all in such a regulation.[1]

The 'Articles for government' ordered that no cleric 'minister or suffer to be ministered the holy communion at any burial'. The authors would have forbidden the practice specifically authorized and encouraged by Elizabeth in her appendix to the Latin Prayer Book. During her reign the only explicit prohibition in an episcopal order came from Bishop Barnes of Durham who, in 1577, ordered 'That no Communion or Commemoration (as some call them) be said for the dead, or at the burials of the dead.'[2] It is uncertain how long the actual practice of communions at burials continued in the Elizabethan church, but in spite of militant efforts no known legal barrier appeared except in this diocesan regulation.

Finally one of the 'Seven articles' reveals the true attitude of the most militant reformers towards the entire Prayer Book in 1563.

---

[1] Guest, or whoever was the author of the letter to Cecil describing a Prayer Book version, made a similar proposal (see above, pp. 109–10).

[2] W. P. M. Kennedy, *Elizabethan Episcopal Administration*, 3 vols. Alcuin Club Collections, xxv–xxvii (London, 1924), II, 72; cf. Frere, *Visitation Articles*, III, 167, for an injunction which skirted the issue.

They asked that the thirty-fourth Article of Religion, on traditions of the church, be changed to mitigate the section which states that those who break traditions and ceremonies of the church 'ought to be rebuked openly...as one that offendeth against the common order of the Church, and hurteth the authority of the magistrate, and woundeth the consciences of the weak brethren'. On principle, the precisians would have disliked the inclusion of any such defence of ceremonies in a formal confession of doctrine, but their protest here seems much more practical. Even assuming that the 'Seven articles' were adopted as they hoped, apparently even these modifications of the Prayer Book would not have satisfied many of them, and they wanted to be assured that they might change or omit rubrical ceremonies without danger of violating the official doctrinal articles. In effect, these clergy wanted to retain the right of conscientious disobedience to the prescribed liturgy without jeopardizing their ministries in the church. They dared not ask for more sweeping changes in the liturgy than the relatively few points they proposed, but they served notice that even these proposals would not satisfy tender consciences that the Church of England really had returned to 'the godly purity and simplicity used in the primitive church'.

Taken as a whole, the plans and proposals of the precisians for changes in the Prayer Book were minor but significant. Forty-three Convocation-men, who came within one vote of winning the approval of the Lower House for their 'Six articles', would have abrogated saints' days, eliminated the cross in baptism, left kneeling at communion to the discretion of the bishop, and required the officiant at offices to face the congregation. Those who had supported the 'Articles for government' would have kept the holy table permanently in the chancel, ordered common bread for communion, and forbidden communions at burials. The large majority of the Lower House who supported the 'Twenty-one articles' would have modified baptism by forbidding lay baptism and by requiring sponsors at baptism to profess their own faith and not to answer in the name of the infant; in the Holy Communion they would have added a repudiation of the Latin Mass, and they would have required non-communicants to leave before the general confession.

Of course not one of these changes of the Lower House proceeded beyond the bishops. Even their minor proposals for liturgical modification ran up against the finality of the settlement which had been achieved in the 1559 Parliament. Only the resolution of the queen could have been responsible for the wholesale rejection of Prayer Book modification. Many of the bishops would unquestionably have welcomed some of these changes, but they had accepted the Prayer Book, and they were prepared, even if they themselves were not entirely happy, to support the queen's wishes.

Parliament, not Convocation, made the only positive contribution to the Prayer Book in the spring of 1563 when they authorized the production of a Prayer Book and Bible in Welsh. Under the leadership of Bishop Richard Davies, both were produced within four years. A. L. Rowse has recently commented that without these two books the language of Wales 'would have declined to the status of Breton—a peasant *patois*'.[1] Like Elizabeth's Welsh bishops, the vernacular Prayer Book and Scripture were not only a consistent extension of Reformation principles, but they also helped to identify the reformed church as the religion of Wales. Had subsequent rulers been as solicitous and wise in their treatment of the Welsh dioceses, non-conformity might not have swept the country as it did in the nineteenth century.

The Elizabethan Prayer Book, the most important single element in the definitive settlement of the independent Church of England, was the product of a bitter behind-the-scenes struggle between the militant reformers and the queen in 1559. The reformers, whose determination and organization gave their members in the Commons a dominant voice in the Lower House, had for their nucleus a hard core of clerics and laymen who had fled abroad to practise their reformed religion in the protestant cities of the continent. These men all regarded the second Edwardian Prayer Book as a minimum liturgical framework, and many of them would have wished to push the Reformation much closer to the pattern which they had

[1] *JHC*, i, 66, 67, 71, and 72; Clarke and Harris, *Liturgy and Worship*, p. 814; *Parker Corr.*, p. 265, Davies to Parker, 19 March 1566; A. L. Rowse, *The Expansion of Elizabethan England* (London, 1955), p. 74.

observed abroad. The queen had, on the contrary, intended to introduce an interim settlement during which an independent English Church would continue the Latin rites with only minor modifications.

In the queen's view, the church through its clerical leadership could then proceed to frame a Prayer Book more closely resembling the earlier 1549 book than that of 1552. The united opposition of the Marian hierarchy to a new break with Rome and the militancy of the reformers forced Elizabeth to foreshorten her policy and to accept the best compromise that she could make with the reformers in the Commons. The bargain drew serious concessions from both queen and reformers, and they both thought that they would be able in the future to modify the liturgy more to their liking.

The Injunctions, the Latin Prayer Book, and the new calendar slightly modified the liturgical settlement in the queen's conservative direction. These minor modifications served notice on the militant reformers that they could expect no gradual improvement. They would have to fight for their programme and turn the bishops' sympathy for many of their aims into active support. They came to the 1563 Convocation determined to alter the most offensive liturgical practices. As the 'Seven articles' suggest in their request for mitigation of the Articles of Religion, had the precisians won this battle, they would have made further demands until they had hammered the English Church into that pattern of godliness which many of them had observed abroad. Although 'Six articles', with its largely liturgical content, missed the support of the Lower House by one proxy vote, the precisians added other parts of their liturgical programme to 'Twenty-one articles' and 'Articles for government'. These died in the Upper House.

The Book of Common Prayer, supported by a resolute queen, stood in the way of the precisians' drive for 'godly purity and simplicity'. Protests against the Prayer Book were to recur with monotonous frequency in the years ahead, but never with such strength in Convocation. The considerable portion of traditional catholic worship that was preserved in the Elizabethan Prayer Book was safe for the future, and the spirit of moderate reform which permeated the book continued to dominate the liturgy of the Church of England.

4. The Supreme Governor: administration and finance

THE defeat of the proposals for liturgical reform disappointed the precisians in the 1563 Convocation, but had they been able to put over a sizeable part of the rest of their programme they would have effectively neutralized the Prayer Book. Near the end of Convocation, a 'most learned' militant reformer told the bishops: 'We thought the queen was the author of this business, but we now perceive that you yourselves are.'[1] Although this is one of the rare recorded instances when the militant reformer openly admitted that he and his party usually blamed Elizabeth herself for impeding the course of a 'more godly reformation', this must have been their common assumption. Although the queen was their chief defence against a return to Rome, she was also the chief obstacle to the accomplishment of the reforms they so zealously sought.

The precisians never directly attacked Elizabeth's role as Supreme Governor of the church. When they proposed changes, for example, in the Royal Injunctions, they never mentioned the fact that the regulations they put forth would have rescinded one of these orders of the queen. The only direct reference to the injunctions in all the Convocation documents is a positive incidental comment in 'Certain articles' asking for better execution of discipline on church attendance 'as prescribed by laws and injunctions of the queen's highness'.[2] The precisians freely wrote of the 'imperfections' of the Prayer Book, but only tacitly would they seek to undo those royal orders which offended their consciences. They maintained the pretence that she was above their ecclesiastical disputes.

The bishops increasingly took the blame for implementing the queen's policies. The angry reformer who in 1563 accused the bishops of the authorship of 'this business' was one of the first of a

[1] ZL, II, 150, George Withers and John Barthelot to Bullinger and Gualter, August 1567; see above, p. 2.
[2] For references to Convocation documents, see below, appendix I.

long series of precisians to attack the bishops. Criticisms of the queen could only discredit the militant reformers and their cause, but bishops could be openly accused with relative impunity.

Queen Elizabeth herself fought passionately to establish her vision of the national church. She battled with the reformers in the Commons at the time of her first Parliament. She carefully chose the bishops. We have already seen how she used her authority as Supreme Governor to order and to encourage liturgical practices to her liking, and in subsequent chapters we shall consider her role in matters of vestments, doctrine, and the treatment of Roman Catholics. More immediately, we turn to some of the more mundane aspects of church discipline and the means by which Elizabeth exercised her governorship of the church.

Was Elizabeth's use of royal supremacy motivated only by political expediency? Increasingly historians have recognized the importance of the queen's concern for church affairs, but old clichés have a way of outliving the evidence on which they were based. A mass of evidence reveals Elizabeth's intimate involvement in religious matters, and I am wholly persuaded that we cannot explain it on the common assumption that she treated religion as a tool of political policy.

This is not the place to argue, as I believe, that Elizabeth's religious convictions consistently and profoundly influenced her ecclesiastical policies, but it may not be amiss to point out one facet of her devotional practice. Canon de Silva, writing to King Philip in 1566, mentioned in passing that Elizabeth 'usually attends' the morning service. The previous year the imperial ambassador accompanied the queen to her chapel, and he reported it all as if it were simply a part of her daily routine. Camden wrote that Elizabeth prayed daily 'at set houres in her private Chappell'. Francis Bacon noted that 'seldom would she be absent from hearing divine service, either in her chapel, or in her privy closet'. Apparently, Queen Elizabeth assisted so regularly at Morning Prayer that her attendance merited no special notice.[1] It is common historical knowledge that Henry VIII

[1] *CSP, Sp.* I, 511, de Silva to Philip, 28 January 1566; Victor Von Klarvill, ed. *Queen Elizabeth and some Foreigners, Being a Series of...Letters from the Archives of*

had Mass said daily in his chamber. How has it been so easily overlooked that his daughter Elizabeth attended the church's daily morning office—usually at its sung recitation in the Chapel Royal?[1] When the queen laid down liturgical regulations, she acted upon knowledge that can come only from regular disciplined participation in the church's worship.

THE STATUTORY ECCLESIASTICAL COMMISSION

Henry VIII had exercised his royal headship of the Church of England largely through his lay Vicar-General, and Edward's Privy Council simply appropriated the royal authority to themselves along with ordinary affairs of state. Queen Elizabeth, in contrast to both, usually employed her powers as Supreme Governor through the central Ecclesiastical Commission which she established at London. The Supremacy Act declared that the queen might 'assign, name, and authorize' natural-born subjects to exercise whatever powers of the royal supremacy she delegated to them. Although English kings had used special heresy commissions from the fourteenth century, this *permanent* statutory commission was an innovation of the Elizabethan legislation which the queen used consistently and effectively.[2]

Before the end of May, it had become known that Elizabeth intended to appoint a commission in accord with the statute, and on 19 July 1559, she issued a writ naming its members and defining its authority. The purpose of the commission was to ensure that the Acts of Supremacy and Uniformity be 'duly put into execution, and such persons as hereafter offend in anything contrary to the tenor

---

the Hapsburg Family, tr. T. H. Nash (New York, 1928), p. 234, Zwetkevich to Maximilian, 4 June 1565; Camden, *Annales*, p. 7; *The Works of Francis Bacon, Lord Chancellor of England*, ed. Basil Montagu, 16 vols. (London, 1825–34), III, 469.

[1] The Chapel Royal with its staff of clerics and choristers kept the regular round of church offices; see Strype, *Annals*, II, part II, 613.

[2] E.g. the Henrician Six Articles Act, *Statutes of the Realm*, III, 739–43, 31° Henry VIII, c. 14; Philip Tyler has recently traced the history of such commissions with great emphasis on their continuity in his D.Ph. thesis at Oxford, 'The Ecclesiastical Commission within the Province of York' (pp. 21 f.).

and effect of the said several statutes to be condignly punished'. She gave the commissioners wide authority to investigate church affairs, to adjudicate disputes, and to punish offenders:

> We do give and grant full power and authority...to visit, reform, redress, order, correct, and amend in all places...all such error, heresies, crimes, abuses, offences, contempts, and enormities spiritual and ecclesiastical wheresoever, which by any spiritual or ecclesiastical power, authority, or jurisdiction can or may be reformed, ordered, redressed, corrected, restrained, or amended.

The so-called Court of High Commission, which developed out of this body, reached the height of its judicature under Archbishop Laud eighty years later, but the commissioners probably acted as a court from the beginning. They never needed more authority than this. During Elizabethan years, however great its theoretical powers, its activities were more modest and restrained.[1]

The choice of commissioners, like the choice of bishops, is instructive. Parker and Grindal were the bishops-elect named in the first commission, and throughout Elizabeth's reign she chose the archbishop of Canterbury and the bishop of London to be members of the commission, always including them in the select inner group, one of whose members was required to be present for any official action. When the commissioners were authorized to receive the Oath of Supremacy in October 1559, the name of Cox was added, and when the entire commission was renewed in 1562, Bishop Guest took his place beside the three other bishops. The membership reflected Elizabeth's consistent policy of governing the church through its own hierarchy.[2]

Elizabeth appointed three other clerics to the first commission: William Bill, William May, and Thomas Huick. Bill, Elizabeth's

---

[1] CSP, For. I, 287, Nowel (?) to Abel, 28 May 1559; writ in G. W. Prothero, Select Statutes and Other Constitutional Documents Illustrative of the Reigns of Elizabeth and James I, 4th ed. (Oxford, 1913), pp. 227–32. Dr Tyler's thesis has important implications for the London commission whose early records have been lost.

[2] Commissions of 19 July 1559 (Prothero, Select Statutes, p. 227), of 20 October 1559 (Rymer, Foedera, VI, part IV, 86–7), of 20 July 1562 (Prothero, p. 232), of 11 June 1572 (p. 235), of 23 April 1576 (p. 237), December 1583 (p. 472a), 3 February 1601 (p. 240).

almoner and subsequently dean of Westminster, and May, dean of
St Paul's, had both supported the Edwardian reforms and also may
have conformed to the Roman discipline in the years of the Marian
reaction. Huick was a clerical lawyer who had been deprived of his
canonry at St David's in 1554.[1]

The fourteen lay members of the commission represented a
spread of former ecclesiastical loyalties. Seven of them had been in
some degree associated with the Edwardian reforms: Thomas
Smith, Anthony Cooke, Francis Knollys, Walter Haddon, Richard
Goodrich, Robert Weston, and Francis Cave.[2] All but two, however,
had come to terms with the Marian reaction. Smith, the most
eminent of the group, conformed under Mary, and his modern
biographer has concluded that

the stout defender of 'reform' was a figment of Strype's imagination....
Smith had nothing but a shuddering dislike of the fiery religious passions
of his time which he neither shared nor understood. Attacked more than
once for being a 'neutral' in religion, he found no trouble in accepting
with alacrity in their turn, the Edwardian reformed religion, Marian
Catholicism, and the Elizabethan Church settlement.[3]

Walter Haddon served in minor government capacities under
Mary, Robert Weston took his doctorate in law from Oxford in

---

[1] See above, pp. 44–5, 48; Foster, *Alumni Oxon.*, under Thomas Huick. 'Le Livre des
Anglois' lists a 'Thomas Duwick' in December 1558 which Miss Garrett identifies
with Huick—a possible but highly conjectural identification (Martin, *Protestants
anglais*, p. 336; Garrett, *Marian Exiles*, under Thomas Duwick).

[2] Sir Thomas Smith's recent biographer effectively disposes of the recurrent notion
that Smith was in holy orders (Mary Dewar, *Sir Thomas Smith* [London, 1964],
pp. 29–30; cf. *DNB* and Venn, *Alumni Cantab.*). I here follow the common tradition
that Weston was a layman, but I suspect he may actually have been in orders and
identical with the Robert Weston who represented the clergy of Coventry and
Lichfield in the Convocation of 1563 (cf. *DNB*, Foster, *op. cit.* IV, 1604; Myles V.
Ronan, *The Reformation in Ireland under Elizabeth, 1558–1580* [London, 1930], p. 399;
Shirley, *Original Letters*, p. 301). For the reform records of these lay commissioners,
see Dasent, *Privy Council*, II, 125, 183, 343–5, and 517; III, 73, 78, 368–9, 382, and
410; IV, 112; Frere, *Visitation Articles*, II, 132–3, 146, 147, and 150; Wilkins, *Concilia*,
IV, 66–7; John Strype, *The Life of Sir John Cheke, Kt.* (Oxford, 1821), p. 70; Foster,
op. cit. IV, 1604; Venn, *op. cit.* II, 280; *CSP, For.* I, 287; VI, 352, Smith to Cecil,
19 May 1563; Strype, *Memorials*, I, part I, 382–93; *DNB*, under Cook, Haddon,
Goodrich, and Weston.   [3] Dewar, *Smith*, p. 5.

1556, and Goodrich and Francis Cave presumably also remained quietly in England throughout the reign. In contrast, Cooke and Knollys had both been religious exiles who had taken a lead among the reformers in the 1559 Commons. Abroad, Cooke had stayed largely in the conservative congregation at Strasburg, and as a father-in-law to both Cecil and Bacon was an intimate of some of the queen's closest advisers. Knollys, a subscriber of the New Discipline at Frankfort, was the most militant reformer on the queen's Privy Council.[1]

The seven other lay commissioners have left no record of strong ecclesiastical loyalties. Ambrose Cave had served in Parliaments of Edward and Mary before his appointment to Elizabeth's Privy Council.[2] Rowland Hill has been called 'the first protestant mayor of London', and yet in 1557 he served as one of the commissioners against heretics.[3] William Chester won Foxe's commendation for shedding tears 'at the death of Christ's people' while he served as sheriff of London in 1555, and yet he burned the reformers notwithstanding the tears, and was knighted by Mary.[4] Gilbert Gerard, a perennial M.P., became serjeant-at-law near the end of Mary's reign.[5] Thomas Sackford had been a Master of Request under Queen Mary and retained the position under Elizabeth. Randall Cholmeley and John Southcote seem to have been young lawyers in Mary's reign.[6] On the whole, it was a body of men undoubtedly prepared to follow the lead of the clerical members in questions of theological and religious distinctions.

The commissioners were equipped by professional training and experience to enforce the legal requirements of the settlement. Knollys and Cave were privy councillors, Hill and Chester had held local public office, and two of the clerical members and nine of

---

[1] Garrett, *Marian Exiles*, pp. 124–6, 210–13, and 358; *Troubles at Frankfort*, pp. 134 and 174.

[2] *DNB* and Venn, *op. cit.*, under Ambrose Cave.

[3] *DNB*; Foxe, *Acts*, VIII, 301.

[4] Foxe, *Acts*, VII, 194–5; *DNB*; Venn, *Alumni Cantab.*, under William Chester. He was unaccountably left out of the writ of October 1562.

[5] *DNB* and Venn, *op. cit.* II, 207; Dasent, *Privy Council*, VII, 17.

[6] Venn, *op. cit.* IV, 2; Dasent, *Privy Council*, VII, 7, 17–18, 19, and 84.

the laymen had been trained in law.[1] By the time of the 1563 Convocation, there were a few changes in the commission. In addition to Bishop Guest's new membership, the deans of St Paul's and Westminster, Nowell and Goodman, replaced their deceased predecessors May and Bill, and nine other men found places on the Commission, including Thomas Watts, like Nowell, a reformer of militant convictions, and Thomas Yale, Parker's chancellor.[2]

The writ for the commission gave its members authority over the entire realm, but Elizabeth also established another body for the northern province alone and, from time to time, she authorized special diocesan commissions. Royal letters patent for a commission in the province of York were issued on 5 May 1561, and the members included Archbishop Young, the bishops of Durham and Carlisle, and fourteen other clerics and laymen. Philip Tyler's important new studies on the neglected records of the commission have demonstrated that from the beginning the northern commissioners sat as a quasi-ecclesiastical court, acting quite independently of their southern counterparts. However, the York commission did not share the status of the London commission as the body of men whom the queen entrusted with the initiation and definition of church policy.[3]

The episcopal commissioners seem to have enjoyed a special status among the bishops of the realm. Although many bishops of both provinces agreed in 1561 upon a set of regulations known as the 'Lambeth Articles', Parker, Grindal, and Cox were those who actually signed the articles, presumably because of their authority as commissioners. When Elizabeth wrote to Parker in January 1565 demanding that uniformity be established in the church, she specifically asked that in determining a course of action he 'confer with

[1] The two clerical lawyers were May and Huick; the laymen, Smith, Haddon, Goodrich, Gerard, Weston, Sackford, Cholmeley, Southcote, and Francis Cave.

[2] In this 1562 writ, Elizabeth also named privy councillor William Petre and six others, mostly lawyers. Of the commissioners from 1559, Bill, May, Goodrich and Hill had died, and Francis Cave, the only other name dropped, may also have died in the intervening years.

[3] Rymer, *Foedera*, VI, part IV, 112; see *Parker Corr.*, p. 225, Elizabeth to Parker, 25 January 1565; see above, p. 130, n. 2.

the bishops your brethren, namely such as be in commission for causes ecclesiastical'. When Parker's 'Advertisements' were finally released a year later in response to the request, the preface referred specifically to this group and, although other bishops also signed it, the names of the four episcopal commissioners head the list: Parker, Grindal, Cox and Guest.[1]

The moderate reformers who dominated the clerical membership of the statutory commission undoubtedly set its theological tone. Led by bishops prepared to carry out the queen's mandate, the commission played an important role in the government of the English Church under Elizabeth.

THE ROYAL VISITATION AND THE INJUNCTIONS

The queen authorized her only royal visitation of the kingdom in the summer of 1559 in order to win loyalty of the English clergy to the religious settlement and to deprive the obstinate of their benefices. She established six temporary commissions to carry Reformation into all parts of England and Wales. The visitation was planned before the end of May, and by mid-June Cecil could write that 'the injunctions and articles of inquisition be redy formed'.[2]

If the authorization for the commission in the north may be taken as typical, the queen authorized the commissioners to investigate the clergy, to punish and deprive those who 'obstinately and peremptorily refused to subscribe' to 'the received religion' (*susceptae religioni*), and to enforce the annexed injunctions. As Henry Gee has pointed out, the commissioners required clerics to subscribe to royal supremacy, to the Book of Common Prayer, and to the queen's Injunctions, the threefold legal foundation of the settlement.[3]

---

[1] Frere, *Visitation Articles*, III, 96, 171–2, and 180; *Parker Corr.*, pp. 225–6.
[2] Forbes, *A Full View*, I, 131, Cecil to Throckmorton, 13 June 1559; *CSP, For.* I, 287, Nowel (?) to Abel, 28 May; *CSP, Ven.* VII, 96, Il Schifanoya, 6 June.
[3] Gee, *Elizabethan Clergy*, pp. 89–93, transcribed from the State Papers (*CSP, Dom.*, 1547–80, p. 149 [X]) the oath administered at York: 'We, the clergy of the Cathedral,...do humbly confess and acknowledge the restoring again of the ancient jurisdiction over the state ecclesiastical and spiritual to the crown....We confess

The visitors named to the six commissions totalled an unwieldy one hundred and twenty-five, men who can be divided into four groups: the county lord-lieutenants, the clergy, the lawyers, and the country gentry. The lord-lieutenants, who were designated to make their authority available to the commissions, included such religious conservatives as the earls of Northumberland and of Arundel.[1] The lesser gentry on the commission seem also to have been added to give local weight to the visitation, for their names seldom appear in records of the working commissions. However, in contrast to the lord-lieutenants, greater selectivity determined the choice of these men, and they were largely favourers of the new ecclesiastical policies.[2]

The real work of the commissions was carried out by the relatively small number of clerics and lawyers, and the queen had expressly ordered this in her instructions. In addition to the clerical commissioners, preachers were assigned to four of the six commissions to justify the proceedings from the pulpit. In the commissions without assigned preachers, the whole preaching load fell on the clerical commissioners themselves.[3] The chief working cleric in each case was a Marian émigré: Becon, Horn, Bentham, Jewel, Richard Davies, and Sandys. In four commissions other clerics with legal training joined them: Thomas Huyck with Horn in visiting London, Ely, and Norwich; Thomas Young, Rowland Merrick, and George Constantine with Davies in visiting the Welsh dioceses, Hereford,

---

also and acknowledge the administration of the Sacraments, the use and order of divine service in the manner and form as it is set forth in...the Book of Common Prayer,...and the orders and rules contained in the Injunctions given by the Queen's Majesty...to be according to the true word of God, and agreeable to the doctrine of the primitive church' (Gee, pp. 77–8).

[1] Gee, *Elizabethan Clergy*, pp. 71–101; list of commissioners from the P.R.O. in C. G. Bayne, 'The Visitation of the Province of Canterbury', *EHR*, xxviii (1913), 636–77, appendix I, pp. 658–9; see p. 637.

[2] Bayne, *EHR*, xxviii, 638.

[3] Instructions for the London–Norwich–Ely commission were directed to clerics Robert Horn and Thomas Huick and to lawyer John Salvyne: 'It is not ment by her Majestie that any of the said noble men shall be otherwise molested with execuson of the said commission, but as occasion shall arise when the foresaid speciall visitours shall come in to any of the said shieres for execucion of the forsaid comission that they shall have nede to require the ayde of the said noble men being her Majesties Lieutenauntes' (Bayne, *EHR*, xxviii, 660 from Inner Temple Library, Petyt MS no. 538.42, 592).

and Worcester; Stephen Nevinson and William Masters with Bentham visiting Oxford, Lincoln, Peterborough, and Coventry and Lichfield, and Henry Harvey with Sandys in the province of York.[1] Becon's group visiting Canterbury, Rochester, Chichester and Winchester, had the eminent and presumably lay ecclesiastical lawyer Robert Weston. Jewel, visiting Salisbury, Bristol, Exeter, Bath, and Gloucester, had H. Parrye, who was later to become his diocesan chancellor. Lesser-known clerics were also attached to some of the commissions.[2] In each group, at least one lay lawyer, usually known to have been sympathetic to reform, was also a member.[3]

Except for Becon all the Marian exile commissioners were soon to be named bishops, as were the clerical lawyers Young and Merrick. Of the attached four preachers, William Alley, who had remained at home under Mary, was also to be soon raised to the episcopate; the other three, Robert Wisdom, Alexander Nowell, and Thomas Lever were, like Becon, unsuccessfully proposed for episcopal office.[4] The slight differentiation here foreshadowed later policy: the more militant exiles were encouraged to preach, but it was generally their more conservative brethren who were entrusted with administrative responsibilities.

The actual visitations took place during the late summer and early autumn of 1559. The small travelling teams found the work exhausting. Jewel, before he left, had predicted that the visitation would be 'long and troublesome'; when he returned, he described it as 'a most fatiguing journey'. None the less, he apparently regarded his time as well spent, for although he had on occasion met 'inveterate obstinacy', everywhere he had found people 'well disposed towards religion, and even in those quarters where we expected most difficulty'.[5]

[1] I am assuming Masters was in orders since he received livings in 1564 and 1571 (Venn, *Alumni Cantab.*).
[2] Ralph Morice with Becon, Peter Lylly with Horn, and Thomas Wyllett with Jewel.
[3] Bayne, *EHR*, XXVIII, 637. Weston and Robert Nowel with Becon; John Salvyn with Horn; William Fleetwood with Bentham; Henry Parry and William Lovelace with Jewel; Richard Pate with Davies; and Richard Kingsmill with Sandys.
[4] See above, pp. 43–8.
[5] *ZL*, I, 39 and 44, Jewel to Peter Martyr, 1 August and 2 November 1559.

Whereas the permanent Ecclesiastical Commission chosen by Elizabeth in 1559 was weighted on the side of clerics who had remained in England during Mary's reign, the queen clearly gave the Marian exiles the dominant role in her visitation. The exiles were, of course, available for the time-consuming work, since, unlike such men as May and Bill, they were unemployed. Unequivocally committed to the cause of an independent reformed church, they were men of learning and ability who could be expected in sermons and examinations to make every effort to win over reluctant priests and to ferret out those who would not accept 'the received religion'. If Elizabeth worried about possible over-zealous reforming activity, the specific terms of the parliamentary settlement and of the injunctions must have seemed an adequate guarantee.

The Articles of Inquiry, which the visitors brought with them, were largely drawn from the articles which Cranmer had used in his diocesan visitation of 1548 in Edward's reign. Of the fourteen articles whose wording was changed, only five were altered in substance, and these were largely adaptations to the new conditions.[1] One such alteration is interesting: inquiring of people who kept in their homes 'images...or other monuments of feigned or false miracles, pilgrimages, idolatry, and superstition', the Elizabethan article proceeded to single out 'especially as have been set up in churches, chapels, or oratories'. Elizabeth did not want her subjects to hoard popish furnishings from the parish church in hope of a future swing of the ecclesiastical pendulum back to Roman obedience. Twelve completely new articles were drawn up in 1559, including one which asked whether or not the parish had used the English litany and vernacular Epistle and Gospel in accordance with the queen's proclamation of 27 December 1558.

The Articles of Inquiry as a whole illustrate how the church maintained its concern for ordinary order and discipline even in the midst of controversial religious changes. Two-thirds of the articles

---

[1] Frere, *Visitation Articles*, II, 176–89 and III, 1–7. Thirty of the Elizabethan articles correspond verbatim; 14 in part; the remaining 12 have no analogue in Cranmer's work (1 and 46–56); the *STC* lists 16 editions from 1559 to 1600 (nos. 10118–33); Articles nos. 9, 17, 21, 24, and 45 changed their meanings.

were concerned with the perennial practical matters of ecclesiastical administration and of clerical and lay morals. Less than one-third were designed to uncover the continuation of Romish practices and resistance to reforming innovations.[1] Although we may well suspect that it was these latter which received the largest share of the Visitors' attention, they diligently inquired whether incumbents had gained their cures by 'fraud, guilt, deceit or simony', they wanted to know if clergy refused to visit the sick or to bury the dead, and they urged parishioners to present adulterers and fornicators and 'such men as have two wives living' to the Ordinary.

The Visitors returned tired to London with the firm knowledge that the overwhelming majority of the clergy and laity of England refused to follow the Marian bishops into schism from the national church. Not only the government and legislators, but the church as a whole accepted the threefold base of the settlement: the royal supremacy, the Prayer Book, and the new Injunctions.

Elizabeth's Injunctions were more than temporary orders set forth to accompany the royal visitation. Frequently reprinted throughout her reign, the Royal Injunctions were to be read four times a year in every parish church (no. 14).[2] Elizabeth, who issued them on the authority of her supreme governorship at the opening of her reign, maintained them to the end.

The 1547 Edwardian Injunctions served as a guide, but the changes that Elizabeth introduced are revealing. Of the fifty-three numbered injunctions, twenty-six came from the Edwardian guides, six were imperative versions of Cranmer's 1548 interrogative articles, and twenty-one were newly drawn.[3]

Although most of the changes which Elizabeth made in borrowed

[1] Articles 2, 9, 15, 45, 51, and 52; 3, 6, 12, 24–6, 33, and 54–6. Four others (nos. 46–9) asked of heresy-hunting in Mary's reign. The purpose of some others is ambiguous; e.g. no. 32, asking of disturbers of church services, might ferret out men disaffected with reform or merely those indifferent to any religion.
[2] Frere, *Visitation Articles*, III, 8–29; for collation with 1547 Injunctions, Gee, *Elizabethan Clergy*, pp. 46–65 or Gee and Hardy, *Documents*, pp. 417–42; sixteen STC editions from 1559 to 1600 (nos. 10095–10110).
[3] From 1547: nos. 1–3, 5–18, and 20–8; from Cranmer's 1548 articles: nos. 31–5 and 39; 1547 Injunctions omitted entirely: nos. 3, 5, 6, 9, 11, 19, 21, 26, 30, and 34–6 (of 1547).

Edwardian Injunctions merely clarified them or adjusted them to the new parliamentary settlement, several changes merit mention.[1] Elizabeth increased the minimum preaching of qualified parsons in their cures from quarterly to monthly sermons; a new injunction, however, requiring only quarterly sermons, introduced an ambiguity in the requirement (nos. 3 and 4).[2] She modified the prohibition of processions to permit the Rogationtide 'perambulation of the circuits of parishes', and made liturgical provisions for this annual procession (nos. 18 and 19). When informed of the ceremony, Peter Martyr thought its pagan origins made the procession highly undesirable and advised his English friends 'to get rid of them as relics of the Amorites.'[3] Although Elizabeth kept the section of an Edwardian injunction ordering clerics to teach that 'no man ought obstinately and maliciously to break and violate the laudable ceremonies of the Church', she omitted the section which ordered clerics also to warn against the superstitious abuse of certain abolished ceremonies (no. 22).

If we compare the 1547 and 1559 Injunctions on images, we shall see that Elizabeth clearly intended to avoid the iconoclasm of her brother's reign. Of the three Edwardian injunctions on images, Elizabeth omitted the most crucial and slightly altered the other two. First, the minor alterations: one 1547 injunction had ordered that clerics 'shall not set forth nor extol any images, relics, or miracles for any superstition or lucre;...but reproving the same, they shall teach that all goodness...ought to be both asked and looked for only of God.' In a subtle alteration, the 1559 injunction required clergy not to 'set forth or extol *the dignity of* any images,...but *declaring the abuse* of the same', to teach that all goodness is of God (no. 2). In another injunction retained, Elizabeth called for the destruction of all 'monuments of feigned miracles, pilgrimages, idolatry, and superstition', but she added an order that walls and glass windows be either preserved or repaired (no. 23). Elizabeth also added the injunction drawn from Cranmer's 1548 articles forbidding persons to 'keep in their houses' any such 'monuments'

[1] Of 12 articles altered in substance, 7 merely clarify or bring up-to-date (nos. 1, 9, 12, 16, 17, 20, and 25).
[2] See below, p. 163. [3] *ZL*, II, 40, Peter Martyr to Sampson, February 1560.

(no. 35). So far the injunctions forbade the superstitious use of images and called for the destruction of monuments of 'idolatry and superstition'; presumably crucifixes and the fuller rood scenes of Calvary, along with other figures of biblical characters and historical incidents, would have been left untouched.

The Edwardian Injunctions had included a third regulation on images, ordering the removal of *any* which had given occasion to 'idolatry' of any sort.[1] This injunction had subsequently legalized the wholesale destructions of all statues and paintings when the Privy Council had ordered 'all images remayninge in any churche or chappell' to be removed, on the grounds that too much contention had arisen in the attempt to determine which images had given occasion to idolatry.[2] Elizabeth left this key injunction completely out of the 1559 set. Her intentions seem clear: the English Church would continue to use those images which in theory the 1547 Injunctions had considered legitimate, and their superstitious use was not to provide an excuse for their destruction.

The reform-minded Visitors of 1559 who proceeded to destroy all images assumed that any image—whether of the visions of St Anthony in the desert or St Paul preaching in Corinth, of the bodily assumption of our Lady or of the very crucifix itself—was a 'monument of feigned miracles, pilgrimages, idolatry, and superstition'. It was a peculiarly perverse interpretation.[3]

Of Elizabeth's nineteen other newly drawn injunctions, seven were administrative and moral regulations which would have been appropriate to almost any religious settlement. Three of them dealt with laymen at church services: no one was to disturb sermons or services, the congregation was to pay strict attention, and men were to be appointed in each parish to check on their fellow parishioners' attendance (nos. 36, 38, and 46).[4] Concern for a better-educated

---

[1] Edwardian injunction no. 3, which had also explained that images might be properly used as a 'remembrance...of them that the said images do represent'.

[2] See above, p. 12.

[3] J. V. P. Thompson, *Supreme Governor: A Study of Elizabethan Ecclesiastical Policy and Circumstance* (London, 1940), p. 56.

[4] In a similar vein were two injunctions reworded from Cranmer's 1548 articles (nos. 33 and 34).

clergy lay behind an injunction forbidding unlearned priests from exercising their ministries (no. 43). The injunction noted that many such had been made priests 'in these latter days' who could neither say Matins nor Mass. No man was to use the Bible 'rashly or contentiously' (no. 37). In the same spirit of religious peace, false accusations of 'papist, papistical, heretic, schismatic, or sacramentary' were all forbidden (no. 50). All books published were to have the express permission of the queen, her Privy Council, or the ecclesiastical ordinary and one other official; all pamphlets, plays and ballads, together with books coming from abroad, were to be licensed by the statutory Ecclesiastical Commission (no. 51). All of these administrative injunctions served to reinforce the Elizabethan settlement, but they would equally well have reinforced any other establishment.

Another nine new injunctions had a mildly reforming character and could also have been applied to almost any stage of the Edwardian reforms. Schoolmasters were to be qualified in learning and religion and to bear the approval of the bishop; they were to inculcate 'the true religion now truly set forth by public authority', and to encourage their students to memorize selected sentences from the Bible (nos. 40–2). The litany was to be publicly read on Wednesdays and Fridays (no. 48). Clergy were to teach the Prayer Book catechism regularly to the youth (no. 44).[1] Clerics and others reading in church were 'to read leisurely, plainly, and distinctly' (no. 53). Clergy might marry provided their brides met the approval of the bishop and two justices of the peace, or, in the cases of bishops themselves, the approval of the metropolitan and the queen's commissioners (no. 29). Two injunctions were of a temporary character: bishops were to obtain records of Marian persecutions, and churchwardens were to give the Visitors inventories of church vestments, ornaments, plate, books, and old service-books (nos. 45 and 47).

The three other new injunctions were of a distinctly conservative character. In the street clergy were to wear the traditional habits and square hats distinctive of their calling (no. 30). Congregations were to uncover and bow their heads at the name of Jesus (no. 52).

---

[1] See also no. 5, an injunction drawn from those of 1547.

Finally Elizabeth ordered that choral foundations in collegiate and parish churches be maintained, and that 'a modest and distinct song [be] so used in all parts of the common prayers in the church, that the same may be as plainly understood, as if it were read without singing' (no. 49). The injunction also allowed the singing of 'an hymn, or suchlike song to the praise of Almighty God' before or after common prayers.[1]

Elizabeth added several provisions to the numbered injunctions, including those for the position of the holy table and for wafer bread. She also assured her subjects that by the royal supremacy, she did not claim 'the authority and power of ministry of divine offices in the church'. The supremacy asserted that the Crown ruled over both laymen and clerics, the two medieval categories of citizens: 'under God to have the sovereignty and rule over all manner persons born within these her realms,...of what estate, either ecclesiastical or temporal, soever they be, so as no other foreign power shall or ought to have any superiority over them'. Consistent with the substitution of 'Supreme Governor' for the ambiguous title 'Supreme Head', Elizabeth expressly limited the ecclesiastical significance of her supremacy over the church.

When the Royal Injunctions of 1559 as a whole are compared with their 1547 prototypes, they appear remarkably conservative. They present a more advanced stage of reform in that they assume the use of the English liturgy, provide for more frequent sermons, allow clerical marriage and, by asking for inventories, hint that some church goods may be confiscated or destroyed. Yet other changes, providing for Rogation processions, clerical street wear, church music, honouring the name of Jesus, all reassert some of the old familiar customs. The changes regarding images were designed to forestall the wholesale indiscriminate iconoclasm that had occurred in 1548 and that was to be reproduced, in spite of these regulations, in 1559. The appended regulations for the holy table and bread reveal a preference for a reform more conservative than that represented by the 1552 Prayer Book.

[1] In addition to these 19 new injunctions, no. 4 for preaching and no. 19 for Rogation processions were also newly drawn (see above, pp. 139–40).

Elizabeth looked to the early years of Edward's reign for guidance to a much greater extent than has been commonly recognized. In the Injunctions which she adopted, amended, and augmented, Elizabeth demonstrated not only concern for the good order and effective ministration of the English Church, but determination, so far as it was possible within the parliamentary settlement, to endow it with the moderate spirit and character of earlier Edwardian reforms. The initial royal visitation was soon over and forgotten, but the Royal Injunctions remained in force for the forty-odd years of Elizabeth's reign—and many indeed lived much longer in the later life of anglicanism as an accepted part of the 'received religion'.

THE ELIZABETHAN PRIMER

The Royal Injunctions also introduced into the Elizabethan settlement a whole new book:

The Primer, set forth at large, with many godly and devout prayers. Anno. 1559. Imprinted at London by the assigns of John Wayland forbidding all other to print this or any other Primer.

Mason wrote to Cecil on 12 August 1559, asking that 'the little book of private prayers for children and servants' and the Latin Prayer Book be approved for the printers. In Parker's visitations of subsequent years, he described the Primer as the book 'annexed unto' the Royal Injunctions. The injunction ordered that

Every schoolmaster and teacher shall teach the Grammar set forth by King Henry VIII of noble memory, and continued in the time of King Edward VI, and none other.[1]

Which Primer did Elizabeth choose to nourish the devotional lives of the nation's children as they began to learn to read and write? Three main varieties were possible candidates: the mildly reformed first official Primer of her father with its dose of mariology; the

---

[1] Clay, *Private Prayers*, pp. 1–114 (convenient reprint of Primer); *CSP, For.* I, 468, Mason to Cecil; Frere, *Visitation Articles*, III, 85 and 105, Canterbury, 1560 and Norwich, 1561; wording of the injunction seems drawn from Cranmer's 1548 articles.

reformed, but still traditional Primer of 1551 which had been designed to complement the 1549 Prayer Book; and the radically revised 'Primer' of 1553 which had appeared as a part of the reformers' programme at the very end of Edward's reign.[1] The wording of Elizabeth's injunction suggests the 1551 Primer, and the contents confirm the identification.

The 1559 Primer differed from its 1551 model in only three ways. First, the Elizabethan book included a Henrician preface, lacking in 1551, which had first appeared in the 1545 bilingual Latin and English edition of the Primer. Second, the deprecation of the bishop of Rome was removed from the litany, and Elizabeth's name was substituted for Edward's name in the appropriate places.[2] Third, a short new section appeared after the preface with the title: 'An order for Morning Prayer daily through the year.' This insertion is awkward, for it does not really seem suitable either as a guide for participation in the public liturgy or as a penitential introduction for the private use of the primer hours. This awkwardness and an intervening blank page both suggest that the section was a hasty last-minute interpolation designed to exhibit an affinity with the recently adopted Book of Common Prayer. These minor differences do not modify the substantial identity of the 1559 Elizabethan Primer with that of 1551, which shared the moderate reforming spirit of the first Prayer Book.[3]

In 1560 Elizabeth did permit the publication of a Primer of the drastically reformed type, but it was published as a private book of prayers, not as a replacement for, or as an alternative to, the 1559 Primer. The book never carried any suggestion that it was authorized for the instruction of youth. The title eliminated the 1553 phrase

[1] See above, pp. 9, 14–15.
[2] In other respects the 1559 Primer litany was *not* changed to conform with the Prayer Book (e.g. the petition for the queen).
[3] Three other undated and slightly varying editions of the Primer from Elizabeth's first years strengthen the evidence that it was the 1551 Primer which she chose as a model for the new official book: Hoskyns, *Horae*, pp. xxviii, 81, 83, 252–3, and 256–7. The inclusion of the deprecation of the pope in all three suggests that these were all early editions in Elizabeth's reign, and the variety of adaptations with the consistent use of the basic 1551 form suggests that the latter was prescribed by authority.

which had asserted that the book was to be 'taught, learned, read, and used'. The official 1559 Primer, in contrast, repeated Henry's order that

Euery scholemaister and brynger vp of young begynners in learnyng nexte after their A.B.C. now by vs also sette furthe dooe teache this primer or boke of ordinarie praiers vnto theim in Englishe, and that the youthe customably and ordinarily vse the same.

Nor did the version of the 1553 book meet the description of the queen's injunction, a description which was reflected in episcopal visitation articles right down to the end of Queen Elizabeth's reign. As late as 1601, a bishop inquired whether schoolmasters used 'any other Grammer than that which is commonly called the King's Grammer, set forth by the authority of King Henry VIII'.[1] The canons adopted by Convocation in 1571 included a provision that schoolmasters were to teach 'no Grammar, but only that which the Queenes Maiestie hath commanded to be read in all Scholes'.[2] The 1560 edition of the 1553 Primer revealingly calls itself '*A* Primer', a title which contrasts sharply with '*The* Primer' enjoined by the Injunctions. These distinctive modifying articles continued in all subsequent editions of the two books throughout Elizabeth's reign.[3]

It is probable, however, that in violation of the injunction, 'A Primer' was frequently used for the instruction of youth: an alphabet, for example, was inserted into an edition printed about 1564. Why did Elizabeth authorize the publication of the 1553-type Primer even while she gave official status only to the 1551 variety? She could have found little positively wrong with its largely Prayer Book content. In her eyes, it would not have been a dangerous book, but

[1] Hoskyns, *Horae*, pp. 82 and 299–300; Clay, *Private Prayers*, p. 12; Frere, *Visitation Articles*, III, 85, 105, 270, 312, 333, and 380; Kennedy, *Episcopal Administration*, III, 156, 193, and 344.
[2] *A Booke of Certaine Canons concerning some parte of the discipline of the Churche of England* (London, John Day, 1571), second item on schoolmasters. The Latin version makes clear that the words 'that which' refer to only *one* book (Cardwell, *Synodalia*, I, 128). See below, pp. 255–6.
[3] Hoskyns, *Horae, passim*. In the seventeenth–nineteenth-century editions of the 1553-type Primer, the indefinite article in the title was changed to the definite: '*The* Primer' (Hoskyns, *Horae*, pp. 303, 305, 306, and 307).

rather an inadequate one. Having conceded the 1552 Prayer Book, she allowed the publication of its companion devotional manual.

The traditional-type Primer made its mark on the Elizabethan church. The *Orarium* of 1560 and the *Preces Privatae* of 1564 were both authorized Latin varieties of the traditional Primers. The effects of devotional manuals are exceedingly difficult to assess, but the more conservative Primer, consistently maintained as the legal standard of schoolmasters' use, may have been an effective means of retaining much of the traditional catholic devotion that the seventeenth-century English divines were to assert with warmth and clarity.[1]

Elizabeth's choice of the 1551 version of the king's Primer adds another bit of evidence that her preference in religious matters was closer to the spirit of the 1549 Prayer Book than to either Henrician national catholicism or the more militant reforms of the second Prayer Book. We may well imagine that the militant reformers and perhaps many of their more moderate brethren found it convenient to ignore the requirement to use the official Elizabethan Primer.

CHURCH BUILDINGS: CARE AND CONSERVATION

The cathedrals and parish churches of England testify eloquently both to the changes of the Reformation and to the fundamental continuity of the post-Reformation church with its medieval predecessor. In the early years of Elizabeth's reign, much of the iconoclasm of Edward's reign, undone in the intervening years, was repeated. Stone altars gave way to wooden tables, statues were destroyed, and bright walls with their colourful paintings were dulled by antiseptic coats of whitewash. Churchwarden accounts and other surviving parish and diocesan documents record a good many

[1] The *Orarium*, printed at the queen's order, was largely a version of Henry's Latin Primer revised to agree with the 1559 book (Hoskyns, *Horae*, pp. 253–6; Clay, *Private Prayers*, pp. 115–206). The *Preces Privatae*, first printed in 1564 and reprinted in 1568, 1573, and 1574, was a severe revision of the *Orarium*, reducing the seven hours to two by combination of various elements (Hoskyns, pp. 257–70; Clay, pp. 209–428; *STC*, nos. 20378–81).

of these physical changes, but our concern here lies with the efforts of the Supreme Governor to check and limit the iconoclastic enthusiasm of the precisians. Not only has some glass and other medieval art lasted to modern times, but Oliver Cromwell's men found much more to destroy ninety years later. Elizabeth was able to succeed as well as she did because of the resistance of many ordinary clergy and laymen to drastic alterations of their familiar places of worship. The traditional appearance of English churches today cannot be explained merely as a result of nineteenth-century gothic enthusiasm. Not only the old medieval churches, but subsequent church buildings in succeeding centuries illustrate the continuity of physical arrangements. Even when the 'auditory church' of Wren and his successors did away with the two-chambered Elizabethan adaptation of the medieval church, the holy table remained the focus of the new buildings. The appearance of the churches changed in Elizabeth's reign, but not nearly as drastically as militant reformers desired. Had they had their way, English cathedrals might have been transformed into vast barren preaching halls akin to St Peter's in Geneva, with its medieval apse curiously useless in the pulpit-centred rearrangement of the cathedral.[1]

We have already seen how Elizabeth ordered the holy table 'decently made' and, out of the communion service, 'commonly covered' at the east end just like the old stone altars. It is difficult to see how Archbishop Laud could have ordered the erection of altar rails and the celebration of the communion at the east end of the church had Elizabeth not modified the order of the 1552 Prayer Book to this extent.

Elizabeth's indignation at wanton destruction in the churches burns through a proclamation of 19 September 1560 against defacers of monuments in churches. Most of these regulations were reasonable attempts to ensure that memorials in churches would remain for reasons of family affection and historical record, but the queen included an order that no 'image in glass windows' was to be

---

[1] For a discussion of the changes in English church architecture, see G. W. O. Addleshaw and F. Etchells, *The Architectural Setting of Anglican Worship* (London, 1948).

broken—a provision that went beyond the historical concern for 'ancient monuments'.[1]

Four months later, in the letters to the commissioners in which Elizabeth ordered that the new calendar be prepared, she also complained of neglect in the care of the churches:

There is such negligence and lack of convenient reverence used towards the comely keeping and order of the said churches, and especially of the upper part, called the chancel, that it breedeth no small offence,...permitting open decays and ruins of the coverings, walls, and windows, and by appointing unmeet and unseemly tables with foul cloths for the communion of the sacraments, and generally leaving the place of prayers desolate of all cleanliness and of meet ornaments for such a place, whereby it might be known a place provided for public service.[2]

She instructed the commissioners to take measures to correct these conditions, and she specifically told them to order churches to set up tables of the Decalogue 'to be not only read for edification, but also to give some comely ornament and demonstration that the same is a place of religion and prayer.' If the churches were not to have paintings and statues, at least they might have decorative words of scripture. Elizabeth's aesthetic judgment may be called in question for this order, but her intention was clear: the church was not to be left barren and bare.

When Elizabeth was on progress in the following summer of 1561, she learned that services were being slovenly conducted without rubrical vestments and that, in spite of her orders, many church buildings were still carelessly maintained. On 10 October she angrily issued more explicit orders to correct some of these conditions. Again these were directed to the members of the statutory commission for execution. Since her commissioners had seemingly lacked the imagination or the will to implement her general order of the previous January, Elizabeth detailed the steps that were to be taken. Chancels were to be kept clean and repaired. It was assumed that the rood statuary and the upper apparatus were to be removed,

---

[1] Edward Cardwell, *Documentary Annals of the Reformed Church of England...*, 2 vols. (Oxford, 1839), I, 257–60.
[2] *Parker Corr.*, pp. 132–3, 22 January 1561.

but Elizabeth insisted that the rood beam remain, together with the rood screen separating chancel from nave. If the partition were missing, it was to be rebuilt. Elizabeth suggested that 'some convenient crest' be placed on top of the rood beam, and this almost invariably became the royal arms. Chancel seats were to remain as they had been. If steps had not been taken out, they were to be left untouched. The net effect of these requirements was to keep the medieval structure of the church with its clear-cut division of nave and chancel.[1]

Elizabeth repeated her previous order about the Decalogue on the wall, adding that in cathedrals they should be 'more largely and costly painted out'. The communion table out of service was to have on it 'a fair linen cloth, with some covering of silk, buckram, or other such like'. Earlier that same year Parkhurst had ordered that in his diocese of Norwich clergy must *not* 'suffer the Lord's Table to be hanged and decked like an altar'. It would seem that this was just what Elizabeth had in mind. A few years later Bishop Bentham ordered the table covered 'in as beautiful a manner as it was being upon the altar'. Parkhurst never quite reversed his earlier injunction; in 1569 he circumvented the queen's wording by asking that the table be 'furnished and placed as becometh'. Cox matter-of-factly inquired in 1571 whether 'the East wall of the choir be hanged with a fair cloth and the paper of the Ten Commandments fastened in the midst thereof'. Such a dossal hanging would have drawn attention to the covered holy table as the traditional focal point of the building.[2]

Elizabeth also struck at some popular baptismal practices of the militant reformers. She ordered that fonts be left where they had been—traditionally near the door of the church—and she forbade militant clerics from performing baptisms in basins apart from the font. Apparently in the manner of some liturgical movement clerics of our own day, the precisians preferred to baptize in front

[1] *Ibid.* p. 148, Cecil to Parker, 12 August 1561; Frere, *Visitation Articles*, III, 108–10.
[2] Frere, *Visitation Articles*, III, 98; injunctions exhibited on 2 May 1561; III, 165, Coventry and Lichfield, 1565; III, 210, Norwich, 1569; III, 301, Ely, 1571.

of the congregation rather than in the often obscure corners to which medieval piety had relegated the baptistery.[1]

Elizabeth's detailed instructions, to the extent that they were carried out, ensured that although churches had been stripped of much of their medieval finery and colour, they would retain a simplified beauty and, on the whole, a traditional appearance. Just like her injunctions, these various orders found their way into the articles of episcopal visitations and into the national Advertisements. English churches retained their wonted dignity partly because of the pertinacity of a queen who refused to equate spiritual reform with a barren severity in the material setting of Christian worship.

THE CROWN AND CHURCH FINANCES

The medieval financial machinery of the Church of England creaked on through the reign of Elizabeth much as it had in the preceding centuries, with three important changes. Monastic communities no longer controlled any purse strings; income and fees did not leave England for Rome; and the national government made more constant and direct appropriations of church income than they had done before the nationalization of the church. The most serious financial problem facing the church lay in the gross inequalities and injustices in ministerial livings. Many of the poorer beneficed clergy lived on a pittance, and unbeneficed clerical hirelings on less.[2] Not until the beginning of the eighteenth century was even a start made at meeting this crucial inequity. Clerical marriage intensified the problem for many priests, who had to support not only themselves but a family as well. Confronting the unusual ecclesiastical problems of adjusting to a new settlement of religion and ever-present crisis in the national treasury, Elizabeth and her advisers turned a blind eye to possible changes in the varying scales of clerical incomes which they had inherited from previous centuries.

---

[1] Among other miscellanea, Elizabeth also insisted that godparents alone answer for children in baptism, a defence of Prayer Book practice which, as we have seen, was attacked by the precisians (see above, pp. 121–2).

[2] Roland G. Usher, *The Reconstruction of the English Church*, 2 vols. (New York, 1910), I, 219–22 and 236–7; II, 54–5.

The story of Elizabethan church finance really remains to be written. Both Roland Usher and Christopher Hill, who have made the most complete modern studies, have been primarily interested in the Elizabethan church finances in the last decades of her reign, in order to provide a Tudor background for their more detailed analysis of seventeenth-century Stuart church finances. Their studies of Elizabeth's reign are far too sketchy.

Since the new factor in church finances was the crown's now unchallengeable pre-eminence, our discussion of church finances comes in a chapter on the role of the Supreme Governor—or 'Supreme Plunderer', as Hill has argued. Until a thorough study has been made of the subject, only a few observations can be made—observations which suggest that the matter has not been quite as one-sided as it has usually been thought to be.[1]

Few laymen in the sixteenth century had scruples about the sanctity of church property. Too many corrupt prelates had violated their trust for children of the Renaissance to regard that canon as more than a smokescreen for clerical avarice. Erasmus provided an epigram for a common observation when he commented that it was in 'raking in moneys' that prelates played 'the bishop, overseeing everything—and overlooking nothing'. In July 1559 Cecil wrote to the Scottish nobility in these plain terms:

In our first reformation here in King Henry VIII's time, although in some points there was oversight for the help of the ministry and the poor, yet if the prelacy had been left in their pomp and wealth, the victory had been theirs. I like no spoil, but I allow to have good things put to good use, as to the enriching of the crown, to the help of the youth of the nobility, to the maintenance of ministry in the church, of learning in schools, and to relieve the poor members of Christ, being in body and limbs impotent.

Thomas Lever, a militant member of the 1563 Convocation, had spoken from St Paul's Cross in 1550:

The entente of [Henry VIII and Edward VI] is verye godlye...that... suche abundaunce of goodes as was superstitiously spente vpon vayne

[1] Usher, *op. cit.*; Christopher Hill, *Economic Problems of the Church...* (Oxford, 1956), p. 32.

ceremonies, or voluptuously vpon idle bellies, myght come to the kynges handes to beare hys great charges, necessarilie bestowed in the comen-wealthe, or partly vnto other mennes handes, for the better releue of the pore, the mayntenaunce of learning, and the settinge forth of goddes worde. Howebeit couetouse officers haue so vsed thys matter, that ... those goodes ...be now turned to maynteyne worldly, wycked, couetouse ambition.

Both the statesman and the reformer assume that, in spite of abuses in the appropriation of church funds, the Crown was entitled to their use. They regarded the church endowments as public funds for the benefit of the one society in its two aspects of church and state. A portion of the funds were assigned to maintain church property, benevolences, and ministers, but the funds could be reallocated when it seemed advisable for the benefit of the whole nation. 'Good things put to good use.' Elizabeth, her advisers, and the members of Parliament all acted upon such principles, and English church leaders tacitly accepted them, however much they might protest against particular applications.[1]

Two bills, introduced by the government into the Parliament of 1559 and easily approved, defined the bulk of Elizabeth's claims on church incomes. One bill restored payment to the Crown of first-fruits and tenths of all benefices with incomes of more than ten pounds a year.[2] These payments were largely deflected from the papacy, and the charges established by the bill, the first year's income and ten per cent thereafter, constituted a form of taxation on clerical incomes to aid the Crown on its 'huge, innumerable and inestimable charges'. The bill also restored to the Crown those impropriated tithes which Henry had taken over from the monasteries and Mary had bestowed upon the church. Elizabeth treated the tithes as a normal part of her revenues and during her reign sold or granted such tithes in 2,216 parishes.[3]

[1] Erasmus, *Praise of Folly*, tr. Hoyt Hopewell Hudson (Princeton, 1941), p. 97; *CSP, For.* I, 424, Cecil to the earls of Argyll, Glencarne, and others, 28 July 1559; Thomas Lever, *Sermons, 1550*, ed. Edward Arber (London, 1871), p. 32; sermon on Septuagesima Sunday, 1550.

[2] *JHL*, I, 544, 552, 563, and 568; *JHC*, I, 54–5; *Statutes of the Realm*, IV, 359–64 and 381–2, 1° Eliz., c. 4 and c. 19; Hill, *Economic Problems*, pp. 188 and 245. The minimum for rectories was actually £6 13s. 4d.; £10 for vicarages.

[3] Hill, *Economic Problems*, p. 14.

Christopher Hill has described the other bill as 'an act for the plunder of the Church'.[1] It ensured the crown's traditional right to the income of episcopal sees during vacancies and, in addition, allowed the queen in such periods to exchange episcopal properties for impropriated tithes of the same values.[2] Another provision of the bill was perhaps more important in the long run: it forbade bishops to lease their lands for more than twenty-one years, or for less than the usual rent, to anyone but the queen. In 1571 the restrictions were extended to include cathedral and parochial livings as well.[3] Since laymen eager to profit from church property could receive long-term or profitable leases only through the queen, in Hill's words, the provision 'centralized the plunder of the church'.[4] This accurate comment reveals the bill to be a two-edged sword, not fully described by Hill. In addition to giving the queen an influential source of patronage, the regulations also enabled her to control and, indeed, to limit the alienation of church property. This point has been too often forgotten. If the bill enabled Elizabeth to 'despoil the church', it also forced others to seek their spoils at the queen's hands. Impecunious clerics could no longer make long-term deals with avaricious gentry for immediate funds at the expense of their successors—except by the queen's explicit permission. Some of the parliamentary opposition to the bill may have come from M.P.s who wanted no obstacle to their share of church loot rather than, as Neale thought, from the 'irreducible Puritan core...who... would not betray the Church in the interest of the State'.[5]

One effect of the bill was to load the dice against Elizabeth when later generations sought historical evidence concerning her use of church properties. Since the law required the queen to be the middleman in all such contracts, our records reflect the ensuing

[1] Hill, *Economic Problems*, pp. 14–15; Hill refers to Strype, but the phrase seems to be his own (*Annals*, I, part I, 142–3). For the bill's course through parliament, see *JHL*, I, 570; Davis, *EHR*, XXVIII, 535; *JHC*, I, 59–60.
[2] The Privy Council had already assumed the Crown's right to vacancies (Dasent, *Privy Council*, VII, 28).
[3] Hill, *Economic Problems*, p. 30.
[4] *Ibid.* p. 14.
[5] *JHC*, I, 60, 17 April 1559, division of 134 to 90; Neale, *Parliaments*, I, 74–5.

disputes between the queen and the prelates.[1] With present evidence, we cannot tell how much or how little Elizabeth spared the church from rapacious Englishmen eager to establish and extend their holdings as landed gentry. We know some of the demands for favourable leases which she did make; we know nothing of her resistance to what she once termed 'the insatiable cupidity of men' who incessantly begged for financial favours.[2] If she had not resisted most of these pleas, we can be sure that the church would rapidly have become impoverished beyond recovery.

The queen's right to exchange episcopal properties for impropriated tithes was a disadvantage to the bishops. The tithes were charged with the repair of chancels and were far more difficult to collect than rent from profitable farms. Early in the autumn of 1559 five bishops-elect requested Elizabeth to cancel the planned exchanges. She refused, but she rebated them half of the first-fruits due the Crown, and the clerics accepted with as much grace as possible. Elizabeth discriminated in making the exchanges, for eight of the poorer sees were left untouched in the first round of vacancies.[3]

The real effect on episcopal income of the exchanges has not been accurately determined. Most of the statistics of Usher and Hill lump together the sixteenth-century depletions of episcopal income beginning with the 1535 *Valor Ecclesiasticus* in the reign of Henry VIII. These depletions occurred during parts of the reigns of

---

[1] E.g. Strype, *Annals*, III, part I, 687, 13 April 1587; III, part II, 226–7 and 476, *c.* 1581 and 11 June 1587; IV, 19–21 and 287, March 1590 and 10 January 1594; *CSP, Dom.*, 1547–50, p. 159 (XIII, 37), 23 September 1560; *CSP, For.* IV, 225, Pilkington to Cecil, 2 August 1561; Hill, *Economic Problems*, 315–16 and 15–38.

[2] I have not found the source of this quotation which Neale mentions in his biography (*Queen Elizabeth I* [Garden City, New York, 1957], p. 297).

[3] *Parker Corr.*, pp. 97–101, bishops-elect to Elizabeth, between 29 September and 25 October; pp. 101–2, Elizabeth to Lord Treasurer *et al.*, 26 October; *CSP, Sp.* I, 108, de Quadra to Feria, 29 October; Machyn, *Diary*, p. 214, 8 October; Strype, *Annals*, I, part I, 144–7, Cox to Elizabeth; *ZL*, I, 51 (no. 22), Jewel to Simler, 2 November; *CSP, For.* II, 137, R...ny to Challoner, 25 November 1559. Patent letters for Bangor, St David's, St Asaph's, Rochester, Carlisle, Chester, Gloucester, Oxford (and two wealthier sees, York and Lincoln) restored the temporalities after the vacancies with no mention of exchanges. In 1566 Elizabeth did make some exchanges at Bangor (Rymer, *Foedera*, VI, part IV, 99–135, *passim*).

four Tudors. Whitgift, for example, writing to Burghley in 1584, complains about the difference between the valuation of bishoprics in 'the Queen's books' and actual income. He mentions four reasons for the discrepancy: not only the exchanges of Elizabeth's reign, but also long leases granted by the bishops' 'Popish pre-decessors', increase in the amount and number of fees since 1535, and the loss of income from religious houses which had been counted in the original valuation.[1] The few hard statistics available make a few generalizations possible for the entire reign. The total income of the twenty-six mainland bishoprics at the end of Elizabeth's reign was almost exactly what it had been at the outset. Since prices rose during those years, the queen apparently reduced the overall value of her bishops' income by the effects of the inflation. The final incomes averaged £865. At the end of her reign the bishops' incomes were a little more evenly distributed, for Elizabeth had substantially reduced the incomes of the wealthy sees of Durham and Winchester while leaving some of the poorer sees virtually untouched.[2]

Through first-fruits, tenths, the exchanges, and the exaction of special subsidies, Elizabeth exercised her authority to siphon off episcopal revenues, but she exercised it with more discretion than has been generally acknowledged.[3] The bishops faced financial difficulties, but they were not impoverished.

Elizabeth has been accused since the days of John Harington of keeping episcopal sees vacant in order to enjoy their revenues. The charge suggests that she allowed whole dioceses to manage as best they could without a chief pastor so that the income might fill her treasury. Elizabeth's delays in appointing bishops at the beginning of her reign seem to have been due to the difficulties in finding suitable

[1] Strype, *The Life and Acts of John Whitgift*, 3 vols. (Oxford, 1832), I, 406.
[2] In 1600 Thomas Wilson estimated the total income of the English bishoprics at £22,500 (*Camden Miscellany: XVI*, Camden Society, Series 3, LII [1963], 22). In mid-1559 Cecil had estimated the value of all but five of the sees; making allowances for his omissions, his total came to £21,778 (Strype, *Annals*, I, part I, 227). For the large drop in the incomes of Durham and Winchester, compare Cecil's estimate with later figures (Strype, *Annals*, I, part I, 227; II, part I, 575; Hill, *Economic Problems*, p. 26; Rymer, *Foedera*, VI, part IV, 110–11, 131, and 163).
[3] For the effect of the subsidies, see Hill, *Economic Problems*, pp. 192–3.

candidates; it is the subsequent appointments which need to be tested.[1]

Vacancies in three dioceses stand out: Bristol and Oxford were vacant most of her reign and Ely was vacant for nineteen years. Otherwise out of seventy-nine subsequent episcopal appointments, only six vacancies lasted more than two years.[2] Five lasted between two and three years and one see was vacant for three and a half years. The pattern of these vacancies does not fit a financial interpretation: Gloucester and Llandaff were poor sees, Chichester and Bath were moderately well off, and only Salisbury was comparatively wealthy. If Elizabeth had wanted to keep sees vacant for their revenues, she could have made far more frequent and judicious choices than these.

The vacancies in the impecunious Henrician sees of Bristol and Oxford did not add much to the Crown's wealth and, as a matter of fact, the income of Bristol was attached for most of the reign to the bishop of Gloucester *in commendam*. Only during the final ten years of the reign did its meagre income trickle into the royal treasury. Elizabeth apparently preferred to have other provisions made for the episcopal care of these small dioceses; the alternative meant allowing the appointed bishop to retain pluralities to maintain what was deemed a suitable episcopal income.[3]

John Harington quipped that Cox's funeral seemed likely to prove the funeral also of the bishopric, and the vacancy of Ely from 1581 to 1600 has too often been taken as typical of Elizabeth's subordination of the church's welfare to her financial needs.[4] On the contrary, the nineteen-year vacancy in the wealthy diocese stands out in sharp contrast to the queen's usual policies. Archbishop

---

[1] John Harington, *Nugae Antiquae*, selected by Henry Harington and ed. by Thomas Park, 2 vols. (London, 1804), II, 41–2 and 106; Hill, *Economic Problems*, p. 15; Thompson, *Supreme Governor*, p. 41; see above, pp. 45–6.

[2] The information was primarily drawn from William Stubbs, *Registrum Sacrum Anglicanum...* (Oxford, 1897), pp. 105–12; Bath and Wells, 1581–4 and 1590–3; Chichester, 1582–6; Gloucester, 1579–81; Llandaff, 1563–6; and Salisbury, 1596–8.

[3] See above, pp. 46–7.

[4] Harington, *Nugae Antiquae*, II, 106; in 1595 Lord Keeper Puckering assumed that the queen's interest in Ely was financial (Strype, *Annals*, IV, 343–6, three papers prepared by Pickering for Elizabeth).

Whitgift exercised his authority as ordinary in Ely as he did in Oxford: both were relatively small dioceses.[1] As a matter of fact, Whitgift's 'peculiar charge' in the university diocese seems to have enabled him to deal effectively and directly with the troublesome puritan problems of Cambridge.[2]

One other question has been raised about Elizabeth's use of episcopal appointments for the benefit of her treasury: did she translate her bishops from see to see so that she could gain more frequent first-fruits? Someone in 1575 prepared a list for the queen showing how she might pocket a year's income from all the dioceses by moving all her bishops 'without any just cause of much offence'. In 1595 Lord Keeper Puckering demonstrated the profits accruing from the successive moves of five bishops.[3] Elizabeth never adopted such schemes.

After her initial appointments, 35 per cent of the appointments were translations.[4] Under James I, the proportion was 36 per cent

[1] Strype, *Whitgift*, III, 297–8, Whitgift to All Souls, Oxford, 12 January 1593; I, 260. For episcopal ministrations, Whitgift may have regularly employed his suffragan of the diocese of Canterbury, for in a fresh licence issued to Richard Rogers, bishop of Dover, Whitgift authorized him to catechize, to confirm, and to ordain, not only in the diocese, but throughout the province of Canterbury (III, 69, 11 December 1583). Rogers died in 1597, and in that same year Whitgift licensed an Irish bishop to ordain in Oxford (Edward Marshall, *Oxford*, SPCK diocesan histories [London, 1882], p. 117).

[2] In a letter to the vice-chancellor in 1586 ordering preachers to subscribe to the anti-puritan articles, Whitgift wrote as if exercising normal episcopal diocesan jurisdiction (Strype, *Annals*, III, part II, 445, 2 May 1586). In the 1595 dispute over William Barrett's anti-Calvinist sermon, Whitgift berated the heads of colleges because they knew 'That in matters of religion, it hath pleased her Majesty to commit the especial care to me, that university also being within my peculiar charge, in respect of the vacancy of the Bishopric of Ely, yet they would not vouchsafe to make me acquainted therewith as in duty they ought to have done' (19 June 1595; H. C. Porter, *Reformation and Reaction in Tudor Cambridge* [Cambridge, 1958], p. 349; see also Strype, *Whitgift*, II, 239).

[3] Powel M. Dawley, *John Whitgift and the English Reformation* (New York, 1964), p. 108; Strype, *Annals*, II, part I, 575–6; IV, 345. Puckering also suggested that by translating the elderly bishop of Norwich to Ely, she would soon have the see back in her hands for another disposition. When Elizabeth finally did appoint to Ely in 1599, she chose forty-six-year-old Matthew Heton (IV, 491).

[4] She translated in 28 out of 79 appointments based on Stubbs. Both in the statistics of Elizabeth's reign and later, translations from Irish sees and from Sodor and

and under Charles I, 45 per cent.[1] From 1689 to 1800 translations averaged 43 per cent; in the nineteenth century they dropped to 32 per cent.[2] Furthermore, the first translation tended to be from a poorer diocese; it was subsequent translations from wealthier sees that were most lucrative. Elizabeth translated only six men to a third see. In the subsequent forty years of Stuart rule, twelve men were moved to their third dioceses, and of these, two moved on to a fourth diocese and one, Richard Neile, held six sees in succession.[3] Elizabeth's translations do not seem excessive in the light of these comparisons.

Elizabeth's management of church revenues does not bear out the charge that she was its 'supreme plunderer'—or at least the limited evidence available does not prove this. Older clerical historians, like Canon Dixon, have tended to see Elizabeth's financial exactions from the church as a part of

a general racking of the kingdom, which was going on to supply an extravagant court, under the usual pretence of the necessities of the Crown.

On the contrary, the necessities of the Crown were no pretence. Lord Burghley near the end of his life commented that 'the parsimony of her Majesty' had greatly contributed to the success of her reign. Modern historians have tended to agree. A. L. Rowse comments that England was almost the only European government to remain solvent in the sixteenth century:

It was not only the wealth of her country but the excellence of her administration that made the Queen of England the most desirable *partie* in Europe.

Man are considered new appointments; their first-fruits were usually far too small to have been a factor of importance.

[1] Under James I there were 22 translations out of 61 appointments; under Charles I, 28 out of 62.
[2] In 1661 Charles II had to supply an almost entirely new episcopate. The years from 1689 to 1800 held 110 translations out of 257 appointments; from 1800 to 1897, 58 out of 184.
[3] Elizabeth moved Grindal, Sandys, Freke, Piers, Fletcher, and Babington to third sees. Under the first two Stuart kings, Vaughan, Andrewes, Abbott, Harscutt, Morton, Field, White, Curll, and Wren held three sees; Monteigne and Laud held four sees, and Neile moved from Rochester to Lichfield to Lincoln to Durham to Winchester to York.

The Supreme Governor: administration and finance

Neale remarks that

for all its drabness and difficulty, finance is the essence of Elizabeth's story...

It was essentially a personal achievement, not managed without constant vigilance, and an attitude towards additional expenditure that made ministers fear to mention charges.

When de Maisse visited England he marvelled that people paid their taxes with 'no talk of robbery', and he also commented:

At London there are infinite houses of charity and hospitals, and almost throughout the whole realm, the greater part of the goods of the Church having been employed to that end, insomuch that one hardly sees a beggar; several fair colleges where the children are taught at the expense of the Queen and the public, and there is no youth in the world, poor or rich, that has greater chance of learning than in England.

While continental courts foundered on the rocks of bankruptcy, Elizabeth's England sailed through safe channels with neatly trimmed sails. Church finances played their own restricted part in this success, which not only preserved England but her distinctive form of Christianity as well.[1]

Elizabeth and her advisers, like many other responsible and committed Christians of their day, regarded church property as part of the nation's wealth, and she herself felt competent to reassess the portions allowed clerics and ministers of state. In an age of personal monarchy, royal favours were not capricious bounty, but a necessary part of government. Official salaries were wholly inadequate and, as Professor Neale has pointed out, 'Queen, courtiers, and servants [were] the victims of a pernicious system for which there was no real remedy.'[2] Church revenues provided one of the few sources Elizabeth could tap to reward her courtiers and to sustain indigent members of the nobility. Elizabeth can certainly be criticized for

[1] Dixon, *History*, v, 190; Burghley, quoted in A. L. Rowse, *The England of Elizabeth* (New York, 1961), pp. 327–8, from S.P. 12/255/84; Rowse's comment, p. 329; Neale, *Queen Elizabeth I*, pp. 294 and 296; De Maisse, *A Journal of All that was Accomplished by Monsieur de Maisse...*, tr. and ed. G. B. Harrison and R. A. Jones (Bloomsbury, 1931), pp. 8 and 12–13 (hereafter called 'De Maisse').
[2] *Queen Elizabeth I*, pp. 297–8.

making injudicious choice of favourites or particularly inappropriate allocations, but she can hardly be blamed for using the only
system available to her.

One important innovation in Elizabeth's church policies arose out
of her implicit assumption that bishops and other clerics would be
largely concerned with diocesan administration and church responsibilities. In the past, men living off ecclesiastical livings had
formed a high proportion of officers of state and diplomats—at little
additional expense to the Crown. Under Elizabeth, laymen such as
Thomas Smith with the deanery of Carlisle, and Robert Weston,
with the deaneries of St Patrick's and Wells, were few and far
between.[1] Clerics in diplomatic service such as Nicholas Wotton,
dean of Canterbury and York, and John Man, dean of Gloucester,
stand out by their singularity. It was not wholly unjust that some of
the church revenues which in the past had so handsomely supported
clerics in royal service should be diverted to support their successors.

Elizabeth taxed clerical incomes heavily, rewarded courtiers with
favourable leases of church property, kept impropriated tithes, and
collected vacant episcopal revenues. By her favourable leases and
exchanges of episcopal property, she substantially reduced Durham
and Winchester and, in general, did not allow the bishops to share
in the rising prosperity of the land. With the probable exception of
Ely's long vacancy, she did not misuse her control of episcopal
appointments for financial gain; for greater rewards were easily in
her grasp had she been willing to sacrifice the church. She probably
judged the church's financial condition by the well-beneficed
clerics whom she usually saw at court, for no attempts were made to
reform the church's financial structure to alleviate inadequate
clerical incomes at the bottom. Her exactions seem to have been
heavy, but not unfairly applied. The financial exactions of her father
and of her brother's government had been incomparably greater.
Although the charge of 'supreme plunderer' must be said to remain
unproven, church reform under Elizabeth did not reach beyond
doctrine and liturgy to touch the antiquated and unjust system of
church finances.

[1] See above, p. 132, n. 2.

THE BISHOPS: VISITATIONS AND 'INTERPRETATIONS'

Many of the more militant reformers in 1559 looked forward to the time when the new bishops would sweep away the substantial bits of popish refuse which still cluttered liturgy and discipline. Parkhurst, who hoped for improvement at the 1563 Convocation, and Sandys, who introduced specific proposals for reform, were not the only bishops to share such hopes. Yet in the years between 1559 and 1563, they had done little collectively to press for reforms beyond those initially laid down.

The bishops tightened up the discipline of their dioceses through the normal machinery of episcopal visitations. In May 1560 Archbishop Parker inhibited the bishops of his province from visiting, pending a metropolitical visitation, and for this, he issued his Articles of Inquiry later in the year.[1] The articles ascertained whether or not the settlement was being established according to the requirements of the Prayer Book and the Royal Injunctions. Parker did not take the visitation in person, but licensed commissioners, frequently the bishop himself, to carry it out in the several dioceses. The whole process took a period of years, beginning in Canterbury and Rochester in the autumn of 1560. Both Strype and Brook point out that the archbishop kept close check on the proceedings by appointing as scribe to all the commissions his own registrar John Incent, who also kept our record of the meeting of the bishops in the 1563 Convocation.[2] Extant articles, injunctions, or other evidence indicate that from 1559 to 1565 diocesan bishops held at least fourteen diocesan and seven cathedral visitations, and others may well have taken place without their records surviving.[3]

[1] *Parker Corr.*, 115–17, Parker to Grindal, 27 May 1560. Brook described the visitation (*Parker*, pp. 91–5). The Articles are reprinted in Frere, *Visitation Articles*, III, 81–6; cathedral articles, III, 74–7.

[2] Strype, *Parker*, I, 205; Brook, *Parker*, p. 92; Cardwell, *Synodalia*, II, 495 ff.

[3] For these, I rely on the summary statistics presented by Kennedy, *Episcopal Administration*, I, iv–xxiv, which suggest that Bullingham may have visited in 1560 and 1563 as well as in 1566. Articles for some of these are printed in Frere, *Visitation Articles* (1560 Canterbury Cathedral, III, 78–80; 1560 Salisbury Cathedral, III, 94; 1561 Norwich, 97–107; 1561 St Asaph's, III, 111–14; 1561–2 London Cathedral,

The bishops: visitations and 'interpretations'

During this period the bishops also consulted with each other, and one fruit of their consultations was the 'Interpretations of the Bishops', which in its final form was clearly described as a temporary measure looking forward to a full Convocation: 'Resolutions and orders taken by a common consent of the bishops, for the present time until a synod may be had for observation and maintenance of uniformity in matters ecclesiastical throughout all dioceses in both provinces.' We have already met the Interpretations briefly for their reinforcement of the queen's orders for the holy table and wafer bread, and we shall return to them in recounting the development of the vestiarian controversy.[1] The bulk of the provisions were straightforward applications of the queen's orders, which the more militant bishops accepted because of their hope for improvement at the future Convocation.

Several provisions affected church services. Preaching licences given out by the royal visitors of 1559 were revoked, presumably to bring the preachers under closer control of the bishops. Preachers were to urge people to the 'often and devout receiving' of holy communion and to obedience to the Prayer Book and the queen's Injunctions. They were not to 'exact or receive unreasonable rewards' for their preaching 'abroad'. Interpreting Elizabeth's injunctions on frequency of sermons, they declared that an able parson ought to preach monthly, but if non-resident with the ordinary's approval, a quarterly sermon would serve as a minimum.

As Elizabeth ordered later in 1561, the bishops insisted that baptism must be performed in the font, which was not to be removed 'by any private advice'. Although the 'chrisom' cloth was no longer used in baptisms, curates were to retain the fee of at least fourpence which had been associated with it. Children were not to be admitted to communion until twelve or thirteen years old.

The bishops specified psalms and the litany and a newly prepared homily for use at Rogation processions. They expanded the

III, 115–18; 1562 Salisbury Cathedral, III, 122–30; 1562 Winchester Cathedral, III, 134–9; 1563 Canterbury, III, 140–2; 1565 Rochester diocese and cathedral, III, 148–62; 1565 Coventry and Lichfield, III, 163–70).
[1] Frere, *Visitation Articles*, III, 68. The text continues to p. 73; earlier drafts are on pp. 59–68; see above p. 120, and below, pp. 197–200; also p. 240.

injunction of keeping Sunday by forbidding shops to open, but they realistically conceded that 'fairs and common markets' need remain closed only 'before service be done'. Bells for the dying were to toll only before death with 'but one short peal' after death and two others before and after burial; forbidden was the old custom to toll to bid for prayers for the departed.

The bishops adopted a few regulations concerning ordinary church discipline for the laity. The injunction directing churchwardens to report to bishops parishioners who did not attend church was made more specific by requiring them to report in writing once a month to diocesan officials. Teachers were not to be employed as local officers, in farming, 'or otherwise worldly encumbered', but to remain devoted to their vocation. Marriage was prohibited within the degrees of family affinity set out in a table issued by Archbishop Parker.

The bishops expanded the provisions in the queen's Injunctions for clerical education. Archdeacons were to require clergy under Master of Arts to memorize chosen texts of the New Testament for examination. Young clerics were to master 'some catechism to be prescribed'—presumably that which emerged as Nowell's work. No curate was to serve without examination of the ordinary, and written testimony was to accompany clergy changing dioceses. Any University student holding a prebend was to face a yearly examination by his bishop to be sure he was not wasting the fruits of the living. Ordinands who knew Latin were also to exhibit competence in the 'principal articles of the faith' and 'some competent matter to comfort the sick and weak in conscience'. Required was at least rudimentary knowledge of dogmatic, pastoral, and moral theology.

For ordination the bishops insisted on character testimonials for all but holders of degrees. The traditional canonical impediments were still to be observed—an interesting early example of the reformed church's recognition that applicable canon law was still in force. Facing a clergy shortage, the bishops permitted men to be ordained who did not know Latin, provided they—and their wives— were 'well testified of'; after a 'good time of experience' as deacons, they might be advanced to the priesthood. Lay readers also ministered in vacant cures, and the bishops regulated their examination and prohibited them from serving in any large parish or where an incumbent was resident.

Bishops were to take care to expose any simoniacal agreements between patrons and clergy, already forbidden by the Royal Injunctions. No bishop, without the approval of the majority of his fellows in Convocation, could promise a benefice before it was void, grant a benefit with cure for a specific term, or approve any new appropriation on a church living. The bishops were to police their own administration in order to retain church incomes intact.

These regulations of the bishops are simply practical applications of the queen's regulations or necessary orders to meet new problems. Except for a vestiarian change to be considered in the next chapter, the only regulation which extended reform was one limiting the tolling of bells after death of parishioners. Otherwise the orders are unexceptionable—except to those precisians who would have disliked the revocation of visitors' preaching licences and the reinforcement of the queen's regulations about the holy table, wafer bread, baptismal fonts, and Rogation processions.

In the Lambeth Articles, dated 12 April 1561 and signed by the three episcopal commissioners, the bishops added a few regulations which they agreed commonly to enforce for discipline.[1] Readers were to be examined once again in order to weed out the incompetent. At every institution of clergy into their benefices, the bishops were to examine them by oath for simoniacal pacts. The old Latin service books were to be defaced and destroyed at visitations. No cleric was to be permitted to serve in any cure unless the bishop was convinced of his 'meetness' for the charge—a regulation that probably proved most difficult to apply effectively. A curious regulation ordered 'priests deprived and other private chaplains' to minister at the bishop's orders in cures 'in this great necessity' or face excommunication. Apparently the bishops felt the clergy shortage so keenly that they were willing to have clerics who had refused the Supremacy Oath minister the sacraments rather than see the parishes untended.

---

[1] Frere, *Visitation Articles*, III, 95–6. The repetition of some of the Interpretations in the Lambeth Articles suggests that the relationship of the documents is more complicated than Frere implies (p. 95 n.).

In the years between the parliamentary settlement and the first re-formed Convocation, the bishops took measures to enforce the Prayer Book and the queen's orders. Grumble they did, but, with varying degrees of zeal and effectiveness, they tried to make the settlement work. Some of them might look ahead to Convocation for more thorough reform but, in the meantime, they were giving the precis-ians a first taste of disappointment with reformed episcopal leadership.

THE SUPREME GOVERNOR AND THE CONVOCATION OF 1563

The long-awaited synod arrived, and the precisians were ready with their proposals for reform in those many areas of church life which, in the queen's eyes, fell under her own general supervision as Supreme Governor. Without any foolish direct attack on the royal prerogatives, the precisians sought to modify or even reverse many of the regulations which Elizabeth had established and maintained. Encouraged by the active support of some bishops and wide sympathy from many more, the militant reformers in the Lower House drew up their specific reforms which we may consider for convenience here in three parts: church services; lay discipline; and clerical education, administration, and finance. Although the pre-cisians' proposals for clerical attire and images also fell largely within the queen's prerogative I am leaving these for special consideration in the next chapter.

In addition to the changes which the militant reformers desired in the Prayer Book and its rubrics, they wanted more preaching, less music, and tighter control of the ringing of bells.

All of the more militant reformers, and probably most of the bishops as well, placed more emphasis on preaching than did the queen. Elizabeth had indeed increased the frequency of parish preaching in her Injunctions, but she retained a sceptical view of the effective homiletic abilities of the clergy in general. Once, many years later, Archbishop Whitgift commented in her presence that there were not enough learned preachers to fill the 13,000 parishes of England; Elizabeth burst out:

Jesus! Thirteen thousand! It is not to be looked for....My meaning is not that you should make choice of learned ministers only, for they are not to be found, but of honest, sober, and wise men and such as can read the scriptures and the homilies well unto the people.

Preaching was clearly in a bad state when some cathedrals could not boast a single preacher on their staffs of resident clergy. Such was the case in Carlisle, and perhaps in Exeter as well, for Bishop Alley, who was no militant reformer, proposed that in such cases the cathedral officials should be required to contribute the salaries of two 'godly learned preachers' for the cathedral pulpit and in attached cures.[1]

Somewhat more universal in application were the proposals of 'General notes' to put a financial premium on preaching. Its authors suggested that only licensed preachers be granted livings over £30, or permission to hold a second benefice.[2] 'Articles for government' carried over these proposals of 'General notes', allowing some wider discretion to the ordinary to make exceptions.[3] These same regulations required those who held the tithes of impropriated churches to provide quarterly sermons under penalty of fines. No one, not even the queen, opposed better preaching. Convocation did not, of course, enact these proposals, but bishops and other patrons were free to use the rewards of the more lucrative livings to encourage sermons and to enforce the provisions for preaching in the Injunctions. In 1571 Parliament, not Convocation, enacted the rule that benefices over £30 were to go only to preachers or 'B.D.'s'.[4]

'General notes', followed by 'Articles for government', picked

---

[1] Neale, *Parliaments*, II, 71; from S.P. Dom., Eliz., 176/68; Grindal, *Remains*, p. 285, to Cecil, 27 December 1563.

[2] 'General notes' required that to hold the second benefice, a cleric must also at least hold an M.A. degree and the benefices must be within twelve miles of each other.

[3] 'Articles for government' allowed the ordinary to allow a non-preacher to hold a benefice over £30 if he judged him worthy 'for his knowledge in the scriptures, gravity, and wisdom in ecclesiastical regiment'. These more finished regulations also applied the limitation on two benefices only when one benefice was worth more than £20 yearly, allowed the ordinary discretion about the academic degree of the cleric, and raised the maximum distance between the two benefices to twenty miles.

[4] *Statutes of the Realm*, IV, 547; 13° Eliz., c. 12. This is the bill for subscription to the Thirty-nine Articles forced through by the puritans in the Commons.

up the bishops' prohibition of excessive tolling of bells for a death, and specified that peals might not be longer than forty-five minutes or an hour. No ringing was to be done at 'Allhallowtide and at All Souls' day with the two nights next before and after'.[1]

The precisians who were enamoured of Genevan liturgies always disliked the traditional church music which continued in the English Church. The metrical psalms were the only musical components of the service which they would admit. The queen's injunction on music plainly called for the continuation of choirs of men and boys with their plainsong and polyphonic music. Although organs were not specifically mentioned, the injunction certainly assumed their continued use. The Chapel Royal maintained a distinguished succession of organists during Elizabeth's reign. The precisians later complained that Archbishop Parker had 'caused an organ to be erected in his metropolitan church at his own expense'. In 1564 Parker reported to Cecil that the French ambassador and his entourage were pleased with English 'reverent mediocrity' in religion, and was especially pleased to observe that 'we did not expel musick out of our quires'.[2]

In the Convocation of 1563 the precisians attempted to do away with the harmonious strains grating in godly ears. The preliminary 'General notes' flatly proposed that 'the use of organs and curious singing be removed'. The militant petitioners of the 'Seven articles' repeated this request and added an interesting corollary. They wanted the psalms at the office either 'sung distinctly by the whole congregation'—presumably in the metrical versions—or else 'said with the other prayers by the minister alone'. They wanted neither a choir singing the psalms nor a responsive reading between the minister and the clerk with others who might have access to a psalter. The clericalism of the precisians again shows through: worship is fundamentally an act of edification performed by the minister for the spiritual benefit of the congregation rather than the

---

[1] This wording is from 'Articles for government'. 'General notes' limited the peal to one hour after death and one half-hour at the burial; 'Articles for government' reduced the peal after death to forty-five minutes.

[2] *ZL*, II, 150, Withers and Barthelot to Bullinger and Gualter, February 1567; *Parker Corr.*, pp. 214–17, Parker to Cecil, 3 June 1564.

harmonic combined acts of adoration by minister, clerk, choir, and congregation. The milder terms of the 'Six articles', which commanded the majority of the members present in the Lower House, left singing untouched but still asked that 'the use of organs be removed'. The request did not contravene the explicit terms of the queen's injunctions as the earlier proposals had done.

The majority of whatever committee—if it was not the whole Lower House—who were responsible for the final form of 'Articles for government' refused to go along with this wholesale abolition of most church music. The only mention of music was an endorsement of the queen's policy which redundantly asked that her injunction 'concerning music in the churches may be put in execution'. Had the solid core of precisians had their way, the whole tradition of English Church music would have been reduced to the narrow confines of the metrical psalms.

These various reforms proposed in the 1563 Convocation for church services touched on areas in which the queen and the bishops had already laid down some guidelines. Like the proposals to 'perfect' the rubrics of the Prayer Book, they would have brought parish worship in the English Church much closer to that of continental protestant churches.

Writing to Bullinger in 1560, Thomas Lever commented that 'No discipline is as yet established by any public authority'.[1] Lever and his friends hoped to correct this in the Convocation. Two of the preliminary papers for Convocation called for a revival of the efforts begun under Henry and Edward to examine and revise the canon law, undoubtedly along the lines of the abortive *Reformatio Legum Ecclesiasticarum* which had died with King Edward. Sandys proposed that the queen appoint 'certain learned men, bishops and others' to frame orders and rules 'for the good government of the church of England'. He also unrealistically wanted Parliament to give the committee a blank cheque—'whatsoever they shall order or set down within one year next to be effectual'. The 'General notes' also called for a revival of the old committee of 'thirty-two persons' and specifically proposed the *Reformatio* as the basis for a new body

[1] *ZL*, I, 85, 10 July 1560.

of canon law.[1] The authors must have been sceptical of their possibilities for success in this project, for they went on to detail great quantities of laws and order to be established 'in the mean time'.

This was not the first time such a proposal was made in Elizabeth's reign. A bill to revive the committee had been introduced in the Commons on 27 February 1559, and after a rapid passage through the house, it died with its first reading in the Lords.[2] Although no action was taken on the bill in the 1563 Parliament, after the publication of the old *Reformatio* in 1571 under the sponsorship of John Foxe, the bill was again unsuccessfully proposed to the 1571 Parliament.[3]

The term 'discipline' had one particular application among the precisians: the local supervision of the morals and religious practices of ordinary church members. Bucer and also many Calvinists would have linked discipline with doctrine and sacraments as one of the *essential* marks of the church.[4] Although Calvin himself never granted discipline this status in theory, he emphasized in practice the importance of strict discipline to the *well-being* of the church. The disciplinary proposals of the militant reformers in 1563 reached out in a number of directions.

One of the sets of regulations running through various Convocation documents would have made the parish priest responsible for fining and excommunicating parishioners who did not cooperate in the instruction of youth and adults.

The Royal Injunctions had called for clerics to train their parishioners by reading the Creed, the Lord's Prayer, and the Decalogue each Sunday when there was no sermon and to catechize on holy days and every other Sunday before Evening Prayer. Bishop Sandys suggested that catechizing be stepped up to every Sunday. 'General notes' laid down a set of penalties for those who did not do their share in lay instruction. Parents and masters whose children,

[1] The committee of persons was to collect and gather ecclesiastical laws and to view those that had been gathered by commissioners appointed in Edward's reign.
[2] The bill was introduced 27 February, engrossed 1 March, and approved 17 March (*JHC*, I, 55, 56, and 58). In the Lords it was received on 20 March, read on 22 March, and not heard from again (*JHL*, I, 566).
[3] Neale, *Parliaments*, I, 193–7.　　　[4] See below, p. 275.

servants, and apprentices could not say the catechism and had not been regularly attending catechism instruction were to be fined. All parsons were yearly to examine their parishioners between Christmas and the fourth Sunday in Lent, to determine if they knew by heart the Creed, Lord's Prayer, and Decalogue. Those who failed to appear were to be excommunicated and fined before absolution; a cleric who failed to make himself available for such examinations was to be fined or even deprived. Laymen who could not say these three fundamentals were not to receive communion, nor to be married, nor to be godparents, 'saving that there be some consideration of those that be very aged...for one or two years, and no longer'. Every parson was to keep a book of all offenders to exhibit during the visitations. The 'Articles for government' reproduced all of these proposals in detail, making churchwardens responsible, along with the clergy, for presenting the book of the parishioners at visitations. Few clerical or lay leaders in England would have disagreed with the desirability of everyone learning the threefold summary of the Christian faith and life, but many would have objected to this manner of requiring it. Not only was the procedure complicated and arduous, but the annual examination with the application of fines and excommunications would have shifted the pastoral relationship of the priest to his people to emphasize more heavily his role as a disciplinary officer.

Proposals made in 1563 would have tightened the discipline requiring attendance and enforcing decorum at Sunday services in the parish church. The mild fines of the Uniformity bill for non-attendance, and the provisions of the Royal Injunctions, were to be made more severe. Bishop Alley merely wanted some punishment laid down for those who, contrary to the injunctions (no. 36), did 'walk and talk in the church at time of common prayer and preaching, to the disturbance of the ministers, and offence of the congregation'. The 'Articles for government' provided an article authorizing churchwardens to levy a fine of 12*d.* on 'disturbances of divine service'. Two other of its articles proposed to fine churchwardens who were negligent in reporting faults of fellow parishioners and to protect dutiful churchwardens from legal reprisals from the persons they detected. 'Certain articles' wanted loopholes plugged which had allowed some to escape the penalties of the Uniformity bill for recusancy.

The 'General notes' had a far more serious proposal, that 'such as do not communicate thrice a year at the least be severely punished'. Persistent offenders were to be treated 'as in case of heresy' or given a 'grievous fine' to be increased 'as the contumacy increaseth'. 'Articles for government' repeated these penal regulations and specified that offenders be treated as heretics after two years without communicating. This would have meant that the full scale of legal penalties, including eventual confiscation of all goods and imprisonment, would have been laid upon all those who did not communicate for any reason whatsoever. It may have been primarily directed against Roman Catholic recusants, but its potential scope was much wider. All the excommunicate would have been subject to these additional penalties and, if the precisians had had their way, the excommunicate would have included a great variety of additional moral offenders—even those who had failed to memorize the Ten Commandments! Furthermore, just as the Clarendon Code (which required English public officials to receive holy communion) one hundred years later turned the central religious act of the Christian church into a political test, these rules would have imposed such a test on the whole population of England. It was an intolerable proposal, but one which reveals the depth of the attachment of many of the militant reformers to a church discipline enforced by all the coercive power of the state.

The precisians also urged that marriage discipline be tightened. Sandys would have had marriages celebrated only in home parishes with the asking of banns. 'Certain articles' and 'General notes' wanted to eliminate all dispensations from the asking of banns.[1] 'Articles for government' repeated the proposals of 'General notes', and added the penalties of deprivation or deposition for clerics who solemnized marriages without the proper banns. 'General notes' also proposed a series of regulations forbidding 'clandestine con-

---

[1] 'General notes' also wanted to allow marriages during traditionally prohibited seasons except Christmas, Holy Week, Easter, and Pentecost.

tracts' and requiring such reasonable tests of free consent as an age of at least fifteen years for the bride, and parental approval for all minors.

Some men in every generation are convinced that the sexual offences of their own age represent the final decline of public morals, and the militant reformers who castigated the libertines of 1563 voiced such sentiments in their times. The author of 'Certain articles' asked that secular courts should not be permitted to impede ecclesiastical proceedings 'for the suppressing of the horrible licence and boldness now used in the variety of adulteries and fornications, and incest'. The 'Articles for government' would have ordered that 'no ecclesiastical judge...be molested' in a temporal court for 'the correction of incest, adulteries, fornications, swearing, blaspheming God's name, drunkenness, sorcery, and such other like causes'. 'General notes' would have had adulterers and fornicators 'punished by strait imprisonment and open shame', and went on to comment that 'some think banishment and perpetual prison to be meet for adulterers'. Some penalties for 'adultery, etc.' were presumably provided in the unidentified schedule which the Lower House returned to the bishops on 5 March.[1]

Swearing was another target of the disciplinarians. Sandys proposed that the bishops might authorize parish clergy to ex-communicate a 'common swearer' after two warnings. 'General notes' suggested that owners of houses penalize those who 'swear by God, or any part of Christ, by the mass,' and it added that the owners ought to 'give good examples themselves'. 'Articles for government' specified that after 'notorious swearers' were twice admonished by the parson or churchwarden, they were to be ex-communicated and fined 2s. 6d. for every offence.

The members of the Lower House who agreed to 'Articles for government' would have enforced discipline with public penances, establishing in each parish and cathedral church a 'place of penitents' where offenders might appear during church services. The ordinary was to determine times for offenders in 'gross faults, as apostasy from the faith, obstinate forbearing to receive the holy communion

---

[1] See above, pp. 68–72.

above one year, incest, adultery, fornication, falsewitness-bearing, perjury, blasphemy, abominable swearing, drunkenness' and murder, theft, and other felonies. Anyone refusing to occupy his penitential place would have been formally excommunicated and, after six months, punished as for heresy. What a point of interest such a place of penitents might have become in the average English parish church!

At the same time as tightening this Calvinistic discipline, 'General notes' and 'Articles for government' would have deprived and deposed any priest who under cover of the annual examination of his parishioners practised 'auricular confession'. The practice authorized in all but name in the Prayer Book's office for the sick was not necessarily forbidden at other times, but it was clearly suspect.

The local discipline of the parish would have been supported by items in both 'General notes' and 'Articles for government' for 'Deans rural'. These officials between the parish priest and the archdeacon would have had the authority to call and examine laymen and clerics who offended against church laws and to pass on the case to the archdeacon or bishop for judgment.

One point of protest in the preliminary papers of Convocation apparently had widespread support, for it led to a parliamentary act. The bishops had not always been able to persuade the lay authorities to apprehend those who had failed to appear in church courts. Both 'Certain articles' and Bishop Alley's paper proposed that better procedures be established. 'Articles for government' contained one article urging that Parliament enact legislation to facilitate the serving of process *De excommunicato capiendo*. Apparently the bishops passed on these proposals for correction to Parliament, for a bill was passed which defined the causes of excommunication and set up procedures by which the bishops might enforce their regulations through sheriffs and other lay officials.[1] This, it should be noted, strengthened the bishops' authority, but did not touch the authority of the local parson or churchwardens except as they might report offenders to the ordinary.

[1] *Statutes of the Realm*, IV, 451–4; 5° Eliz., c. 23; see above, pp. 74–5.

If the parson were to enforce such discipline as the 'Articles for government' envisaged, it was perhaps well that they also included a provision for the excommunication of any who railed or jested against the clergy, or who laid violent hands upon them.

Had a large portion of the disciplinary measures proposed by the precisians in Convocation been adopted by the Church of England, the whole kingdom of England would have been patterned like the Geneva of John Calvin or like some of the puritan communities of New England in the early years of the next century. The parish priest would have become primarily a judge of his flock aided in ferreting out sinful behaviour and practices by his sleuthing church-wardens. No wonder a Londoner wrote in late January 1563 that 'there is great labour made by the clergy for discipline, whereof some suppose the Bishop of Rome has gone out at one door and comes in by another'.[1]

A final series of proposals in the Convocation of 1563 touched the clergy, their income, and the administration of the church. Clerical education posed a serious problem and one directly related to the short supply of preachers. The medieval church could tolerate a substantial number of 'mass-priests' with minimal preparation for their ministry, but a reformed church which emphasized the edification of its people demanded higher educational standards. The loss of religious orders with their varying degrees of concern for education aggravated the situation. Elizabeth recognized the in-solubility of the problem and ordered the homilies to be read by serious and sober, if unlearned, clerics. Both moderate and militant reformers tried to improve the learning of the clergy. What galled the precisians and their puritan successors was their inability to move as far ahead in the roads of church advancement as their education and talents qualified them. They saw non-preaching 'dumb-dogs' enjoying comfortable livings while they were refused higher ministerial responsibilities. On occasions, in subsequent years, some were even to be deprived of the livings they held. Over and above the concern for a better educated clergy which they shared with the bishops, they knew that the upgraded requirements for the

[1] *CSP, For.* VI, 62; Georges Ferness to Challoner, 22 January 1563.

education of the spirituality would increase the influence of their party.

The 'General notes', followed by 'Articles for government', proposed a divinity lecture three times a week in every cathedral church—and all 'ministers and singing-men' of the church were to attend. 'General notes' would have required all clerics who were not licensed preachers to study scriptures, and 'Articles for government' in more detail would have them study assigned topics in the scriptures and catechism—presumably Nowell's—under the direction of bishops, archdeacons, and rural deans. After quarterly examinations, negligent clergy would have been fined, and bishops might deprive beneficed priests who refused to report on their studies.

If a cleric did not know Latin well enough to answer the catechism, again presumably Nowell's, 'General notes' would have barred him from a rectory worth more than £8 or vicarage of more than 20 marks (£13 6s. 8d.). 'Articles for government' seem to have repeated these proposals, stepping up the minimum to 20 marks and £20 respectively. The order allowed the bishop to make exception for a cleric 'with singular knowledge of scripture, and special gift of utterance'.

Sandys proposed that bishops ought to ordain only men who had a cure to serve and only after the 'consent of six learned ministers', all of whom would share in the laying on of hands with the bishop, presumably only at the ordination of priests, which provided for such presbyteral participation. Sandys' suggestion for granting presbyters an authoritative voice in the bishop's choice of 'fit men' is interesting as a means by which an element of presbyterian polity might have been introduced quite naturally into the episcopal Church of England.

The militant reformers attempted to eliminate the abuses of simony and non-residence which arose out of the old financial systems. Three of the preliminary papers proposed penalties for simony. The queen had already ordered by injunction (no. 26) that any priest guilty of simony was to be deprived and unable 'at any time after' to receive any other living and that the patron was to lose the right of presentment for that time. Bishop Alley repeated these penalties without any reference to the injunction, but wished the patron to lose his next appointment as well. 'General notes', commenting that *patroni* were not to be *praedones*, would have taken the gift of the living away from a guilty patron for his lifetime. The authors also proposed granting the bishops wider powers to investigate suspected instances of simoniacal pacts. 'Certain articles', while improving investigation procedures, would have reduced the penalties of the injunction by making the guilty minister incapable of receiving another living for only seven years—not for life. The repetition and even proposed lightening of the penalties for simoniacal priests suggests that the problem was by no means solved by the injunction. Apparently, however, the Lower House could not decide on any new penalties for simony, for none of the papers produced by the Convocation refers to it.

Pluralities and non-resident clergy were also evils which the Elizabethan church inherited from medieval days. Although even the militant reformers did not try to eliminate them completely, they tried to introduce laws to minimize the abuses. 'Certain articles' simply wanted that 'some good order be devised to reform dispensations for pluralities and non-residence'. 'General notes', in addition to limiting pluralities to preachers and the better-educated clergy, would have allowed no priests to have more than two benefices with cure; it would have required the permission of the bishops of the parishes concerned; and it would have given bishops the right to deprive any licensed non-resident who failed in any six weeks out of a year to provide a 'meet curate' and who did not deliver or arrange for the four annual sermons. Chaplains to noblemen were desirable, provided the minister were a preacher who might deliver 'an ordinary sermon every Sunday'. Such chaplains could hold a prebend and might also be dispensed for non-residence from a benefice with cure not more than twelve miles from the nobleman's house. The queen's chaplains, 'if they be preachers', might also be dispensed, but only while 'they shall be occupied in her majesty's service'. Except for these specified pluralities and chaplaincies no dispensation for non-residence was to be granted but for sickness, and even that no longer than six months. 'Articles for government' contained the same regulations for pluralities and noblemen's chaplains, but it did not reproduce the articles concerning the queen's chaplains, the limitations of non-residence, or the specific authorization to deprive non-residents who did not supply curates to serve their parishes. Perhaps too many members of the Lower House had stakes themselves in the comfortable continuation of the old practices of non-residence.

'General notes' also would have prohibited any spiritual living, whether with cure or not, from being held by anyone not ordained a priest, with exceptions being made for cathedral prebends with no cure of souls which might be held by full-time University students and by graduate lawyers exercising some spiritual jurisdiction. 'Articles for government' repeated the substance of these proposals.

Reformers wanted to eliminate the anomaly of 'peculiar jurisdictions', areas within dioceses exempt from the bishop's jurisdiction. Bishop Alley, whose diocese contained a long list of peculiars, wanted bishops to have the right to call all criminal causes and 'to reform other disorders' in these 'dens of robbers'.[1] 'General notes' would have simply abolished all 'peculiar jurisdictions'. 'Articles for government' made no such sweeping rule. It would have granted bishops jurisdiction in peculiars arising from former exempt monasteries, but not in peculiars which belong to 'any cathedral or collegiate church or college'. The cathedral chapters, which were strongly represented in the Lower House, were not about to lose their quasi-episcopal jurisdictions.

Convocation men attempted to improve the unreformed financial structure of the church, beginning with the impropriated tithes in secular hands. The queen in her injunctions had merely ordered that the traditional tithes be paid without excuse (no. 15), but 'Certain articles' proposed that Henry VIII's legislation for tithes be reviewed and that holders of impropriated tithes of poor vicarages in towns be required to augment the clerical incomes. 'General notes', realistically admitting that the ideal solution of universal restitution of impro-

---

[1] Frere, *Visitation Articles*, I, 172–86, appendix II; 1565 list of peculiars, Exeter, on pp. 176–7.

priated tithes 'can hardly be hoped for', proposed an elaborate scheme by which the tithes would be annexed to the parishes, a yearly pension paid to the present owners of the impropriations, and commissioners given authority to ensure a sufficient income for the clergy. These do not appear in 'Articles for government'. For better payment of tithes, 'Articles for government' would have enabled a bishop to cite owners of lands who actually resided outside his diocese, but the drastic proposals of 'General notes' were apparently dropped by the Lower House.

'General notes' also pointed to the evil of leases of benefice lands 'by avarice and practice of evil bishops, pastors, and priests... with the confirmation of the bishop and patron'. The authors' radical solution was to cancel all present leases in three years and to prohibit any future leases of more than one year.[1] Sandys would have merely limited a bishop from leasing his lands for longer than his own episcopal tenure. Bishop Alley would have similarly ordered the bishops not to approve any lease made by their diocesan clergy for more than the priest's own incumbency. 'Articles for government' took up none of these proposals, but it would have required parsons entering a benefice to swear that they would not lease church property unless it were to their own curates or else during the first two years of their incumbency. This latter provision was to enable them to raise the money to pay the first-fruits due to the queen.

'General notes' pointed to another source of the impoverishment of town and city parishes, in that 'personal tithes' were notoriously difficult to collect in contrast to tithes of agricultural products. The authors proposed some kind of rating for every person, possibly based on the rent of their houses. 'Articles for government' approved no such innovation, but it would have authorized bishops to examine men about the payment of their personal tithes by means of corporal oaths, a procedure which the existing statutes prohibited.

Parliament made two stabs in 1563 at improving the financial lot of poorer clergy. When the Speaker of the House presented himself to the queen on 15 January, among national conditions needing

---

[1] A marginal note proposed that three-year leases be permitted, and that present leases be allowed to run their term.

correction, he pointed to the towns without preachers because 'the vicar hath but only £20, and the rest, being so small sum, is impropriate'.[1] The Lords passed a bill allowing the bishops to unite churches in cities and towns provided that the united value remained under £24, but the Commons did not approve it.[2] Some members of the Commons came up with two separate proposals, one of which, supported by Cecil, would have allowed commissions to review each parish and assure every 'parson, vicar, or curate' £20 annually. Unfortunately for the welfare of the church and its clergy, the bill ran into the usual resistance that meets measures which threaten property rights, and neither it nor its alternative reappeared after the first readings.[3] None of the efforts made in Convocation or Parliament of 1563 to alleviate the financial conditions of the poorer clergy was successful.

The proposals of the reformers for the finances and education of the clergy attacked problems which were to plague the Church of England for many decades. Whether they would have solved these problems without creating others we do not know, but they would have altered the old structure of the Church of England. The drastic financial measures in 'General notes' were, by and large, *not* taken up in 'Articles for government'. The Lower House was apparently not prepared to go so far. Yet even the mild reforms codified in 'Articles for government' died along with those which would have 'purified' the church services and established a much more rigorous and Calvinistic parochial discipline.

As Elizabeth's reign progressed, the bishops were able to make some improvements, especially in better education for the clergy, but they did this without changing the traditional administrative and financial structure of the English Church. Whenever the reformers tried to alter orders which the queen had issued as Supreme Governor,

[1] Neale, *Parliaments*, I, 99; from Cotton MS. Titus F I, fols. 69 ff.
[2] See above, p. 75.
[3] The bill, listed in the Journal 'nova', was read on 30 March: 'The Bill, that the Lord chancellor may direct commissions to the Bishop, and other Persons, for the Increase of Living of Ministers in Churches of small Values in Towns' (*JHC*, 71). It would seem to be this bill which Strype describes in *Annals* (I, part I, 513–14; see Read, *Cecil*, I, 271).

they utterly failed. In church services, lay discipline, and clerical education and finances, the programme of the militants was ignored.

The role of Elizabeth as Supreme Governor was crucial for the course of the Church of England. Had she encouraged or even permitted the reforms urged by the more militant part of reforming clerics, the shape of the settlement, and subsequent anglicanism, would have been quite different. Just as the queen was determined not to permit alterations of the liturgy agreed upon in 1559, in those areas of discipline which she believed expressly hers to determine as part of the adiaphora, she implemented a more conservative settlement than that of the final years of her brother's reign. She exercised her supremacy neither through a lay vicar nor her Privy Council, but through a commission dominated by the conservative reforming prelates whom she had chosen. Her initial visitation swiftly ensured the loyalty of the overwhelming majority of English clerics to the new ecclesiastical conditions. Her Royal Injunctions were remarkably moderate and she authorized a version of the reformed but traditional 1551 Primer which had been the companion of the 1549 Prayer Book. Her orders for church buildings reveal a concern both for repair of the fabric and for the traditional dignified beauty of their interiors.

In financial matters, Elizabeth used church incomes for the benefit of the national government, but she drew on these funds with restrained discretion. She did nothing to overhaul the antiquated system of church finance, but allowed the medieval machinery to keep turning as best it might. The poor clergy continued in their poverty.

The administrative regulations of the bishops remained within the general framework of the queen's injunctions and orders. The sympathy of many bishops for the programme of the precisians never developed in the 1563 Convocation into open wholehearted support, and their inaction defeated the militant attempts to alter church services, to impose a stricter moral discipline on the local parish, to ameliorate the level of clerical education and income, or to correct financial abuses and administrative anomalies. The bishops had said, in effect, 'Wait until the synod.' The synod came and went, and the proposals of the militant reformers lay on the table stillborn.

The Supreme Governor: administration and finance

The Church of England had made its reforms in 1559, and further steps to change its remaining traditional structures ran up against the queen's settled convictions and determined policies and the willingness of the bishops to accept them. Elizabeth carefully qualified her ecclesiastical supremacy in the appendix to her injunctions, but she regularly exercised the authority that remained to her. Amidst the mass of conflicting religious convictions at the court among her advisers and her clergy, only the strong personality of the queen could have framed the policies that were ordained in her name. A complex but consistent purpose shines through the subtle maze of her successes and failures in ecclesiastical affairs.

5. The queen and her bishops: images, vestments, and apparel

HISTORIANS writing of the Elizabethan settlement of religion have all paid some attention to the vestiarian controversy and have given passing notice to the queen's 'little silver cross'. Yet partly because of past misunderstandings of the crucial struggle in the 1559 Parliament, their accounts have missed the close connection between vestments and images and the extent to which controversies over these matters illuminate the shifting relationship between the queen and the bishops in the opening years of the reign.

At the time of Elizabeth's initial Parliament, most of the clerical reformers, both moderate and militant, stood together in support of the party in the Commons which would not tolerate the queen's original legislative programme for religion. In 1563 the reformers were sufficiently divided so that the bishops, a majority of whom had been Marian exiles, squarely blocked the militant programme for fuller Reformation. In 1566 the bishops began to deprive and even to imprison the more recalcitrant nonconformists. How did this come about? What happened to persuade sincere reformers on the episcopal bench to move from the side of their former comrades-in-exile to the side of the queen? The controversies over the vestments and images were not the most substantial ecclesiastical issues over which men fought in these years, but the intense emotions which they generated can shed a few glimmers of light upon the human dynamics among the leaders of the church.

The 1559 religious settlement rested upon the compromise between the queen and the Marian exiles, and like most compromises it had borne the seeds of future dissent. Two details of the settlement provided the friction points which ignited the first serious struggle within the Elizabethan church: the ornaments rubric of the Prayer Book and the royal injunctions concerning images.

From the beginning, the ornaments rubric, requiring cope or

Mass vestments at Holy Communion and surplice at other services, drew differing interpretations from the protagonists who had accepted the Prayer Book compromise. Elizabeth clearly intended it to settle the whole question of the vestments to be worn at church services; it was one of the few changes she had demanded in the 1552 Prayer Book.[1] The Marian exiles interpreted the regulation quite otherwise. Sandys wrote to Parker just two days after the Uniformity bill had been concluded in the Lords:

The last book of service is gone through with a proviso to retain the ornaments which were used in the first and second year of King Edward, until it please the Queen to take other order for them. Our gloss upon this text is, that we shall not be forced to use them, but that others in the meantime shall not convey them away, but they may remain for the Queen.

To most reformers, and certainly to the former exiles whether devotees of Cox or Knox, the 'scenic apparatus of divine worship', in Jewel's phrases, comprised only 'tawdry...fooleries' inappropriate in any properly reformed church. Christopher Goodman cited the 'binding of ministers to Papist apparel' as one of the things that so 'offended him and wounded the hearts of the faithful' that he left England for the godlier pastures of Scotland.[2] Many reformers also resented the royal injunction which required them to wear outdoors the customary priest's gown and cap. Parkhurst, as he looked forward to the 1563 synod with hope for reform, must have remembered the vestiarian scruples which had sent his friend Hooper to a stay in prison in Edward's reign.

The clerics who led the royal visitations in the summer and autumn of 1559 perversely interpreted the queen's injunctions when they ordered all images to be destroyed. In London, where the Visitors had been sitting in late August, the St Bartholomew's Day fair provided an occasion for public burnings; Machyn reports two

---

[1] See above, pp. 106–11.

[2] *Parker Corr.*, p. 65, Sandys to Parker, 30 April 1559; *ZL*, I, 23, Jewel to Peter Martyr, spring 1559; *CSP, For.* II, 63; Goodman to Cecil, 26 October 1559; see also *ZL*, I, 63, Sampson to Peter Martyr, 6 January 1560; I, 85, Lever to Bullinger, 10 July 1560.

great bonfires 'of rodes and of Mares and Johns and odur emages' in conspicuous locations, and the Imperial ambassador reported to Ferdinand that at the fair 'images and other Church ornaments were publicly burnt'.[1] The actions in London were repeated around the kingdom. As the Visitors made their rounds, they were either oblivious of the queen's real intentions in her injunctions or they deliberately pushed the terms of the settlement in the direction which they believed to lead to a more scriptural and primitive Reformation. Although both queen and reformers had accepted the compromise, the reformers were united in 1559 in their opposition to the queen's intention of keeping the vestments and the images.

CROSSES AND COPES

In mid-April 1559 John Jewel wrote to Peter Martyr that if Elizabeth would only abolish the Mass from her chapel, it might be banished from the kingdom for 'of such importance among us are the examples of princes'. The liturgics of the Chapel Royal in the first weeks of the reign had presaged religious changes, and Jewel hoped that Elizabeth might ignore the legalities and introduce a reformed fully vernacular service. In November, after the English liturgy had been in use for six months, Jewel still wrote with dismay of the Chapel Royal:

The doctrine is every where most pure; but as to ceremonies and maskings, there is a little too much foolery. That little silver cross, of ill-omened origin, still maintains its place in the queen's chapel. Wretched me! This thing will soon be drawn into a precedent.

Before a single new bishop was consecrated, that little silver cross had become the centre of a bitter controversy.[2]

Bishop de Quadra's report of 9 October provides the earliest notice of the dispute:

[1] Machyn, *Diary*, p. 207 and pp. 206–9 *passim*; von Klarvill, *Foreigners*, p. 121, Baron Breuner to Ferdinand, 31 August 1559; see also *CSP, Sp.* I, 89, de Quadra to Philip, 13 August 1559; Wriothesley, *Chronicle*, II, 146.

[2] *ZL*, I, 18 and 55, Jewel to Peter Martyr, 14 April and 16 November 1559.

On Thursday [5 October] the Queen had ordered the marriage of one of her lady servants to take place in her own chapel and directed that a crucifix and candles should be placed upon the altar, which caused so much noise amongst her chaplains and the Council that the intention was abandoned for the time, but it was done at vespers on Saturday, and on Sunday the clergy wore vestments as they do in our services, and so great was the crowd at the palace that disturbance was feared in the city. The fact is that the crucifixes and vestments that were burnt a month ago are now set up again in the royal chapel, as they soon will be all over the kingdom.

A few days later Knollys wished Parker success in what he believed to be the archbishop-elect's opposition to the 'enormities yet in the Queen's closet retained, although without the Queen's express commandment these toys were laid aside till now a late'. The latter part of the comment is a remarkable admission from a militantly reform-minded layman who belonged both to the Privy Council and to the Ecclesiastical Commission that the queen's injunctions did *not* order the destruction of all images.[1]

One crucial question must be answered: when were the ornaments originally removed from the chapel? Gee argued from silence that they had been removed at Easter, assuming that the Prayer Book had been regularly used in the chapel from that date. He was mistaken on all counts. The Prayer Book was introduced in the chapel only after Parliament rose on 8 May, and none of the three accounts of that change mentions any alteration of the physical arrangements except for the removal of the reserved sacrament.[2] The argument from silence in these accounts tells against Gee, for all our reporters would have been interested in as important a change as the removal of the central crucifix. The disputed ornaments remained not only after Easter, but after the introduction of the English liturgy in May. Since there is not one piece of evidence to the contrary, we may assume that the chapel ornaments in Whitehall Palace were removed at about the same time that crucifixes were removed from St Paul's

---

[1] *CSP, Sp.* I, 105; de Quadra to the bishop of Arras, 9 October 1559; *Parker Corr.*, p. 97; Knollys to Parker, 13 October 1559.
[2] Gee, *Elizabethan Prayer Book*, p. 152; *CSP, Sp.* I, 66 and 69, Feria to Philip and de Quadra to Philip, 10 May 1559; Machyn, *Diary*, p. 197; see above, pp. 92 f.

and other London churches, namely, during the visitation in mid-August when similar ornaments were publicly burned.

Such a timetable makes it readily apparent why the dispute did not break out until the first week of October. Elizabeth had been in Kent and Surrey, providing the country with a foretaste of her yearly summer progresses. She had left London on 21 June, and she did not return until 28 September.[1] Perhaps on Sunday 1 October she first viewed the full liturgy celebrated in her chapel without cross and candles. Her order to return the crucifix for the imminent wedding threw the court clerics into confusion. Elizabeth relented—but only for the wedding. By next Saturday evensong, cross and candlesticks were back, and a major ecclesiastical struggle had been joined.

This reconstruction of events is crucial to an understanding of Elizabeth's convictions and policies, since such eminent historians as Maitland, Rowse, and Read have followed Gee in his opinion that the crucifix reappeared as a gesture towards the marriage suit with Archduke Charles. It is unfortunate to discard so delightfully graphic a symbol of Elizabeth's supposed lack of religious principles as the evanescent crucifix, but there is not one shred of evidence to suggest that the ornaments ever disappeared and reappeared in response to the political situation. They were removed in Elizabeth's absence, and she ordered them to be restored as soon as she returned. They indeed aroused Roman Catholic hopes of winning the queen, but that was incidental to her consistent determination to keep the 'little silver cross'.[2]

[1] Von Klarvill, *Foreigners*, p. 103, Breuner to Ferdinand, 12 July 1559; *CSP, Sp.* I, 98, de Quadra to Emperor, 2 October; Arthur Clifford, *The State Papers and Letters of Sir Ralph Sadler*, 2 vols. (Edinburgh, 1809), I, 464, Cecil to Sadler, 27 September; Machyn, *Diary*, pp. 201–7 *passim*. In addition, a whole swatch of Elizabeth's own letters demonstrate her continued absence from London during the crucial weeks of August and September (*passim* in Rymer, *Foedera*, VI, part IV, 83–4; *CSP, For.* I, 449–573; *CSP, Dom., 1547–80*, pp. 137–8; Clifford, *Sadler*, I, 392–446).

[2] Gee, *Elizabethan Prayer Book*, p. 152; Frederick William Maitland, 'The Anglican Settlement and the Scottish Reformation', *Cambridge Modern History*, II (Cambridge, 1934), p. 575; Rowse, *The England of Elizabeth*, p. 395; Read, *Cecil*, I, 155; Forbes, *Full View*, I, 259–60, Killigrew and Jones to Elizabeth, 14 November 1559; *CSP, Sp.* I, 103, de Quadra to Philip, 9 October 1559; Sander, *Anglican Schism*, p. 271.

The queen and her bishops

The crucifix and the candles were probably kept on the holy table, except during the time of communion when the table was moved out and the crucifix moved to a shelf on the wall.[1] Machyn remarked on 'the cross and ij candylles bornyng' at sermons in the spring of 1560. Sampson in a letter early that same year implied that the 'image of the crucifix' was near the table during the Lord's Supper—to his scandalized horror.[2]

In the summer of 1562 a vandal—of presumably militantly protestant conviction—broke the cross and candlesticks, and Bishop Parkhurst jubilantly informed Bullinger with the comment, 'a good riddance of such a cross as that'. Eight months later he had sadly to report that the ornaments had been 'shortly after brought back again to the great grief of the godly'. The one grain of hope Parkhurst offered the Zurich reformer of Elizabeth's conversion to more godly liturgics was that the candles were not now lighted during service.[3]

Canon de Silva reported in January 1565 that the earl of Leicester ordered that the cross be removed, but that Elizabeth kept it on the altar—a typical reaction of the queen to the occasional high-handedness of her favourite.[4] In February Thomas Lever, writing to Cecil and the earl of Leicester, put Elizabeth's crucifix alongside Mary Stuart's Mass as 'old stombling blockes...seen of idolators and traitors with rejoicing and hoping'. Two years later Elizabeth told de Silva that 'her Protestants...would like to abolish [her cross], but they would not do it'. A zealot threw down the cross and candlesticks in the midst of service in 1567, and a tapestry depicting

[1] For mention of the shelf in 1565, see *Joannis Lelandi Antiquarii de Rebus Britannicis Collectanea*, ed. Thomas Hearn (London, 1774), II, 691–4, 'The maner of the Christening of the Child of the Lady Cicila'.
[2] Machyn, *Diary*, pp. 226 and 229; *ZL*, I, 63–4, Sampson to Peter Martyr, 6 January 1560.
[3] *ZL*, I, 122 and 129, 20 August 1562 and 26 April 1563; see also an account of a 1600 Epiphany Eucharist in Leslie Hotson, *The First Night of Twelfth Night* (New York, 1954), pp. 189–90; from the report of Grigori Ivanovich Hikulin to the Tsar, printed in *Sbornik Imperatorskago Russkago Istoricheskago Obshchestva*, St Petersburg, Tom XXXVIII (1883), ed. K. N. Bestuzhev-Riumin, pp. 302–63.
[4] *CSP, Sp.* I, 401, de Silva to Philip 2 January 1565; see also I, 387, 9 October 1564; see above, n. 1; Elias Ashmole, *The Institution, Laws and Ceremonies of the Most Noble Order of the Garter* (London, 1672), p. 369, service on 24 January 1565.

the crucifixion temporarily replaced the metal crucifix. Some time before 1571 the cross was returned to the chapel.[1] The cross remained prominently in the Chapel Royal.

With the relative permanency of the 'little silver cross' established, we must return to the controversy which it kindled in the first year of the settlement. By the beginning of 1560 records suggest that more was at stake in the dispute than the appointments of the queen's chapel. On 6 January Sampson lamented to Peter Martyr that although altars and images were removed throughout the kingdom, he feared that the 'wretched multitude' would imitate the queen's use of the crucifix and candles. He asked what he should do if the queen were to 'enjoin all the bishops and clergy either to admit [these]...into their churches, or to retire from the ministry of the word'.[2]

Early in February Bishop de Quadra, characteristically imputing political motives to the Queen, wrote that she

is trying to please [the catholics] somewhat by ordering the restoration of the crosses on the altars which would have been already ordered but for the confusion and dissensions amongst the heretic bishops themselves and others who have charge of religious matters.

Jewel described the seriousness of the controversy and explained more about these 'dissensions' among the bishops in a letter of 4 February:

This controversy about the crucifix is now at its height. You would scarcely believe to what a degree of insanity some persons, who once had some show of common sense, have been carried upon so foolish a subject. There is not one of them, however, with whom you are acquainted,

---

[1] Strype, *Parker*, III, 140, 24 February, [Strype supplied the year,] 1565; *CSP, Sp.* I, 604, 682, 683, 687, and 690, de Silva to Philip, 16 December 1566 and 1 and 8 November, 1 and 29 December 1567; *Parker Corr.*, p. 379, Parker to Cecil, 6 February 1571. The distinction which has been drawn between a plain cross and the crucifix with a *corpus* seems to have been irrelevant to the English dispute and was introduced only by the German Cassander in his letter to Cox (W. M. Southgate, *John Jewel and the Problem of Doctrinal Authority* [Cambridge, Massachusetts, 1962], pp. 46–8; *ZL*, II, 43). 'The little silver cross' *was* the crucifix.
[2] *ZL*, I, 63.

excepting Cox. A disputation upon this subject will take place tomorrow. The moderators will be persons selected by the council. The disputants on the one side are the archbishop of Canterbury and Cox; and on the other, Grindal...and myself. The decision rests with the judges. I smile, however, when I think with what grave and solid reasons they will defend their little cross. Whatever may be the result I will write to you more at length when the disputation is over; for the controversy is as yet undecided; yet, as far as I can conjecture, I shall not again write to you as a bishop. For matters are come to that pass, that either the crosses of silver and tin, which we have every where broken in pieces, must be restored, or our bishoprics relinquished.[1]

The controversy had reached the point at which Jewel thought he would be required to resign his see for refusing to readmit crucifixes in his diocese. He clearly set himself and Grindal on one side against Parker and Cox on the other. The dispute now involved not merely the cross in the Chapel Royal, but crucifixes in parish churches throughout the land. As Sandys informs us in a letter to Peter Martyr summarizing the whole controversy, Elizabeth wanted 'the image of Christ crucified, together with Mary and John... replaced, as heretofore, in some conspicuous part of the church'. Elizabeth was insisting that the whole rood statuary be restored. Sandys, just like Jewel, reported that he being 'rather vehement' could not have consented to such a resoration and therefore was 'very near being deposed...and incurring the displeasure of the queen'. Jewel, Sandys, and probably Grindal as well, were prepared to give up their bishoprics rather than admit the crucifixes to their churches.[2]

The stand of Parker and Cox is a bit obscure, but an unsigned letter to the queen among Parker's papers helps to unravel the mystery. The editor of Parker's correspondence ascribed the letter to 'Archbishop Parker and others' but, as Parker's latest biographer recognizes, no evidence identifies the archbishop as one of its authors.[3]

The letter is undated, but it was written some time between the episcopal consecrations on 21 December 1559 and the resolution

[1] *CSP, Sp.* I, 126, de Quadra to the duchess of Parma, 7 February 1560; see also his letter of 12 February (I, 128); *ZL,* I, 67–8, Jewel to Peter Martyr, 4 February 1560.
[2] *ZL,* I, 74, 1 April 1560; see also I, 65, Sampson to Peter Martyr, 6 January.
[3] *Parker Corr.,* pp. 79–95; Brook, *Parker,* p. 78.

of the dispute over images early in 1560. It argued against the 'erecting of and retaining' of images, a possibility which the authors clearly regarded to be imminent; they insisted:

The profit of images is uncertain, the peril by experience of all ages and states of the church (as afore) is most certain. The benefit to be taken of them (if there be any) is very small. The danger ensuing of them, which is the danger of idolatry, is the greatest of all other. Now to allow a most certain peril for an uncertain profit, and the greatest danger for the smallest benefit in matters of faith and religion, is a tempting of God, and a grievous offence...

   It is evident that infinite millions of souls have been cast into eternal damnation by the occasion of images used in places of religion. And no history can record that ever any one soul was won unto Christ by having images.

The writers hesitated before claiming outright that images were absolutely forbidden, *de jure divino*, but in due course they arrived at precisely this conclusion:

If by virtue of the second commandment images were not lawful in the temple of the Jews, then by the same commandment they are not lawful in the churches of the Christians. For being a moral commandment, and not ceremonial,... it is a perpetual commandment, and bindeth us as well as the Jews.

The authors significantly admitted that Elizabeth's orders had not yet forbidden images in English public law:

The establishing of images by your authority shall not only utterly discredit our ministries, as builders of the things which we have destroyed, but also blemish the fame of your most godly brother, and such notable fathers as have given their lives for the testimony of God's truth, who by public law removed all images.

They besought Elizabeth 'to refer the discussment and deciding' of these matters 'to a synod of your bishops and other godly learned men', a procedure which they knew would effectively prevent the erection of the superstitious stumbling-blocks of idolatry. From the writings of Epiphanius, they strove to show that, of all images, those of Christ himself—the image on Elizabeth's chapel altar—are 'most perilous in the church'.

The authors of this letter were clearly men of the party of Jewel, Grindal, and Sandys—men prepared to resign rather than consent to an action which they were persuaded 'doth tend to the confirmation of error, superstition, and idolatry, and finally, to the ruin of the souls committed to our charge'. In a curiously complicated sentence which requires close reading, the authors distinguished two groups among the bishops:

We have at this time put in writing...those authorities of the Scriptures, reasons and pithy persuasions, which as they have moved *all such our brethren*, as now bear the office of bishops, to think and affirm images not expedient for the church of Christ, so will they not suffer *us*, without the great offending of God, and grievous wounding of our own consciences, ...to consent to the erecting or retaining of the same in the place of worshipping.

The authors could never in conscience consent to images, a position one step beyond that of *all* the bishops who agreed only that it was not *expedient* to erect them at this time. Therefore, *some* bishops regarded the images as inexpedient, but scripturally lawful and tolerable if the queen so ordered.

We would naturally include Archbishop Parker among the latter group, since Jewel so clearly identified him with Cox, as his opponent in the disputation. Other evidence has tended to obscure his roles and to lead to the conclusion either that he was inconsistent, eventually capitulating to the queen's wishes, or that the disputation was merely an academic exercise in which Parker assumed a position which he really did not accept. I am convinced that, on the contrary, Parker held and defended a consistent position throughout the dispute. Like all the bishops, he thought images to be inexpedient, but he was among those who, nevertheless, did not think them forbidden *de jure divino*.

Knollys in his letter to Parker of 13 October assumed Parker's 'good enterprise' against the 'enormities yet in the Queen's closet'.[1] We

---

[1] *Parker Corr.*, p. 97.

would expect the primate-elect, who did not believe the crucifix expedient, to make some effort to persuade Elizabeth to rescind her orders.

Parker wrote to Cecil on 6 November 1559 of Elizabeth's recent
favour in a cause he had argued before her, and he wished he might
speak with her again 'to continue our humble supplication to the
finishment and stay of that offendicle'. The editor of Parker's
correspondence has followed most historians in identifying the
'offendicle' with the little silver cross. This is, of course, possible,
and it would be consistent with Parker's attitude that the crucifix,
although lawful, was not expedient. However, I am inclined to
think that Parker's words in this letter fit better with another hot
issue of the moment: the exchange of episcopal properties. Parker
and other bishops-elect had written to the queen requesting her not
to reduce episcopal incomes by exchanging solid properties for
less-certain tithes as parliamentary statute permitted her. Elizabeth
issued an order on 26 October which slightly modified the exchange
to the bishops' advantage, but her concession fell far short of the
bishops' request. Parker's letter to Cecil said that although the
queen had given him 'much comfort', the principal cause was 'not
yet fully resolved'—a good description of the state of the financial
suit, but hardly consistent with anything known about the dispute
over the crucifix. No evidence suggests that Elizabeth gave any
ground on the chapel cross in the autumn of 1559. To modern ears
the archaic word 'offendicle' somehow conveys the sense of an
object of offence, but its sixteenth-century meaning was simply a
cause of offence. Parker used the word in at least two other letters.
He referred to himself personally as an 'offendicle' to Thomas
Cartwright. He also described Thomas Sampson's refusal to wear
prescribed vestments as a 'great offendicle'. Although the 'offendicle'
of Parker's 1559 letter cannot be identified with certainty, the additional information in the letter suggests the property exchanges
rather than the crucifix.[1]

[1] *Ibid.* p. 105, Parker to Cecil, 6 November 1559; pp. 97–101, Parker, Grindal, Cox,
Barlow, and Scory to Elizabeth (mid-October, 1559); pp. 101–2, Elizabeth to the
Lord Treasurer *et al.*; p. 454, Parker to Lord Burghley, *c.* 1573; p. 244, Parker to
Cecil, 4 June 1565; see above, pp. 154–5.

Neither Knollys' comment nor the possible identification of the cross as the 'offendicle' is inconsistent with Parker's stand on the images as scripturally lawful, but presently inexpedient. In 1571 Parker told Cecil that one nobleman blamed him for the restoration of the cross in Elizabeth's chapel; he commented that 'I never knew of it, nor yet in good faith I think it expedient it should be restored'.[1] No evidence suggests that Parker ever wavered from the position which he held as an opponent of Jewel in the disputation.

Cox's position on the crucifix is far more ambiguous. Jewel not only identified him as one of his opponents in the disputation, but singled him out as the only acquaintance of Peter Martyr among those 'who once had some show of common sense', but were now carried away to an unbelievable 'degree of insanity'. Yet there is a draft of a letter to the queen among the Petyt manuscripts which, although unsigned, is endorsed in a sixteenth-century hand: 'Reason of B: Cox why he cold not celebrate in ye Q: chappell the crosse and lights being there.' An important section of the letter has corrections in Cox's handwriting in which he begs Elizabeth 'to peruse the consyderations which move that I dare not minister in yor grac chappell the lights and crosse remayning'. The letter then goes on to argue, as did the joint petition to the queen, that the second commandment forbids men from setting up 'an image in the temple of God'. Lumping all the 'learned and godly clergy' together, the author declares that they think this commandment 'undispensable', and he squarely puts the issue to Elizabeth as a clear-cut decision between 'the protestants as thei terme them on the one syde and the papists on the other'. On a second sheet of biblical proof texts in Cox's own hand, he closes his letter to the queen with the plea that she 'force not my conscience' lest he be consigned to hell. We have no way of knowing whether or not Cox ever sent the letter, but we do know that the queen's insistence, aided perhaps by persuasions of such men as Parker, brought Cox to the point where he was even willing to argue the legality of setting up the images once again in the churches.[2]

[1] *Parker Corr.*, p. 379, Parker to Cecil, 6 February 1571.
[2] Inner Temple Library, Petyt MSS. 538: 47, fos. 555–6. Strype has reprinted the letter (*Annals*, I, part II, 500–3). I am most grateful to Dr J. Conway Davies for his

A letter which Cox wrote to Peter Martyr shortly after his con-secration on 21 December 1559 contains a hint of his change of mind:

We are only constrained, to our great distress of mind, to tolerate in our churches the image of the cross and him who was crucified: the Lord must be entreated that this stumbling-block may at length be removed.

Cox might be in great 'distress of mind', but he seems willing to tolerate the stumbling-block if it cannot be removed. Unlike Jewel and Sandys, he never suggests that he might resign or be deposed from the episcopate. By 4 March 1560, Cox wrote quite neutrally of the disagreement to the Lutheran George Cassander, asking for his opinion on the use of the cross:

There does not exist an entire agreement among us with respect to setting up the crucifix in churches, as had heretofore been the practice. Some think it allowable, provided only that no worship or veneration be paid to the image itself: others are of the opinion that all images are so universally forbidden, that it is altogether sinful for any to remain in churches, by reason of the danger so inseparably annexed to them. But we are in that state, that no crucifix is now-a-days to be seen in any of our churches.

As Cox undoubtedly expected, Cassander replied in defence of the use of the image of Christ on the cross which he 'was unwilling should be regarded as superstitious'.[1]

The ranks of the reformers which closed against Elizabeth's policies during the parliamentary session in the spring of 1559 began to split before the end of the year. The queen had determined not only to keep her chapel cross, but to restore to parish churches the rood crucifix acompanied by the 'Mary and John'. Some reformers so opposed the queen in this matter that they were prepared to sacrifice advancement to the demands of conscience for the second time in their lives. Parker and others disagreed with the queen's judgment, but not thinking images absolutely forbidden, they were

opinion identifying the handwriting as that of Cox. The section of the letter which specifically mentions the chapel appears not only to have been corrected in the words quoted, but subsequently completely crossed out.

[1] ZL, I, 66, Cox to Peter Martyr; II, 41–2, Cox to Cassander, 4 March 1560; II, 42–7; quotation on p. 44; Cassander to Cox.

prepared to obey. The persuasion of Cox was a signal victory for Elizabeth. Her brother's tutor had been a significant figure in the English Reformation since the latter days of King Henry, and even though the more militant reformers bitterly resented his role at Frankfort, he had, if anything, increased his stature during the Marian exile. Initially agreeing with the more militant reformers, he came over to join Parker and other moderates who were willing to restore the images. I would hazard the guess that of the other bishops chosen by early March 1560, Barlow, Bullingham, Guest, Merrick, and Young also belonged to this group of moderate reformers. The division among the new bishops stood in striking contrast to the unity of the reformers a year earlier. In the course of a dispute arising later in 1560 out of Sandys' visitation in Worcester, Parker accused the former exile with his 'Germanical nature' of scheming with Grindal to undermine his metropolitical authority. The breach did not heal easily.[1]

In spite of the fears of Jewel and Sandys, no one resigned, nor was anyone deposed. The tempestuous controversy was over in March as quickly as it had begun in October, and since images were not restored to parish churches, the records of the controversy have lain largely neglected by historians. When Jewel wrote to Peter Martyr on 5 March, he calmly remarked that 'religion is now somewhat more established than it was'. Sandys, in his tantalizingly brief summary of the controversy, described the dénouement:

God, in whose hands are the hearts of kings, gave us tranquility instead of a tempest and delivered the church of England from stumbling blocks of this kind: only the popish vestments remain in our church, I mean the copes; which, however, we all hope will not last very long.

The most curious part of Sandys' account provides the clue to the resolution of the controversy. He concludes his discussions of the dispute over the *crucifix* with a comment about *copes*. The concession of copes would have contributed to the peace only if the dispute over images had been broadened to include vestments.[2]

---

[1] *Parker Corr.*, pp. 124–7, Sandys to Parker, 24 October 1560.

[2] *ZL*, I, 71 and 73–4, Jewel to Peter Martyr and Sandys to Peter Martyr, 5 March and 1 April 1560.

Vestments have been on the periphery of our accounts of the controversy. When de Quadra on 9 October told of the queen's restoration of the ornaments, he also noted that the clergy wore vestments 'as they do in our services'. The ornaments rubric had prescribed the vestments but, at least in London, both copes and 'vestments' had been burned, presumably with the approval of the Visitors. In St Paul's on 12 August, clergy were ordered to wear 'onelye a surplesse in the service time'.[1] The surplice at the Eucharist may have been another innovation to greet Elizabeth on her return to Whitehall. It is difficult to know if de Quadra referred to copes or to the traditional Mass vestments in the Chapel Royal, alternative uses for the Holy Communion according to the ornaments rubric.[2] De Quadra, as a bishop, would have been able to distinguish between them, but his reports were probably secondhand. Sampson in January wrote of the three ministers wearing the 'golden vestments of the papacy'.[3] Since, in the fifteenth century, the general word 'vestment' was also specifically applied to the chasuble, the main garment of the celebrant, Sampson just might mean that the three ministers were decked out in chasuble, dalmatic, and tunicle, but his words may merely refer to three copes. Although the main controversy in these months had been over images, a dispute over vestments hovered in the background.

The clue to the resolution of the controversy may lie in the regulations of those elusive documents, the 'Bishops' Interpretations'. They incorporated a compromise on the use of vestments which no longer authorized the use of a chasuble ('vestment'):

That there be used but only one apparel as the cope in the ministration of the Lord's Supper, and the surplice at all other ministrations. And that there be no other manner and form of ministering the Sacraments, but as the Service book doth precisely prescribe, with the declaration of the Injunctions, as for example the communion bread.[4]

[1] See above, pp. 184–6; Wriothesley, II, 146.
[2] The 1549 Prayer Book ordered either vestment, perhaps intending the cope to be worn when only the ante-communion was to be said.
[3] *ZL*, I, 63, Sampson to Peter Martyr, 6 January 1560.
[4] Frere, *Visitation Articles*, III, 61; cf. III, 70.

May not this article preserve the substance of a compromise already achieved between 4 February and 5 March 1560? The antagonists were, on the one hand, Queen Elizabeth, reluctantly represented by Parker and Cox and, on the other hand, more militant reformers, represented by bishops who were willing to lose their sees rather than to restore images to their churches. But what mention of images or crucifixes? None—for that was the compromise! Silence confirmed the pragmatic *status quo*. Elizabeth would continue to keep her chapel crucifix and candlesticks, but she would not put the consciences of the exiles to the test by insisting that the cross and Mary and John be set up elsewhere. When she gave specific orders a year and a half later for the retention or reconstruction of rood beams and screens, she ordered no statues, but only a 'convenient crest'. Had Elizabeth had her way, it would have been the traditional statuary rather than her royal arms which would have adorned the roods. According to this agreement the chasuble would not be used at Holy Communion, but the cope would invariably take its place. This reconstruction of the compromise makes sense out of Sandys' statement that by conceding copes, he and like-minded bishops had won their battle to keep images out of the churches—and to hold their episcopal offices as well.

Why did Elizabeth give ground and compromise again? She had designed the Injunctions to allow legitimate images, such as the crucifix, to remain in the churches, but the Visitors had so interpreted them as to justify a wholesale destruction. Off on her progress, Elizabeth either did not know of the iconoclasm, or she felt unable to restrain the Visitors who were, after all, securing the subscription of the great majority of English clerics to her settlement. When she returned to London to face an ecclesiastical *fait accompli*, she immediately ordered the ornaments to be restored to her chapel, and by the beginning of 1560 she was pressing to restore crucifixes throughout the kingdom. But she could only implement the policy by insisting on it against the better judgment of the whole body of her chosen episcopate, and she contemplated the possibility that a good portion of these bishops would refuse to continue in their posts. Such a consequence could wreak havoc on the adjustment of the church to its new conditions. During Holy Week of the previous year, she had concluded that she dare not risk the success of the whole settlement in possible religious chaos. She arrived now at a similar conclusion. Once again she drove a hard bargain—a bargain which wholly satisfied neither herself nor the bishops, but one with which she and they could both live.

In an undated letter to the queen, the three episcopal members of the Ecclesiastical Commission wrote:

We have of late in our consultations devised certain orders for uniform and quiet ministration in religion. We trust your gracious zeal towards Christ's religion will not [disapprove] our doings, though such opportunity of time hath not offered itself as yet to be suitors to your princely authority to have a public set synod to the full determination of such causes.

Whenever the letter may have been written, we may safely assume that certain orders constituted the 'Bishops' Interpretations' at some stage of their evolution.[1] The only item of the Interpretations to which the queen would be likely to take exception is that on vestments, for this explicitly modified the legal terms of the 1559 settlement by abolishing the chasuble. The commissioners were not seeking royal assent but they 'trust' that she will not disapprove. This suggests that she had already indicated that she would tolerate the compromise—even if she refused to confer her royal assent upon its provisions. The commissioners, with their episcopal brethren, were free to enforce them. The three commissioners included, of course, three of the principals in the disputation over the images: Parker, Cox, and Grindal.

The queen's refusal to grant her royal assent to the compromise over images and vestments would explain the multiplicity of titles in the three extant MSS of the Interpretations:

(1) Resolutions concerning the Injunctions.
(2) Declarations of Injunctions and Articles for ministers and readers.
(3) Resolutions and orders taken by common consent of the bishops,

---

[1] *Parker Corr.*, p. 130. W. P. M. Kennedy's reasons for dating the letter after February 1561 are not completely convincing (*Studies in Tudor History* (London, 1916), p. 159).

for the present time until a synod may be had for observation and maintenance of uniformity in matters ecclesiastical throughout all dioceses in both provinces.

The commissioners could act independently of the queen, whose governing rights they, as commissioners, represented. Since she withheld specific authorization, they eventually secured the approval of their fellow bishops who agreed to enhance the Interpretations with the authority of their 'common consent'. The bishops were forced to reach, perhaps unconsciously, towards rights inherent in their episcopal office.[1]

The controversy arising from the 'little silver cross' produced the first serious disagreement among reforming clerics of the Elizabethan church, and the new bishops found themselves ranged on both sides of the issue. Only by giving up enough ground to win the unanimous conformity of the bishops did Elizabeth assure the church of a continuation of the relatively smooth transition to the new settlement under the leadership of the men she had chosen.

MARRIED CLERICS AND AN ANGRY QUEEN

Elizabeth unquestionably would have preferred a celibate clergy. Reports reached Roman Catholic exiles on the continent that she would never receive wives of clerics at court, and her godson John Harington described several incidents illustrating her aversion to clerical marriage. Elizabeth's parting words to Mrs Parker after an entertainment at the archiepiscopal palace may be apocryphal, but the anecdote illustrates her well-known attitude: 'And you,... *Madam* I may not call you, and *Mistris* I am ashamed to call you, so I do not know what to call you, but yet I do thank you.'[2]

In the very choice of Parker for the primacy at the outset of her reign, Elizabeth had committed herself to married clerics. But her injunction on clerical marriages with its requirement for official

[1] Frere, *Visitation Articles*, III, 59, 59n., and 68.
[2] Sander, *Anglican Schism*, p. 280; John Harington, *Nugae Antiquae*, II, 16, 17, 46, 122, 151; Neale, *History*, x (1925), 224.

approval bespoke her conviction that priests' wives did not often adorn the church's ministry. She did not reintroduce Edwardian legislation on the subject, and before the first Parliament was out, Sandys angrily wrote to Parker that she 'will wink at it, but not establish it by law, which is nothing else but to bastard our children'.[1] Many of the reformers would have preferred the greater assurance of a statutory declaration.

The summer royal progress in 1561 through Suffolk and Essex had revealed to Elizabeth a distressing 'nakedness in religion', and led, for one thing, to her royal order of October demanding the proper appointments and repair of parish churches.[2] Cecil warned Parker on 12 August of the queen's anger and of her insistence that lack of clerical discipline was related to clerical marriage:

I have had hitherto a troublesome progress, to stay the Queen's Majesty from daily offence conceived against the clergy, by reason of the undiscreet behaviour of the readers and ministers in these counties of Suffolk and Essex. Surely here be many slender ministers, and such nakedness of religion as it overthroweth my credit. Her Majesty continueth very evil affected to the state of matrimony in the clergy. And if [I] were not therein very stiff, her Majesty would utterly and openly condemn and forbid it. In the end, for her satisfaction, this injunction now sent to your Grace is devised. The good order thereof shall do no harm.... The bishop of Norwich is blamed even of the best sort for his remissness in ordering his clergy. He winketh at schismatics and anabaptists as I am informed. Surely I see great variety in ministration. A surplice may not be borne here. And the ministers follow the folly of the people, calling it charity to feed their fond humour. Oh, my Lord, what shall become of this time?

Three days earlier from Ipswich Elizabeth had issued the injunction of which Cecil wrote. No 'head or member of any college or cathedral church' in the realm was to have 'his wife or other women... haunting' his cathedral or collegiate lodgings. The presence of 'wives, children, and nurses' had created 'no small offence...to the intent of the founders, and to the quiet and orderly profession of

---

[1] *Parker Corr.*, p. 66, 30 April 1559.
[2] See above, pp. 149–51.

study and learning'. The order reached the ears of Machyn in London before the end of the month.[1]

The bishops were dismayed. Cox wrote to Parker that the rule was reasonable enough for colleges where students 'should be in all quietness among themselves', but that it was disastrous for cathedrals. He thought it would only encourage non-residency, and he cited Ely where he had one permanent resident prebendary—a married priest.[2]

Parker who was shortly 'daily and hourly' deluged with complaints, needed no help to reach the same conclusion:

Horsekeepers' wives, porters', pantlers' and butlers' wives, may have their cradles going, and honest learned men expulsed with open note, who only keep the hospitality, who only be students and preachers, who only be unfeigned orators, in open prayers for the Queen's Majesty's prosperity and continuance; where others say their back pater-nosters for her in corners.

The archbishop had a painful interview with the queen, hoping to persuade her to rescind the order. He described it to Cecil:

I perceived her affection to be such toward the state of her clergy that I can but lament to see the adversary so to prevail....I was in horror to hear such words to come from her mild nature and christianly learned conscience, as she spake concerning God's holy ordinance and institution of matrimony. I marvelled that our states in that behalf cannot please her Highness....The Queen's Highness expressed to me a repentance that we were thus appointed in office, wishing it had been otherwise...

I have neither joy of hours, land, or name, so abused by my natural sovereign good lady: for whose service and honour I would not think it cost to spend my life....I have, for the execution of her laws and orders, purchased the hatred of the adversaries, and also, for moderating some things indifferent, have procured to have the foul reports of some Protestants, yet all these things thus borne never discomfited me, so I might please God and serve her Highness. But yesterday's talk, with such earnest forcing that progress-hunting Injunction made upon the clergy with conference of no ecclesiastical person, have driven me under the hatches, and dulled me in all other causes.

---

[1] *Parker Corr.*, pp. 148–9, 12 August 1561, Cecil to Parker; p. 146, Order of Queen Elizabeth, 9 August 1560; Machyn, *Diary*, p. 265.
[2] *Parker Corr.*, pp. 151–2; Cox to Parker, undated.

The outburst of such heartfelt despair on the part of the sober archbishop could only have arisen from what was to him an unprecedented and unjustifiable display of royal fury.[1]

What had caused the intensity of Elizabeth's anger? It does not seem likely to have been merely the incongruous sight of the effects of family life in cathedral closes and collegiate quadrangles. She had bargained for that at the beginning of her reign. Now she told Parker she regretted his appointment, and probably, in the luxury of temper, she did regret it. The unusual relationship between the slovenly worship in Suffolk and the queen's order against married clerics suggests that the anger was born out of her resentment and frustration as she had, for her standpoint, given ground to the reformers on point after point. After the crisis of Parliament, she had thought that by conceding the slightly revised 1552 Prayer Book, she had won the honest support of the conservative wing of the exile party. As she saw it, they betrayed her confidence and support time and again. They had deliberately misinterpreted her visitation articles and had made them instruments of an iconoclasm she had never intended and yet could not recall. They had blocked her efforts to restore the rood statues, and it was only by the most vigorous assertion of will that she even retained the crucifix in her own chapel. The ornaments rubric had prescribed the traditional vestments at services, but she had been forced to accept a working compromise of copes at communion and surplices at other services. She undoubtedly had heard that some clerics, unrestrained by their bishops, seemed to tolerate the Prayer Book rites, which they conducted in an outrageously slipshod manner, only in order to provide an occasion for preaching. Through all of this, she knew that she depended upon the very bishops who, from her standpoint, were not keeping faith with her. The clerics who owed their fortunes—and perhaps their very lives—to her continued rule were undermining ecclesiastical foundations which she considered important and which she had expected them to secure.

Elizabeth must have known in moments of honesty that her injunction of 9 August could never be enforced. She could not deny

[1] *Ibid.* pp. 156–8; Parker to Cecil, undated.

the advancements of prebends and deaneries to all married clerics, nor could she force them to live apart from their wives and children. The arguments of Cox were unanswerable. Yet when she toured ill-disciplined sections of the dioceses of Grindal and Parkhurst, and realized that great numbers of ministers ignored even the watered-down rules which she had conceded to the bishops, she could not contain herself. She issued the order without consulting a single prelate. When the archbishop appeared in her presence to complain, she unleashed the torrent of emotion that she had constricted into the legalities of her injunction.

Elizabeth made some additional attempts to enforce her order in the next few months, but by her own action, not through the bishops. In the royal peculiars of Windsor and Westminster, no more wives were to be resident. Puritans continued to carp at the regulation, which was never formally rescinded, but the rule never obtruded itself into episcopal injunctions and seems to have been largely a dead letter.[1]

Former exiles formed the core of episcopal resistance to her policies, and Elizabeth's experience may have influenced her subsequent appointments. After the fateful March 1560 when she gave up the attempt to restore crucifixes, only two more former exiles received bishoprics out of the nine new men she named.[2] After the summer progress of 1561, to the one bishopric remaining to be filled, she appointed Richard Cheyney, the most conservative of all the new men of the episcopal bench.

Elizabeth's order against wives in cathedrals and colleges reveals her deep-seated dislike of married priests, but it also measures the intensity of her disappointment with her bishops, who were failing to maintain traditional liturgical standards under the new conditions of the Prayer Book settlement.

[1] Machyn, *Diary*, p. 267, 20 September 1561, Windsor; *CSP, Dom.*, *1547–80*, p. 187 (xx, 9), 18 October, Elizabeth to Dean Goodman; *ZL*, I, 164, Laurence and Humphrey to Bullinger, July 1566; II, 129–30, Beza to Bullinger, 3 September 1566.
[2] See above, pp. 44–6; included in the nine are Gilpin, who refused, but not Pilkington, who had already been named to Winchester and was later reappointed to Durham; the two are Parkhurst, named in March 1560, and Horn, named in November. Years later she appointed two other exiles: John Aylmer (1577) and Thomas Bickley (1586).

Married clerics and an angry queen

The relationship between Elizabeth and her bishops may be likened to the marriage of a couple after a very short engagement. Initially, in their ignorance of each other, each partner saw in the other only a projection of his own goals and aspirations. When, in the practical issues of life, the realities of their characters and convictions emerged, they were both disillusioned and considered themselves to have been deceived. The queen's disappointment reached its height in the summer of 1561, but even then, neither she nor the bishops wanted a divorce.

VESTMENTS AND IMAGES IN THE CONVOCATION OF 1563

As the militant reformers came to Convocation in 1563, they set great store by their plans to do away with the traditional vestments and the outdoor clerical caps and gowns. Images were of less immediate concern, but reformers in both houses were prepared with proposals to eliminate them as well.

The precisians in the Lower House made one specific proposal against images in 'Twenty-one articles', which won the overwhelming support of members of the house. 'Articles for government' also authorized bishops and their officials to search out 'books, images, beads, and other superstitious ornaments used in time of papistry', but this was merely a call for a more intensive application of the royal injunction against ornaments hidden away against another papal restoration. The item in 'Twenty-one articles' asked 'That all images of the Trinity and of the Holy Ghost be defaced; and that roods, and all other images, which have or hereafter may be superstitiously abused, be taken away out of all places, public and private, and utterly destroyed'.[1]

The test of 'superstitious abuse' was precisely that of the Edwardian injunction which Elizabeth had omitted from her own orders—a test which again might be expected to justify the elimination of all images. It is possible that the article was designed so that the queen

[1] For references to Convocation documents, see below, Appendix 1. The royal injunction (no. 35) did not mention books, but otherwise seems to have covered similar ground.

herself might keep the 'little silver cross'. Who would dare accuse her of superstitiously abusing her ceremonial oddity?

This item suggests that the reformers had exaggerated during the height of the controversy over the roods when they claimed that all crucifixes outside the Chapel Royal had been removed and destroyed. It furthermore suggests that the 1560 compromise between queen and bishops to keep the *status quo* in images may have restrained them from embarking on any more widespread iconoclastic campaigns. Undoubtedly statues continued to be removed and church interiors whitewashed, but a parson and congregation determined to keep the more restrained and scriptural evidences of medieval artistry just might have been able to do so. In general the contemporary episcopal articles of inquiry and injunctions are ambiguous in their orders about images, although both Parkhurst and Horn were particularly concerned to eliminate images of the Trinity, and Sandys and Grindal specifically included 'crosses' in their lists of monuments of idolatry and superstition.[1] The precisians proposed in 'Twenty-one articles' to destroy all the images which legally remained under the regulations in force.

In the bishops' draft of the Thirty-nine Articles of Religion, they incidentally authorized a new book of homilies which they had prepared in advance of Convocation. One of these homilies demands our attention at this point of the Convocation story, for it bears the title 'Against Peril of Idolatry'. This homily stands out by its size alone: four times longer than any other sermon either in this book or in the first Edwardian set of homilies. Its arguments are yet more remarkable. To be expected are the warnings to the people not to keep devotional images lest they fall into superstition. But that is not the main thrust of the sermon. Rather, it seeks to prove by scriptures, the fathers, and common sense that the second commandment forbids any images to be set up in Christian churches. The author took special pains to demonstrate that the image of Christ himself is especially offensive.[2]

[1] Frere, *Visitation Articles*, III, 90, 104, 226, 255, 285, and 323.
[2] Nineteenth-century edition with modern spelling: *Certain Sermons or Homilies Appointed to be read in Churches in the Time of the Late Queen Elizabeth...and Now*

To whom is the homily directed? The laity in parishes without a regular licensed preacher who would hear it read? The author warns them of bishops and other clergy who would lead their people astray:

If they be bishops, or parsons, or otherwise having charge of men's consciences, that...reason [that] it is lawful to have images publicly, though it be not expedient, what manner of pastors show they themselves to be to their flocks?

Some bishops seem to have been trying to convince episcopal colleagues from the pulpits of unlicensed clerics.[1]

The homily touches not only prelates, but princes as well. In a passage which came as close to the queen as the writer dared, he declared:

God's horrible wrath, and our most dreadful danger cannot be avoided, without the destruction and utter abolishing of all such images and idols out of the church and temple of God, which to accomplish, *God put it in the minds of all Christian princes*. And in the mean time, let us take heed and be wise.

The reference is unmistakable. Forbidden by the laws of God, idols and images are still tolerated by England's queen. Bishops and other clergy who concede that such images are lawful, however inexpedient they might think them to be, aid and abet sinful idolatry.[2]

This homily was undoubtedly prepared by bishops who had belonged to the party of Jewel, Grindal, and Sandys in the controversy of 1559–60, and it is, in effect, a lengthy expansion of the arguments in the letter which that party addressed to the queen when the dispute was at its height. We do not know why Parker, Cox, and other bishops of their views agreed to a homily which implicitly condemned them as poor pastors unconcerned about the salvation of their flocks. Perhaps the bishops, when assigning the various topics for the homilies, had agreed that they should respect

...*reprinted*...*Anno MDCXXIII* (Oxford, 1840; hereafter referred to as '*Homilies*'), pp. 199 and 158–9; see also pp. 173, 195–6, and 200; see below, pp. 273–6.
[1] *Homilies*, pp. 226–7; see also pp. 159, 216, 219, and 221.
[2] *Ibid.* p. 239; italics mine.

each other's work, and they honoured this promise. Perhaps Parker and his supporters conceded the homily in order to secure the support of the other bishops on issues which they regarded to be far more crucial. After they had resolved the practical issues of the controversy in the spring of 1560, the theoretical distinctions between the positions of the two groups of bishops had become rather academic and sterile. In 1560 the iconoclastic bishops had won the *de facto* right to enforce their convictions in most places in England; now they won the *de jure* right to assert their teachings against the images.

The advocates of iconoclasm might urge their people to pray that God might put their purpose 'in the minds of all Christian princes'. In England the prayers never effected their goal. The crucifix stayed in the queen's chapel, and the 'images' which in subsequent centuries reappeared in many English churches could do so without the slightest hint of illegality. Elizabeth's stand ultimately proved to be far more than a gesture of royal pique.

The more militant reformers came to Convocation determined to eliminate and simplify clerical vestments and apparel. The émigrés who became bishops had disliked the vestments from the start but, as Grindal later wrote, they had accepted their sees rather than desert their 'churches for the sake of a few ceremonies'. Hoping that they might eventually rid the church of Romish garments they would have repudiated not only the more colourful and elaborate Mass vestments and copes, but even the plain white surplice, tainted as it was with popish associations. Jewel, who had been obediently wearing the required vestments for over two years, wrote early in 1562 that the surplice was one of the 'vestiges of error' which must 'as far as possible, be removed together with the rubbish'. Jewel and other bishops would have been glad to see Convocation take some positive action against the 'rags of popery'. At the beginning of Convocation, while many reformers hoped for a positive reduction in the vestiarian requirements, the queen wanted the present requirements more strictly enforced. In Lord Keeper Bacon's opening address on behalf of Elizabeth to Parliament, he attacked clerical non-conformity: 'Many ceremonies agreed upon with the right ornaments thereof, are left undone or forgotten.' He publicly warned the bishops that the queen expected them to enforce the regulations. Some of the new prelates, who were willing enough to wear vestments themselves, were reluctant to force their more scrupulous former brethren-in-exile to wear them. The bishops sitting in the Lords were served notice by the Lord Keeper's speech that the queen was in no mood to permit further deterioration of the ornaments rubric.[1]

Vestments figured prominently in the proposals of the precisians in 'General notes', which simply asked that 'the use of vestments, copes, and surplices, be from henceforth taken away'. 'Vestments' here surely refers to the chasuble, an interesting testimony to the acknowledged legality of the traditional garb of the eucharistic celebrant, if not to its actual use.

In the Upper House, the moderate Bishop Alley wanted some action in such matters 'indifferent', since some preachers called vestments 'things of iniquity, devilish, and papistical'; he included the queen's orders for outdoor clerical apparel along with the vestments, pointing out that

it be all one in effect, to wear either round caps, square caps, or button [?] caps, yet it is thought very meet that we, being of one profession, and in one ministry, should not vary and jangle one against the other for matters indifferent; which are made politic by the prescribed order of the prince.

The broad-minded bishop would have it decided either that 'they may go as we go in apparel, or else that we may go as they do'. 'Certain articles' did not mention vestments, but in outdoor apparel it took a stand similar to Alley's: 'that ministers may be enjoined to wear one grave, prescribed form in extern apparel; and such as have ecclesiastical living, not agreeing to the same, to be discharged upon three monitions of the ordinary'. Grindal added a marginal note that this outdoor apparel should have a 'difference, although not altogether' from that used in popish times.

[1] D'Ewes, *Journals*, p. 60; *ZL*, 100 and 169, Jewel to Peter Martyr, 7 February 1562 and Grindal to Bullinger, 27 August 1566. For early examples of the Marian exiles vested, see account of Parker's consecration (Strype, *Parker*, I, 114) and Machyn's reports of court sermons (*Diary*, pp. 226 and 228).

The precisians in the Lower House wrote the drastic proposal of 'General notes' into their 'Seven articles', which thirty-four Convocation men subscribed. They would have abolished copes and surplices and substituted 'a grave, comely, and side-garment, as commonly they do in preaching', in effect, the Geneva gown. These articles also asked that clergy should not be compelled to wear the outdoor apparel of the 'enemies of Christ's gospel'. When these failed to win majority, the precisians reduced their demands in the 'Six articles' which fell short by only one proxy vote of a majority of the house. These regulations would not have touched the clerical gowns and caps for street wear, and concerning vestments they would have declared it 'sufficient for the minister, in time of saying divine service, and ministering of the sacraments, to use a surplice; and that no minister say service, or minister the sacraments, but in a comely garment or habit'. The concessions for continued use of outdoor apparel and the surplice were the most significant differences between the 'Seven' and 'Six' articles, and these changes may have won most of the additional support for the revised liturgical and vestiarian reforms. But the vote still fell one short, and the Lower House placed no proposals for vestiarian reforms before the bishops.

The majority of both houses of Convocation in 1563, if left without the queen's orders, would probably have favoured the abolition of most traditional vestments and images in the churches of England. Yet under the actual circumstances, when the precisians tried to push their reforms in these matters through the synod, the Lower House stopped some of their proposals by one vote, and the bishops disposed of the rest. The more militant bishops, on their own, scored one crack against Elizabeth's chapel cross in a homily but otherwise, in spite of many bishops' enthusiasm for further reforms, they were willing to continue the settlement of 1559 with the few modifications they had wrested from the queen. The bishops must have had many disagreements amongst themselves in Convocation, but there was no open split as there had been in 1560. As the militant reformers in the Lower House angrily declared, it was not only the queen, but the bishops who supported her who could be accused of the authorship of 'this business'. Elizabeth and her episcopal bench had successfully passed through their crises of 1560 and 1561. The queen found that she now had the tacit support of the bishops against the militant reformers who dominated the Lower House of Convocation. In the coming years, she would demand from the bishops more active support than they were yet prepared to give her, but already the division between the bishops and the militant reformers was rapidly becoming wider than that between the bishops and the queen. The reformers' unity of 1559 was in serious disarray.

THE 1565 CAMPAIGN FOR CONFORMITY

Elizabeth bided her time after Convocation, and the relative quiet which had marked her relations with the bishops since 1561 continued until 1564. Many clerics conscientiously continued to disobey the regulations for vestments and apparel, and in the autumn of 1564 portents of coming battles began to appear. The new Spanish ambassador, de Silva, reported that Cecil had warned the bishops that Elizabeth was determined to 'reform them in their customs, and even in their dress'. A few weeks later the militant-minded Lord Bedford wrote to Cecil from Berwick that he had heard of 'much ado for caps and surplices', and hoped that the church would not lose godly and learned pastors. Two other voices from the north were heard at court when the bishop and dean of Durham wrote letters to the Earl of Leicester urging that non-conformity be tolerated.[1] In December Parker put a questionnaire before Sampson and Humphrey, two of the leading and most respected non-conformists, and on the basis of their responses unsuccessfully attempted to find a form of conciliation.[2] By the beginning of 1565, de Silva thought that Leicester had managed to have the issue dropped.[3] He did not know that the real war was about to be joined.

---

[1] *CSP, Sp.* I, 387, de Silva to Philip, 9 October 1564; *CSP, For.* III, 232, 27 October 1564, Bedford to Cecil; Strype, *Parker*, III, 69–73 and 76–84, Pilkington, Whittingham to Leicester, 25 [and 28] October 1564.

[2] Strype assigns this date to a paper sent from Parker to Cecil summarizing the questions and replies of Sampson and Humphrey (Strype, *Parker*, I, 329–33 and 343–5). Parker and Guest prepared or had prepared replies to the non-conformists (I, 334–40 and III, 98–107; see also 340–3). [3] *CSP, Sp.* I, 401, de Silva to Philip, 2 January 1565.

Queen Elizabeth initiated the intense campaign against vestiarian non-conformity in a famous letter to the primate dated 25 January:

There is crept and brought into the church by some few persons...an open and manifest disorder...by diversity of opinions and specially in the external decent, and lawful rites and ceremonies to be used in the churches....Yet we thought, until this present, that by the regard which you...would have had hereto according to your office, with the assistance of the bishops your brethren,...these errors...should have been stayed and appeased....But perceiving very lately...that the same doth rather begin to increase than to stay or diminish, We...mean not to endure or suffer any longer these evils thus to proceed, spread, and increase in our realm, but have certainly determined to have all such diversities, varieties, and novelties amongst them of the clergy and our people...to be reformed and repressed and brought to one manner of uniformity...

And therefore, we do...straitly charge you...to confer with the bishops your brethren, namely such as be in the commission for causes ecclesiastical, and also all other head officers....And, thereupon, as the several cases shall appear to require reformation, so to proceed by order, injunction, or censure...so as uniformity or order may be kept in every church.

And for the time to come, we...charge you to provide and enjoin in our name...that none be hereafter admitted or allowed to any office, room, cure, or place ecclesiastical,...but such as shall be found disposed and well and advisedly given to common order...

And in the execution hereof we require you to use all expedition.

Since the bishops had failed to enforce uniformity, the Supreme Governor herself formally ordered Parker to investigate diversities, take action against the non-conformists and, in the future, to refuse church livings to clerics who would not conform.[1]

A few days earlier Cecil, who had prepared the draft, had sent it on to Parker asking him to 'alter or abridge any part thereof'. In the most recent and fullest account of the vestiarian controversy, J. H. Primus credits Cecil and Parker with 'the original impulse for the enforcement of conformity'. This is misleading. The timing and wording were details to be proposed by archbishop and secretary. That the letter expressed Elizabeth's own wishes seems unquestionable. Cecil's only doubt about his wording was 'whether she will

---

[1] *Parker Corr.*, pp. 223–7.

not have more added than I shall allow'. The queen herself probably did change Cecil's advice to the primate to use 'all good discretion' in executing the order to her own phrase that he was to use 'all expedition'.[1]

After formally receiving the queen's command, the archbishop lost no time. On 30 January he wrote to Grindal describing her orders in detail and ordering him to relay them to the other bishops of the province. The bishops were to execute 'the laws and ordinance already established', and within one month to return full accounts of the 'varieties and disorders' in their dioceses.[2]

After the prescribed month had passed, on 3 March Parker sent Cecil a rough draft of 'a book of articles' to present to the queen at an opportune time. These articles had been drawn up by an *ad hoc* six-man committee of the four bishops on the ecclesiastical commission, Parker, Grindal, Cox, and Guest, plus Horn and Bullingham. On 8 March, Parker sent the finished book to Cecil requesting him to ask Elizabeth to grant the articles her royal assent so that he and his fellow commissioners might enforce them. He warned Cecil that 'if this ball be tossed unto us and then have no authority by the Queen's Majesty's hand, we will set still'. Queen Elizabeth tossed the ball back to Parker; she refused her assent.[3]

These articles which Parker proposed in 1565 were the proto-types of the Advertisements which he and his fellow commissioners were to issue on their authority a year later, and Strype has reprinted a MS which seems to be that sent by Parker to Cecil in 1565. The preface is drafted in a form which would have clearly stated that the Queen herself decreed the regulations on her authority as Supreme Governor, but otherwise only relatively minor changes distinguished the proposed 1565 MS from the 1566 Advertisements.[4]

[1] *Ibid.* p. 223, Cecil to Parker, 15 January 1565; J[ohn] H[enry] Primus, *The Vestments Controversy: An Historical Study of the Earliest Tensions within the Church of England in the Reigns of Edward VI and Elizabeth* (Kampen, 1960), pp. 93–4; Strype, *Parker*, III, 69. It seems unlikely that Parker made the change, for in his full outline of the queen's letter for Grindal he did not include the phrase (*Parker Corr.*, pp. 227–30). [2] *Parker Corr.*, pp. 227–30, 30 January 1565.
[3] *Ibid.* pp. 233, 235, and 263, Parker to Cecil, 3 and 8 March 1565 and 12 March 1566.
[4] *Ibid.* pp. 263 and 272, Parker to Cecil, 12 and 28 March 1566; Strype, *Parker*, III, 84–93; see below, pp. 241 n. and 255.

In Parker's letter of 3 March 1565, he described the book of articles as 'partly of old agreed on amongst us and partly of late these three or four days considered'. Almost half of the items repeat directions of the 'Bishops' Interpretations', and several more regulations merely repeat Prayer Book rubrics or royal orders.[1] Several new items were designed to bring preachers under tighter episcopal control: all licences issued before March 1564 were voided, listeners were to denounce to bishops any preacher who urged any matter 'tending to dissension, or to the derogation of the religion and doctrine received', and no unlicensed person was to preach, expound, or exhort except from the homilies and other prescribed works (items 4, 5, and 9). No child was to be a godparent unless he had already been admitted to communion, and no 'superstitious ceremonies heretofore used' were to be added to the Rogationtide processions (items 17 and 21). The new articles also regularized the monthly celebrations of the Holy Communion in collegiate and cathedral churches which many bishops had already authorized in place of the weekly celebrations envisaged by the rubrics of the Prayer Book (item 10).[2] The officiant at the offices was henceforth to stand where the bishop 'shall think meet for the largeness and straitness of the church and choir, so that the people may be most edified' (item 8). This gave the bishop the right to move the officiant's place from the Prayer Book's 'accustomed place' if it seemed advisable—a sensible modification to the reformers' liking.

The outward apparel required of clergy by the Articles was clarified in nine items (30–8). Bishops were to wear their 'accustomed apparel', and the dress of other higher clerics was described in detail. The square caps and gowns were ordered for other 'ecclesiastical persons' outside their homes although 'poor parsons' were permitted

---

[1] Frere, *Visitation Articles*, III, 171–80 (Interpretations, III, 68–73).

[2] The following sets of cathedral articles and injunctions called only for monthly celebrations: Parker, Canterbury, 1560 (Frere, *Visitation Articles*, III, 79); Jewel, Salisbury, 1560 (III, 94); Grindal, London, 1562 (III, 116); Horn, Winchester, 1562 (II, 135); for Winchester College (III, 123). In Guest's inquiries of 1564, he asked whether the cathedral celebrated the Eucharist each Sunday (III, 148), but in his subsequent injunctions, he ordered celebrations only once every three weeks (III, 152).

to substitute 'their short gowns'. Clerics who were not exercising their ministry or who had refused the Supremacy Oath were forbidden to wear clerical dress. The traditional outdoor apparel was to continue to mark out the clergy as it had in the past.

The vestiarian requirements of the bishops' proposals introduced the most significant innovations. At Holy Communion in cathedral and collegiate churches, the celebrant and two assistants were to wear copes (item 11). The dean and canons of cathedrals were to wear surplice and silk hood in choir and the hood when preaching (item 12). These requirements were substantially those of the Bishops' Interpretations. Changed were the regulations for parish churches: during the Holy Communion as in other services, the celebrant was required to wear no cope, but only 'a comely surplice with sleeves' (item 13). Finally all clerics before admission to any living were to subscribe to eight simple articles promising their faithfulness to their duties and conformity in 'all external policy, rites, and ceremonies'. The concession of the surplice at Holy Communion outside collegiate and cathedral churches went a step beyond the Bishops' Interpretations and made an additional modification in the standards set by the Act of Uniformity.

Why did Queen Elizabeth refuse the sanction of the royal supremacy to these proposals by Parker? The usual answers of historians have not been satisfactory. Primus conveniently summarizes the possible reasons that he and his predecessors have proposed:

Perhaps the non-conformists' sympathizers on the queen's council effectively opposed authorization; perhaps for political reasons the queen did not want to become officially associated with measures which could prove to be very distasteful to a part of her populace; perhaps she felt that, having enforced the January 25 letter, the ecclesiastics should be able to cope with the people alone without further civil interference; perhaps, with specific regard to the book of articles she considered those articles superfluous since they required nothing more, with the exception of the voidance of preaching licenses—and in the case of vestments even a little less—than the... Act of Uniformity and her injunctions.[1]

[1] Primus, *Vestments Controversy*, pp. 95–6.

Even collectively these reasons seem inadequate. Parker desperately wanted the royal assent to enable him to establish that uniformity which Elizabeth had so forcefully demanded in her letter of 25 January. Yet she still held back. The reason most frequently imputed to her is her aversion to being officially responsible for imposing rules. This reason proves too much; it totally ignores the fact that she permitted the archbishop to refer specifically to herself and to her letter in the title and the preface of the Advertisements when they appeared in 1566. The printed Advertisements proclaim unequivocally that since Queen Elizabeth demanded uniformity, the episcopal commissioners in response devised these articles: 'Advertisements partly for due order, ... and partly for apparel of persons ecclesiastical, by virtue of the Queen's Majesty's letters commanding the same, the 25th of January, in the seventh year of the reign....' Elizabeth's willingness to send the letter and to be known to have done so would also rule out the explanation that reform-minded councillors persuaded her to withhold her assent. The queen's refusal to grant her assent affected neither the ultimate outcome of the enforcement of the regulations nor the image of her own role in initiating them.

The last two reasons proposed by Primus are closer to the mark, but they still miss the main point which is that *Queen Elizabeth would not alter the legal standards of the 1559 settlement.* She believed that her prelates had sufficient authority to proceed on their own to enforce the vestiarian requirements of the Advertisements. If she issued the Advertisements with her royal assent, she would *legally* supersede the vestiarian requirements of the ornaments rubric.

Just as in the dispute over the crucifix and the roods, Elizabeth would permit the bishops to *enforce* a standard lower than that decreed by the settlement, but she would not sanction it by her authority as Supreme Governor. The puritans could later consistently claim that, although no chasuble was in use in the Church of England, the old Mass vestments were still legally established; their episcopal opponents never directly denied it.[1] Three centuries later English

[1] The evidence on this point is summarized in the 1908 report to the Upper House of the Convocation of Canterbury: *The Ornaments of the Church and its Ministers*, by a subcommittee appointed February 1907 (no. 416), pp. 55–6 and 83.

ecclesiastical lawyers became embroiled in hopelessly tangled controversies as they sought to determine the authority of Parker's Advertisements. The ornaments rubric of 1559 could claim until 1965 to be the law of the land.

Elizabeth's determination to keep the terms of the 1559 settlement even while she would permit a lower standard to be enforced explains what otherwise seem to be capricious decisions. She refused to grant her assent to the canons of 1571 which would have raised the vestiarian requirements of the Advertisements to full legal status; she assented to the canons of 1575, 1585, and 1597 which did not touch the compromise of 1559.[1] She gave her wholehearted support to Whitgift's campaign of 1583–4 for uniformity and the eleven articles which were the scourge of puritans, but she never gave them her assent as Supreme Governor. Whitgift informed his suffragans she had yielded 'her most gracious consent and allowance' to his regulations, but this was not a formal exercise of her governorship.[2] Whitgift's articles endorsed the vestments of the Advertisements. Francis Bacon commented on Elizabeth's constancy in religious matters: 'Within the compass of one year she did so establish and settle all matters belonging to the church, as she departed not one hair's breadth from them to the end of her life.[3]

Elizabeth would not lower the legal standard upon which she had insisted in the compromise of 1559. In spite of her primate's warning in 1565, she tossed the ball back to him and his fellow bishops, and she expected them to continue the game.

The queen had judged her archbishop aright. Parker did not 'sit on his hands' as he had threatened when she failed to authorize the articles. Early in March he and other bishops met informally with

[1] Cardwell, *Synodalia*, I, 119, 126, 127, 132–8, 139–46, and 147–63. The authorization for the 1575 articles may be something less than full royal assent (pp. 132–8).

[2] Strype is misleading here, for he flatly states that Elizabeth gave these articles her 'royal assent' (*Whitgift*, I, 228). When he transcribed the letter of Whitgift to Aylmer of 19 October 1583, he changed the phrase 'consent and allowance' to 'assent and allowance', but Cardwell fortunately preserved the word *consent* (Strype, *Whitgift*, I, 233; Cardwell, *Documentary Annals*, p. 405; taken from Whitgift, I, fo. 90b). When Elizabeth granted her royal assent, the fact was unequivocally stated in the documents.

[3] Francis Bacon, *Works*, III, 477.

Sampson, Humphrey, and other non-conformists. The bishops requested Cecil to attend the meeting and, according to de Silva, he did so and warned the recalcitrants: 'Do the queen's will or worse will befall you.'[1] Later in the month, writing to Cecil, Parker sought more formal support from the Privy Council: 'If my lord of Leicester and your honour would consult with my lord keeper how to deal in this cause to do good and to pacify the Queen's Majesty, I think ye shall spend a piece of your afternoon well.' Parker suggested that these three key members of the council confer on positive action against the vestiarian offenders—an action which Leicester, at least, would probably have opposed. Parker appealed to the known will of Elizabeth; only by taking action would they pacify her. He was to be disappointed. No formal help came from the Privy Council.[2]

In their only related action the Privy Council pressed for a mitigation of the campaign at its end. In June they held an emergency meeting to consider the danger created by the imminent marriage of Mary of Scotland and Lord Darnley. As Roman Catholics, each with hereditary claims to the English throne, their marriage posed the threat that they might try to unseat Elizabeth on the plea of religion. Among various counter-measures, the councillors wanted to unite all protestants. They all agreed that since 'by the Queen's command', the bishops had raised papal hopes by enforcing 'certain apparel', Elizabeth ought 'to notify to the two Archbishops that her former command was only to retain uniformity, and that she determined to maintain the form of religion as established, punish such [Roman Catholics] as did herein violate her laws'. Some councillors—surely Bedford, Leicester, and Knollys among them—would have gone further and asked her, if the papal threat continued, to advise the archbishops to 'use moderation therein until the next Parliament, when some good uniform order might be devised for such ceremonies'. No evidence suggests that Elizabeth implemented

---

[1] *CSP, Sp.* I, 406, de Silva to Philip, 12 March 1565; see *Parker Corr.*, p. 233, Parker to Cecil, 3 March. I assume that the occasion mentioned by de Silva was the meeting held on 3 March as Parker planned; Cecil did not attend the meeting with Sampson and Humphrey on 8 March (p. 234, Parker to Cecil, 8 March).

[2] *Parker Corr.*, p. 236, 24 March 1565, Parker to Cecil; see p. 237, 7 April.

either recommendation. The Privy Councillors considered Elizabeth responsible for the vestiarian campaign; they themselves
remained out of it in 1565.[1]

Parker felt that he was fighting a lone battle without support from
the Privy Council or even from the queen who had ordered him to
take action. She disappointed him twice in March 1565. Not only
did she refuse her assent to his proposed ordinance, but she also
refused his request for a private royal letter to Grindal ordering him
to execute the law. Grindal had told Parker that with such a letter
in hand he would 'see reformation in all London'. Parker judged
that if London could be brought in order 'then is the matter almost
won throughout the realm'.[2]

A few days later, the archbishop wrote to Cecil that he marvelled
'that not six words were spoken from the Queen's Majesty to my
lord of London for uniformity of his London, as he himself told me;
if the remedy is not by letter, I will no more strive against the stream,
fume or chide who will'.[3] Parker expected Elizabeth to issue a
special order to Grindal. It does not seem likely that she failed to do
so from lack of interest in uniformity nor from a desire to put the
onus of unpopularity on the archbishop. She had abundantly
demonstrated concern for uniformity, and Grindal certainly knew
that she had initiated the present campaign.

Elizabeth probably did not think it her place to order one of
Parker's suffragans to obey an unequivocal command that she had
already relayed to the archbishop in proper form. It could set a
precedent that would allow any bishop to refuse the metropolitan's
order until he heard directly from the queen. She refused to write to
Grindal probably because she would not subvert ecclesiastical order—
even at the primate's own request. Ironically, it was to be Grindal's
own refusal as archbishop of Canterbury in 1575 to obey her order
to end the 'prophesyings' that forced her to disregard this policy
and write directly to the bishops.[4]

---

[1] *CSP, For.* VII, 384–7, Cecil's summary of the meeting of 4 June 1565; see also Read,
Cecil, I, 320 f.   [2] *Parker Corr.*, pp. 233–4, Parker to Cecil, 3 March.
[3] *Ibid.* p. 235, Parker to Cecil, 8 March 1565.
[4] Grindal, *Remains*, pp. 467–9, Elizabeth to the bishops of the southern province,
May 1577; Strype, *Annals*, II, part II, 612–13, to the bishop of Lincoln.

Parker's position was difficult. Throughout the controversy the non-conformists publicly blamed him and his bishops as if they had foisted the campaign for uniformity on the queen. Parker felt the sting, and early in April he wrote to Cecil:

I alone, they say am at fault. For as for the Queen's Majesty's part, in my expostulation with many of them I signify their disobedience, wherein, because they see the danger, they cease to impute it to her Majesty, for they say, but for my calling on, she is indifferent.[1]

The recalcitrant clerics knew they could criticize Parker with comparative impunity. Criticism of the queen, and open avowal of disobedience to her orders, was sedition. The reluctance of the non-conformists openly to criticize Elizabeth must not blind our modern eyes to her consistent role in the struggle.

Protestant Scottish lords wrote to Cecil and Leicester to encourage them in their work for the suspense of the 'late edict set forth by the Queen for tippets and caps'. De Silva reported to Philip that 'the Queen must need get angry, and has again given stringent orders that the rule is to be enforced'.[2] On Ash Wednesday 1565 Dean Nowell had the ill-timed misfortune to preach before the queen against images, an issue too closely associated with the vestments. Elizabeth interrupted him: 'Leave that, it has nothing to do with your subject, and the matter is now threadbare'.[3] The preacher stopped, and the queen departed in anger. A month later, Cardinal Charles Borromeo in the Vatican took heart from the incident and from the enforcement of clerical apparel:

The Queen is reported to give some sign of holding things Catholic in less abhorrence than she did at first, having made a decree that churchmen are to wear habits in the streets as of yore, and having also censured the preacher that preached against images and the Saints.[4]

[1] *Parker Corr.*, p. 237, Parker to Cecil, 7 April 1565.
[2] *CSP, For.* VII, 314, Lords Murray and Lethington to Cecil and Leicester, 13 March 1565; *CSP, Sp.* I, 416, 7 April 1565, de Silva to Philip.
[3] *CSP, Sp.* 405, de Silva to Philip, 12 March 1565; see also *Stowe's Memoranda*, p. 132; *CSP, For.* VII, 324, Randolph to Cecil, 30 March 1565; Strype, *Parker*, III, 94, Nowell to Cecil, 8 March 1565.
[4] *CSP, Rome*, I, 171, Borromeo to Santacroce, nuncio in France, 21 April 1565.

Alexander Nowell was an earnest and zealous reformer, but he made a bad mistake when he tried to play John Knox at the court of Elizabeth.

Parker's difficulties multiplied. On the day after the archbishop had taken Nowell home from his sermon to dinner 'for pure pity', Sampson and Humphrey tried to persuade Parker that Bucer and Peter Martyr would have supported their refusal of the vestments. A month later, in recounting his woes to Cecil, Parker complained that the non-conformists claimed Grindal 'is but brought in against his will', that Bishop Pilkington 'will give over his bishopric rather than it shall take place' in Durham, and that Archdeacon Cole went about court in his non-conforming 'hat and short cloak'. At this time however, Parker was able to invalidate the preaching licence of George Withers who had preached in Cambridge for reformation of 'the university windows'. This must have reassured Parker about his own archiepiscopal authority, for a month earlier he had warned Cecil regarding Withers, that, 'if you the council lay not your helping hand to it, as ye did once in Hooper's days, all that is done is but to be laughed at'.[1]

Parker had singled out Sampson and Humphrey from the beginning of the 1565 campaign. He was aghast to find out that Grindal or the Lord Mayor had invited these eminent non-conformists to preach at Paul's Cross. He wished that they had been 'at the first, put to the choice, either conformity or depart; but they abuse their friends' lenity, on whom they trust'. Finally on 29 April Parker himself put them to the choice: either they would depart their livings or agree 'to wear the cap appointed by Injunction, to wear no hats in their long gowns, to wear a surplice with a non-regent hood in their quires at their Colleges, according to the ancient manner there, to communicate kneeling in wafer-bread.' Both men refused to observe the orders.[2]

Parker, in spite of all his doubt about authority and his desire for

[1] *Parker Corr.*, pp. 234–5, 236 and 238, Parker to Cecil, 8 and 24 March and 9 April 1565.
[2] *Parker Corr.*, pp. 239–40 and 240–1, Parker to Cecil, [about Easter] 1565 and 30 April [1565].

Privy Council support, prepared to move against both men at the queen's pleasure. He thought that he might be able to deprive Sampson of the deanery of Christ Church for, with the vacancy in Oxford, the archbishop was the ordinary. But he judged that Horn, as Visitor of Magdalen, must take action against Humphrey, president of that Oxford college. By June Sampson was deprived, and a new dean was established in Christ Church. Parker continued to try to persuade Sampson to conform and, characteristically, he also sought to mitigate the mild arrest in which Sampson had been placed.[1]

Horn seems not to have deprived Humphrey, who kept all his offices. Later in the year Horn even presented Humphrey to a benefice in Jewel's diocese. Even though Humphrey promised Jewel that he would conform when preaching in the parish if granted the living, Jewel refused to admit him.[2] In spite of Bishop Jewel's close friendship with Humphrey and his own personal distaste for vestments, he held to his principle of obedience in matters indifferent. Jewel disliked the prescribed vestments and street clothes as much as anyone, but they did not touch his conscience. He had been prepared to resign his see when the queen had threatened to restore the rood crucifixes, for that, in his opinion, would have violated God's express commandment. He took clerical garb, on the other hand, to be part of the adiaphora, and he would obey his queen in these matters. By her difficult but wise decision in the spring of 1560 to bend to the reformers' wishes in images, Elizabeth had saved John Jewel's valuable services for the church and had won his loyalty to her rule. In any judgment of Queen Elizabeth's governorship of the Church of England, Jewel's episcopacy ought to be counted full measure.

In spite of all Parker's grumblings, uncertainties, and admini-

---

[1] Dixon, *History*, VI, 60–61 n.; *ZL*, I, 175–6 (no. 75), Grindal and Horn to Bullinger and Gualter, February 1567; II, 162 (no. 62), Withers to Elector Palatine; *Parker Corr.*, pp. 243–5; Sampson to Parker, Parker to Cecil, Parker to Sampson, and Parker to the earl of Huntingdon; 3 and 4 June 1565.

[2] Jewel, *Works*, ed. John Ayre, Parker Society, 4 vols. (Cambridge, 1845–50), IV, 1265; Jewel to Parker, 22 December 1565; Strype, *Parker*, I, 370, Humphrey to Jewel, 20 December 1569.

strative loneliness, he carried through the campaign successfully as far as he could. He did the queen's bidding in her way by using his own ecclesiastical authority. Whether or not the Privy Council's June worries had anything to do with the relative quiet of the summer and autumn of 1565, the spring campaign had really run its course. A year later he could even look back on the difficult months with satisfaction, commenting that the campaign had brought 'to the most part of the realm an humble and obedient conformity', although 'some few persons...more scrupulous than godly prudent' still refused obedience.[1]

The example of Sampson may have convinced many priests that it was foolish to suffer deprivation for the sake of a few garments. As Bullinger later wrote to Coverdale, when he had been consulted on the dispute, he had limited his advice to the vestiarian issues and his 'chief object was this, to convince those who think it better to desert the churches of Christ than to adopt those habits, that it would be more advisable to adopt the habits, and at the same time remain with the churches committed to their charge'. The episcopal former exiles and their Swiss correspondents saw a sinister danger in pursuing too rigorous a policy. If they pushed the queen too far, she might entrust the church's leadership, as Bullinger once warned, to 'papists or else to Lutheran doctors and presidents'. They were well aware that her most recent episcopal appointment had been Richard Cheyney, and they wanted no more of his conservative convictions beside them on the episcopal bench. When the bishops who were reluctant to enforce vestiarian requirements realized the queen's determination, for the most part they were to come around to Parker's position and at least make some show of enforcing them.[2] Parker bore most of the responsibility for executing the 1565 campaign. In the next year he was to shift some of the load on to his fellow bishops.

[1] *Parker Corr.*, p. 273, Parker to Grindal, 28 March 1566.
[2] *ZL*, II, 136, Bullinger to Coverdale, 10 September 1566; I, 234 (appendix II), Bullinger to Horn, 3 November 1565; see also I, 169 (no. 73), Grindal to Bullinger, 27 August 1566; I, 176–7 (no. 75), Grindal and Horn to Bullinger and Gualter, 6 February 1567.

Elizabeth opened the 1566 campaign to establish uniformity in an interview on 10 March with Parker, Grindal, and possibly Horn and Young. When Parker informed the queen that some 'precise folk' would prefer prison to conformity, 'her Highness willed [him] to imprison them'.[1] If we may believe the reports reaching the Spanish ambassador, Elizabeth may have told Grindal what she had been unwilling to put in writing the previous year: 'The Queen believed, or was informed, that the bishop of London would not execute the order very zealously, and she rated him soundly and threatened to punish him for an anabaptist, with other expressions of the same sort.' Since the queen spoke in the archbishop's presence, her action could not be as easily interpreted as a circumvention of his metropolitical authority.[2]

Parker suggested in a letter of 12 March to Cecil that he had delayed pressing for the conformity of remaining recalcitrants because of pressure put on him to yield to 'the state of the times'.[3] Probably this was the work of the same councillors who had made similar pleas the previous June. Parker also complained that some preachers had not worn the tippet at court 'and had nothing said to them for it'. Just possibly these preachers had, in fact, reminded the queen that it was time to demand that her bishops renew the campaign for uniformity.

On 26 March, Archbishop Parker and Bishop Grindal, assisted by their fellow commissioner Dean Goodman and other lesser clerics, held a meeting of ninety-eight London priests, demanded written promises of conformity, and suspended the thirty-seven who refused to sign.[4] The archbishop had understood that the queen was pre-

---

[1] *Parker Corr.*, p. 278, Parker to Cecil, 12 April 1566; p. 273, Parker to Grindal, 28 March; *CSP, Sp.* I, 553, de Silva to Philip, 25 May (these may not all refer to the 10 March meeting).

[2] *CSP, Sp.* I, 553, de Silva to Philip, 25 May 1566.   [3] *Parker Corr.*, pp. 262–4.

[4] *Parker Corr.*, pp. 269–70, Parker to Cecil, 26 March 1566; *ZL*, II, 148 (no. 158), Withers and Barthelot to Gualter and Bullinger, August 1567; *Stowe's Memoranda*, p. 135; Strype, *Grindal*, pp. 144–6.

pared to send 'some honourable' to such a meeting, and he had
attempted to secure the presence of Cecil, Bacon, and Northampton,
but no privy councillor appeared. The non-conformists were faced
with their own ecclesiastical superiors and not a mixed clerical and
civil tribunal. An interesting change from the previous year is the
wholehearted support which Grindal seems to have given the archbishop. Perhaps the queen's hard words had persuaded him that she
would not be likely to change either her mind or her policies.[1]

Parker made one more attempt in March 1566 to gain the royal
assent for the ordinances drawn up the previous year, hoping that
the queen might at least authorize those for 'particular apparel'. The
queen did not yield, but this time Parker was finally ready to act on
his own without her formal assent. On 28 March he sent Grindal a
printed copy of the Advertisements with orders to enforce them in
London and to convey them to the other bishops of the province.
On the same day the archbishop wrote to Cecil: 'And where the
Queen's Highness will needs have me assay with mine own authority
what I can do for order, I trust that I shall not be stayed hereafter.'
Parker was now convinced that he might count on the queen's
support if he went ahead to issue the requirements. He boldly told
Grindal, 'We have full power and authority to reform, and punish
by censures of the church all and singular persons which shall offend.'
Parker informed Grindal that the non-subscribing London clerics
were to remain suspended for three months, and if they had not yet
agreed to conform, patrons might present new candidates 'as though
the...persons so offending were dead'.[2]

The Advertisements were published with the title and preface
which, as we have noticed, explained that the queen had ordered the

[1] *Parker Corr.*, pp. 267–9; Parker and Grindal to Cecil and Parker to Cecil; 20 and
25 March 1566. An undated letter from Grindal to Cecil probably belongs here and
not as calendared in November: 'The Archbishop...hopes to meet the Lord
Keeper, you and others of the Council tomorrow at Lambeth on this matter of
apparel. I have moved my Lord Keeper, and I find him very willing.' (*Calendar of
State Papers, Domestic Series, of the Reign of Elizabeth, Addenda, 1566–79*, ed. Mary
Anne Everett Green (London, 1871), p. 20 (XIII, 40), hereafter called *CSP, Dom.
Add., 1566–79*.)
[2] *Parker Corr.*, pp. 263 and 272, Parker to Cecil, 12 and 28 March 1566; pp. 272–4,
Parker to Grindal, 28 March.

primate to enforce uniformity and that consequently he and other episcopal members of the ecclesiastical commission issued these orders. Parker might argue that there was nothing in the regulations against the 'law of the realm', but Elizabeth knew that the surplice at Holy Communion in parish churches was not the vestment envisaged by the ornaments rubric.[1] Both archbishop and queen apparently agreed that, given the leadership and state of the church, the full requirements of the ornaments rubric were unenforceable, and that only a lower standard could be maintained in practice. The solution pleased Parker; Elizabeth realistically tolerated it. The Advertisements carried royal approbation, but not royal assent.

So far the campaigns for conformity seem to have been limited to the southern province. The previous summer Bishop Pilkington of Durham and the earl of Bedford attempted to procure the services of Sampson as a preacher in the border town of Berwick; Bedford left the problem of ceremonies to the queen's pleasure, although as far as he knew 'the same were never seen to have been observed in these rude parts'. Except for the possible attendance of Archbishop Young at the meeting with the queen on 10 March, the records contain no evidence of earlier efforts for conformity in the northern dioceses. But before the end of April Parker commented that the queen had 'willed my lord of York to declare her pleasure determinately to have the orders go forward'. The Advertisements were to be enforced throughout the land.[2]

Parker, having finally moved ahead on a large-scale assault on the non-conformists by his own authority, expected that at some point his orders would be backed up by the Privy Council. In the first part of April the archbishop ordered Robert Crowley to be confined to his house until the council should call him to judgment. In addition to Crowley's archdeaconry of Hereford, which had entitled him to attend the 1563 Convocation, he also held a canonry of St Paul's and a London parish. A signer of the New Discipline in Frankfort and the 'Seven articles' in Convocation, he had refused to allow clerks

---

[1] Strype, *Parker*, III, 84–5; *Parker Corr.*, p. 272, Parker to Cecil, 28 March 1566.
[2] *CSP, For.* VII, 408 and 415; Pilkington to [Bedford] and Bedford to Cecil, 20 and 29 July 1565; *Parker Corr.*, p. 280, Parker to Cecil, 28 April 1566.

vested in surplices into his church for a funeral. When the council had still not called Crowley after three weeks, the disconsolate primate complained to Cecil:

I utterly despair,...and therefore must sit still, as I have now done, alway waiting, either her toleration or else further aid. Mr. Secretary, can it be thought, that I alone, having the sun and moon against me, can compass this difficulty? If you of her Majesty's council provide no otherwise for this matter than as it appeareth openly, what the sequel will be *horresco vel reminicendo cogitare.*

Parker cited the council's support for uniformity under Edward, and asked how he could possibly hope to accomplish 'that the Queen's Majesty will have done'.[1]

Before May was out, the council finally called Crowley and four other recalcitrant clerics. After the offenders fell on their knees and pleaded for mercy, the council sent them as prisoners to Horn, Cox, and Parkhurst for 'so long as the queen and her council shall think fit'.[2] About 6 June, Parker wrote with satisfaction to Walter Hadden: 'With the assistance of the Queen's Majesty's council we have dispersed a few of the heads of them...to school them, or else at least to have them out of London, till we see cause to restore them their liberty.'[3]

The sequence of events suggests that Elizabeth deliberately withheld the support of the Privy Council until Parker had done all he possibly could on his own authority. Then, when his orders were openly flouted, the Privy Council acted to punish open contempt of episcopal authority. Parker's invocation of Edwardian precedent was much to the point, but not as he thought. In Edward's years the council had not only supplemented episcopal authority, but at times it had for all practical purposes supplanted normal ecclesiastical authority. What Parker failed to realize was that if councillors were brought in at an early stage, as he wanted, the independent Privy Council would not be merely a support to his archiepiscopal

[1] *Parker Corr.*, pp. 275–80, Parker to Cecil, 3, 4, 12 and 28 April 1566.
[2] *ZL*, II, 119, Abel to Bullinger, 6 June 1566; *Stowe's Memoranda*, pp. 138–9.
[3] *Parker Corr.*, p. 285 (*CSP, Sp.* I, 564, de Silva to Philip, 29 June; see Dasent, *Privy Council*, VII, 313, 27 October).

authority, but would become the real judge in ecclesiastical issues. Although Parker did not apparently recognize the distinction, Elizabeth must have insisted upon it. Her council never exercised ecclesiastical jurisdiction in the manner of her brother's council—and as some Elizabethan councillors would have wished to do.

The two major campaigns for conformity in the springs of 1565 and 1566 concluded the first major engagement between the bishops and the precisians. The tacit division which had been apparent at Convocation in 1563 had turned into open warfare. Significantly, the battle for uniformity was won in Grindal's diocese of London. The militant reformers were shortly to emerge in a new generation as full-blown puritans who would seek not only to purify the doctrine, liturgy, and discipline according to their standards, but their more advanced members would want to overthrow the episcopal government of the Church of England. They had hoped that the sympathetic bishops would bring the English Reformation to its conclusion. When this did not come to pass, the new reformers proclaimed the moral and spiritual bankruptcy of the whole prelatical ministry of the English Church, and the open struggle between puritan and 'anglican' would be on.

The queen and her bishops learned much about each other during these early years of the reign. Images and vestments provided much of the grist for the mill of their mutual education. The vestiarian debate under Edward had been only a minor flurry compared with this long and difficult struggle. The militant reformers' demands for vestiarian and decorative changes in the 1559 settlement formed only a small part of their total programme, but the first major public battles were fought over these issues. In one way this was not surprising, for these things forcefully introduced themselves in a clergyman's life. A crucifix, if present at all, was inevitably in a central position in his church or chapel. He must wear a vestment every time he conducted a service—a duty which constituted the focal point of his vocation. The clothes he was required to wear on the street were a part of his daily life. It was more than an irritation for a precisian to be forced to use these ever-present reminders of the papal past. He had rejected Roman Catholic religion in what he may have regarded as the most important decision of his life. Many such men were willing enough to muddle on with the antiquated system of finance, bad as that might be, but it was intolerable to be forced repeatedly and regularly to minister before a 'seducing idol', or to wear a 'rag of popery', or to dress in the ridiculous costume of the adversary in order to carry out daily pastoral duties. Sampson and Humphrey perhaps expressed the feelings of many militant reformers when they wrote to Bullinger: 'We must indeed submit *to* the time, but only *for* a time; so that we may always be making progress and never retreating.'[1] They could see no progress, and therefore they had stood their ground.

Although Parker led the campaigns, Queen Elizabeth was responsible for retaining the legality of images in the church and the actual use of some traditional vestments. In the year after the Advertisements were issued, several of the former émigrés explained to their friends at Zurich that Elizabeth had been unmovable. Grindal wrote that unless the non-conformists relented, they could not be reconciled, for he and his fellow bishops were 'unable to effect anything with her majesty, irritated as she is by this controversy'. Grindal and Horn wrote that by the outcries of the non-conformists against the habits, 'we have alas! too severely experienced that the mind of the queen, otherwise inclined to favour religion, has been much irritated'. Jewel commented that it was certain that 'the queen will not be turning from her opinion; and some of our brethren are contending...as if the whole of our religion were contained in this single point'.[2]

Elizabeth found that she could count on Parker's loyal compliance in the adiaphora of religion. By and large the bishops who stayed in England for most of Mary's reign seem to have followed the archbishop's lead. The queen did not so easily win the cooperation of former exiles in enforcing the settlement. The episcopal

---

[1] *ZL*, I, 161, Humphrey and Sampson to Bullinger, July 1566.
[2] *ZL*, I, 168–9, Grindal to Bullinger, 27 August 1566; I, 176–7, Grindal and Horn to Bullinger and Gualter, 6 February 1567; *ZL*, I, 185, Jewel to Bullinger, 24 February 1567; see also *ZL*, II, 138, Bullinger and Gualter to earl of Bedford, 11 September 1566; II, 144, Bullinger and Gualter to Beza; I, 287–8, Pilkington to Gualter, 20 July 1573.

émigrés were reluctant to punish men who had shared the same dangers during the reign of Mary. In exile together for similar reasons of conscience, they had known privation and insecurity, and together they had accepted the hospitality of continental protestants. They were bound in those unique human bonds that are forged when men choose to face a common adversary for the sake of some great cause. In spite of the differences among them that had arisen abroad, these mutual bonds were strong. The émigré bishops agreed with their non-conforming brethren that the church would be better off without the remaining 'relics of popery'. When it came to images, and possibly to the chasuble as well, some of them were prepared to resign the ministry rather than accept their use. Cox first refused images, then wavered, and finally came over to Parker's side in obedience to the queen. Others may have had similar doubts and changes of mind. It was not easy for the bishops to deprive fellow exiles for being true to conscience; they could not forget that they had fled England together for conscience in another day. Nevertheless, the bishops had fatefully decided in favour of obedience in things indifferent, and among these they numbered the old clerical apparel, episcopal rochets and chimeres, surplices, and even copes. For several years they wore the vestments themselves, but by and large permitted freedom to conscientious objectors. The day came to pay the price for their decision in favour of obedience, and Queen Elizabeth forced them to accept the consequences of their decisions. Some, like Jewel and Grindal, once convinced of the necessity of action, performed their painful duties with consistency and resolve. Others, like Pilkington and Jewel's old tutor Parkhurst, continued to equivocate and perhaps never fully assumed the consequences of their decisions and the responsibilities for the settlement. The non-conformists were quick to attribute the bishops' decision to worldly ambition. Human motivation is always too complex for the rough tools of the historian, but the *religious* reasons demanding obedience to the magistrate in these issues were at least as convincing as those against it—as the advice of such Zurich protestants as Bullinger and Peter Martyr testifies.

The Marian exiles returned to England with enthusiastic plans to mould the English Church into a godlier form similar to the models that they had seen abroad. They looked upon the 1559 settlement as an interim on the way to a fuller Reformation. To Elizabeth, the settlement was a greater concession to continental protestant tastes than she had ever intended to make. She discovered that her bishops were to demand even more. She conceded the images in parish churches, but retained the crucifix in her chapel. She gave up Mass vestments, and finally even the cope at communion in parish churches. She would not budge one step farther. Standing firm on the line drawn in the Advertisements, she gave the bishops no choice but to accept or give up their cures. Horn looked back in 1571 over the past twelve years:

Our church has not yet got free from those vestiarian rocks of offence, on which she at first struck. Our excellent queen, as you know, holds the helm, and directs it hitherto according to her pleasure. But we are awaiting the guidance of the divine Spirit, which is all we can do; and we all daily implore him with earnestness and importunity to turn at length our sails to another quarter.[1]

The queen never relinquished the helm, and the divine spirit never guided her to change her course. After she had weathered the storm of the vestiarian controversy, the course was never in doubt.

After the campaigns of 1565 and 1566, it became increasingly rare to find any of the non-conformists in the more important posts in the English Church. To them, their exclusion from high office was persecution. To the queen, it was merely logical policy that the clerical representatives of the church be expected to support its liturgy and discipline.

From Elizabeth's standpoint, she had been forced to concede far too much in the first seven years of her reign. While giving ground in matters of practical enforcement, she retained the legal standards of 1559. The return of crucifixes and chasubles to common use in the Church of England in later centuries can be credited in no small measure to the pertinacity of Queen Elizabeth, who refused to supersede the ornaments rubric or to concede the reformers' interpre-

[1] ZL, I, 248, Horn to Bullinger, 8 August 1571.

tations of her injunctions. The Advertisements represented the farthest variance from the 1559 standards which the queen would allow to be enforced. From the exiles' standpoint, the settlement remained a 'leaden mediocrity', although some of them came to find that they could minister and live quite happily within it. William Cole, however, probably expressed the disillusionment of many when he wrote to Gualter in 1579:

> You see how small a number they are reduced who sometime lived with you as exiles....But if you wish to know what is the state of religion throughout all England, it is precisely the same as it has been since the beginning of the reign of our most gracious queen Elizabeth. There is no change whatever.[1]

Was the Elizabethan church 'Erastian'? The queen determined many church policies, and, to this extent, it was Erastian—along with much of Christendom from the fourth to the nineteenth centuries. If, on the other hand, Erastianism requires that the governmental apparatus control ecclesiastical affairs, then the Elizabethan church fails to meet the test. Two centuries later, royal supremacy was to become an instrument of party politics, and the church thoroughly enmeshed in governmental machinery of the age. Yet at that same time, non-jurors, and later, tractarians would emphasize the church as a spiritual society inherently free from government control. The conflicting traditions both owed a debt to Elizabeth who had insisted on her prerogative over the spirituality, but had employed it in such a way as to free the bishops from interference from Parliament and Council.

From the time of the angry outburst of the queen against clerical marriage, the relationship of Elizabeth and her bishops unevenly but steadily improved. The outcome of the 1563 Convocation is evidence of their mutual alliance. By the middle of 1566 the united body of reformers of 1559 was completely split asunder. As upholders of the settlement, the queen and the main body of bishops were prepared to stand together against the rain of puritan attacks.

[1] *ZL*, II, 308, 28 February 1579.

6. Doctrine: definition and discipline

MARTIN LUTHER always insisted that right doctrine was what really mattered, and that if doctrine were properly reformed right Christian living and ecclesiastical policies would naturally follow. Calvin and other leaders of the Reformed tradition put much greater stress on proper reform of the worship and discipline of the church, but they really treated these as aspects of the 'edification of the members of Christ'. Edification had a wider connotation than mere 'correct teaching', and yet the Reformed vision of the church as a great 'school of Christ' is one of their glories. In differing ways, correct doctrinal formularies were absolutely central in both Lutheran and Reformed traditions. This has never been quite true in the Church of England.

Historians of the English Reformation have all given some place to the undeniable influences of the continental reformers, but far too often they have written, especially when treating of Elizabeth's reign, as if every theological breeze which crossed the sea from Germany and Switzerland brought some kind of strange alien spirit to the pure air of English religious thought. We are in the midst today of a healthy reaction against such nonsensical distortions of history. Yet we too shall err badly if we mistake parallels in the wording of continental and English doctrinal formulae for an identity of purpose and character. The doctrinal accomplishments and failures of the Convocation of 1563 provide an excellent vantage-point from which to view the English Reformation in relation to the continent, for the decisions made there in matters of doctrine reveal both the large extent to which the English Church shared in the greater European movement and also the ways in which it was a unique historical phenomenon.

The Convocation of 1563 can justly claim to have made the most significant decisions about doctrinal statements in the history of the Church of England. All the reformers came to the synod resolutely determined to nail down the church's teaching in unequivocally authoritative statements, and Convocation authorized the durable Thirty-nine Articles of Religion. The Scots in 1560 had initiated their Reformation with a Confession of Faith. Their southern neighbours only got around to definitive doctrinal statements four years after they had established their liturgy. If the symbolism of this chronology is not pushed too far, it can help us understand why the great debates in anglican churches have often centred on Prayer Book revision, and not, as in Lutheran and Reformed churches, on doctrinal statement and interpretation. But that is hindsight. Doctrine was not far from the centre of concern of many reformers in 1563. Undoubtedly it loomed large in the mind of Bishop Parkhurst when he wrote to Bullinger of his hope 'for an improvement at the approaching convocation'.

TENTATIVE DOCTRINAL DECLARATIONS

The Elizabethan reformers inherited a series of documents from the English Church during the years of independence under Henry and Edward, and they were free to draw on the plethora of doctrinal statements which had emanated from continental churches ever since Melanchthon had drawn up a confession for the Diet of Augsburg in 1530.[1]

Theologians who remained under papal obedience reacted to the doctrinal challenges of the reformers by drawing new sharp lines to delimit what they understood to be orthodoxy and heresy. In the three sessions of the Council of Trent from 1545 to 1563, the Roman Catholic Church carefully defined its teaching in extensive and lengthy decrees.

The Lutherans were perhaps most prolific in the multiplication of theological definition. After the fundamental Confession of Augs-

---

[1] The standard English collection and commentary is still Philip Schaff's 3-volume work, *The Creeds of Christendom* (New York, 1877); see also W. A. Curtis, 'Confessions' in James Hastings' *Encyclopedia of Religion and Ethics* (Edinburgh, 1910), III, 831–901; two recent collections: B. A. Gerrish, *The Faith of Christendom* (Cleveland, Ohio, 1963); and John H. Leith, *Creeds of the Churches* (Garden City, 1963); new English translation of Lutheran symbols, Theodore G. Tappert, ed., *Book of Concord* (Philadelphia, 1959).

burg, itself more than twice as long as the English Forty-two Articles of 1553, they defined and redefined their doctrine as a consequence of their own internal disputes and their controversies with Roman Catholic and Reformed. The gathering of six major Lutheran confessions in the *Book of Concord* in 1580 filled a very substantial volume. Subscribed by most of the German Protestant states, it became the doctrinal standard of much of German Lutheranism.

As the earlier works of Zwingli were largely superseded in the Reformed churches by those of Calvin, the much revised *Institutes of the Christian Religion* became the most important theological work, but it was hardly a confession of faith. Its relationship to the formal reformed doctrinal statements is rather like that of St Thomas Aquinas' *Summa* to the decrees of Trent. The Zwinglian First Helvetic Confession and Calvin's Genevan Confession, both of 1536, and the 1559 Gallican Confession are all brief declarations, roughly the length of the Forty-two Articles. But lengthier statements of Reformed teaching became common and popular. Calvin's Genevan Catechism of 1545 (French, 1541), the 1560 Scottish Confession, the 1563 Heidelberg Catechism, and Bullinger's Second Helvetic Confession of 1566 are all at least twice as lengthy and detailed as the Forty-two Articles. The 1549 *Consensus Tigurinus* and the 1552 *Consensus Genevensis* comprised extended expositions on the Eucharist and predestination. Of the major Reformed churches, only the French maintained a relatively brief standard of teaching through the sixteenth and seventeenth centuries.

Of the sixteenth-century continental churches, the Anabaptists were least tied down to long official statements of faith. A complexity of factors was responsible, including their universal status as dissenters from established religions, their isolation from the educational centres of Europe, and their primary concern for a holy life based on gospel principles rather than on theological precision.

In setting the terms of the religious settlement in 1559, queen and Parliament drew heavily on the precedents of earlier stages of the English Reformation. In doctrine the Elizabethan church inherited a series of formularies which were available for their use. The various

Henrician doctrinal statements were largely irrelevant after the Uniformity Act had been passed, but Edward's reign provided several viable possibilities for use in 1559. Of greatest significance were the Forty-two Articles of 1553—a briefer statement of Christian doctrine than almost any of the definitions of continental churches. Among the lengthier works which had been endorsed with a lesser degree of Edwardian ecclesiastical authority were the 1547 homilies and the 1553 catechism.[1]

Many decisions affecting the doctrine of the church were determined by the initial terms of the settlement. By the end of Queen Elizabeth's first year the Acts of Supremacy and Uniformity, the Royal Injunctions, and the choices of clerical leadership had determined the general doctrinal orientation of the Church of England, but they had not laid down doctrinal definitions.

The Prayer Book expressed a great many fundamental Christian convictions, but only the three catholic creeds and the brief children's catechism could qualify as formal doctrine.

The Supremacy Act as a whole implied certain doctrines concerning the church and its polity, and it also contained a proviso that the queen's commissioners might not call any teaching heresy unless so proven

by the authority of the canonical Scriptures, or by the first four general Councils, or any of them, or by any other general Council wherein the same was declared heresy by the express and plain words of the said canonical Scriptures, or such as hereafter shall be ordered, judged, or determined to be heresy by the High Court of Parliament of this realm, with the assent of the clergy in their Convocation.

The clause expresses what came to be a characteristic anglican appeal to scriptures and the patristic church. Significantly the proviso also limits the royal supremacy in the definition of doctrine. Any definition of heresy which went beyond the plain words of the Bible and the first four Councils was reserved for the joint action of Parliament and Convocation. In Elizabeth's unpublished defence prepared at the time of the rebellion of 1569 she echoed this limitation by

[1] See above, pp. 9–11, 16–17.

insisting that she claimed no 'superiority to our self to define, decide, or determine any article or point of the Christian faith and religion'.[1]

Queen Elizabeth reinstated the Edwardian Book of Homilies in her Injunctions of the summer of 1559. Non-preaching parsons were to

read in their churches every Sunday one of the Homilies, which are and shall be set forth for the same purpose by the queen's authority, in such sort, as they shall be appointed to do in the preface of the same.

To implement the requirement, the book was reprinted in 1559, and its title included the new royal authorization:

Certayne Sermons appoynted by the Quenes Maiestie, to be...read, by all persones...euery Sonday and holy daye:...And by her Graces aduyse, perused & ouersene.

In the new preface Elizabeth explained that she had had her brother's book 'to be printed anew', and that she commanded non-preachers with spiritual cure

every Sunday and holyday in the year, at the ministering of the holy communion,...after the gospel and creed...to read and declare...one of the said homilies in such order as they stand in the book, except there be a sermon.[2]

Churchwardens such as those in Prescot, Lancashire began to procure the 'homelye book' for their parishes. Using these homilies parsons began again to exhort English congregations to read holy scriptures, for 'how can any man say that he professeth Christ and his religion if he will not apply himself...to read and hear...the books of Christ's gospel and doctrine?'. They heard the emphases of the Reformation declared from pulpits in the words of Cranmer:

[1] *Statutes of the Realm*, IV, 350, 1° Eliz., cap. 1; for proviso, see *JHC*, I, 59 and 61; *JHL*, I, 574; E. J. Davis, *EHR*, XXVIII, 336, 337 and 339; Maitland, *Collected Papers*, III, 197–8; Neale, *EHR*, LXV, 330–1n.; Elizabeth's Defence (I follow her own marginal alterations), *Queen Elizabeth's Defence of her Proceedings in Church and State*, W. E. Collins, ed. (London, 1899), p. 42.

[2] See above, p. 16; Injunction no. 27 (see also no. 4); Edwardian Homilies, Jugge and Cawood, 1559, STC no. 13648; also editions in 1560 and 1562; quotations from nineteenth-century edition, *Homilies*, pp. xiii–xiv.

We be justified by faith in Christ only (according to the meaning of the old ancient authors)....We put our faith in Christ that we be justified by him only, that we be justified by God's free mercy, and the merits of our Saviour Christ only, and by no virtue or good work of our own.

Cranmer also warned them not to misinterpret this teaching, for a true lively faith 'worketh by charity', but he clearly asserted the primacy of faith. In almost contradictory words composed by Edmund Bonner, the deposed bishop of London, congregations were also warned that 'of all things that be good to be taught unto Christian people, there is nothing more necessary...than charity'. Priests exhorted their people to practise the virtues and to avoid the vices vividly described in the several other homilies. This Edwardian inheritance became the first teaching staple of the Elizabethan religious settlement.[1]

Even earlier, while the Parliament of 1559 was still sitting, two groups of opposing ecclesiastical loyalties, the Marian clergy and the Marian émigrés, issued doctrinal statements. As we have seen, the staunch Roman Catholics who dominated the 1559 Convocation protested the course of reform being debated in the Commons, and the Lower House passed a set of five articles affirming the real presence, transubstantiation, the sacrifice of the Mass, the authority of the pope, and the incompetency of laymen to define matters of faith, sacraments, and discipline.[2]

Some time before the end of April 1559 a group of Marian émigrés prepared a 'Declaration of doctrine' for the queen. John Jewel reported in a letter to Peter Martyr that it did not depart 'in the slightest degree from the confession of Zurich'. If 'confession' refers to formal doctrinal statements, then the First Helvetic Confession of 1536 as it was qualified in eucharistic doctrine by the

[1] *The Churchwardens' Accounts of Prescot, Lancashire, 1523–1607*, ed. F. A. Bailey (Preston, 1953); see purchases in 1560 and 1561, *Churchwardens' Accounts of the Town of Ludlow in Shropshire from 1549 to the End of the Reign of Queen Elizabeth*, ed. Thomas Wright, Camden Society, cii (Westminster, 1896), p. 107; *The Churchwardens' Accounts of S. Edmund and S. Thomas, Sarum, 1443–1702*, ed. H. J. F. Swayne (Salisbury, 1896), p. 105; *Homilies*, pp. 5, 24, 32, and 55; on authorship of homily on charity, see Gibson, *Articles*, p. 724.
[2] Cardwell, *Synodalia*, ii, 491–4; Strype, *Annals*, i, part i, 81; see above, pp. 86–8.

Consensus Tigurinus would have been intended. Jewel probably meant something less precise by the comment: the Declaration adequately expressed his own convictions, and he had found these convictions compatible with those of the church of Zurich.[1]

By and large the exiles' Declaration followed the Forty-two Articles. In its most striking doctrinal differences from the Articles, the Declaration omitted the specific condemnation of the scholastic phrase '*ex opere operato*' to explain the effectiveness of the sacrament, and it substituted a more positive statement of Christ's presence in the Supper.

The Declaration contains several long new expositions of doctrine. In the preface the signers claimed themselves to be 'true members of the Catholic Church of Christ'. They affirmed the dogmatic decisions of the ancient councils and claimed to be at one with the church 'according to the ancient laws of the Christian Emperors Gratianus, Valentinianus, and Theodosius'.

The émigrés appended a long explanation to the article on predestination in order to enumerate the reasons for delving into this 'most deep mystery'. They submitted an exposition of justification for three of the Forty-two Articles and added a lengthy defence to assure their readers that they did not exclude fasting, prayer, or 'other good works'. They protested their conscientious loyalty to magistrates in general, to women rulers in particular, and to their lawful Queen Elizabeth most explicitly.

The declaration is one of the minor links between the Forty-two Articles of 1553 and the Thirty-nine of 1563. Subsequent generations of Anglicans may be glad, however, that they have not had to give allegiance to the verbose meanderings of the Declaration.

Two years later the English bishops issued the one *authoritative* statement of doctrine between the parliamentary settlement of 1559 and the adoption of the Thirty-nine Articles of 1563. Usually known as Archbishop Parker's Eleven Articles, it was authorized at a meeting of the bishops at Lambeth Palace on 12 April 1561:

[1] *ZL*, I, 21, Jewel to Peter Martyr, 28 April 1559; Strype, *Annals*, I, part I, 167–72; Dixon, *History*, v, 107–16, notes, from MS.cxxi, 20, Corpus Christi College, Cambridge.

A Declaration of certain principal Articles of Religion set out by order of both archbishops metropolitan, and the rest of the bishops for the uniformity of doctrine, to be taught and holden of all parsons, vicars, and curates;...to be read...at their first possession-taking or first entry into their cures, and also after that, yearly at two several times...immediately after the gospel.[1]

Some months earlier, at least before February, the bishops who were members of the Queen's Ecclesiastical Commission had prepared the first two drafts of the 'Interpretations of the Bishops'. In one of the items of both these drafts they called for the preparation of 'one brief form of Declaration...setting out the principal articles of our religion' to be read when clergy entered their cures and twice yearly thereafter. For the time being a set of Latin articles, 'prescribed to ministers', was appended to the drafts, and this has been dubbed by Strype, 'Principal Heads of Religion'.[2]

The final edition of the 'Interpretations', possibly also adopted at the April 1561 meeting of the bishops, dropped the Latin Articles entirely and was able to refer to the English Declaration now 'already devised'. The Spanish ambassador probably misinterpreted rumours of the preliminary preparation of these Eleven Articles, for he reported to Philip on 25 March that 'the bishops frequently meet in the archbishop of Canterbury's house and are drawing up a profession of faith to send to the Concilio'.[3]

The Eleven Articles bore authority, but only that of the collective voice of the bishops who issued them, for neither queen, Parliament, nor Convocation sanctioned them. Surprisingly, the Thirty-nine Articles did not displace them. Although not uniformly enforced, church officials inquired of the semi-annual parochial readings of the Eleven Articles as late as 1582.[4] Since the loyalty of the clergy was

---

[1] Hardwick, *Articles*, pp. 357–9, text of Eleven Articles; Wilkins, *Concilia*, IV, 195 ff.; Frere, *Visitation Articles*; III, 95, item 3.

[2] Frere, *Visitation Articles*, III, 59–68; W. P. M. Kennedy, *Studies in Tudor History*, p. 159; see above, pp. 163–5.

[3] Frere, *Visitation Articles*, III, 68–73; *CSP, Sp.* I, 190, de Quadra to Philip; Brook, *Parker*, p. 105.

[4] Frere, *Visitation Articles*, III, 100, 151, 154, 158, 160, 169, 210, 220, 279 (Grindal, York Province, 1571), 297–8, 305, 326, 370, 379 (Parker, Winchester, 1575); Kennedy, *Episcopal Administration*, II, 129 (1582, Middlesex).

better secured by the fuller Thirty-nine Articles, why were the
Eleven Articles continued at the same time? The reason may be
found in their title which asserted that they were not only for the
'testification' or common consent of the clergy, but also 'necessary
for the instruction of their people'. The Thirty-nine Articles were
far too lengthy to be of real use for regular public reading—even in
the sixteenth century.[1]

Both the English Eleven Articles and the Latin Principal Heads of
Religion are largely drawn from the Forty-two Articles, and together
they provide another set of links between these and the Thirty-
nine Articles. Both new statements are brief; the Latin Articles
are more comprehensive in scope, but more sparing of repetitious
verbiage.

Against Roman Catholics, the 'Principal Heads' insist that the
vernacular ought to be the language of liturgy; they deny the authority of the pope in England; and they condemn eucharistic adoration,
the propitiatory sacrifice of the Mass, and scholastic doctrines of
transubstantiation, purgatory, and the invocation of saints. They
establish scripture and the three catholic creeds as doctrinal
authorities and declare that particular churches have the right to
determine their own ceremonies. Against Anabaptists, the 'Principal
Heads' demand an outward call to the ministry, and uphold infant
baptism. In their discussion of royal supremacy, they expressly
approve of women rulers. These Latin Articles furthermore declare
justification by faith to be a certain doctrine, explain sin against the
Holy Spirit, insist on the indissolubility of marriage, and justify the
civil death penalty, participation in war, and clerical marriage. A
section on the sacraments makes a stronger assertion of the reality of
sacramental grace in general and of Christ's eucharistic presence in
particular.

The Eleven Articles are, on the whole, far less controversial.
Unlike the 'Principal Heads', they avoid definitions of the sacraments, justification, sin against the Holy Spirit, executions and war,

[1] Hardwick, *Articles*, pp. 355–9; Kennedy, *Episcopal Administration*, I, xlviii; see below,
pp. 255–6. The first draft of Parker's Advertisements called for the reading of both
the Thirty-nine and the Eleven Articles (Strype, *Parker*, III, 85, items 2 and 3 of I).

marriage, and the defence of women magistrates. In place of the condemnation of scholastic doctrines of purgatory and invocation of saints, the English Articles are content to censure extolling of images and other 'vain worshipping of God'. They open with a new trinitarian article, and they specifically endorse the Prayer Book with its simplification of baptism and communion in two kinds. Significantly they approve the book not only as a liturgy but 'for doctrine' as well. In all other respects, the Eleven Articles echo the 'Principal Heads'.

In the Eleven Articles, the bishops promulgated a doctrinal statement which condemned certain Roman Catholic teachings and practices, but otherwise asserted little more than the doctrinal standard of the Book of Common Prayer. Apparently the mild 'Principal Heads' took stands on too many of the controversial issues of the sixteenth century for the bishops to be willing to support it or to enforce it without wider authoritative approval. In the Eleven Articles, the bishops fully preserved the doctrinal comprehensiveness which had been implicit in the terms of the settlement of 1559.

'APOLOGIA ECCLESIAE ANGLICANAE'

An Apology of the Church of England by John Jewel stands as the single major theological treatise of the earlier years of the Elizabethan church. Not until the reign of James I when Archbishop Bancroft ordered all parish churches to own Jewel's *Works* was the *Apology* to be accorded a national official status, but from its first appearance church leaders held the book in high regard.[1]

Cecil, in May 1561, wrote to Nicholas Throckmorton in Paris that he had 'caused an Apology to be written in the name of the whole clergy,...but I stay the publication of it until it may be further pondered'. Although there has been some historical ambiguity over the authorship of the book, Jewel's most recent commentator John E. Booty accepts Parker's statement that Jewel was the 'chief author', aided and advised by himself and others. Booty

---

[1] Cardwell, *Documentary Annals*, II, 126; Barnes did order the Apology for parish churches in Durham in 1577; Kennedy, *Episcopal Administration*, II, 79 and note.

judges it likely that Jewel altered and expanded the *Apology* during the summer of 1561, and by 1 January 1562 the book was published.[1]

The *Apology* was prepared with an eye to distribution abroad. Cecil immediately sent copies to Throckmorton who received it with a mixed reaction. He was disappointed that its author made no attempt to justify English retention of Catholic elements against the 'Calvinists'. Throckmorton had already written to Cecil that a French Roman Catholic had 'marvelled why the clergy of England did not fortify the ceremonies, rites, and observations retained in their church with the authority of the ancient writers and the examples of the old churches'; he further reported that a Huguenot friend had made a similar request since his own ministers 'fare as men that would pluck down an old building which consists of good and bad stuff, and when they have plucked down that patched building they leave the world often without any covered house'. Throckmorton, who schemed to win the French court to a moderate Reformation like that of England, found the *Apology* too one-sided for his purposes.

Elsewhere the book received a more enthusiastic welcome. Peter Martyr wrote to Jewel that not only he but Bullinger and the other Zurich divines 'can make no end of commending it'. When Henry Knollys and Christopher Mundt were approaching German protestants for a possible alliance with England, they took the *Apology* with them and lent it to the Calvinist Count Palatine and to the Lutheran duke of Würtemberg. The palsgrave took delight in it for its 'brevity and clearness', and the duke, who had heard evil reports of religion in England, advised Elizabeth to send it all abroad to 'serve for a defence against all backbiters'. Thomas Harding was the best of the English Roman Catholics abroad to reply to the *Apology*,

[1] Read, *Cecil*, I, 262, Cecil to Throckmorton, 8 May 1561 (from P.R.O.); John Jewel, *An Apology of the Church of England*, ed. John E. Booty (Ithaca, N.Y., 1963), p. 3, Parker to Lady Bacon in preface (also *Works*, III, 51), pp. xxxvii–xxxviii; John E. Booty, *John Jewel as Apologist of the Church of England* (London, 1963), pp. 51–5; *Parker Corr.*, pp. 148 and 161–2, Parker to Cecil, 11 August 1561 and Cecil to Parker, 1 January 1562; cf. Southgate, *Jewel*, pp. 61–2. Booty has brought to light a most interesting anonymous letter written by Jewel at Cecil's request in defence of the English Church of April 1561 (pp. 209–25).

16-2

and this dispute continued in a series of publications until Jewel's final *Defense of the Apology* in 1570. Jewel himself noted that the book had been translated into French, Italian, Dutch, and Spanish.[1]

English churches at home welcomed the *Apology* from the start. After one unsatisfactory English translation, Lady Bacon, wife of the Lord Privy Seal and sister-in-law to Cecil, provided in 1564 a vernacular version with the full approval of the author and of Parker. The *Apology* remained an unofficial treatise, useful to the government abroad and popular in England.[2]

Recent studies on Jewel's work by W. M. Southgate and John E. Booty have helped to delineate the theology of the *Apology*. Jewel moved in the theological company of moderate reformers who, on the continent, included Bucer, Peter Martyr, and Calvin and, on Lutheran and Zwinglian sides of the group, Melanchthon and Bullinger. This does not mean that Jewel derived all his theological thoughts from these men. C. W. Dugmore has recently warned that the theological writings of the English reformers were not copies of continental works 'as if they had no theological training, no knowledge of the Schoolmen or the Fathers and were utterly incapable of thinking for themselves'.[3]

Southgate's case for Jewel's distinctive use of patristic authority is convincing in spite of Booty's dissent. Southgate concludes that Jewel established not a 'declarative authority' for doctrine, but rather 'a method by which doctrine was to be found, a method fundamentally incompatible with absolute declarative authority'. In the use of that method, the fathers played a unique role:

[Jewel] never departed from the view that as individuals the fathers were but men. They had not received as individuals the special revelation from God which set the apostles as individuals apart from other men. As a

---

[1] *CSP, For.* IV, 462, 504, and 506, Throckmorton to Cecil, 28 December 1561 and 24 and 26 January 1562; V, 514 and 555, Elector Palatine to Elizabeth, 4 December 1562 and Knollys and Mundt to Elizabeth, 14 December; *ZL,* I, 339, Peter Martyr to Jewel, 24 August 1562; Southgate, *Jewel,* pp. 80–7 (Harding controversies); Jewel, *Works,* III, 186.

[2] Jewel, *Works,* IV, xviii; Booty, *Jewel,* pp. 55–6; cf. Southgate, *Jewel,* p. 55.

[3] See above, p. 243, n. 1; C. W. Dugmore, *The Mass and the English Reformers* (London, 1958), p. vii.

group, however, Jewel did regard them as set apart, as superior to other men. The 'consent of the fathers' appears to have had for him deeper meaning than the mere numerical sum of the views of individual fathers. Consent, agreement among them, was an instrument through which God had chosen to instruct his Church.

This way of using the fathers, a way which Cranmer's writings may have suggested, provides an emphasis in the writings of John Jewel which distinguishes them from those of the continental reformers with whom he was in substantial doctrinal agreement.[1]

The *Apology* was first prepared at a time when the English government was considering the admission of a papal nuncio to invite England to send representatives to the Council of Trent. The work bears the marks of that origin, and its final chapter is devoted to councils in general and to Trent in particular. The whole argument is anti-Roman and assumes that Lutheran, Reformed, and English churches can all be grouped together against Rome on one side and against Anabaptists on the other. Countering the charge that Lutherans and Zwinglians cannot agree, Jewel insists:

In very deed they of both sides be Christians, good friends, and brethren. They vary not betwixt themselves upon the principles and foundations of our religion, nor as touching God, nor Christ, nor the Holy Ghost, nor of the means of justification, nor yet everlasting life, but upon one only question which is neither weighty nor great; neither mistrust we, or make doubt at all, but they will shortly be agreed.

---

[1] Southgate, *Jewel*, pp. 217 and 189, and, in general, pp. 161–91; Booty, *Jewel*, pp. 126–49. Booty wrote: 'Southgate views Jewel as considering that the Fathers were a "primary authority in the interpretation of scriptures". Certainly Jewel did not go that far. The authority of the Fathers was limited to whatever *assistance* they might afford the investigator as he attempted to understand a difficult passage' (p. 137; I could not locate the quotation from Southgate in the published work; Booty cited it from the unpublished thesis). This is, in part, a semantic disagreement —the line between Booty's 'assistance in a difficult passage' and Southgate's 'interpretive authority' would be hard to draw. Booty seems to miss Southgate's point: Jewel differed from Calvin and other continental reformers not in his doctrine of scripture, but in his use of the fathers in interpreting scripture. Jewel's understanding of the role of the Holy Spirit, as Booty describes it, is not at odds with Southgate's theory. Jewel's use of the fathers may be close to that of Melanchthon if Peter Fraenkel's recent study rightly assesses the German (*Testimonia Patrum: The Function of the Patristic Argument in the Theology of Philip Melanchthon* [Geneva, 1961]).

Jewel's distinctive use of the fathers contains no hint that he was consciously departing from the continental reformers. Was Jewel's distinctive method, then, the result of his choice of the patristic church as the ground for his battle with Roman Catholics? Perhaps. But the fact remains: Jewel himself chose the battleground and defended it to the end.[1]

Jewel defended the English Church from the charge of departing from the catholic Church by insisting, on the contrary, that Rome had departed 'from God's word, from Christ's commandments, from the apostles' ordinances, from the primitive church's examples, from the old fathers' and councils' orders', and that England had 'returned to the apostles and old catholic fathers'. Although continental reformers also claimed to have returned to patristic standards, Jewel made the congruity of the English with ancient churches a central argument in his *Apology*. Jewel consistently insisted that the only final source of doctrine lay in the Bible, but he looked first to the fathers for help in its interpretation.[2]

In almost four years of independent life before the 1563 Convocation produced the Thirty-nine Articles, the Church of England had no definitive statement of its teaching on the many current theological controversies. Children learned the summary of their religion as they memorized the Creed, the Lord's Prayer and the Ten Commandments and learned the brief expositions in the Prayer Book catechism. At church, men again heard in English the biblical lections set aside in Mary's reign, and they imbibed the implicit teaching of the Prayer Book rites. If they did not hear sermons regularly, they again heard the reformed teachings of the Edwardian homilies. For the last two years, twice a year, they had listened to the bishops' Eleven Articles with its condemnation of selected Roman Catholic teachings, so recently banished from the realm. The lack of doctrinal definition was no great inconvenience for the Christian nurture of the vast majority of people.

---

[1] Jewel, *Apology*, p. 48; see also pp. 44 and 58 (*Works*, III, 69–70, 68 and 74); see Booty, *Jewel*, pp. 36–57. Jewel originally chose the patristic battleground in his challenge sermon at Paul's Cross which led to another literary dispute with Harding (Booty, *Jewel*, pp. 27–35 and 60–1).

[2] Jewel, *Apology*, pp. 97 and 17 (*Works*, III, 90 and 56).

It did pose a problem to bishops who needed guideposts to assure themselves and their clergy of the contents and limits of sound doctrine. The more militant reformers were scandalized, for they believed that only carefully and fully stated doctrinal agreement could provide a common understanding of the Gospel and the right ordering of church life. During these years, only an Anabaptist or a convinced Roman Catholic would find himself as cleric or layman excluded from full participation in the Church of England. The doctrinal limits of the church were as wide as it is possible to imagine them in the sixteenth century. The reformers came to Convocation determined to define those limits more clearly and to narrow them to fit their varying concepts of orthodoxy.

ADOPTION OF THE THIRTY-NINE ARTICLES

The Convocation of 1563 prepared the Articles of Religion, that doctrinal statement which remains four centuries later a classic, if anachronistic, expression of the anglican understanding of the Christian faith. Alley of Exeter put doctrine first in his proposals before the Upper House, and he urged that authorized preachers ought to teach only 'one kind of doctrine'. Although 'Certain articles' suggested that articles should be 'drawn out of the substance' of the Apology, the militant reformers' major prospectus, 'General notes', proposed the course actually followed: the Forty-two Articles 'with addition and correction as shall be thought convenient'.[1]

This, however, formed only a small part of the programme of the precisians for a thorough doctrinal reform that would have had the English Church marching right in step with their continental brethren. I am convinced that the failure of historians to recognize the potential results of this programme has been the most serious consequence of their neglect of the Convocation documents. Before I can lay this case before the reader, we must go over the better-known ground of the Thirty-nine Articles and the accompanying

[1] For references to the preliminary papers for Convocation, see appendix 1, pp. 342f.; see also above, pp. 62–4.

new book of Homilies. The story of the Articles has not been told in detail by contemporary scholars, and so we shall first consider them before returning to the militant reformers' full programme for doctrinal reform.

Although members of the Lower House of Convocation reviewed the Forty-two Articles early in their sessions, the bishops assumed the major, if not exclusive, responsibility for framing the new version. As we have seen, the archbishop of York and two of his suffragans signed the Articles along with most of their southern episcopal brethren on 29 January, and they may well have shared in the work of preparing the Articles. The signed manuscript comprises a revised version of the Forty-two Articles, with further changes indicated in red in Parker's hand. The first stage of revision might represent the consensus of the Upper House at some stage *in the course of* their ten-day deliberations on the Articles, but historians have assumed that Archbishop Parker himself, with the help of Guest and others, presented his fellow bishops with the proposed revision at the opening of discussions on 19 January. In either case, the *second* group of red-penned revisions were certainly introduced in the course of the bishops' discussions.[1]

The changes introduced in the first stage of the revision of the Forty-two Articles can be divided into several natural categories.[2] One series of changes completed and clarified the Articles as a summary of doctrine. Trinitarian dogma was filled out by a new article on the Holy Spirit and a new phrase on the eternal consubstantiality of the Son (5 and 2 of the Thirty-nine). The ecclesiastical establishment of the biblical books and a list of the Old Testament canon were added to the article on scripture (6). The articles on

---

[1] See Appendix 1, p. 352; Lamb, *Thirty-nine Articles*, pp. 13–19; Hardwick, *Articles*, pp. 123–30; Gibson, *Articles*, pp. 30–1; northern bishops signing were Young, Pilkington and Downham; these men and Best were attending Parliament (D'Ewes, *Parliaments*, p. 62).

[2] Anyone familiar with the literature will recognize my debt to the various standard discussions of these revisions, although I find none totally satisfactory: Hardwick, *Articles*, pp. 126–39; Gibson, *Articles*, pp. 38–42; Dixon, *History*, v, 393–408; B. J. Kidd, *The Thirty-nine Articles*, 3rd ed. (New York, 1906), pp. 45 f.; E. J. Bicknell, *A Theological Introduction to the Thirty-nine Articles*, rev. ed., H. J. Carpenter (London, 1957), pp. 15–16.

justification and free will were rewritten, one on good works added, and one on grace eliminated.[1] The alteration clarified but did not substantially change the 1553 statements, and was partly anticipated by the émigrés' 1559 Declaration (10, 11, and 12). The Lutheran Confession of Würtemberg, prepared in 1552 for presentation at the Council of Trent, probably provided the basis for the wording of most of these alterations. This second direct Lutheran influence on the Articles took its place alongside that which came from the Confession of Augsburg by way of the Thirteen Articles of 1538.[2]

The revisers omitted denials of doctrines thought to be held by the various radical groups called 'Anabaptist'. Blasphemy against the Holy Ghost was left undefined. Millenarianism was no longer condemned. The separate article on the authority of the Old Testament moral commandments was omitted, although a summary sentence was added to the article on scripture (7). The description of Anabaptists as modern Pelagians was dropped (9).[3]

Another set of changes strengthened the anti-Roman Catholic stance of the Articles. The Forty-two Articles had blandly called vernacular worship agreeable to scripture; the revision vigorously declared that worship in an unfamiliar language was repugnant to the word of God (24). Every national church was now said to be competent to 'ordain, change, and abolish' ceremonies and rites (34). The wording of both these changes followed propositions argued by the reformers in the 1559 Westminster disputation.

Following the Eleven Articles, a new article insisted that holy communion ought to be administered in two kinds (30). In direct opposition to the decision of Trent, canonical books of the Old Testament were distinguished from apocryphal books (6). The Roman definition of seven dominical sacraments was specifically denied (25). The Forty-two Articles had negatively declared that God's law did not forbid marriage to clergy; the revision positively asserted that they might marry or not 'as they shall judge the same

[1] Article 10, 'Of Grace' of the Forty-two.
[2] Hardwick prints the relevant sections of the Würtemberg Confession, *Articles*, pp. 124–6, notes; see above, 10–11.
[3] Eliminated were articles 16, 19, and 41 of the Forty-two; see Hardwick, *Articles*, pp. 99–105.

to serve better to godliness' (32). Erroneous teachings of the 'school authors' were more pointedly named 'Romish doctrine' (22). Finally, to the condemnation of the doctrine of transubstantiation, was added the accusation that this teaching 'overthroweth the nature of a sacrament' (28).[1]

The words 'in Christ' were added to a phrase in the article on predestination which described the elected as those whom God has 'chosen *in Christ* out of mankind' (17). The revision also omitted the Edwardian words, 'although the Decrees of predestination are unknown to us'. Both minor changes give additional emphasis to the statement in the last paragraph that men ought not to attempt to fathom God's decisions, but to content themselves with his revealed will 'expressly declared unto us'—namely, salvation in Christ.

The most significant doctrinal shift in the first stage of revision lies in the most fiercely debated topics of sixteenth-century theologians, the sacraments. The Edwardian article on the sacraments had expressly condemned the use of the phrase *ex opere operato* which in the opinion of many reformers including Luther and Calvin implied that the sacraments worked their effects automatically apart from the faith of the recipient (25). The Elizabethan revisers eliminated the condemnation.[2] The statement on the presence of Christ in the Lord's Supper was reworked (28). In a manner similar to its Edwardian pattern, the revision declared that Christ's body had remained in heaven since the ascension; it was proper for human nature to have a definite location rather than to be diffused in many places or to be everywhere at the same time. Therefore, Christians ought not to believe in the 'real and corporal presence of Christ's body and blood'. This argument was common to Swiss theologians of both Zwinglian and Calvinist convictions. Bishop Guest devised an additional positive statement that the 'body of Christ is given, taken, and eaten in the Supper only after an heavenly and spiritual manner', and is received and eaten by means of faith. When Bishop Cheyney in 1566 objected that the word 'only' denied the presence of the

[1] The sentence in Article 34 about the rights of national churches had appeared also in similar form in the 'Principal Heads'.
[2] Augsburg Confession, XXIV, 22 (Latin); Calvin, *Institutes*, IV, xiv, 26.

body of Christ, Guest replied that it 'did not exclude ye presence of Christis body fro the Sacrament, but onely ye grossnes and senseblenes in the receavinge thereof'. The proposed revision also added a new article which sided with the Reformed against the Lutherans in the current continental Supper dispute: the wicked, in receiving holy communion, were not 'partakers of Christ' (29). This new article and the stronger assertion of Christ's presence emphasized the revisers' rejection of both strict Lutheran and Zwinglian positions on the Eucharist in favour of more central teachings closer to those of Calvin's *Institutes*.[1]

The revisers changed three other articles which applied to the English scene. A second set of homilies to be read by non-preaching ministers were authorized to take their place alongside the first set (35). The article on royal supremacy was altered to conform with the queen's title of 'supreme governor' in place of 'supreme head', and it included limitations similar to those which Elizabeth had herself set out in the Injunctions of 1559 (37).

The revisers changed the article which had asserted the 'godliness' of the Prayer Book and Ordinal into the affirmation of the Ordinal alone (36). Bishops, priests, and deacons ordained by its rites were declared to be 'rightly, orderly, and lawfully consecrated and ordered'. Nothing in the book was of itself 'superstitious or ungodly'. The article would seem directed both against Roman Catholics who would deny the validity of English ordinations and against those protestants who considered the English rites and the form of ministry to be unscriptural and popish.

This first stage of revision, possibly supervised by Parker in advance of Convocation, still included forty-two articles, although they did not correspond to those of 1553.[2]

In the additional revisions, indicated on the Convocation MS by Parker's red notations, the bishops dropped three more articles condemning 'anabaptist' eschatological peculiarities: against an immediate resurrection at death, against 'soul-sleep' between death

---

[1] White, *Elizabethan Bishops*, p. 131, Guest to Cecil, 22 December 1566; see also Stone, *Holy Eucharist*, II, 210.

[2] The first stage also introduced other minor revisions in articles 6, 8, 27, and 37.

and resurrection, and against universal salvation.[1] Bishop Alley had singled out disputes over Christ's descent into hell as a source of unnecessary theological strife, and urged the bishops to decide between conflicting interpretations. He personally argued for the views of 'all the fathers...both of the Greeks and the Latins' against those of 'Erasmus and the Germans,...Mr. Calvin and Mr. Bullinger'. The reverend fathers merely eliminated part of the appropriate article, leaving the unembroidered credal statement. Apparently they preferred to avoid the issue rather than adjudicate it. In the article on church traditions, the bishops decided that diversity of 'times' in addition to diversity of 'countries and men's manners' might require national churches to modify their ecclesiastical ceremonies (34).[2]

The bishops were unsatisfied with the strengthening of the teaching on the presence of Christ in the Supper in the initial revision, for they excised the entire rewritten paragraph on the local presence of Christ's body in heaven with its explicit denial of his 'real and corporal' presence in the supper (28). In the first stage, the Edwardian Swiss argument on the ascension had stood side by side with Guest's new positive assertion of the giving of the body after a spiritual manner and its reception by faith. Now the latter stood alone, moving the teaching of the Articles yet further away from the Zwinglian implications of 1553. A strong assertion of the presence of Christ in the communion was now qualified only by Guest's carefully chosen words, by the condemnation of transubstantiation, and by the new article denying the wicked's participation in Christ.

By these two stages of revision, the bishops rounded out and clarified fundamental teachings, eliminated trivial condemnations of sectarian doctrines, emphasized their rejection of current Roman Catholic teachings and practices, modified ever so slightly the teaching of predestination, strengthened the positive affirmations in sacramental doctrine, and finally they authorized new homilies, affirmed the Ordinal, and clarified the role of the Supreme Governor.

[1] Articles 39, 40, and 42 of the Forty-two.
[2] Further minor revisions included the change of the title of article 16 and a few words in articles 9 and 21 (Hardwick, *Articles*, pp. 137, 301, and 319).

In this form the Articles were subscribed by most of the members of the Convocation of Canterbury. Bishops Guest and Cheyney and some members of the Lower House appear to have been reluctant to subscribe the Articles. Whatever may have been the reason for the reluctance of the Lower House clerics, the two bishops apparently felt that even the revisions had not sufficiently strengthened the sacramental doctrine of the articles. Guest did subscribe eventually; Cheyney probably did not.[1]

The official Latin edition of the Articles of Religion appeared some time before 25 March 1564. Queen Elizabeth formally authorized them after she had, according to the declaration, 'herself first diligently read and examined them'. But two changes had been introduced into the text after it had been subscribed by the bishops: a sentence had been added on the authority of the church in Article 20, and Article 29 on the wicked at the Lord's Supper had been entirely omitted. The queen is the only authority likely to have introduced such alterations into the text approved by Convocation.[2]

The Edwardian article on the authority of the church, adopted intact by the 1563 Convocation, had been solely negative: the church must not ordain anything 'contrary to God's word written'. The new version prefaced a positive preamble: 'The Church hath power to decree rites or ceremonies, and authority in controversies of faith.' Although the sentence disappeared and reappeared in a bewildering succession of sixteenth-century editions of the Articles, no evidence of any *controversy* concerning it remains from Elizabeth's reign. The inconsistency in Elizabethan texts seems to be due

[1] An extract from the Convocation records made by William Laud bears Guest's subscription (Laud, *Works*, VI, James Bliss, ed. [Oxford, 1837], p. 66n.). Guest did sign a 1571 draft of the Thirty-nine Articles (Lamb, p. 39 and reproduction of MS). Less reliably Strype states that he found both Guest and Cheyney in 'certain extracts out of the registers of convocations' (*Annals*, I, part I, 487; cf. I, part II, 282; see also Wilkins, *Concilia*, IV, 237). For the sacramental doctrine, see below, p. 254, n. 2; for Lower House subscriptions, see above, pp. 63–4 and see appendix II, pp. 357–9. Names missing from the MS of subscriptions form no pattern of ecclesiastical loyalties: e.g. Thomas Becon, former exile; George Carew, conforming dean of the Chapel Royal; John Ellis, reform-minded dean of Hereford, and even Prolocutor Nowell.

[2] Hardwick reproduced this Latin edition, *Articles*, pp. 289 and 349–51. Grindal in a letter to Cecil of 17 July 1563 implied that the Articles were changed after they were 'first offered' to the queen (*Remains*, p. 57).

to nothing more than carelessness. The addition was thoroughly in agreement with the convictions and policies of the queen.[1]

Elizabeth's omission of Article 29 carried the conservative revision of the sacramental doctrine of the Forty-two Articles one step beyond the bishops' final version and two steps beyond the partial revision. The article, with its anti-Lutheran polemic, offended Cheyney, who held a eucharistic doctrine close to that of the Lutherans, and Guest, who held similar but more flexible views.[2] Elizabeth, in word and action, consistently supported a stronger doctrine of the presence, and she disliked quibbling over the doctrine. In this case, she probably saw no need to include a new article which would appear to some to deny the real presence.[3]

After eight years of Thirty-eight authorized Articles, the bishops reconsidered them in Convocation in 1571. They reconfirmed all thirty-nine, and the members of the Lower House subscribed them. Guest, through a letter to William Cecil, Lord Burghley, urged that

[1] The supposed dependence between this article and the Confession of Würtemberg is dubious (cf. Hardwick, *Articles*, pp. 126n. and 317). For details of the inclusion and omission of the sentence, and the seventeenth-century controversy over it, see Hardwick, pp. 133, 140n., 142–3, and 317; Laud, *Works*, VI, 66n. and 68; Gibson, *Articles*, pp. 512–13; Cardwell, *Synodalia*, I, 40-1n. These writers state that all the editions after 1571 contain the sentence. This is not quite accurate, for at least one English edition by Jugge of 1573 and one Latin edition by John Day of 1575 omit the sentence.

[2] No explicit evidence suggests that Cheyney adopted the full Lutheran doctrine, including 'ubiquity', but he at least held a conviction which had in common with Luther a close identification of the consecrated elements with the body and blood (see above, pp. 23–4; Strype, *Annals*, I, part II, 284–5; Stone, *Holy Eucharist*, II, 210 or White, *Elizabethan Bishops*, pp. 131–2, Guest to Cecil, 22 December 1566; ZL, I, 185–6, Jewel to Bullinger, 24 February 1567). For Guest's views, see his 1566 letter to Cecil and another of May 1571 (White, pp. 130–1 or Stone, II, 211–13); de Silva's comment to Philip of 1 November 1567 (*CSP, Sp.* I, 682); and Guest's eventual subscription (see above, p. 253, n. 1). Guest in his 1571 letter also proposed changes in his own composition in article 28 and changes in articles 17 and 25 (Gibson, *Articles*, p. 45n.).

[3] For arguments that Elizabeth was trying to placate those of Roman persuasion, see Gibson, *Articles*, p. 32; Kidd, *Articles*, pp. 41 and 236; that she was attempting to soothe Lutheran sensibilities, see W. H. Griffith Thomas, *The Principles of Theology* ... (London, 1951), pp. xliv–xlv; Maitland in *Cambridge Modern History*, first edition, II, 588; J. V. P. Thompson, *Supreme Governor* (London, 1940), p. 72. She seems to have been placating men like Guest and Cheyney whose traditional convictions were close to her own (see above, pp. 109–11).

article 29 be repudiated once again. When Burghley passed the request on to Parker, the archbishop refused to reconsider the exclusion of the article. The willingness of the newly created peer to pursue Guest's case provides an interesting sidelight on his supposedly puritan personal sympathies.[1]

All thirty-nine articles appeared in Latin and English with the ratification that the book had been 'again approved and allowed… by the assent and consent of our Sovereign Lady Elizabeth'. Firm insistence by most of the bishops, led by Parker, must have persuaded the queen to assent to the article she had vetoed in 1563. The article, as even Guest apparently persuaded himself, did not rule out a real spiritual presence. It might 'cause much busynes', but it was hardly a matter of fundamental principle for either the queen or her almoner.[2]

In addition to reasserting all thirty-nine articles, the bishops in 1571 also defined the status of the declaration in the life of the Church of England. For eight years, the officially authorized statement of the church's teaching had no real function. In the first proposed version of the Advertisements prepared in 1565, Parker had included rules prohibiting any preacher from impugning the Articles and requiring their reading twice yearly in parish churches. However, the version officially issued in 1566 left out these doctrinal requirements in deference to the queen's wishes, and preachers were required to conform only to what was euphemistically called 'unity of doctrine established by public authority'. In 1571 the bishops drew up a series of canons which never received royal assent, but which were generally enforced, and included several specific disciplinary applications of the Articles. The fully authorized Canons of 1604 gathered up the various Elizabethan ecclesiastical regulations in force and are still technically authoritative today, and among these we find almost all the disciplinary regulations concerning the Articles from the 1571 Canons.[3]

Clergy were required to subscribe the Articles as the standard of

[1] Stone, *Holy Eucharist*, II, 212; *Parker Corr.*, p. 381, Parker to Burghley, 4 June 1571; Hardwick, *Articles*, p. 351 (ratification of 1571 Articles); Read, *Cecil*, I, 214.

[2] Hardwick, *Articles*, p. 349; Bicknell, *Articles*, pp. 399–400.

[3] 1565 draft of Advertisements, Strype, *Parker*, III, 85; final form, Frere, *Visitation Articles*, III, 172; see above, pp. 213–15; *Parker Corr.*, p. 272, Parker to Cecil,

the church's public teaching. Every minister 'before he enters a sacred function', presumably including ordination and admission to a benefice, was to subscribe 'all the articles of the Christian religion'. A further requirement, one which did not reappear in 1604, enabled a bishop to demand that his clergy publicly reveal their conscience concerning any part of the Articles.

Preachers were to teach doctrine agreeable to scripture and to the 'catholic fathers and ancient bishops'. Since the Articles, together with the Prayer Book and Ordinal, contained nothing contrary to such teaching, they were to confirm the Articles 'not only in their preaching, but also by subscription' before they received licences to preach. Cathedral deans were to report any preacher whom they should discover preaching to the contrary.[1]

Diocesan 'chancellors, commissaries and officials', sometimes now laymen, were required to subscribe to the Articles in order to assure their loyalty to the official teaching of the church whose disciplinary standards they served and upheld.[2]

The only possible application of the Articles to the ordinary laity lies in the canon on preachers. After declaring the necessity of preachers' subscriptions, the canon declares: 'Whoever does otherwise, and will disturb the people with contrary doctrine, let him be excommunicated.' If this 'whoever' is intended to be general and to apply to the laity, the order contains the germ of the 1604 canon which excommunicated any person who declared that the Articles contained error or superstition. I am inclined to think that the 1571 regulation applied only to preachers. The Canons of 1571 applied the test of the Articles only to the clergy and other church officials; other laity were, at the most, only forbidden to disturb the church by actively and publicly opposing them.[3]

---

28 March 1566; Cardwell, *Synodalia*, I, 112–31, Canons of 1571. Guest required the clergy of Rochester Cathedral to have copies of the Articles in 1565, and possibly Horn required them of fellows in New College, Oxford in 1566 (Frere, III, 151, 153, 183, and 192).

[1] Cardwell, *Synodalia*, I, 120, 126, 112, and 116–17; Canons 36, 37, and 51 of 1604.
[2] Cardwell, *Synodalia*, I, 118; canon 127 of 1604.
[3] Cardwell, *Synodalia*, I, 127; canon 5 of 1604. I assume that '*Articulos fidei*' and '*articulis christianae religionis*' in other canons refer, as they normally do, to the Apostles'

In 1571 Parliament, as well as Convocation, dealt with the Articles of Religion and gave them their legislative sanction. All clergy had not been ordained by the Prayer Book rites and all clergy who were to receive benefices in the future were to subscribe the Articles. Every newly beneficed clergyman was to read them in church on a Sunday and to declare his assent to them. Any 'person Ecclesiastical' who affirmed a doctrine 'directly contrarie or repugnaunt' to the Articles was to be deprived of his living.[1]

Parliament made one important modification which distinguished the Act from the bishops' canons. They specified that subscription need be made to 'all the Artycles of Religion, wch onely concerne the Confession of the true Christian Faithe and the Doctrine of the Sacraments'. The 'onely' was to permit puritans of tender conscience to subscribe the doctrinal articles but not such 'disciplinary' articles as those on the traditions of the church and the consecration of bishops. To the dismay of the puritan clergy and to the anger of the puritan party in the Commons, the bishops stuck by their canonical legislation and required subscription to all the Articles and not merely to that selection implied by the Act of Parliament.

The bishops enforced their regulations of 1571 on the basis of their inherent episcopal authority, just as they had required the Eleven Articles and the Advertisements. These canons imposed the fully authorized statement of the church's teaching on her clergy and other officials, but they laid no burden on the conscience of most lay men and women. The place of the full Thirty-nine Articles of Religion in the Church of England was firmly secured.

Creed (Cardwell, I, 120). An isolated visitation article of Bishop Wickham for Lincoln in 1588 asked if any of the laity 'holdeth and maintaineth' doctrine contrary to the Prayer Book or the Articles (Kennedy, *Episcopal Administration*, III, 246). The bishops in 1571 proposed in their meetings that the Articles be read four times yearly, but the only record of episcopal attempts to enforce regular public readings seems to be in Archbishop Whitgift's articles for the deanery of Shoreham in 1597 which asked if the Articles were read twice a year—presumably a transferal of the order for reading the Eleven Articles (Lamb, *Articles*, p. 28; Kennedy, III, 287). The laity did hear the Articles of Religion read by newly inducted parsons as the Act of Parliament provided, but that was a test of clerical doctrine, not a form of lay instruction.

[1] *Statutes of the Realm*, 13 Eliz., c. 12, IV, 546f.

Doctrine: definition and discipline

It was not only Englishmen who were concerned about the outcome of the Elizabethan religious settlement. Many continental countries and churches had a stake in the English struggle. England had rejected Rome in 1559, but the Vatican and other Roman Catholic observers believed that the closer the Church of England stayed to the faith and practices of Rome, the easier it would be to recover the people when the opportunity came to restore papal authority. England was a key to the religious politics of Europe. Even though the Lutheran princes never formed an alliance with Henry VIII, the threat of it had been useful to them in their dealings with Emperor Charles V. Already in Elizabeth's reign, the ambitious and staunchly Roman Catholic family of Guise had felt the weight of English aid to protestants in Scotland and France. In a few years Elizabeth's brother-in-law Philip would be equally stung by England's support of his rebellious Dutch protestants. Nor was England's importance in European religious affairs limited to the papal–protestant struggle. The Reformed churches were continually feeling pressed by both Lutherans and Roman Catholics, and it was with real concern that Swiss religious leaders urged their English friends to avoid Lutheran infection lest it spread to all 'the purer churches'. Ever since Luther had met Zwingli at Marburg, the Supper dispute had been close to the centre of differences between Lutheran and Reformed, and it was one of the major issues exacerbating relations among the Lutherans themselves. The position which England adopted in the issues of European theological controversies was important to contemporaries, and an assessment of the Articles today can only be made in the light of those controversies.

England has often been an ambiguous member of the European community, and we must take account of that ambiguity as it applies to religion. The Articles reflect both the European theological controversies and distinctively English concerns. One non-anglican commentator declares the Thirty-nine Articles to be 'in sympathy with moderate Calvinism'; another writes that, with the exception of two articles, they are 'in the tradition of the Wittenberg Reformation'. John Henry Newman was even able to make out a fairly good case for their congruity with the decrees of Trent. Such a variety of competent judgments itself warns against too simple a categorization.[1]

The mere reduction of articles from forty-two to thirty-nine is significant at a time when Roman Catholic, Lutheran, and Reformed all tended to expand their doctrinal declarations into lengthy expositions. By not defining too much detail, the English reformers left room for differences of interpretation and emphasis.

The Articles can be considered under four main headings: catholic teaching, evangelical teaching, the eucharistic presence, and distinctly English emphases and provisions.[2] More than one-third of the articles express catholic or ecumenical doctrines which the English Church held in common with the mainstream of Orthodox, Roman Catholic, Lutheran, and Reformed Christianity. Articles 1 to 5, together with article 8 on the three ancient creeds, reaffirm the catholic dogmas on the Trinity and the person of Christ which had been formally adopted in the fourth and fifth centuries.[3]

'Anabaptist' was a catch-all epithet in the sixteenth century for many forms of radical sectarianism. Six of the articles, in part at least, refute doctrines which were alleged to be held by these groups. Article 7 insists on the value of the Old Testament and declares that Christians are still bound by its moral commandments. Articles 15 and 16 assert the humanity, sinlessness, and atonement of Christ, and they condemn the teaching that real Christians must be free from all

---

[1] W. A. Curtis in Hastings' *Encyclopedia of Religion and Ethics*, III, 854 b; Carl S. Meyer, *Elizabeth I and the Religious Settlement of 1559* (St Louis, 1960), p. 167; Newman's judgment is, of course, the substance of his famous Tract XC.

[2] Many divisions of the Articles have been made by different authors. I have found B. A. Gerrish's discussion to be the most helpful, although I differ at a number of points (*Faith*, pp. 173–83).

[3] The Ascension in article 4 has been said to be designed against the Lutheran doctrine of the ubiquity (Gibson, *Articles*, pp. 193–4; Bicknell, *Articles*, pp. 111–12). Although the revisers of the Articles largely rejected ubiquity, the wording here hardly goes beyond the language of the creeds. Neither the American Carl Meyer nor the Norwegian Einar Molland, two recent Lutheran commentators, found the issue worthy of notice (*Settlement*, p. 156; Molland, *Christendom*, 2nd Eng. ed. [London, 1961], p. 152).

sin and that the church ought not to forgive sin after baptism.[1]
Article 23 requires a preaching and sacramental ministry of men who
have been publicly called and authorized to minister in the church.
Article 26 reaffirms the traditional doctrine that an unworthy
minister cannot negate the effect of the sacraments. Article 27 upholds
infant baptism and denies the Anabaptist, and possibly Zwinglian,
teaching that baptism is no more than 'a sign of profession and mark
of difference'. Three articles seem to be aimed at the moral teachings
of some of these groups. Article 38, which contains the only remaining identification of Anabaptists by name, denies that the
'riches and goods of Christians' are common; article 39 sustains
oaths taken before a magistrate; and the last two sentences of article
37 vindicate capital punishment and participation in just wars. The
Articles repudiate this catena of sectarian doctrine and morality.

Article 33 on the avoiding of the excommunicate would be
acceptable to most Christian bodies. There is a faint whiff of possible
penalties, but even the Lutherans, who tended to deprecate such
penalties for spiritual censures, could easily interpret the article in
terms of their own understanding.[2]

The most important influence on the wording of many of these
catholic articles came from Lutheran formularies, and many are
couched in expressions characteristic of continental protestant
churches, but they could as well have been endorsed by Roman
Catholics.[3] In these articles, Canterbury was at one with Rome,
Wittenberg, and Geneva.

An even larger number of articles can be called 'evangelical', for
they substantially agree with the doctrinal teachings of the Lutherans
and Calvinists. Scriptures, containing 'all things necessary to salvation', provide the basis for doctrinal authority (6). After listing the

[1] Article 15 and the sinlessness of Mary, see Gibson, *Articles*, pp. 439–41; cf. Hardwick,
Articles, pp. 100 and 402; Article 16 and predestination, see Gerrish, *Faith*, p. 178.
[2] Article IX of Smalcald; Article XXVIII of the Apology of the Augsburg Confession,
and item 7 among the errors of the Schwenkenfelders in Article XII of the Formula
of Concord (*The Book of Concord*, pp. 314, 283, and 499).
[3] Meyer, *Settlement*, pp. 153–67; Henry Eyster Jacobs, *The Lutheran Movement in
England during the Reigns of Henry VIII and Edward VI* (Philadelphia, 1890), pp. 340–
2; Hardwick, *Articles*, pp. 61–3, 123–6, and 260–76.

canonical books of the Old Testament, the article comments on the list of apocryphal books which follow. These are not to be used to determine doctrine but only as an 'example of life and instruction of manners'. In this particular, the English Church approximated to Luther's estimate of these books, for Calvinists tended to reject them outright.[1]

Articles on original sin, free will, and works before justification expounded the Augustinian doctrine of man in language agreeable to Lutheran or Calvinist (9, 10, and 13). The English reformers avoided the more extreme expressions of man's depravity and bondage to sin which sometimes characterized continental writings. Although later puritans wanted to strengthen the wording on free will and works, yet the articles as they stand agree with most continental formularies.[2]

The article on predestination was acceptable to Lutheran and Reformed (17). To say this is to insist that the article leans closer to Lutheran than to Calvinist convictions, for the article avoids those Calvinistic assertions to which Lutherans took exception: irresistible grace, limited atonement, and double predestination. To argue, as one commentator does, that the mere mention of predestination reveals a Calvinistic bias is to miss the point. By mid-century, no theologian familiar with Calvin's work could easily avoid the issue. Lutherans fully accepted the predestination of the elect, but they urged men not to concern themselves with the 'secret counsel of God', resting content with his revealed will in Christ to save mankind. This would seem to be the plain teaching of the English article, especially after the minor revisions of 1563. In this issue, Bullinger's views were closer to Luther than to Calvin, and hence substantially similar to those of this English article.[3]

---

[1] Luther prefaced his translation of the apocryphal books with the comment that they are 'not equal to Scriptures, but are useful and good to read' (*Works*, xxxv, ed. E. T. Bachman and H. T. Lehmann [Philadelphia, 1960], p. 333 n.). The incomplete 1563 list of apocryphal books was corrected in 1571.

[2] *Cf.* Gibson, *Articles*, pp. 376 and 417.

[3] W. A. Curtis, Hastings' *Encyclopedia*, iii, 863 b; *Book of Concord*, pp. 494–7 and 616-32, Formula of Concord; Schaff, *Creeds*, iii, 252–4, second Helvetic Confession, ch. 10, sections 4 and 7; André Bouvier, *Henri Bullinger, réformateur et conseiller œcuménique* (Paris, 1940), pp. 53–9.

Doctrine: definition and discipline

Calvinists could have accepted article 17, and many so did. Some unequivocally Calvinist confessions went no further. Yet only extrapolations and uncertain implications of this teaching could convert the article into an explicit expression of Calvin's teaching in the *Institutes*. Even if Lutheran Carl Meyer overstates the case in terming the article 'anti-Calvinistic', he correctly assesses it as 'Lutheran, or better still, Scriptural'.[1]

The articles on justification and good works are brief terse statements wholly congruous with the teachings of Luther and Calvin, and the cavils of some English commentators who deny this are wholly unjustified (11 and 12). The brevity of these articles enabled them to avoid the phrases whose misinterpretations have sometimes plagued continental protestants. Article 11 explicitly endorses the homily 'of salvation', containing Cranmer's remarkably balanced discussion of the doctrine.[2]

Article 18 warns that a man can be saved only by Christ and not 'by the law or sect which he professeth'. The article may have been directed against a rationalist variety of Anabaptists, but it also effectively repudiates a common misunderstanding of the monastic vocation.[3]

Six articles condemn medieval teachings and practices which, in the opinion of the reformers, denied the scriptural gospel of salvation: theories of works of supererogation; the 'Romish doctrine' of purgatory, pardons, image-worship, and invocation of the saints; a liturgical language 'not understanded of the people'; communion in one kind; the 'sacrifices of masses'; and the necessity of clerical celibacy (14, 22, 24, 30, 31, and 32).

Three articles on the church fall within the area of agreement among continental protestants (19, 20, and 21). In defining the

[1] Meyer, *Settlement*, pp. 161–2; Schaff, *Creeds*, III, 367, 401, and 444–5, Gallican, Belgic, and Scottish Confessions; Calvin, *Institutes*, III, xxi, 1–7 and III, xxiv, 14–17; Molland, *Christendom*, p. 152; Gerrish, *Faith*, pp. 141 and 177–9.

[2] Gibson, following other English writers, distorts Luther's views of justification and of good works, and then distinguishes the English article (*Articles*, 389, 410–12). Bicknell is more judicious (*Articles*, p. 206).

[3] Hardwick, *Articles*, pp. 101 and 407; Gibson, *Articles*, pp. 489–90; Dixon, *History*, V, 397 n.; Bicknell, *Articles*, p. 228.

visible church as a congregation 'in which the pure word of God is preached, and the sacraments duly administered', the English reformers used Luther's phraseology which Calvin had also taken over. Calvin, however, derived his definition of the church from his doctrine of election, and many reformed confessions follow him in this. By not following Calvin in this respect, the English Articles avoided what Geddes MacGregor terms the 'methodological error' of his doctrine of the church.[1] All churches rejecting papal authority agreed that the Church of Rome might err, and, indeed, had erred. The assertion of the church's authority in article 20 was to prove an irritant to the puritans, but both Lutherans and Calvinists would have found its wording unexceptionable. The puritans objected to the way authority was constituted within the English Church, not to authority itself. The limitations on the authority of general councils would have found general agreement among the reformers, although the 'commandment and will of princes' was more congenial to Lutheran than to Calvinist notions of church and state.

The description of the sacraments in article 25 follows the two chief continental reformers in repudiating an Anabaptist or minimizing form of Zwinglian doctrine. It also follows them in describing sacraments as witnesses and signs of grace and God's good will, in distinguishing Baptism and Holy Communion as the sole sacraments 'ordained of Christ...in the Gospel', and by insisting that Christ did not ordain them 'to be gazed upon or to be carried about'.

The first paragraph of the article is similar to the Augsburg Confession, but included the words 'effectual signs of grace', a phrase added to the Augsburg wording in the Thirteen Articles of 1538. Neither Luther nor Calvin used this scholastic expression which implied to them that the sacraments conferred grace apart from faith. Peter Martyr, however, without reducing the necessity of faith, declared 'the signification of the symbols potent and effective',

---

[1] Geddes MacGregor, *Corpus Christi* (Philadelphia, 1958), pp. 48 f.; Calvin, *Institutes*, IV, i, 1–9; Schaff, *Creeds*, III, 418–19, 458–61, 324–5, and 375; Belgic, Scottish, and Heidelberg symbols reflect the relation of election to ecclesiology; Gallican does not.

and he wrote that the bread and wine 'are made the effectual signs of the body and blood'. In all likelihood, either Peter Martyr had influenced the English authors of the 1553 Articles in continuing the 1538 phrase or he had adopted it from their use.[1] This stronger assertion that grace is communicated in the sacraments had been mirrored in the unpublished 'Principal Heads', which declared that grace was 'conferred on those appropriating' the sacraments rightly.[2]

The 'five commonly called sacraments' were carefully distinguished from the Gospel sacraments, but they were still allowed a sacramental character. That the article permitted such an interpretation can be clearly seen in a passage from one of the new homilies:

In a general acceptation, the name of a sacrament may be attributed to anything, whereby an holy thing is signified. In which understanding of the word, the ancient writers have given this name not only to the other five,...but also to...other ceremonies...not meaning thereby to repute them as sacraments, in the same signification that the two forenamed sacraments are.... And although there are retained by the order of the church of England...certain other rites and ceremonies about the institution of ministers in the church, matrimony, confirmation of children,... and likewise for the visitation of the sick [absolution had been mentioned in a previous paragraph]; yet no man ought to take these for sacraments, in such signification and meaning as...baptism and the Lord's Supper are; but either for godly states of life,...worthy to be set forth by public action or solemnity, by the ministry of the church; or else judged to be such ordinances as may make for the instruction, comfort, and edification of Christ's church.

This flexible attitude toward the application of the word sacrament is closer to Lutheran teaching than that of most Calvinists who rigidly limited the New Testament use of the word to the two.[3]

These evangelical articles represent the common cause which the

[1] Hardwick, *Articles*, p. 270, no. 9 of the Thirteen; Luther, 'Babylonian Captivity', *Three Treatises* (Philadelphia, 1947), pp. 176–80; Calvin, *Institutes*, IV, xiv, 17; Joseph C. McLelland, *The Visible Word of God* (Edinburgh, 1957), pp. 163, 223–4, 227, and 276.

[2] *Quibus confertur gratia rite sumentibus*, Frere, *Visitation Articles*, III, 65.

[3] *Homilies*, pp. 316–17. Luther preferred to restrict the name to the two, with penance a kind of sacramental appendage to baptism. Melanchthon in the Apology of the

English reformers believed they shared with the two great reforming movements on the continent. Not one of these articles is entirely incompatible with either Lutheran or Calvinist. Yet their emphases are frequently closer to the Lutherans, and Lutheran confessions contributed more directly to the wording of some of the articles. The English statements on common doctrines were more restrained and compact than most of their counterparts in continental confessions. These articles declared to sixteenth-century Christendom that the Elizabethan church stood with Lutheran and Reformed against what all three believed to be the perversions of the teachings of the Church of Rome.

The articles which treat of the eucharistic presence cannot be fitted into the category of general evangelical teaching because continental protestants were themselves at such odds on this doctrine. In the two articles on the presence of Christ in holy communion, the English reformers opposed the teaching not only of Roman Catholic and Zwinglian–Anabaptist formularies, but the developed sixteenth-century Lutheran teaching which achieved its final definition in the Formula of Concord in the late seventies. According to article 28, Christ's body is eaten by means of faith after 'an heavenly and spiritual manner'. The strict Saxon interpreters of Luther condemned such language, insisting that the 'sacramentarians' who used it meant by the word spiritual 'no more than the presence of Christ's spirit, or the power of Christ's absent body, or his merit'. Article 29 would also have come under the Lutheran anathema against the teaching that 'unbelieving and impenitent Christians do not receive the body and blood of Christ, but only the bread and wine'.[1]

Both Lutheran and Reformed modern commentators on the

Augsburg Confession stated that 'no intelligent person will quibble about the number of the sacraments or the terminology, so long as those things are kept which have God's command and promise' (*Book of Concord*, pp. 211–13). Calvin freely called many Old Testament ceremonies 'sacraments', but he limited New Testament sacraments to two—although he grants at one point he might allow ordination to be a kind of sacrament (*Institutes*, IV, xix, all; xiv, 20).

[1] *Book of Concord*, pp. 481–2, 485–6, 587–91, and 668–70; 572, 580–2, 585, and 590. Although the accusations that 'Zwinglian' teachers were constantly twisting words to insinuate themselves into the Augsburg Confession were directed against Calvinists of Germany, there is no reason to think that the Saxons looked more kindly on

Doctrine: definition and discipline

English Articles classify 28 and 29 as 'Calvinistic'. This is an inexact adjective, for it implies too exclusive a dependence on the writings of John Calvin. In the doctrine of the presence, a rejection of a minimizing Zwinglianism, on the one hand, and of strict Lutheranism and Roman Catholicism, on the other, inevitably put the teaching of the English Articles in that body of Supper doctrine which lay between Zwingli and Luther: the Reformed and the Lutheran 'crypto-Calvinists'. The doctrines of this group of mediating theologians span a wide range, but the chain runs from Melanchthon, whose views touched those of Luther, through Bucer, Calvin, and Peter Martyr to Bullinger, whose views touched those of Zwingli. The chain has no broken links; each felt substantially at ease with the eucharistic doctrines of the men next to him, and the shadings between them have few sharp lines of distinction. Yet the differences between the ends of the chain are patent. The two English articles do not specifically *oppose* the teachings of any of this group of theologians, but they leave out the qualifications beloved by Bullinger and usually included by Peter Martyr and Calvin. Humphrey and Sampson, writing to Bullinger in 1566, included among their grievances against the Elizabethan church the 'mutilation' of the Edwardian article which had included some of these significant qualifications on the presence.[1]

English formularies. The Formula of Concord even expressly condemned the distinction of the Wittenberg Concord between the wicked (*impii*) and the unworthy (*indigni*), see p. 484; Schaff, *Creeds*, III, 140.

[1] ZL, I, 163 (no. 71), July 1566. For the doctrines of continental theologians, the relevant documents are: the Augsburg Confession; Melanchthon's modification in his 1535 edition of the *Loci Communes* (*Corpus Reformatorum*, ed. H. E. Bindsell, XXI [Brunsvigae, 1854], 479]; the 1540 *variata* Augsburg Confession (Schaff, *Creeds*, I, 241); the Wittenberg Concord between Melanchthon and Bucer (B. J. Kidd, *Documents Illustrative of the Continental Reformation* [Oxford, 1911], pp. 318–19; and the *Consensus Tigurinus* between Calvin and Bullinger (Kidd, pp. 652–6); and chapter XXI of the second Helvetic Confession (Schaff, III, 291–5). Recent useful discussions of the comparative doctrines can be found in: McLelland, *Visible Word*, especially pp. 181–220 and pp. 272–88; Cyril C. Richardson, *Zwingli and Cranmer on the Eucharist* (Evanston, 1949), especially pp. 1–24 and 35–40; G. J. Van de Poll, *Martin Bucer's Liturgical Ideas* (Assen, 1954), pp. 81–93; André Bouvier, *Henri Bullinger* (Paris, 1940), pp. 110–63; François Wendel, *Calvin* (Paris, 1950), pp. 251–71; and Ronald S. Wallace, *Calvin's Doctrine of the Word and Sacrament* (Grand Rapids, Michigan, 1957), pp. 197–218.

The 1559 Declaration of the Marian émigrés had moved in this direction by explicitly insisting that they did not 'deny all manners of Presence of Christ's Body and Blood', but only the 'corporeal, carnal, and real presence' of their adversaries. They also maintained that although the wicked eat only to their damnation, believers are 'truly given and exhibited whole Christ, God and man,...and inwardly by faith and through the working of God's Spirit...made partakers *vere et efficaciter* of the Body and Blood of Christ'. The 'Principal Heads' briefly reflect a similar change of emphasis when they state that 'to the faithful are truly given and exhibited the communion of the Lord's body and blood'. The doctrine of the eucharistic presence in the Forty-two Articles was close to the ethos of Bullinger, and the added positive statements in these unofficial documents moved it into the ethos of Calvin and Martyr. When Convocation removed the insistence that Christ's body was locally in heaven and the explicit rejection of the real and bodily presence from the Articles, the doctrine moved on to the ethos of Martin Bucer and Philip Melanchthon.[1]

So far, I have ignored C. W. Dugmore's thesis that the eucharistic theology of English reformers was largely based on a long stream of 'non-papist Catholic' tradition classically expressed in the 'realist–symbolist' teaching of St Augustine. Dr Dugmore's evidence demonstrates that the sixteenth-century reformers could draw on the work of a long stream of theologians who taught the reality of Christ's presence, but did not teach that the substance of bread and wine were obliterated in the consecrated elements.

I find two main problems with Dr Dugmore's arguments as they apply to the Thirty-nine Articles. The first lies in his attempt to interpret the Forty-two Articles by reading into them the higher sacramental doctrine of the Declaration of the Marian exiles, of the Thirty-nine Articles themselves and, finally, of Guest's own understanding of his contribution to article 28. This is ingenious, but not convincing. These four documents cannot be wrapped up in one uniform package as if they share one single theological stance, simply because *some* continuity of purpose and authorship runs

[1] Dixon, *History*, v, 112–13 n.; Strype, *Annals*, I, part I, 323.

through them all. Their differences in emphases are typical of the distinctions on which bitter and complex eucharistic controversies were based, and to ignore them is to miss all the subtle changes of direction in English eucharistic theology as circumstances changed.[1]

The second problem I find in Dr Dugmore's thesis is the arbitrary distinction which he makes when he emphasizes every possible influence of the 'non-papist Catholic' tradition on the English reformers and, at the same time, never suggests that their continental friends might have made use of the same tradition. This leaves the reader with the impression that continental reformers did not really share in the common heritage of catholic Christianity, but rather inaugurated a new 'purely protestant belief that the reception of the body and blood of Christ depends solely on the subjective faith of the recipient'. Dr Dugmore here echoes a common English prejudice about the supposedly 'subjective' character of classical continental protestantism. The arbitrary distinction between English and continental reformers underrates the simple reality that together they shared both the tradition and the new ideas of sixteenth-century theology. If we are to make use of Dr Dugmore's rather precious terminology, I suspect that Bucer and Melanchthon, and perhaps Calvin and Martyr as well, belong to the mainstream of the 'realist–symbolist' tradition.[2]

In spite of these reservations about Dr Dugmore's interpretation, his work warns us that the teaching of the Articles on the presence of Christ did not arise out of a scissors-and-glue exercise performed on the writings of contemporary theologians. The bishops who framed

---

[1] Dugmore, *Mass*, pp. 217–23.

[2] Dugmore, *Mass*, *passim*, quotation on pp. 225–6. Dugmore occasionally suggests this at several points himself: Bucer's teaching was like that of Ratramm (p. 126); there is an 'echo of Augustine's belief' even in the *Consensus Tigurinus* (p. 162); Calvin at least ought to have escaped the Lutheran description of him and Peter Martyr as 'sacramentaries' (p. 208); yet Dugmore, for example, wrote that Jewel 'does not go the whole way with Calvin or the *Consensus Tigurinus*, and talk about Christ's body being present in the sacrament merely in virtue, force or efficacy' (p. 231). In such a statement Dr Dugmore ignores Calvin's paradoxical assertion of the receiver's substantial participation in Christ's body. As for the *Consensus*, although the words 'virtue, force, and efficacy' are not foreign to its ethos, they do not appear in the document.

the Articles of Religion brought to them an amalgam of convictions formed out of their knowledge of traditional teachings, their studies in the scriptures and in the fathers, their past involvement in heated controversies, and their knowledge of the convictions of one another and of their continental contemporaries. The bishops adopted the eucharistic teaching of articles 28 and 29 because they believed it to be scriptural and patristic. Dr Dugmore reminds us that their conviction was not wholly specious.

The strengthened doctrine of the eucharistic presence in the Thirty-nine Articles went hand in hand with the revised Prayer Book liturgy.[1] With its suggestion of an offertory and its remnant of a consecration canon, the rite was more traditionally catholic than most Lutheran and far removed from the Reformed liturgies. Wedded to this liturgy was an official eucharistic doctrine akin to that of those continental theologians who stood just on the Reformed side of the borderline between Lutheran and Reformed teachings. The marriage goes a long way to explain why for many years continental Lutherans and Calvinists, with their myopic preoccupation with doctrinal formularies, assigned the English Church a place among the Reformed churches in spite of the obvious similarities in liturgy with the Lutheran bodies.

The remaining articles were much more exclusively English. All the churches of the Reformation agreed that traditions and ceremonies need not be everywhere alike and that national churches might change ceremonies and rites ordained of mere human authority. However, article 34 went on to rebuke those who would 'openly break the traditions and ceremonies of the Church which be not repugnant to the Word of God, and be ordained and approved by common authority'. The independent Church of England has had more extensive and frequent disputes over the use of prescribed ceremonies than any church of western Christendom. If the issues in themselves were inevitably trifles, the protagonists believed the principles more significant. The church is a society with discipline in its liturgical life, and congregations are entitled to some protection against the particular idiosyncrasies of their pastors—even when the

---

[1] See above, pp. 106–10.

idiosyncrasies are matters of conscience. As the Lutheran Molland has observed, the inclusion in a doctrinal statement of the need for obedience to ceremonies is 'typical of the Anglican temper'.[1]

Article 35, authorizing both the Edwardian and the new books of Homilies, bestows on them a general assurance that they contain 'a godly and wholesome doctrine'. These lengthy exhortations and expositions formed no part of the English confession of faith itself, and the phrase 'necessary for these times' suggests that the bishops recognized that the subjects of the homilies and their treatment might not be appropriate *in perpetuum*. The most important doctrinal implication of the article lies in its very promulgation: preaching, however desirable, is not the *sine qua non* of Sunday worship; in the absence of licensed preachers, the reading of a homily constituted a tolerable substitute.

The main section of article 37 that treats of civil magistrates states the peculiarly English understanding of royal supremacy. To the queen belonged 'the chief government of all estates in this realm, whether they be ecclesiastical or civil'. This article reflects the concept of the unified medieval commonwealth, now writ small within the confines of one nation.

The article specifically refers to the queen's own statement in her 1559 Injunctions that she never thought her responsibilities allowed her 'to challenge authority and power of ministry of divine offices in the church'. She later expanded on this statement in the 1569 'Defence'; she wished

to provide that the Church may be governed and taught by archbishops, bishops, pastors, and such other ecclesiastical ministers and curates as by the ecclesiastical ancient policy used in the realm hath been in former ages ordained. Whom also we know that our duty is to assist with the power which God hath given as they, being the ministers of the Church, may... retain our people in obedience to their Almighty God and to live as Christians to the salvation of their souls which Christ hath redeemed.

The workings of royal supremacy and the whole relationship of church and state had to be worked out pragmatically, but the doctrine

[1] Molland, *Christendom*, p. 153.

of the Articles does not substitute royal supremacy for the authority of the pope. Elizabeth's insistence on the title of 'governor' instead of 'head' was more than a verbal game. She determined to place limits on the exercise of the supremacy—even if these limits were in fact hers to define.[1]

Elizabeth's concepts of her responsibilities are not greatly different from those that Philip Melanchthon included in the 1535 edition of the *Loci* which he initially dedicated to her father:

The magistrate is guardian [*custos*] not only of the second table [of the Decalogue], but also of the first, as it pertains to external discipline. Thus, not only care for guarding the tranquillity of citizens and for dispelling injuries to bodies and fortunes pertains to the magistrate, but also care for preserving discipline in religion. For even though corporal punishments do not produce piety in souls, nevertheless, for the sake of discipline, magistrates ought to restrain outward contumelies in religion, manifest idolatry, blasphemies, impious teachings, and perjuries....The wise magistrate considers this one principle to be the purpose wherefore men are put together in society, that God may be clearly known and glorified. ...The magistrate ought to forbid impious worship and the profession of impious doctrines and to punish heretics. However, the knowledge of doctrine pertains to the church, that is, to pious and well-learned men. And yet the magistrate himself is the member of the church whose eyes ought to observe most of all.[2]

The English concept is unique, however, in two respects. Both Lutheran and Reformed sought to abolish the distinction between the estates spiritual and temporal, believing it to be an erroneous form of sacerdotalism. Elizabeth based her concept of the royal supremacy on that distinction. And secondly, in England the 'magistrate' was not a civil authority of alterable form, but the regnant sovereign, anointed of the Lord.

[1] Appended orders to the Injunctions, Frere, *Visitation Articles*, III, 25–6; *Queen Elizabeth's Defence*, p. 43; Elizabeth added the last sentence quoted in her own hand.
[2] Melanchthon in *CR*, XXI, 553–4; my translation. For other continental views on the magistrate, see Calvin, *Institutes*, IV, 1, 4, 6, 9, 26, and 28 (he even calls them 'vicars of God' [6]); second Helvetic Confession, chapter XXX (Schaff, *Creeds*, III, 305–6); Gallican Confession, article XXXIX (III, 391–2); Belgic Confession, article XXXVI (III, 432–3); Scottish Confession, article XXIV (III, 474–6).

Doctrine: definition and discipline

Finally, the English Church ratified its episcopal form of government in article 35. The article affirms no theory of episcopacy, but the Ordinal which it endorsed states as historical fact the continuation of the threefold ministry from apostolic times and declares that no one not already a deacon, priest, or bishop may minister in the English Church without this ordination. Taken together with article 23 which insists on an outward public call to the ministry, this article is patent of two interpretations: (1) the form of the ministry is a matter of indifference as long as some public discipline is established; since the threefold episcopal ministry has continued from apostolic times, it is to be continued in the English Church; or (2) the threefold ministry which has continued from apostolic times is an integral part of the form of the Catholic church and, therefore, the Articles order it to be continued within the Church of England, which comprises their sphere of influence. Probably most of the bishops who framed this article would have inclined to the first interpretation, but they simply proclaimed the fact of history and ordered the traditional discipline followed without insisting that their own theological convictions be a part of the doctrinal definition.

In framing the final form of the Articles of Religion, the bishops did not allow themselves to be carried away by continental example to pile definition upon definition. The relatively brief declaration avoided unnecessary speculation and argument. Continental protestants, from their several positions, could take comfort in the renewed repudiation of Rome, but except for the slightly anti-Lutheran touch of eucharistic teaching which pleased the Reformed, they could find little ammunition for their intra-protestant battles. The moderation of the Articles must have made them seem as bland to most continental protestants as they were to the precisians at home. At the 1563 Convocation, the precisians signed the articles, for they had other plans for tightening the doctrinal standards of the English Church. In the midst of the theological controversies of the Reformation the bishops defined the position of the Church of England, unrealistically hoping that, with the Articles, all those who taught in her name might avoid 'diversities of opinions' and establish 'godly consent touching true religion'.

THE NEW BOOK OF HOMILIES

The book of Homilies already figured in our consideration of the controversy over images because of its oversized second sermon on the topic. Finally authorized by the Thirty-nine Articles, the book had been a long time in coming. An appended note in the 1547 Book, which Elizabeth had re-authorized in 1559, promised another collection and proposed twelve new subjects. Elizabeth had implied in her Injunctions that these would be forthcoming, and the initial drafts of the Bishops' Interpretations had called for the writing of about thirty-six homilies on the proposed and additional topics. When the more formal version of the Interpretations was drawn up in 1561 the homilies had still not been prepared.[1] By the time the bishops signed the Articles at the end of January 1563, at least twenty new homilies had been prepared, for the titles of these appear in the Articles. Whether some bishops had failed to prepare the sixteen or so other assigned sermons or whether their brethren in the episcopate did not approve their efforts remains a mystery.[2]

Queen Elizabeth balked at the bishops' new book. Parker wrote to Cecil some time after Convocation that he wished the queen 'would resolve herself in our books of Homilies', for he wanted to deliver them in a coming visitation. Elizabeth resolved herself before 25 March 1564, for four editions of the second book of Homilies with the twenty sermons bear the date 1563.[3]

The royal authority granted to the second book of Homilies turns out to be far more ambiguous than that with which Elizabeth had authorized the Edwardian book when she had rewritten its preface. Bishop Cox prepared a MS draft of a preface which would have granted

---

[1] See above, pp. 163–5, 240; the appended note is on p. 137 of *Homilies*; Frere, *Visitation Articles*, III, 18, 60, and 70. Proposals in the first drafts of the Interpretations specified that every bishop was to have two homilies and the bishop of London, four. By the end of 1560 there were 17 bishops, not counting the infirm Kitchin.

[2] The Latin MS signed by the bishops on 29 January contained the names of the twenty homilies in English. It seems likely that more than these twenty were assigned, for not only were the bishops to have two each, but three topics mentioned in the Edwardian book and two in the Interpretations never appeared in the second book.

[3] *Parker Corr.*, p. 177, 'shortly after midsummer'; for visitation, see Frere, *Visitation Articles*, III, 140 f. The four editions of the homilies are STC 13663–6.

the second book a status exactly that of the earlier homilies. The draft would have declared that the queen annexed the new homilies,

and hath with like authority set them forth, to be read unto her loving people and faithful subjects, in such order, as in her said brother's time they were; that is to say, that every Sunday or holyday in the year,...the parson, vicar, or curate of every parish do plainly and distinctly read... one whole homily, or such parts of one as are in this book set forth, and divided, in such place and order, as in the Book of Common Prayer is appointed. And where the whole book shall in such order be read through and ended, there her majesty's pleasure is, that it be begun again; that by often repeating, those most necessary points may more firmly be fastened in the memories of her said subjects.

The draft was never used.[1] The new book appeared with only an anonymous 'Admonition to all Ministers Ecclesiastical'. It declared that among other ministerial duties, the clergy ought

prudently also to choose out such homilies as be most meet for the time, and for the more agreeable instruction of the people committed to your charge, with such discretion, that, where the homily may appear too long for one reading, to divide the same, to be read part in the forenoon, and part in the afternoon.

The minister was under no obligation to read these homilies through in order, as Elizabeth's authorization for the first book expressly required and as Cox proposed for the second. The seasonal sermons in this second book offer some reason for the option, but scarcely sufficient for such a drastic change in the format and contents of the directions. Even while the first book of Homilies continued to be reprinted with Elizabeth's original full authorization, the second book was reprinted to the end of the reign with no authorizing preface but that of the ambiguous 'Admonition'.[2]

After 1570 the title page explicitly declared that the book was

---

[1] Strype, *Annals*, I, part I, 516–17.

[2] *Homilies*, p. 141. The first book of Homilies was reprinted at least eleven times in Elizabeth's reign, and the ten of these which I examined all conform to one another with respect to the preface: STC 13648–53 (1559–69) and STC 13655–8 (1576–95). The second book was printed at least twelve times, and the ten editions I examined all contain the Admonition in the same form: STC 13663–5 (1563) and STC 13668–74 (1570–95).

'set out by the authority of the Queen's Majesty'. In earlier editions, the same words appeared, but the punctuation and the typographical layout made it uncertain whether the phrase applied to the second book or only to the earlier Edwardian book.[1]

The peculiarities of this authorization suggest the studied subtlety of the queen herself. As Parker hinted in his letter, something in the book had aroused her displeasure—presumably the implicit attack on the little silver cross. And so instead of granting the book the full authority of her explicit assent, she allowed the book to be printed with only a vague suggestion of her authorization and with a specific proviso that would allow a clergyman to select those homilies he would read. The party of bishops who thought images forbidden by divine law won the right to teach their doctrine through non-preaching ministers who chose to do so, but the queen made it possible for the priests and readers who shared *her* convictions to leave this homily entirely out of their preaching cycle.

The second book of Homilies was, like its predecessor, a mixed bag. Some of the seasonal homilies for Christmas, Good Friday, Easter, Whit Sunday, and Rogationtide could equally well be employed at other times. The Whit Sunday homily described the three essential notes of the church in Bucerian terms of doctrine, sacraments, and discipline. Attacking Roman claims, it launched into an incredible 'historical' account of the abominations of the papacy including the accouchement of 'Pope Joan' in the course of a public procession.[2]

[1] The title of STC 13663 of 1563 appeared as follows:

The Seconde
Tome of homelyes of
such matters as were pro-
mised and Intituled in
the former part of ho-
melyes, set out by
the aucthoritie
of the Quenes Maiestie:

And to be read in euery paryshe Churche agreablye.

STC 13665 is substantially the same, but STC 13668 of 1570 has altered the arrange-ment, and the comma after 'former part of our homilies' has become a period and the next phrase is on a separate line, clearly referring the authorization to the second book.
[2] *Homilies*, pp. 413 and 417, see above, p. 170.

Homilies discussed such practical ascetical matters as fasting, alms-giving, prayer, repentance, and the reception of holy communion. The doctrine of the last-mentioned homily more explicitly expressed Calvin's own teaching than did the Articles. It spoke of the body of Christ in the Supper as a 'ghostly substance', and it also exhorted listeners 'to lift up your hearts' to seek spiritual meat 'where the sun of righteousness ever shineth'.[1]

One homily dealt with certain difficulties in scripture, another with marriage, and three more warned against idleness, excess of apparel, and gluttony and drunkenness. Four homilies concerned the liturgy and the building which housed it, one dealing with the very practical matter of 'repairing and keeping clean the Church'.

With such authorization as the second set of homilies had, the book was enforced throughout the remainder of Elizabeth's reign. In the aftermath of the northern rebellion of 1569 came another extended homily, about half the length of that against idolatry. Entitled 'An Homily against disobedience and willful rebellion', its title appeared in the 1571 revision of the Articles, and it became the twenty-first homily in all subsequent editions of the book.[2]

The second book of Homilies, framed by the bishops and adopted at the Convocation of 1563, took its place as an element in the doctrinal orientation of the Elizabethan church. Neither it, nor its earlier companion, could claim officially to *define* doctrine in the English Church, but thousands of Englishmen grew up and lived their lives with the weekly sound of its contents droning past their ears and occasionally impressing its teaching upon their minds. The homilies hardly deserve oratorical or literary fame, but we must wonder if their teaching and style is not at least as good as the average fare of preaching in most ages of the Christian church.

[1] *Homilies*, pp. 399–400.
[2] STC 13679, *An Homilie agaynst disobedience and Wylful rebellion*, Jugge and Cawode, 23 June 1570; Second Tome of Homilies, STC 13669; Hardwick, *Articles*, p. 541. Specific episcopal inquiries about the *two* books: Guest, 1565, Rochester, and Grindal, 1571, province of York; Frere, *Visitation Articles*, III, 157 and 254; see also III, 278 and 283, and Kennedy, *Episcopal Administration*, II, 79, 91, 111, 140; III, 210, 227, 262, and 286.

Doctrine: definition and discipline

NOWELL'S CATECHISM AND DOCTRINAL DISCIPLINE

The militant reformers' striking victory in the Lower House of Convocation in 1563 has been passed unnoted and unheralded in the histories of England's church. The precisians' pre-Convocation prospectus, 'General notes', began with a call for doctrinal reform. 'A catechism is to be set forth in Latin, which is already done by Mr. Dean of Paul's and wanteth only viewing.' Next they called for the revision of the Edwardian Articles of Religion to be prepared along with a revised version of the *Apology*. Their key proposal followed: 'These three to be joined together in one book, and by common authority to be authorized, as containing true doctrine, and enjoined to be taught.' Then the authors proposed a series of regulations to enforce this book as the doctrinal standard of the English Church. Strype's omission of most of these regulations partly explains why subsequent historians have missed the significance of the proposals. 'Certain articles' had more loosely proposed that articles be taken out of the *Apology*, and that Nowell's catechism be authorized for universities and schools, but there was no hint that these might be joined together as one great book of symbolical dogma.[1]

By the time members of the Lower House subscribed 'Twenty-one articles' the *Apology* had dropped out of the picture, but otherwise the Lower House bought the doctrinal proposals of 'General notes' lock, stock and barrel.

The catechism was central to the precisians' plans. The prolocutor of the Lower House, Alexander Nowell, came to Convocation with his draft for a Latin catechism, the *Catechismus Puerorum*, which the Lower House presented to the bishops on 3 March. Nowell later wrote to Cecil that in the 1563 Convocation, the 'whole clergy' of the Lower House had subscribed the catechism and the bishops had 'allowed' it after Convocation members had made some alterations. The description aptly fits the suggested reconstruction of events. By 'allowing' the catechism, the bishops permitted its use without

[1] See above, pp. 60–73; for Convocation documents, see appendix I, pp. 342–56.

granting it the official status which the Lower House had requested and which the bishops gave to the Articles and Homilies.

Nowell sent the book to Cecil in June hoping for the 'Queen's majesty's authority' to make the catechism public, and Cecil did not return it for more than a year. Elizabeth never granted the book the slightest hint of her royal approbation, and when Nowell finally published it in 1570 with Parker's encouragement, he dedicated it to the bishops, but made for it no claim of synodical authority.[1]

The year after publication, Nowell's catechism received its minor official status in the Elizabethan church. The canons of 1571, adopted and promulgated by the bishops of both provinces, ordered all schoolmasters to use the Latin catechism of Nowell and none other in the instruction of their charges and to use the English translation for those who knew no Latin. A series of metropolitical and diocesan injunctions and articles testify to the continued attempt to enforce this regulation throughout the rest of the reign.[2]

The Jacobean canons of 1604, which regularized and gave full authority to many of the Elizabethan episcopal regulations, included the requirement that 'all schoolmasters shall teach in English or Latin,...the larger or shorter Catechism heretofore by public authority set forth'. The shorter catechism mentioned, Nowell's so-called 'Middle Catechism', was an abridgement of the larger work which appeared in English in 1572 and in Latin two years later. Nowell's book thus eventually became an authorized text-book for schoolchildren to learn both Latin and doctrine until,

---

[1] Both the 1570 Latin edition and its English translation of the same year by Thomas Norton are available in the Parker Society volume (Nowell, *Catechism*). Also see above, pp. 68–73; Strype, *Annals*, I, part I, 526–7, Nowell to Cecil, 22 June 1563; Nowell, *Catechism*, p. vi, Nowell to Cecil, 16 June 1570. When Cecil had the book, he had 'some learned men' examine it and suggest certain changes which Nowell adopted.

[2] Cardwell, *Synodalia*, I, 128; see above, pp. 254–5. A series of episcopal directions designated only the Latin catechism: Frere, *Visitation Articles*, III, 270, 291, 312, and 333; Kennedy, *Episcopal Administration*, II, 15 and 49; III, 156 and 193. Other directions called for the catechism to be taught in both languages according to the children's ability: Frere, III, 371; Kennedy, II, 98 and III, 177. Most directions mentioned the catechism without specifying language: Frere, III, 327; Kennedy, II, 118; III, 177, 184, 204, 291, 303, 323, and 344.

later in the seventeenth century, it gradually faded from the English scene.[1]

All the standard commentaries state either that Nowell took Poynet's 1553 catechism as his model or that he was indebted to both Poynet and Calvin. Such statements are seriously misleading. A careful comparison of the Latin texts—or even of the English translations—of the three catechisms will show that Nowell's primary debt was to John Calvin alone. In composing his work, Nowell's chief guide was the catechism of Geneva, which had formed a part of the 'New Discipline' he had subscribed at Frankfort. Nowell rewrote Calvin's work in his own style and considerably amplified it both with his own expositions and with some sections of Poynet's work. Like Calvin in his early writings, Nowell referred only obliquely to double predestination. Especially in his exposition of the sacraments, Nowell closely reflected Calvin's teaching. Expressing a strong doctrine of the presence of Christ in the Supper, Nowell also included Calvin's characteristic qualification that the body of Christ is in heaven and that recipients must communicate by the act of the *sursum corda*. Nowell wished that the English Church would establish a godly discipline in the local congregation: elders as censors of morals with the right of excommunication. The realistic dean of Paul's also expressed right in the catechism his despair that such an ideal might ever be established in England. Nowell defined the church in Calvin's fashion as the society of the elect, and he adopted the consequent distinction of the visible and invisible church.[2]

Archbishop Whitgift and Bishop Cooper, in their defences of the establishment against puritan attacks of Cartwright and Martin Marprelate, referred to the catechism which, if it did not defend episcopal polity, did not demand the establishment of a synodical

---

[1] Canon 79 of 1604, Cardwell, *Synodalia*, I, 291.

[2] E.g. *DNB*, under Alexander Nowell; Dixon, *History*, V, 409; Procter and Frere, *Book of Common Prayer*, p. 602. For Poynet's catechism, see Ketley, *Two Liturgies*, pp. 495–525 and 545–71 (Latin and English); for Latin and French texts of Calvin's catechism of Geneva, see *Corpus Reformatorum*, XXXIV, Joannis Calvini, *Opera Quae Sunt Omnia*, VI (Brunsvigae, 1867), 9–134; convenient English translation in *Calvin: Theological Treatises* (Philadelphia, 1954), ed. J. K. S. Reid, pp. 91–139. For the study, I collated the texts of the three Latin catechisms.

presbyterianism. The advanced and doctrinaire puritanism which dominated the most militant reformers after 1570 left Nowell's relative moderation far behind.[1]

The 1571 canons required schoolmasters to use both the 1559 Primer and Nowell's catechism in teaching the young. It is curiously characteristic of the Elizabethan church that, in one breath, its leaders could require a catechism substantially based on John Calvin and, in the next, require a devotional manual solidly rooted in the medieval books of hours.

Mild Calvinism though it was, had Convocation and the queen in 1563 seen fit to approve the proposal to enforce the catechism as part of its doctrinal standard, the Church of England would have been committed officially and unequivocally to a large body of Genevan doctrine as one of its main bonds of unity.

The bishops not only refused to include the catechism as part of their confessional standards; they also repudiated the discipline with which the precisians sought to enforce doctrine throughout the English Church. The militant reformers in 1563 would have protected the entire confessional book, articles and catechism alike, by laws which would have imposed penalties on

whosoever, being either of the clergy or laity, shall preach, declare, write, or speak any thing in derogation, depraving, or despising of the book...or against any doctrine therein contained, and be thereof lawfully convicted before any ordinary, and will stand in the maintaining thereof.

In the canons of 1571 the bishops used far less forceful legal language in protection of the Articles of Religion alone. Throughout the extant copy of the 'Twenty-one articles' the penalties to be applied are replaced by an uninformative '&c.'. In the corresponding proposed item of 'General notes' an offender was to suffer 'as in case of heresy'. Since the Supremacy Act, however, had repealed Mary's heresy laws, 'General notes' suggested an alternative: the penalties of the Uniformity Act for those that 'offend and speak against the Book of Common Prayer'. There were increasingly stiff fines for the first two offences and, for the third, confiscation and life imprisonment.[2]

---

[1] Strype, *Parker*, II, 18; *Annals*, I, part I, 528–9.
[2] *Statutes of the Realm*, IV, 355–8; 1° Eliz., c. 2.

The authors of 'General notes' hoped either for a parliamentary revival of the old heresy laws or for the Uniformity Act to become the model for a new heresy law. The Lower House may have omitted penalties from their petition of 'Twenty-one articles' because they thought the bishops would receive it better if they left the penal determination to the episcopal judgment. It would be, after all, the bishops who would have to take Convocation's proposals into the Lords to seek parliamentary sanction for any such measures. But the stiff penalties proposed in 'General notes' show what the precisians had in mind. They would have protected both the Articles and Nowell's catechism with penal teeth that ultimately led either to execution or, at the least, to life imprisonment.[1]

Although the entire book was to serve as a doctrinal standard for the church and the Articles were to be interpreted in the light of the catechism, the precisians did distinguish the Articles from the catechism. They proposed to enforce the Articles with a thoroughness that would have done credit to the Church of Geneva.

Subscription to the Articles was to be immediately introduced in the universities. 'General notes' would have required that masters, fellows and all 'that take degrees' subscribe. Recusants, and those masters who failed to impose subscription, were to be deprived, expelled, and 'disabled to take any degree'. If the vice-chancellor failed to require the subscription of masters within four months he was to be stiffly fined for each offence. The Lower House extended the list of those required to subscribe to include 'beadles and other officers' and all admitted to any 'living place of students'. Also in 'Twenty-one Articles', they would have required beneficed students of canonical age for ordination to preach two public sermons a year on assigned topics. The precisians intended to permit no deviation in doctrine among those teaching or studying in English institutions of higher learning.[2]

For the clergy in general, the militant reformers proposed

---

[1] See also Nowell's sermon, appendix to *Catechism*, p. 226; see below, pp. 330–1.
[2] From 1573 Oxford required subscription for a degree; from 1576, for matriculation. In 1618 James I ordered Cambridge to require all taking degrees to subscribe to the three sections of canon 36 of 1604 (Hardwick, *Articles*, p. 231).

requirements substantially similar to those actually imposed by the bishops in the canons of 1571. Clergy were to subscribe the Articles of Religion before entering a benefice, and a bishop might demand that any beneficed clergyman publicly consent to the Articles at any time under threat of deprivation. As additional insurance that these requirements would be carried out, the Lower House in 'Twenty-one articles' specified that a note of the subscription was to be included in the institution records and that penalties would be applied to bishops and their officials who failed to require subscription.[1]

The precisians in the Lower House added a provision in 'Twenty-one articles' to provide better indoctrination of the laity. They proposed that the Eleven Articles of 1561 be reviewed and expanded, and that this revised version be regularly read in English churches. They undoubtedly desired revisions which would have made these articles far more specific and rigorous on many controverted issues.

The regulations with the most far-reaching potential for the imposition of doctrinal uniformity would have affected both the clergy and the laity of England. In an item not in the original proposals of 'General notes', the Lower House would have punished any person 'lay or ecclesiastical' who denied 'directly or indirectly, publicly, or privately, by writing or speaking, any article of doctrine contained in the said book' and who 'obstinately' stood in his opinion when 'lawfully convicted'. In a second item, which also originated with 'Twenty-one articles', every bishop was to have authority to call before him any person, clerical or lay, in his diocese 'whom he suspects concerning religion', and to require the suspected heretic to subscribe and publicly consent to the Articles. If the recalcitrant refused, the bishop, after notifying the queen and allowing one month to pass, could impose the unspecified penalties for such heresy. This provision would have given the bishops inquisitorial powers to ferret out any doctrinal deviations which Englishmen might harbour in their inner minds and hearts. Had the

---

[1] The requirement to make a public declaration of conformity was dropped in 1604 when it was not taken up in the new canons.

regulation been combined with a revival of the old penalties for heresy and enforced with vigorous zeal, it could have made the persecutions of 'bloody Mary' look like a tea party in comparison. In effect, this rule would have required the laity of the Church of England to be prepared to subscribe the Articles of Religion along with the clergy. In actual fact, laity were expected to listen to the reading of the Prayer Book and conform to its rites, but never were they required to subscribe and publicly declare their approval of its contents. These proposals of the Lower House would have raised the 'confession of faith' in anglicanism to a status superior to that of the liturgy.

The hopes and plans of the militant reformers for strict doctrinal discipline were not entirely unknown to those who would have been touched by them. A group of former Marian émigrés who reaffirmed their continued abhorrence of 'all papistry and foreign power' petitioned the bishops not to enact and enforce heresy laws against them. They stated that they could not accept the convictions of many of their protestant brethren about predestination. Rather in the fashion of the later Lutherans, these Englishmen distinguished God's foreknowledge and predestination of all goodness from his foreknowledge *alone* of wickedness. They claimed their views were like those of 'all the learned fathers unto this our age'.

The petitioners insisted that the upholders of strict predestination called them

free-will men, Pelagians, papists, epicures, anabaptists, and enemies unto God's holy predestination and providence, with other such like opprobrious words and threatenings of such like, or as great punishments and corrections, as upon any of the aforesaid errors and sects is meet and due to be executed, what time discipline (which of all things is most meet and necessary to be had in a Christian congregation) shall be fully committed into the hands of the clergy...

Please it your gracious fatherhoods therefore, that it may be provided and enacted, that none of these corrections, punishments, and executions, which the clergy hath in their authority already, and hereafter by authority of this present parliament from henceforth shall have in their authority... shall in no wise extend to be executed upon any manner of person or persons that do hold of predestination as is above declared.

The petitioners were convinced that the clerical champions of strict predestination might gain disciplinary laws from the Convocation and Parliament of 1563. As the matter came out, the petitioners need not have feared. Not only did Convocation fail to enact the discipline, but the 1553 article on predestination was not made more rigorous, but was slightly liberalized.[1]

The programme of rigorous doctrinal discipline had the support of a large majority of the Lower House, including a majority of those who had voted against the controversial 'Six articles' on ceremonial. Yet in spite of this wide support, the 'Twenty-one articles' died in Convocation. The bishops again were the roadblock to the militants' programme. Some of the bishops may not have wanted such fierce doctrinal discipline but others, knowing their sovereign's distaste for binding theological definition in matters of secondary importance, perhaps feared that their support of such a programme would turn her against the Articles of Religion which they had so carefully framed.[2] The bishops approved the Articles of Religion, moderated to their own tastes—and nothing more. Never again was the Lower House of Convocation to contain such a powerful concentration of members determined to force the doctrinal Reformation of the English Church closer to the pattern of the 'best reformed churches' of the continent.

The precisians did not give up their plans for doctrinal reform on account of their defeat; they changed their base of operations. John Neale pointed out the change that the 1563 Convocation made in the tactics of the militant reformers:

Having failed to mould their own assembly to their wishes and thus exploit the proper constitutional machinery, the left-wing of the clergy was driven back, for future occasions, on the irregular expedient of 1559—on organizing its agitation through the House of Commons.

[1] The MS is in the Inner Temple Library (Petyt MSS. 538.38, fos. 59–60). The MS states it was exhibited by Thomas Talbor[t?], parson of Mary Magdalene, Milk Street, London. Strype reprints it with only minor discrepancies (*Annals*, I, part I, 495–8). For Lutheran later doctrine of predestination, see article 11 of Formula of Concord (*Book of Concord*, pp. 494–7 and 616–32).
[2] See above, pp. 253–4.

Until 1571 when the form of the Articles was finally settled and the bishops had adopted their own discipline for enforcing them, the bishops were uncertain what their policy ought to be. For a fleeting moment in the next Parliament of 1566, they supported a proposal of the more militant reformers to establish some workable discipline for doctrine.[1]

Near the end of the 1566 Parliament, a bill 'with a little book, printed 1562, for sound Christian religion' attached to it appeared in the House of Commons. The 'little book' was almost certainly the English version of the Articles of Religion. Some English Roman Catholics, troubled by 'grave penalties' which they feared from the bill, told the Spanish ambassador that it was 'only another way to molest them and place them in greater straits than they are now'. If the ambassador's informants were correct, the measure must have imposed the Articles on the laity as well as the clergy.[2]

The bill passed the Commons, but Queen Elizabeth 'forbade the discussion of the matter in Lords'. The bishops sought an audience with her to assure her that they had not, as rumour had it, initiated the bill and yet they hoped she would allow the Lords to consider it. De Silva was delighted to report to Philip that Elizabeth refused the bishops audience for two days. When they appeared, she told them that she did not dislike 'the doctrine of the book of religion, for it containeth the religion which she doth openly profess, but the manner of putting forth the book'. Typically, Elizabeth did not want religious legislation to originate in Parliament, and she used the rights of her royal prerogative to prevent it.[3]

Even though the two archbishops with thirteen of their suffragans urged the queen by letter to allow the bill, she refused to budge. Even though an angry protesting Commons held up some minor government measures in retaliation, the bill with 'the little book' for statutory discipline in doctrine proceeded no farther.

[1] Neale, *Parliaments*, 1, 89–90.
[2] *CSP, Sp.* 1, 603, de Silva to Philip, 16 December 1566. The description of parliamentary action follows Neale (*Parliaments*, 1, 166–76).
[3] *CSP, Sp.* 1, 606, de Silva to Philip, 26 December 1566; *Parker Corr.*, pp. 290–4, Parker to Cecil, 21 December; bishops to queen, 24 December.

Doctrine: definition and discipline

The clash between the bishops and Elizabeth has the markings of a fortuitous incident. Parker wrote to Cecil that neither he nor most of his fellow bishops had any part in initiating the Commons bill, nor even knowledge of it until it appeared in the Lords. Apparently, however, the bishops thought that they ought to seize the opportunity to establish some discipline in doctrine, just as they had finally established discipline in clerical apparel and vestments earlier in the year. Either they approved of the provisions of the Commons bill, or they planned to amend it to their tastes in the Lords. The bishops were disappointed with Elizabeth's refusal to allow such a bill, but the incident did not seriously threaten the common purpose which had bound them and the queen closely, if uneasily, together for some years. In spite of their failure in 1566, the bishops' efforts may not have been entirely in vain, for Elizabeth was perhaps more ready to allow them to establish discipline on their own authority in Convocation in 1571.

As we have seen, Parliament in 1571 conferred statutory status on some of the articles. The act requiring clerical subscription only to those Articles of Religion which 'concern the confession of the true Christian faith' was a meagre consolation prize won by the puritans in the Commons who had hoped to persuade their fellow legislators to impose a programme of thorough reform on the Church of England. Strict doctrinal discipline was again a major element in the reformers' programme, and Neale believes that the legislators substantially adopted the proposals of 'Twenty-one articles'.[1]

By 1571, the militant reformers were no longer prepared to accept all of the Articles of Religion. Those on polity and discipline offended their increasingly presbyterian consciences. Two bills which were actually before Parliament in 1571 concerned doctrine. One bill, in Neale's judgment, ratified and enforced *some* of the Articles, omitting those offensive to puritans. The enactment of such a bill would not only have left the omitted articles in an ambiguous status; it would have established an important precedent for Parliament's right to determine doctrinal matters. The second bill required

[1] See above, pp. 255–7; Neale, *Parliaments*, I, 191–217; 'Parliament and the Articles of Religion', *EHR*, LXVII (1952), 510–12.

the clergy to subscribe to the Articles, but allowed them the option of subscribing only to those ratified by Parliament in the first bill.

The Commons passed the first bill with its selected list of Articles. When they heard nothing from the Lords about the bill, they inquired and were told:

The Queen's Majesty having been made privy to the said Articles liketh very well of them, and mindeth to publish them, and have them executed by the Bishops, by Direction of her Highness's Regal Authority of Supremacy of the Church of England and not to have the same dealt in by Parliament.[1]

It was a situation similar to 1566 with one important exception: then the bishops had supported the militant reformers in the Commons, and now they stood with the queen. They knew they had Elizabeth's approval to establish discipline without parliamentary legislation and they wanted no part of a reforming programme to shave the Articles of Religion which many of them had helped to frame eight years earlier.

In anger, the Commons amended their second bill to provide for clerical subscription only to the doctrinal articles. Elizabeth, who needed the political support of the puritans, dared not frustrate their designs *in toto*, and so she allowed the amendment and assented to the bill. As we have seen, the bishops ignored the parliamentary limitation by demanding subscriptions to all the Articles as their own canons required.

The bishops also successfully restored article 29, insisting on the full text of their Articles of 1563 against both puritans and queen. However bitter a pill article 29 may have been for Elizabeth, she was always prepared to distinguish between fundamental and peripheral matters in religion. She accepted the article and assured herself of the wholehearted support of the bishops against the puritan programme of reform.[2]

Although Neale rightly credits Queen Elizabeth herself with

[1] *JHC*, I, 87.
[2] See above, pp. 254–5; Neale, *Parliaments*, I, 207; *EHR*, LXVII, 519–20. Neale here assumes that Elizabeth wanted legislative enforcement of the Articles, an assumption I seriously question.

maintaining the religious settlement in the years between 1559 and 1571, he seriously overstates the case when he suggests that the 1559 'common front' of the reforming clerics was not dissolved until 1571. Elizabeth and the bishops had had a fairly good working alliance since their low point in the summer of 1561. The 'common front' had been substantially dissolved as soon as the bishops made up their minds that they would obey the queen in matters indifferent and that most of the queen's demands, however much they may have disliked them, belonged to this category of the adiaphora. The smooth cooperation of queen and bishops in the Parliament of 1571 may represent a new level of understanding and agreement in the face of a more fully developed puritanism, but it had been the bishops who turned back the forerunners of the puritans in the Convocation of 1563.[1]

The Convocation of 1563 and consequent events in Convocation and Parliament of 1571 established the doctrinal position of the Church of England. The church rejected the attempt of its militant members to raise a contemporary catechism to a position of central importance in its life. The precisians failed to join Nowell's Genevan-like credenda to the Articles of Religion; they failed to require general lay subscription to the Articles; they failed to gain inquisitorial authority for the bishops; they failed to secure severe penalties for 'heresy'; and they failed to raise the Articles to a status equal or superior to the Prayer Book. This wholesale repudiation of the precisians' programme distinguishes anglicanism from the continental churches of the Reformation much more than the minor differences of emphasis between the Articles of Religion and continental confessions. Doctrinal reform and discipline formed a most important part of 'many things of the greatest advantage' which, puritans complained, 'never saw the light' because of the opposition of the bishops in 1563. When hopeful puritans approached James I in 1603 en route to his new throne, they still found it necessary to include among their requests the plea that 'there may be a uniformity of doctrine prescribed'.[2]

---

[1] Neale, *Parliaments*, I, 217.
[2] Millenary petition, Gee and Hardy, *Documents*, p. 509.

The Articles of Religion remained important tests of public teaching in the church, required of the clergy and church officials. Laity were at most enjoined not to speak openly against them. They identified the English Church's acceptance of a great body of common ecumenical traditional teaching, her adoption of the primary themes of the continental Reformation, and a few of her own distinctive characteristics. The English reformers did not rely on any single contemporary authority or group of authorities to frame their doctrinal declarations. They borrowed and adapted and originated those statements which they believed could be tested against scripture as it had been, in general, interpreted by the 'catholic fathers and ancient bishops'. The Prayer Book, in addition to the teaching stated in its simple catechism and implicit in its liturgies, took a similar doctrinal stance in its frequent use of the ancient creeds and its heavy dose of public readings of scripture. The position on the eucharistic presence was most congenial to high Reformed and 'crypto-Calvinist' Lutheran doctrine.

Other writings remained subordinate authorities in doctrinal matters. The Eleven Articles, only gradually falling into disuse, continued to assert their mildly anti-Roman teaching. The proviso in the Supremacy Act, with no formal ecclesiastical ratification, continued to prohibit civil action against heretics unless their doctrine could be proved contrary to the plain words of scripture and the first four ecumenical councils. The Homilies, with full royal assent for the Edwardian sermons and an ambiguous royal permission for the new set, were read and re-read in many parish churches. After 1571, Nowell's Latin catechism was enforced on all schoolmasters. Finally, and certainly of greatest merit among these minor doctrinal authorities, the *Apology* of John Jewel, with the active promotion of the government and the support of church leaders, became the standard defence of English ecclesiastical independence and Reformation.

The Elizabethan reformers did not do, in matters of doctrine, what many of their supporters expected from them. The Thirty-nine articles were briefer, more conservative, and less discursive than their Edwardian predecessors. Had progress in doctrine been made in 1563 as the zealous reformers anticipated, it is difficult to see how the Church of England could have provided fruitful soil for the growth of its distinctive comprehensiveness. In an age when ecclesiastical guards were busy shutting doors to theological alternatives, the Elizabethan reformers left a remarkable number of doors ajar.

7. Roman Catholic recusants: diplomacy and forbearance

MOST of the highest clerical leaders from Mary's reign, a small but significant number of the lesser clergy, and an amorphous body of English laity remained loyal to the unreformed Latin rites and to the authority of the see of Rome. This segment of the English people, whose loyalties were torn between what they regarded to be the claims of God and the claims of Caesar, faced a lacerating conflict of conscience. If we think of the sixteenth century as a time when the broadening influence of Renaissance humanism was inclining men to tolerance, let us balance our view by the recollection that it was also the century of the Spanish Inquisition. English Roman Catholics had little reason to expect any consideration of their problems of conscience, and the memory of the fires of Mary Tudor's reign would have afforded them little comfort.

The policies of the government in the early years of Elizabeth merit our attention, for they show us how Roman Catholics might have been treated throughout the reign if some of their co-religionists had not threatened the rule and the very life of the queen. The presence of Mary Stuart on English soil and the papal bull of excommunication had not yet exacerbated the political threat of a religious rebellion against Elizabeth. Not that the possibility of Roman Catholic revolt was absent during the initial decade of the reign. It was apparent to any moderately observant Englishman that the simplest means of restoring papal jurisdiction would be to replace Elizabeth with a Roman Catholic sovereign. In mid-February 1559 Mary Tudor's ambassador at Rome wrote to Elizabeth of the unsuccessful French attempts to win papal support for Mary Stuart's claims against her.[1] Yet these threats remained quiescent potentialities until armed incidents supported by foreign intrigues aroused alarm. In 1563 it was not primarily Convocation, but Parliament which struggled with the problems of policy towards Roman Catholics.

[1] Haynes, *Collection*, p. 245; Sir Edward Carne to Elizabeth, 16 February 1559 (N.S.).

Inevitably internal policy towards Roman Catholics was influenced by the problems of international politics. The final sessions of the Council of Trent took place during Elizabeth's first years, and rumours and counter-rumours flew across Europe that England might return to the papal fold by participating in the Council. Before turning to the specific events of 1563 and the governmental policies toward Roman Catholic citizens, we shall first need to consider these negotiations over Trent and the lingering hopes of a voluntary submission of England to Rome, for inevitably international and internal policies were intertwined. In this investigation, we shall be able to test A. L. Rowse's judgment that the policy of 'the first decade of Elizabeth's government' was marked by an 'extraordinary leniency' toward Roman Catholics.[1]

TWO PAPAL NUNCIOS

At the time when the Convocation of Canterbury met in 1563, the larger ecclesiastical council at Trent was in adjournment between its twenty-second and twenty-third sessions. Having defined the doctrine of the Mass in September 1562, the Council would proceed in July 1563 to statements on the sacrament of holy orders. As late as 1566 the pope was willing to encourage a scheme to bring the English queen 'back to the true faith'.[2] The very existence of such an ephemeral hope after seven years of Elizabeth's consistent policies illustrates the tenacious character of Roman Catholic attempts to recover 'the Helen that [had] been stolen from them'.[3] In the first four years of Elizabeth's reign, most of these attempts were aimed at persuading her to send representatives to the Council of Trent. Since the Vatican had every intention that the general council would continue to operate within the framework of the medieval canonical structure, English submission to a council would have been, in effect, a renewed submission to papal obedience.

Proposals for the recall of the general council were in the air at

[1] Rowse, *England of Elizabeth*, p. 439.
[2] *CSP, Rome*, I, 192, Bishop of Terni to Bernardino Ferrario, 21 March 1566.
[3] *ZL*, I, 177, Horn and Grindal to Bullinger and Gualter, 6 February 1567.

the time of Elizabeth's accession, and they were reported to Elizabeth in the late spring of 1559.[1] In January 1560 Elizabeth received news that Pius IV had already proposed the council to the 'chief princes'. A month later Throckmorton from France warned Cecil that he must be prepared with 'what ys to be done' if a council were called. And, in his characteristic fashion, Throckmorton went right on to tell the first secretary exactly what preparations he ought to make—even to naming the members of a proposed embassy to the emperor.[2] The ambassador in France had no papal sympathies, and his advocacy of English representation at the council testifies to the conviction of some reformers that a 'free' general council might be able to assert its superiority to the pope. In contrast to Throckmorton, Sir Thomas Challoner dryly remarked to Cecil that the amity of emperor, Spanish king, and pope over the council 'may be unto us a pyllow *in utraque aurem dormire*'.[3]

By the end of April 1560, Pius IV determined to send the abbot of San Saluto to Elizabeth 'to sound her disposition'.[4] The abbot, a layman by name of Parpaglia, was described by de Quadra as a 'staunch Frenchman', and he had been arrested in Flanders a year and a half earlier as a French spy.[5] In the light of the enmity between England and France at the time, the choice must have appeared ominous to the English government, and there is some evidence that Pius had given the envoy a stern, secret letter threatening Elizabeth with war if she would not submit to papal authority.[6] Outwardly, however, the pope wanted to appear conciliatory. Rishton reported that Pius authorized Parpaglia to reassure Elizabeth of his indulgence

[1] *CSP, For.* I, 273, Mundt to Elizabeth, 24 May 1559; I, 303, 7 June; I, 315, Mundt to Mason, 14 June; I, 323, Mundt to Elizabeth, 21 June.
[2] Forbes, *Full View*, I, 302, Killigrew and Jones to council, from France, 17 January 1560; I, 320-1, Throckmorton to Cecil, 4 February 1560.
[3] I.e. 'for us to sleep soundly', Haynes, *Collection*, I, 236-7, minute from Challoner to Cecil, 5 February 1560.
[4] *CSP, Rome*, I, 19, Newsletter, 27 April 1560; *CSP, For.* III, 43, Shers to Cecil, 11 May; *CSP, Rome*, I, 21-2, Pius IV to the duchess of Parma and to de Granvelle, 7 and 8 May.
[5] *CSP, Sp.* I, 159, de Quadra to de Granvelle, 3 June 1560; *CSP, Ven.* VII, 229, Tiepolo to Doge and Senate, 25 June; C. G. Bayne, *Anglo-Roman Relations, 1558-1565* (Oxford, 1913), p. 46.
[6] Bayne, *Anglo-Roman Relations*, pp. 48 and 56.

toward her title, and the abbot carried an official papal greeting
addressed to 'our most dear daughter in Christ'. Pius in this letter
referred to the 'ecumenical and general Council for abolishing of
heresies', but he clearly sought England's representation only if the
queen first submitted to his ecclesiastical authority.[1]

Elizabeth never had to make a formal decision whether or not to
receive Parpaglia, for he had hardly arrived in Brussels in June when
Pius sent orders for him not to cross the Channel. Three months
later the pope recalled him.[2] Philip II, Bishop de Quadra, and the
duchess of Parma had all conspired to prevent the pro-French Parpaglia from representing the pope in London.[3] Yet Elizabeth and
her advisers had expected to be forced to make a decision about the
abbot's entry, and sinister rumours reached her that the nuncio was
to be accompanied by Spanish and French envoys.[4] Although the
dénouement of the incident revealed the improbability of such a
Spanish–French entente at this time, its very possibility must have
given pause to the queen and her advisers.

Throckmorton told the Venetian ambassador in France that
Elizabeth wanted to see Parpaglia's instructions before permitting
him to enter her kingdom. As Throckmorton told it, she had 'already
determined, should the council be free and universal, to send thither
all her bishops and submit to it'. This may be a quite accurate account
of Elizabeth's mind, for these conditions substantially parallel those

[1] Sander, *Anglican Schism*, pp. 290–1; Camden, *Annales*, p. 34, letter dated 15 May
1560; for a convincing assessment of Camden's reports that the pope at the same
time offered to confirm the English liturgy and to grant communion in both kinds,
see John H. Pollen, *The English Catholics in the Reign of Queen Elizabeth...*
(London, 1920), p. 83a; *CSP, For.* IX, 76–7, Walsingham to Burghley, 21 June 1571.
[2] *CSP, Rome,* I, 22, Newsletter, Rome, 17 and 21 May 1560; I, 24, Borromeo to
nuncio, 29 June; I, 26, Borromeo to nuncios in Spain, 17 September; *CSP, For.*
III, 63 and 79, Shers to Cecil, Venice, 18 and 25 May; III, 289, Parpaglia to Elizabeth,
8 September; *CSP, Ven.* VII, 229, Tiepolo to Doge and Senate, 25 June; *CSP, Sp.*
I, 170, de Quadra to Philip, 25 July.
[3] Borromeo's letter of 17 September implied it was Elizabeth's 'obstinate refusal'
which prevented completion of the embassy, but this judgment conflicts with his
own letter of 29 June, with Parpaglia's letter to Elizabeth, and with Tiepolo's report
of 25 June (see above, n. 2).
[4] *CSP, For.* III, 100, Petre to Cecil, 6 June 1560; III, 63 and 79, Shers to Cecil, 18 and
25 May; III, 136, Gresham to Purvey, 22 June.

which the Lutheran princes had laid down the previous year, that the council be 'general, free, Christian, and held in Germany'. The Vatican steadfastly refused to grant conditions which would have abnegated papal control in order to meet English and Lutheran definitions of 'free'. The whole incident in 1560 was a dress rehearsal for the decision which Elizabeth and her government could not so easily avoid in the following year.[1]

Through the summer and autumn of 1560, European diplomatic speculation frequently centred on the general council, and some protestants still hoped that their conditions for a free council might be met. Before the year was out, Pius had issued a bull reconvening the council which would meet under firm papal control: a free council by papal standards, but hardly qualifying as 'free' by the standards of the English and Germans. The pope delegated envoys to carry the bull to European nations in and out of the papal orbit, designating Abbot Martinengo to go to England.[2]

Before news of the bull reached England, Queen Elizabeth was so optimistic about the chances for a council free of papal domination that her Italian fool 'talkd openly of the same, and devisd upon the meanes of sending'. Elizabeth insisted on communications with the German princes; she had in mind a council which would meet their conditions. The cautious Cecil worried about the consequences of English involvement in the council, and he feared Elizabeth's enthusiasms for the project. He regretted that Throckmorton encouraged Elizabeth in thinking of English representation, a matter of too much weight 'for a woman's knowledge'. However, after receiving news of the bull, not only Throckmorton, but the queen herself cooled towards the council. In instructions to her agent Mundt, she delegated him to attend the February 1561 meeting of German protestant princes at Naumberg and to urge them not to

[1] *CSP, Ven.* VII, 233, Michiel to Doge and Senate, 30 June 1560; *CSP, For.* I, 303, Mundt to Elizabeth, 7 June 1559.
[2] *ZL*, I, 90, Jewel to Peter Martyr, 17 July 1560; *CSP, For.* III, 196, Throckmorton to Elizabeth, 19 July; III, 211–12, Giannetti to Elizabeth, 3 August; III, 255, Peter Martyr to Cox; III, 353 and 381, Shers to Cecil, 12 October and 2 November; III, 432 and 451, Giannetti to Elizabeth, 7 and 20 December 1560; III, 453, Shers to Elizabeth, 21 December.

assent to the council 'unless it be held in Germany, and in such place where the parties coming thither may be free from danger or apprehension'. The Germans did not need Elizabeth's persuasions, and they refused to receive the bull.[1]

Elizabeth and her advisers determined in January 1561 to send the earl of Bedford to France to aid Throckmorton in fanning the smouldering anti-papal forces in France. He was to urge the protestant-minded king of Navarre that

There will be no reformation until the Pope and the rest submit themselves in a General Council to the rule of the old Fathers and Bishops of the ancient Church, and conform themselves to Scriptures and the ancient canons, so this manner of assembly will serve but to abuse Christian Princes, and indeed will prove an augmentation to their tyranny.

Bedford found the king of Navarre in substantial agreement, but the earl was less successful in his attempt to persuade the *politique* Queen Mother that the proposed council would not be free. The English hoped either that the French would refuse to participate in the council or that they would be able to force changes in the council's structure which would make it possible for England and protestant Germany to attend.[2]

Abbot Martinengo travelled to Brussels in March and April where he stopped to await English permission to present the formal announcement of the council at the English court. Cardinal Moroni, who expected the envoy to be admitted, urged him to maintain a conciliatory attitude:

He is to wear his ordinary habit,...to tarry in Flanders for a safe-conduct; ...in England he is not to reside with the Spanish ambassador;...in the Queen's presence he is to betray no offence even though she should speak

[1] Philip Hardwicke, *Miscellaneous State Papers from 1501 to 1726* (London, 1778), I, 166–7, Jones to Throckmorton, 30 November 1560, as corrected by Bayne, *Anglo-Roman Relations*, p. 70n.; *CSP, For.* III, 469, Throckmorton to Elizabeth, 31 December 1560; III, 473, Throckmorton to Privy Council, 31 December; III, 463, 30 December, Elizabeth to Mundt; III, 539, princes to Mundt, 6 February 1561; III, 550, John Frederick to Elizabeth, 13 February; IV, 5, Mundt to Elizabeth, 4 March; IV, 13–14, Shers to Cecil, 8 March.
[2] *CSP, For.* III, 505, Instructions for the earl of Bedford, 20 January 1561; III, 567 and 569–70, 575, Throckmorton and Bedford to Privy Council, 26 February 1561.

disrespectfully of the Pope, or evince reluctance to accept the Council because it is summoned by him....If she should refuse him an answer, promising to write herself to the Pope, he is to be content that she do so.

Pius did not intend to make any substantial concessions to 'heretical' princes, but he invited them so that 'those that refuse to come may be convicted of contumacy'.[1]

In England Bishop de Quadra strove with might and main to prepare the way for the nuncio's arrival. The Spanish ambassador believed that he was preparing the way for the return of England to papal obedience. By mid-March he thought that he had made progress, and he forthrightly asked Cecil for his opinion on reunion through a council. To the bishop's surprise, Cecil made what de Quadra judged to be three important concessions:

First, that the Queen would be willing to send her ambassadors and theologians to the Concilio even though it were convoked by the Pope on condition that the meeting was at a place satisfactory to...[Philip], the Emperor, and the King of France....She would be willing that the Pope or his legates should preside...in such a way as did not infer that he was a ruler over it, but only as head or president....They would be in favour of judging questions of faith, as well as others, according to...holy scriptures, the consensus of divines, and the declarations of the ancient [first four] *Concilios*.

Cecil also did insist that the English bishops be seated in the council as they were 'canonically ordained'—a significant claim that the Elizabethan episcopate had legitimately succeeded their predecessors according to catholic order. Reading de Quadra's report, I cannot see what it was that he thought Cecil had conceded, for these are substantially the three conditions which Elizabeth and the German protestants had been requesting for nearly two years to guarantee a free council. De Quadra's reaction reveals his surprising ignorance of the convictions of English reformers—he did not understand what Cecil was asking from the papacy. De Quadra also reported that

[1] *CSP, Rome*, I, 32 and 34, Borromeo to nuncios in lower Germany and Spain, 4 and 7 March 1561, and undated instructions noted on a letter of questions from Martinengo; *CSP, For.* IV, 82, Throckmorton to Elizabeth, 29 April.

English bishops were meeting frequently to prepare a statement of faith for the council when, in fact, the Lambeth Articles, the final form of the Interpretations, and the Eleven Articles seem to have been their main agenda. He was pleased to note that Cecil had reproved Robert Horn for preaching against conciliar authority.[1]

In April, when the papal legates left Rome for Trent, de Quadra was so confident of his success in England that he engaged lodgings near Greenwich so that he would be near at hand when Elizabeth received the papal nuncio. A major reason for his optimism was his intrigue with Robert Dudley, Elizabeth's favourite and councillor. As de Quadra understood the secret negotiations, he would win Philip's support for Elizabeth's marriage to Dudley in return for Dudley's assurance that, through the Council of Trent, England would return to papal obedience. In the course of this bizarre sideshow, the beguiled bishop interpreted all Elizabeth's words as if she enthusiastically supported Dudley's schemes:

> The Queen...told me with her own lips several times that she wished to send representatives to the *Concilio*, and...Cecil...assured me that her Majesty was about to select Ambassadors,...and many other things proved to me...that she approved of what [Dudley] said to me.

Later, when de Quadra insisted that the queen had promised to 'restore religion' by means of the council, 'she got out of it by remarking that this was only on certain conditions'. De Quadra did not remember the conditions, but it is not likely that the queen would have erred in a matter of such moment nor that she found it necessary to lie. The mere word 'free' would have provided an adequate condition from Elizabeth's standpoint, but to the Spaniard a 'free council' would have been one in which the pope could exercise his rightful authority.[2]

By the end of April, de Quadra knew that all was not well. Elizabeth had already informed him that if the nuncio were to be

---

[1] *CSP, Sp.* I, 190–1, de Quadra to Philip, 23 March 1561; see above, pp. 239–40.

[2] *CSP, For.* IV, 51–2, Shers to Cecil, 5 April 1561; *CSP, Sp.* I, 194, 197, and 200–1, de Quadra to Philip, 12 and 25 April and 5 May 1561; (for details of the Dudley diversion, see *CSP, Sp.* I, 179–206, *passim*; Bayne, *Anglo-Roman Relations*, pp. 88–93 and 266–9; Read, *Cecil*, I, 207–8).

received, it must be as the ambassador of the bishop of Rome since English law denied papal supremacy. The bishop was disappointed, and his few remaining hopes evaporated when the government arrested a group of prominent Roman Catholics. De Quadra went to Cecil to ask for the nuncio's safe-conduct, and the secretary informed him that the seditious activities of the recusants had made it impossible for the government to admit Martinengo.[1]

The Privy Council formally decided on 1 May to refuse admittance to Martinengo. The official notes of the meeting state that the councillors, including such conservatives as Arundel, Derby, and William Howard, reached their decision unanimously, but according to a report sent to Rome, Bacon and Cecil gained unanimity by suggesting that a contrary vote would seem like treason. In their statement, the councillors pointed out the papal activities that had already disturbed the realm. In regard to the council itself they wrote:

Nothing can better please her Majesty, than to hear of a General Council: and among all worldly things that might happen unto her, no one thing could be thought more happy, than that she might live to hear of such a General Council, as might tend to make a unity in Christendom.... When she shall understand a Council to be called in such a sort, and meeting at such a place,...and with such conditions of freedom, for all Christian Princes and estates to come,... [she will send] meet persons, as she doubts not shall declare the earnestness of her affection to have one unity in all matters of Christ's religion. But...her Majesty cannot understand that the Council now mentioned is so called.

The councillors also protested the pope's failure to consult Elizabeth along with other Christian princes before calling the council. Except for this minor new note, the paper is an eloquent reaffirmation of all Elizabeth had previously said about a general council.

It was a bitter defeat for the formidable bishop from Spain. By anticipation, he had savoured the joy of presenting a hard-earned victory to king and to pope. Instead, not only had he been defeated,

[1] Bayne, *Anglo-Roman Relations*, pp. 93–4 and 108–9; Read, *Cecil*, I, 209; two of de Quadra's reports are not in the calendar, but both Bayne and Read have taken them from Lettenhove (II, 348–9 and 559–60); on the same day de Quadra wrote an outraged letter to Dudley (*CSP, Sp.* I, 197–8, 25 April 1561).

but he had been made to appear naïve and foolish as well. His subsequent meeting with the councillors at court must have been a painful and humiliating experience.[1]

The diplomatic games and court rumours during this whole series of events produced conflicting reports of the intentions of the government. When historians who were convinced of Elizabeth's fundamental religious indifference have dealt with these reports, they have inevitably found in them evidence that Elizabeth seriously considered betraying the 1559 religious settlement by submitting to the papally dominated Council of Trent. Convinced as I am of Elizabeth's consistent religious policies (apart from the thornier question of her motives), I approach the evidence from a different position, and I find in it nothing to substantiate such a conclusion. Every authentic statement that came from Elizabeth, from her chief secretary, or from foreign envoys abroad made English representation at the council dependent upon conditions which would ensure its freedom from papal domination. Pius' December 1560 bull ruled out the possibility of such conditions.

The court conversations in which de Quadra put such faith and the disagreements which de Quadra reported between Cecil and the bishops suggest that some responsible people, including some bishops, thought that the government might still send representatives to the council planned by Pius. At the end of April, Throckmorton was sufficiently concerned to write to Elizabeth enumerating, in his pedantic fashion, the practical reasons over and above 'the testimony of her conscience' why she ought not to return to Rome if she had been 'no other wise stirred with religion than Numa Pompilius or Sertorius'.[2]

Apparently Elizabeth had either hinted at her willingness to submit to a papally governed council, or she had not put down rumours to that effect when they appeared. It has often been judged that Elizabeth used religion as a tool of political policy; perhaps, at this

[1] Hardwicke, *State Papers*, I, 180–6; *CSP, For.* IV, 94–5; Bayne, *Anglo-Roman Relations*, p. 272, an excerpt from Vatican archives; *CSP, For.* IV, 99–100, answer to de Quadra for the coming of the pope's nuncio, 5 May 1561; *CSP, Sp.* 201–2 and 204, de Quadra to Philip, 5 May 1561, and de Quadra to de Granvelle and the duchess of Parma, 6 May.
[2] *CSP, For.* IV, 86–7, Throckmorton to Elizabeth, 29 April 1561.

juncture, Elizabeth employed politics as a tool of her religious policies. In the spring of 1561 she knew that many of her new bishops were evading their duty to enforce the settlement and would seek to abolish more of the traditional ceremonies if they found opportunity. Rumours of her possible reconversion to Rome may have been 'false and scandalous', but they may have served her purpose by suggesting to the bishops that if they did not fulfil their duties, they might wake up to find the pope back in England. Elizabeth's calculated use of her bishops' fear of Rome may explain the prevalence of rumours that she might submit to a papal council. No firm evidence suggests that she ever seriously contemplated any such submission.

Cecil's attitude diverged from that of Elizabeth in some aspects of the issues, and again I find that I read the evidence differently from most historians. On 8 May Cecil wrote to Throckmorton that he had sent a copy of the notes for refusal of the nuncio

to sundry places 'lest *our former inclinations* had been too hastily spread by the adversaries'. When he saw the Romish influence towards about a month past, he thought necessary to dull the Papists' expectation by discovering certain mass-mongers and punishing them. 'I take God to record I mean no evil to any of them, but only rebating of their Papists' humours, which by the Queen's lenity grow too rank. I find it hath done much good.'[1]

The key to the difference between Cecil and Elizabeth in regard to proposed policies lies in the words '*our* former inclinations'. This could really refer only to the specific question of admitting Martinengo to present his invitation, for no historian has seriously entertained the thought that *Cecil* had been inclined to return England to Roman obedience! The queen and her secretary originally thought it would be well to admit the papal nuncio so that Elizabeth might make a formal reply and lay down her conditions for accepting the council.

The admission of the envoy in no way implied submission to the council. In Cardinal Moroni's instructions, he assumed that Martinengo would be admitted, and then he expected that the nuncio might fall

---

[1] *CSP, For.* IV, 104, Cecil to Throckmorton, 8 May 1561; italics mine.

foul of Elizabeth's heretical intransigence. In the very letter in which
Throckmorton exhorted the queen to remain steadfast in religion,
he advised her to admit Martinengo, who would make 'no greater
inconvenience' than any other ambassador.[1] The Privy Council met
on 1 May only to decide about the nuncio's admission to England—
not about England's admission to the council.

Finally, Cecil wrote another revealing comment to Throckmorton:
'Here hath been no small ado to refuse this Popish Messenger; not
that any counsellor was outwardly unwilling, but no man was
found so earnest and bold to adventure the advising of such as
were of other minds.'[2] Who in England but Queen Elizabeth
would earls and men of state fear to advise? Queen Elizabeth had
apparently wanted to admit Martinengo. This had also been Cecil's
'former inclination' until he saw the extent of Roman Catholic
jubilation. The possible display of domestic papal strength fright-
ened Cecil, who thought that it might prove dangerous to the
government. He deliberately dug out evidence of Roman Catholic
sedition in order to expose the dangers implicit in the visit.

Cecil's 'mass-mongers' and the unanimous opposition of the Privy
Council to Martinengo's entry convinced Elizabeth. She may have
wished to press for a genuinely free council, or she may simply have
looked forward to verbal sparring with the pope's envoy. She had
been nurtured on the independence of the English Church, and
probably felt confident of her ability to handle the Roman cleric in
her facile Latin. The changes of government attitudes from the
autumn of 1560 to the spring of 1561 were changes of tactics—not
of fundamental policies.

LINGERING ROMAN CATHOLIC HOPES

The refusal to allow Martinengo on English soil might have been
expected to end papal attempts to secure English representation at
Trent. Surely English 'contumacy' was proven. Yet the spring of
1562 brought renewed efforts. Two factors may account for the re-

[1] *CSP, For.* IV, 84, Throckmorton to Elizabeth, 29 April 1561.
[2] Hardwicke, *State Papers*, I, 171, Cecil to Throckmorton, May 1561.

vived efforts: first, English diplomats, in reporting abroad the refusal to admit the nuncio, emphasized the queen's willingness to support a council that was truly general and free;[1] second, the French were ambivalent toward the papally controlled council and by the end of 1561 had still not sent a delegation to Trent.[2]

The Cardinal of Ferrara, papal legate in France, initiated the new efforts to woo Elizabeth in November 1561. He sent a messenger to England and solicited Throckmorton's support in Paris. For several months the negotiations remained courteous but casual. In February 1562 Jewel wrote to Peter Martyr that Elizabeth had 'fully made up her mind not to send any representative to the council'.[3]

A new development unexpectedly appeared in early March. Throckmorton jubilantly reported that the Queen Mother had sent Admiral Coligny to propose that English delegates join with France at Trent to demand a new and free council:

The Queen Mother is well affected for a general reformation in the Church, and for the Bishop of Rome and his clergy to be arranged in some order, or that amongst the Protestant Princes some order be taken that the Papists may not be able to give laws to the Protestants....The Queen Mother desires that the Queen will send her Legates [to Trent], ...and employ her credit with the Protestant Princes that they may do the same.

Elizabeth immediately took an interest and appointed a committee of top councillors who proceeded to recommend that no English representative be sent to Trent unless the German princes followed suit.[4]

[1] *CSP, For.* IV, 101, Elizabeth to Throckmorton, 6 May 1561; *CSP, Ven.* VII, 315, Surien to Doge and Senate; VII, 318, Tiepolo to Doge and Senate, 3 July; but cf. *CSP, Rome,* I, 37, Commendone to Gonzaga, 20 May.

[2] *CSP, Ven.* VII, 296, Surien to Doge and Senate, 17 February 1561; *CSP, For.* IV, 398 and 439, Throckmorton to Elizabeth, 14 November and 13 December; IV, 435, Shokerly to Throckmorton, 12 December.

[3] *CSP, Sp.* I, 219, de Quadra to Philip, 27 November 1561; Read, *Cecil,* I, 231–2, Throckmorton to Elizabeth (summarized in *CSP, For.* IV, 432–3); *CSP, For.* IV, 447–8, Throckmorton's instructions for Francis Petowe, 20 December 1561; IV, 527, Throckmorton to Elizabeth, 16 February 1562; IV, 528, Throckmorton to Cecil, 16 February; *ZL,* I, 101, Jewel to Peter Martyr, 7 February 1562.

[4] *CSP, For.* IV, 545, Throckmorton to Elizabeth, 6 March 1562; Bayne, *Anglo-Roman Relations,* p. 287, from BM MS., Cecil to Throckmorton, 24 March 1561.

In secret instructions to her agent Christopher Mundt, Elizabeth told him to propose to the duke of Würtemberg that England and protestant Germany take some concerted action to support French efforts at Trent. The duke told Mundt that the princes were planning a consultation and offered to invite Elizabeth to be represented. The Germans did not treat the proposal with much seriousness, for the meeting was not held until September, long after the project had been abandoned by the French and English.[1]

Elizabeth, meanwhile, wrote to Throckmorton to encourage the Queen Mother without committing England; he was to inform Catherine of Elizabeth's 'conviction that Trent is completely in papal control'. Throckmorton convinced Catherine that she should seek to prorogue the council until English delegates arrived. On her orders, the French ambassador to Trent proposed on 25 May that the council send a special invitation to England, and he even went so far as to ask that it declare itself to be a new council. A new council would have been free to reconsider all the anti-protestant doctrinal decisions reached at Trent to date. Even Ferrara, who had not known of Catherine's anti-papal dealings with Throckmorton, disapproved of these new proposals. The Vatican had never been enthusiastic about Ferrara's restrained intrigues, and the legates at Trent firmly rejected the French proposals. On 1 June Pius himself unequivocally explained in a letter to the French queen:

As to the delay demanded for the Queen of England, would to God she were in earnest in what she says! We put no faith in her because she would not listen to our nuncios. The Council...has refused her Majesty the delay....But, nevertheless, for respect to your Majesty, they have waited and will still wait until the 4th inst. Thereafter We know not what the Council will do, for it is free, though some say the contrary because they would fain have a Huguenot, Lutheran, or Protestant Council, and We are determined that it shall be, as it should be, Catholic. And if the Queen of England shall be minded to return to Holy Mother Church, she has yet time.[2]

---

[1] *CSP, For.* IV, 561–2 and 562–4, Cecil to Mundt and Elizabeth to Mundt, 22 and 23 March 1562; IV, 591, Mundt to Elizabeth, 8 April 1562; V, 391, Mundt to Cecil, 3 October 1562; Bayne, *Anglo-Roman Relations*, pp. 287–8.

[2] *CSP, For.* IV, 550–1, Elizabeth to Throckmorton, undated, but probably March 1562; *CSP, Rome,* I, 75, 77 and 82, Borromeo to Ferrara, 28 January, 15 March,

The embittered de Quadra thought that England only pursued
these negotiations in the spring of 1562 in order to prevent French
representation at Trent. His judgment was a half-truth at best.
Elizabeth's prompt attempt to gain German cooperation suggests
that Throckmorton's enthusiastic reports had revived the hopes of
the queen, if not of her councillors, that a strong anti-papal block
might still be formed at Trent. Her hope was more than wishful
thinking, for papal officials revealed in May their worries that a strong
anti-papal bid could prove difficult to handle. German indifference
and the failure of Catherine's efforts snuffed out England's last
flicker of hope for an international resolution of the disunity of
western Christendom.[1]

By the time Convocation met at the beginning of 1563, serious
negotiations between England and the Vatican were finished. The
inexorable progress of the Council of Trent was approaching its conclusion, and before the year was out it was to delineate the course
of Roman Catholicism for the next four centuries. Elizabeth now dismissed the hope of bringing Rome to reformed convictions, a hope
which her ecclesiastics had dismissed long before.

Vatican leaders, for their part, were becoming increasingly convinced that political and military means were their only hope for
regaining England. The new English exiles at Louvain already believed that strong action was their only hope. Early in June 1563
they requested the Council of Trent to declare Elizabeth worthy of
excommunication.[2] The Council sought the opinion of the pope and
emperor. Ferdinand was furious. The papal nuncio at the imperial
court immediately sent off letters to protest to the Vatican and to the
legates at Trent: 'I know not any thing that has ever moved the
Emperor so much as the proposal now made to deprive the Queen

and 9 May; I, 84, legates at Trent to Borromeo, 21 May 1562; I, 89, Musotti's
summary account of the council, 25 May; I, 93, nuncio with the emperor to
Borromeo, 15 June; I, 87 and 92, Borromeo to legates at Trent, 27 May and 6 June;
I, 95, nuncio with the emperor to legates, 2 July; I, 91, Pius IV to Catherine de
Medici, 1 June 1562.
[1] *CSP, Sp.* I, 240, de Quadra to Philip, 6 June 1562; *CSP, Rome,* I, 83, Borromeo to
legates at Trent, 20 May 1562; I, 86, legate with emperor to Borromeo, 25 May.
[2] *CSP, Rome,* I, 135, de Granvelle to legates at Trent, 27 June 1563; Bayne, *Anglo-
Roman Relations,* pp. 186–8.

of England.'[1] Ferdinand feared that such an action would force the protestant princes of the empire into an active league against Roman Catholic rulers. Cardinal de Granvelle was equally horrified and informed the legates that His Catholic Majesty of Spain knew best how to deal with Elizabeth. Pius at first looked with favour on the exiles' project, but under the pressure from both Hapsburg governments he backed down and rescinded the orders to proceed against Elizabeth.[2]

Futile intrigues and idle negotiations recurred. An Italian by the name of Gerone Bretano began a one-sided correspondence with Cecil in the autumn of 1563, ostensibly to serve Cecil, but in reality to reconcile England to the papacy. In September 1564 Bretano elaborately explained how Cecil might cause Parliament 'to settle the true religion in the kingdom'. At the same time he sent an agent, who was received into Leicester's service, with offers of military support and bribes for the queen, Cecil, and Leicester. Records of the intrigue end with Pius' death in December 1565, but in the meantime the queen and Cecil kept the diverting plot alive by notes of courteous flattery.[3]

Pope Pius revealed his inadequate understanding of the English situation in his two interviews with Thomas Sackville, who was temporarily imprisoned in Rome at the beginning of 1564. Pius told Sackville, the son of a privy councillor, that he thought two things estranged Elizabeth from the holy see: Clement's judgment on her parents' marriage and the alienation of church property. He promised the queen, through Sackville, that if she would submit to his authority, he would satisfactorily remedy these difficulties. When Elizabeth

---

[1] *CSP, Rome*, I, 132, nuncio with the emperor to Cardinal Moroni and to legates at Trent, 17 June 1563; Bayne, *Anglo-Roman Relations*, pp. 188–9.

[2] *CSP, Rome*, I, 135, de Granvelle to legates at Trent, 27 June 1563; I, 137–8, Borromeo to the legates at Trent, 6 July 1563; to the nuncio with the emperor, 10 July; to the legates, 10 July.

[3] *CSP, For.* VI, 593, 594, 607, and 639, Bretano to Antoine Burschetti in London, before November and 18 November 1563; Bretano to Cecil, 18 November, 5 and 18 December; VII, 37 and 208–9, Cecil to Bretano, 29 January 1564; Bretano to Cecil, 19 September; Bayne, *Anglo-Roman Relations*, pp. 208–17 and 311–23, especially pp. 317–18, Cecil to Bretano and Elizabeth to Bretano, 17 April 1565; pp. 322–3, Bretano to Requesens, 2 November 1565.

heard the offer, she showed courteous interest, but she made no move to send the envoy requested by the Vatican. The offer had been made in utter seriousness, and Sackville had met with Cardinals Moroni and Borromeo to confirm the terms. Pope Pius was willing to encourage Bretano and to deal with Sackville; it is surprising that he still thought it worth while, even as an outside chance, to try to win Elizabeth by offers of political and financial support.[1]

Pius IV, by and large, followed Philip's lead in emphasizing conciliation to win Elizabeth. However, in a consistory session on 12 October 1565, shortly before his death, he spoke of heresy in England and English interference in Scotland:

He had never been desirous of war, nay he heartily detested it, and yet, since others engaged in it for religion's sake, it behoved him to support the Catholics with counsel, aid, and money, wheresoever and by what means so ever he might be of service; and other Princes of the Christian commonwealth should do the like. He therefore exhorted the [cardinal] protectors of princes that were present to admonish their princes, the Emperor, the Most Christian King, and the Catholic King, that it belonged to their office to support the Catholics with all the countenance and aid at their command.[2]

Although the pope was primarily concerned with Scotland in this speech, he made a sharp turn in his official English policy as well— a turn he himself had considered when the Louvain exiles had requested Elizabeth's formal excommunication. By implication, he now sought to encourage military action to return England to papal jurisdiction. Pius V's condemnation of Elizabeth in 1570 cannot be attributed wholly to his more aggressive character; he inherited the policy from his predecessor, who had initiated it in the last months of his life.

---

[1] *CSP, For.* VII, 34, notes of Smith in Paris from a recent traveller from Rome, 29 January 1564; *CRS, Miscellanea* (London, 1906) II, 1–11, 'Testimonial by Bishop Goldwell and Others in favour of Thomas Sackville', ed. by H. D. Grissell; also three papers from the Vatican, ed. by J. H. Pollen; *CSP, Rome,* I, 163–4; cf. *CSP, Sp.* I, 390–1, de Silva to Philip, 4 November 1564; Bayne, *Anglo-Roman Relations*, p. 216.
[2] *CSP, Rome,* I, 179, consistory meeting, 12 October 1565.

Philip II had himself finally arrived at the same conclusion. In the same month of October 1565, he declared in a letter to a Vatican official:

When the time comes to throw off the mask and bestir ourselves,...the Pope and I will consider the manner in which we may aid and promote that cause of God which the Queen of Scotland upholds, since it is manifest that she is the gate by which religion must enter the realm of England, all others being now closed.[1]

Philip did not intend to act in the immediate future, but the holy crusade of the Armada was already implicit in these words. A measure of truth underlay the false rumours circulating Europe for the next two years that Roman Catholic powers had formed a league to depose the queen of England.[2] Pius IV and His Catholic Majesty of Spain now understood that they could not persuade or cajole Elizabeth to restore papal authority in England.

At the beginning of the pontificate of Pius V, he made two small conciliatory gestures towards Elizabeth. In March 1566 he gave his unenthusiastic blessing to an Italian scheme to convert Elizabeth, and in December the Vatican asked de Silva to offer Elizabeth papal recognition of her crown in return for her obedience. The scheme came to nothing and de Silva's offer was rebuffed. Pius V probably soon became convinced that his predecessor's last decisions about England's queen were right: she was a notorious heretic who could only be brought to obedience by force of arms.[3]

A whole series of misjudgments seem to have been responsible for the lingering Vatican hope that England might voluntarily return to papal obedience under the queen's leadership. Papal adherents misjudged the significance of the queen's quarrels with protestant non-conformists. They overestimated the influence of nobles who

---

[1] *CSP, Rome*, I, 182, Philip to Cardinal Pacecco, 16 and 18 October 1565; cf. *CSP, Sp.* I, 352-3, Philip to de Silva, 15 January 1564.

[2] *CSP, For.* VIII, 1, Bedford to Cecil, 2 January 1566; VIII, 18, Randolph to Cecil, 7 February (or Wright, *Queen Elizabeth*, I, 219-20); *CSP, Sp.* I, 650, de Silva to Philip, 26 June 1567; *CSP, Ven.* VII, 404, Michiel from Vienna to Doge and Senate, 11 September 1567.

[3] See above, p. 292, n. 2; *CSP, Sp.* I, 600 and 603; de Silva to Philip, 2 and 16 December 1566.

remained loyal to the older ways. They put the most favourable interpretations possible upon her ambiguous statements. And finally they naïvely thought that the whole matter might be solved by her marriage to a Roman Catholic prince. Behind all these misjudgments stood the influence of Philip of Spain, who preferred a heretical Elizabeth on the English throne to an orthodox Mary Stuart who remained more French than Spanish. He eventually was convinced that she was 'the gate by which religion must enter' England, but he wanted Spanish hands alone to place the English crown on her head.

The negotiations over the Council of Trent misled Roman Catholic supporters—perhaps as Elizabeth intended that they should. At no time was the English government prepared to send representatives to the Council unless they were first assured that the Council would be free, according to an understanding of the word which they shared with the German Lutheran princes. By the middle of 1565 the Vatican largely understood the nature of the challenge which they faced in England. All papal efforts to win England by persuasion and political promises had wrecked on the rock of the determination of Elizabeth and her advisers to keep to the settlement of 1559—a settlement which left no room for compromise with a post-Tridentine papacy.

The change in papal policies toward England was to bring its greatest suffering to English Roman Catholics who would increasingly be forced to make the decision they feared and avoided: loyalty to queen or loyalty to pope. Although the efforts at negotiations during the early years of Elizabeth's reign were fruitless, they helped to postpone the days when such decisions were required of English Roman Catholics.

EARLY GOVERNMENT POLICY TOWARDS ROMAN CATHOLICS

When Bishop de Quadra described Dean Nowell's sermon at the opening of the 1563 Parliament, he called it an exhortation 'to kill the caged wolves'. By 'caged wolves' he meant bishops and other prelates who had refused to conform to the settlement. A number of Marian ecclesiastics in prison at the time of Convocation had been there since the spring of 1560.[1]

The first action the English government took against lay Roman Catholics for the practice of their religion came in February 1560 when Englishmen were arrested who had attended Mass at the home of the French ambassador. It was a tense period, for war with France threatened to break out over Scottish policies. Our informant, de Quadra, reported that the queen feared that her subjects carried on 'clandestine communications with the French ambassador'. There may have been substance to the royal fears, for Dr Cole, the deprived dean of St Paul's, had recently warned de Quadra that if the Spanish would not aid English Roman Catholics 'they would appeal to the French, or even to the Turks, rather than put up with these heretics'. It is significant that in this initial action against Roman Catholics, the Spanish ambassador confirms the political motivations which Elizabeth always claimed were her reasons for such measures. Dr Cole and his fellow clerics undoubtedly acted from religious motives in seeking foreign aid, but they were willing to accept the political implications which such aid inevitably involved.[2]

The deprived Marian bishops remained at liberty until the spring of 1560. I feel confident that this is true in spite of Philip Hughes' judgment that twelve of the bishops were in prison from the time of their deprivations. Dr Hughes concludes this as a fact which 'seems certain' on the basis of the 'sworn testimony of Edmund Daniel'. The records, however, in intelligence rumours, contemporary letters, and Machyn's Diary all suggest that the incarcerations which certainly did take place in the spring of 1560 were fresh imprisonments rather than changes in the location and severity of the bishops' imprisonment. Edmund Daniel was giving his evidence ten years later, when the months of episcopal freedom could have telescoped into insignificance in the memory of hindsight.[3]

---

[1] *CSP, Sp.* I, 289, de Quadra to Philip, 15 November 1562; also I, 291, de Quadra to his servant in Brussels, 14 January 1563.

[2] *CSP, Sp.* I, 124 and 126, de Quadra to Philip and to the duchess of Parma, 5 and 7 February 1560; see Philip's instructions to de Quadra, 23 March 1559 (I, 41).

[3] *The Reformation in England*, 3 vols. (New York, 1954), III, 245; Gee, *Elizabethan Clergy*, p. 144, from State Papers Dom., XVIII, 1–5; Machyn, pp. 233, 237, and 238;

The militant protestants were scandalized by the government's easy treatment of the Marian prelates. Christopher Goodman concluded a list of complaints against the English settlement in October 1559 with this:

And last (which sticketh much in the hearts of many), the suffering of those bloody Bishops and known murderers of God's people and your dear brethren, to live, upon whom God hath expressly pronounced the sentence of death; for the execution whereof He hath committed the sword into your hands, who are now placed in authority.

Elizabeth's government, less certain of God's express sentence, withheld any penal action until after a flurry of signs suggested that the bishops were intriguing with the French. Death and flight had reduced the number of Marian bishops in England to nine, and eight of them were imprisoned in the spring of 1560: Bonner to Marshalsea in April; Scot to the Fleet and Watson and Pate to the Tower in May; and Heath, Thirlby, Turberville, and Bourne to the Tower in June.[1]

When de Quadra protested to Elizabeth, she replied that she knew they 'wanted to rise against her, and she could show... proofs of it'. Cecil wrote to Throckmorton that 'if the French begyn oppen playe we maye not dissemble with theis men'. Jewel wrote that the bishops were imprisoned

for having obstinately refused attendance on public worship and everywhere declaring and railing against that religion which we now profess. For the Queen... most manfully and courageously declared that she would not allow her subjects to dissent from this religion with impunity.

Apparently the bishops had not only refused to attend the English liturgy, but had publicly spoken out against the religious changes.

Forbes, *A Full View*, I, 460, Cecil to Throckmorton, 22 May 1560; I, 105, Killigrew to Throckmorton, 29 May; *CSP, Rome*, I, 23, intelligence from England, *c.* May 1560; *CSP, Ven.* VII, 240, Michiel (in France) to Doge and Senate, 22 July 1560.

[1] *CSP, For.* II, 63; Goodman to Cecil, 26 October 1559. Tunstall and Bayne died on 18 November, Morgan on 23 December 1559, White on 12 January 1560, and Oglethorpe 'a short time' after his deprivation (Francis Godwin, *De Praesulibus Angliae* [London, 1616], Canterbury, p. 616, York, pp. 139 and 153; edition of the same by William Richardson [1743], p. 181 n.; Strype, *Annals*, I, part I, 213; *ZL*, I, 71, Jewel to Peter Martyr, 5 March 1560); see above, p. 310, n. 3.

When the former ecclesiastical leaders of the nation openly condemned the national church at a time when their co-religionists in
Scotland and France were virtually at war with England, they posed
a threat which the government could not afford to overlook.
Elizabeth's remark to de Quadra suggests that some evidence had
indicated that some or all of the bishops were in touch with the
French—negotiations which could not but have the odour of
treason.[1]

One bishop remained out of prison—David Pole. Sander reported
to Cardinal Moroni that this was due to 'protracted illness'. Pole
lived on for several years and, for a time confined to the environs
of London, he was never imprisoned, although he conformed no
more than did his episcopal brethren. Illness alone was not sufficient
reason for keeping men out of prison in the sixteenth century. As a
contemporary noted on an official paper, Pole's liberty was the result
of his being 'a man known and reported to live quietly and therefore
hitherto tolerated'. His situation confirms the probability that the
eight other bishops were imprisoned because, rightly or wrongly,
they were considered to be an internal danger in face of the impending
struggle with France.[2]

Tower imprisonment was hardly a holiday, but prisoners of rank
had some comforts provided they could pay for them, and they were
usually allowed to retain servants. In September Parker arranged for
the former prelates in the Tower to eat together at meals. Conditions
may have been more severe for Bonner and Scot at the other prisons.[3]

By the end of 1560, the passing of the immediate crisis with France
brought in its wake a more lenient policy toward English Roman
Catholics. The government offered to release the bishops and other
former prelates 'so as they conclude to come to church, to Common

---

[1] *CSP, Sp.* I, 159; de Quadra to Bishop of Arras, 3 June 1560; Forbes, *A Full View*,
I, 460, Cecil to Throckmorton, 22 May 1560; *ZL*, I, 79, Jewel to Peter Martyr,
22 May 1560.

[2] *CSP, Rome*, I, 64, Sander's Report to Cardinal Moroni; *CSP, Dom. Add.*, 1547–65,
p. 521 (XI, 45); 'Collection of Original Letters from the Bishops to the Privy
Council, 1564', ed. Mary Bateson, *Camden Miscellany, IX*, Camden Society, second
series, LIII (Westminster, 1895), p. 40; Bentham to Privy Council, 10 November
1564.

[3] *Parker Corr.*, p. 122, Parker to lieutenant of the Tower, 6 September 1560.

Prayer, and neither openly or secretly to talk, or do anything pre-judicial to the Queen's proceedings'. Just as English envoys abroad were instructed to attend Latin rites while refraining from active participation or sacramental communion, apparently Elizabeth and her government thought that the bishops ought to be willing to attend the Prayer Book offices. Officials were not prepared at the beginning of 1561 to release the bishops without a demonstrable act of obedience. According to Sander, when Heath had been offered liberty in exchange for mere attendance at service, the former arch-bishop replied,

In principle it is the same to be schismatic in one point as to be schismatic in all, and therefore he was minded to countenance none of these doings either by word or deed, nor to suffer his back to be seen where none could read his heart.

The government thought that they were offering sufficient con-cessions to the prisoners' consciences; the prisoners judged otherwise, and in the Tower they remained until the government relaxed its requirement.[1]

Secret Latin Masses had continued in the homes of some of the gentry, and the first major attack on the practice came in April 1561 when Cecil ordered the arrest of almost two dozen 'mass-mongers' including two of Queen Mary's councillors. Cecil, as we have seen, used the incident to dramatize the danger of admitting the papal nuncio waiting at Brussels. He had either found political significance in the incident or, more likely, he had chosen to endow it with such significance.[2]

By the end of July 1562 the Privy Council had decided to champion the cause of French Huguenots. It is not surprising that they ordered the imprisoned Marian bishops to be 'more straightly shut up than they have been accustomed', that they might not have 'common conference' with each other or with visitors. Elizabeth also established

---

[1] *CSP, For.* III, 462, Jones to Throckmorton, 2 (or 5) December 1560; *CSP, Rome,* I, 62–4, Sander's report to Cardinal Moroni.

[2] *CSP, Dom.,* 1547–80, pp. 173–4 (XVI, 49–51); *CSP, Dom. Add.,* 1547–65, p. 510 (XI, 8); see above, pp. 299–302.

a special ecclesiastical commission for the diocese of Chester, where William Allen had been effectively fortifying Roman Catholic loyalties among the gentry of Lancashire.[1]

Bishop de Quadra's intrigues with English papal recusants typify the complex relationship between international affairs and domestic Roman Catholic policies. The Spanish ambassador to Elizabeth tried to become the leader of English Roman Catholics in order better to serve king and pope. In the intrigues to win Elizabeth's adherence to the Council of Trent, the interests of both masters coincided. But this was not always true. As a bishop loyal to the pope, he did all he could to keep Englishmen in papal obedience. As the envoy of Philip, he strove to keep Roman sympathizers out of French clutches. In January 1562 de Quadra wrote to Philip in almost open anger as he described his frustrations in trying to pose as the hope of English Roman Catholics while he followed Philip's instructions to prevent a rupture between them and the queen.[2]

Many Englishmen loyal to the papacy thought they might, without offence, obey the provisions of the Uniformity Act requiring them to attend church. In the summer of 1562 some of them requested de Quadra to obtain an authoritative Vatican judgment. The Spanish bishop himself clearly argued in favour of a qualified permission:

What...has to be considered...is the great unusualness and novelty of the case,...it being here prohibited by law to be a Catholic and capital punishment assigned to anyone here who will not live as a heretic.... That ...which they call Common Prayer...contains no false doctrine or anything profane, because it is entirely Scripture or prayers taken from the Catholic Church (although from some of them everything has been omitted that mentions the merits and intercession of the Saints), so much so that leaving aside the sin of dissimulation and the harm that would accrue from the example, the act of taking part in this [worship] is not

[1] Dasent, *Privy Council*, VII, 118–19; J. Stanley Leatherbarrow, *The Lancashire Elizabethan Recusants*, Chetham Society, n.s., CX (Manchester, 1947), p. 20; *CSP, Dom., 1547–80*, p. 203 (XXIII, 56), commission, 20 July 1562.
[2] *CSP, Rome*, I, 16, Pius IV to de Quadra, 2 March 1560; *CSP, Sp.* I, 126, de Quadra to duchess of Parma, 7 February 1560; I, 132, to Feria, 7 March 1560; I, 189, 192 and 226, to Philip, 23 March and 12 April 1561 and 31 January 1562.

in its nature evil. The Communion...is not before us now. They only ask if they can attend this service of Common Prayer which I have mentioned.[1]

He also asked for terms of absolution for those who repented of their conformity to the established religion.

At the same time the Portuguese ambassador asked for a similar decision at the Council of Trent.[2] The Office of the Inquisition and the Council's committee which had been assigned the inquiry both gave the same answer: under no conditions might the faithful attend the Prayer Book offices.[3] The resolute stand of the imprisoned bishops was vindicated by the highest councils of the Roman Church.

Pius IV did, however, formally empower Bishop de Quadra to reconcile penitent heretics and to delegate such authority to English priests. The ambassador received the commission with mixed feelings. As he wrote to Philip, he thought it 'convenient and necessary', and yet he knew of the danger of seriously offending Elizabeth if she heard of these new arrangements. She could hardly countenance an ambassador of a friendly nation who absolved her subjects from the sin of obeying her laws.[4]

De Quadra's defeat over the admission of Martinengo must have cast him into the depths of despair, but worse was yet to come. In the autumn of 1562, his secretary betrayed his secrets to the English government, and de Quadra's dual role was fully exposed to his English enemies. Cecil wrote that the bishop appeared more 'like a nuncio of the Pope's than the King's ambassador'. In January, when Convocation opened, de Quadra completely lost his usefulness to both pope and king. The Privy Council called him before them to accuse him of abusing his diplomatic privileges:

[1] Bayne, *Anglo-Roman Relations*, pp. 293–5, 7 August 1562, de Quadra to Vargas; tr. by Canon Jourdan in *History of the Church of Ireland from the Earliest Times to the Present Day*, ed. Walter Alison Phillips (London, 1934), II, 608–9.

[2] *CSP, Rome*, I, 97; Bayne, *Anglo-Roman Relations*, pp. 290–1; 2 August 1562.

[3] *CSP, Sp.* I, 267, de Quadra to Philip, 8 November 1562; Bayne, pp. 165–73, 289–93 and 296–7; Jourdan, *Church of Ireland*, II, 607–8 and 610–11; Arnold Oskar Meyer, *England and the Catholic Church under Queen Elizabeth*, tr. McKee (London, 1916), p. 68.

[4] *CSP, Rome*, I, 106, Pius IV to de Quadra, 11 October 1562; *CSP, Sp.* I, 267, de Quadra to Philip, 8 November 1562.

Roman Catholic recusants: diplomacy and forbearance

A great number of persons...come every Sunday and feast day to hear
your Mass.... It can be proved that certain traitors who a short time ago
conspired against the Queen...have been encouraged by you....To
speak plainly, it is believed that under cover of religion your Lordship
is the cause of a large number of her Majesty's subjects being disposed to
sedition and disobedience who otherwise would have been good and loyal.[1]

In the succeeding weeks, as Parliament and Convocation were
meeting, the Privy Council took stern measures to prevent Englishmen from attending Mass at either the French or Spanish embassies.[2]
Late in February the government arrested even Spanish subjects—to
the horror of de Quadra. He countered English pleas of the precedent
set by the treatment of Englishmen under the Spanish Inquisition:
'We are only doing what we have always done with Englishmen
and all others, and what was done when the treaties of alliance were
made, whereas here they have departed from what they were in the
habit of doing.'[3]

The sudden arraignment of de Quadra and prohibition of recusant
attendance at the embassy chapels were closely linked with the
English commitment to the Huguenots and with domestic plots to
overthrow Elizabeth. With English troops fighting in France at the
side of French protestants against a Roman Catholic government,
Englishmen worshipping at the embassies of the Roman Catholic
powers might have anticipated that their actions would be suspect.
When Lord Keeper Bacon opened Parliament on 12 January, he
referred to a conspiracy against the queen and suggested the need
for legislative response. At the end of February Cecil wrote to
Thomas Smith that traitors had admitted plans to land a force in
Wales to proclaim Mary of Scotland as Queen of England.[4]

De Quadra died in England in August, and his last six months

[1] Wright, *Queen Elizabeth*, I, 98–9, 11 October 1562; Read identifies Cecil's recipient
as Chaloner (*Cecil*, I, 251); *CSP, Sp.* I, 285, de Quadra's notes on the meeting.
[2] *CSP, Sp.* I, 290, de Quadra to duchess of Parma, 10 January 1563; I, 293, to Philip,
27 January; I, 329, testimony of Carlos del Gesse, 22 May; I, 295, de Quadra to
Philip, 7 February; Wright, *Queen Elizabeth*, I, 123, Cecil to Smith, 7 February
1563; I, 128, Mason to Chaloner, 27 February; Machyn, *Diary*, p. 299.
[3] *CSP, Sp.* I, 301, de Quadra to Philip, 15 February 1563; see I, 304, 20 February.
[4] D'Ewes, *Journals*, p. 60; Wright, *Queen Elizabeth*, I, 127, Cecil to Smith, 27
February 1563.

were among the most disappointing of his diplomatic career. Under official displeasure, he could not function effectively in any capacity. In May an English Roman Catholic suspected of sedition, John Storey, escaped from prison, and de Quadra's personal chaplain foolishly aided him. It took all of de Quadra's efforts just to prevent the arrest of his own Spanish bedesman.[1] The ambiguous activities and the frustrating dilemmas of de Quadra's embassy graphically illustrate the complexities in which Roman Catholic recusancy was embedded. The realities of international politics inevitably were weighed as the government varied policy towards its own Roman Catholic subjects. The precisians who wanted strong measures against Roman 'heretics' found natural allies in those Englishmen who wished to cut through the Gordian knot of English papal loyalties by taking stern direct measures against Englishmen who refused to comply with the acts of Supremacy and Uniformity.

LEGISLATIVE SEVERITY AND ADMINISTRATIVE MODERATION

The full programme of the militant reformers in Convocation would have weighed heavily on English Roman Catholics. The penal proposals of their doctrinal discipline alone would have proved violently persecutory, if it had been implemented and enforced. The precisians, moreover, wrote into their prospectus, 'General notes', two items which the Lower House picked up in 'Articles for government' almost without change and these were specifically directed at Roman Catholics:

Whosoever shall at any time hereafter say mass, or procure mass to be said, or willingly suffer it to be said in his house, and...be lawfully convicted...within 2 years...shall be judged in law a felon and shall suffer the pains of death and forfeiture of goods...

Whoever shall hear mass and be...convicted...within 2 years... shall forfeit for every mass that they shall hear 100 marks, if they be worth so much, and if they be not, then they shall forfeit all their goods and chattels...

[1] *CSP, Sp.* 1, 324–5, de Quadra to Philip, 9 May 1563.

These requirements speak for themselves. The prolocutor of the Lower House accurately expressed the attitude of the precisians towards Roman Catholics when he called for severer penalties in his sermon at the opening of Parliament. The only other Convocation proposal directly touching Roman Catholics was the item in 'Twenty-one articles' to require communicants to abjure 'the idolatrous mass' at the time of the General Confession. Of course, these penal regulations were left in limbo when the bishops refused to act on any of the proposals of the Lower House. Yet the bishops themselves, as members of the House of Lords, shared in approving a parliamentary act with severe potential consequences for Roman Catholics.[1]

Parliament heeded Nowell's call. The lay militant members of the House of Commons successfully pushed through a bill which greatly increased the scope and the penalites for those who refused to take the Supremacy Oath with its repudiation of the pope. As early as November 1562 de Quadra had heard rumours that Parliament would act to execute the imprisoned bishops, and Nowell's sermon confirmed his expectation. As the bill emerged, it required subscription to the Supremacy Oath from a greatly enlarged number of clerical and lay officials, including all candidates for ordination and for university degrees, schoolmasters, lawyers, court officials, and members of parliament. Only the nobility were specifically exempt. Bishops might tender the oath to 'every spiritual or ecclesiastical person' in their jurisdiction, and the Lord Chancellor might issue commissions for requiring the oath of any Englishman. The most ominous provision for English Roman Catholics designated 'the same Paynes...and Execucōn as ys used in Cases of Highe Treason' for those who refused the oath when it was tendered to them for the second time.[2]

J. E. Neale convincingly argues that the government had intro-

---

[1] For Convocation documents, see below, appendix 1, pp. 342–56. The sayers or procurers of Masses were to be tried for felony only before temporal judges; ecclesiastical or temporal judges might hear charges against *hearers* of Masses.

[2] *CSP, Sp.* 1, 269 and 291, de Quadra to Philip, 15 November 1562, and to his servant in Brussels, 14 January 1563; *Statutes of the Realm*, IV, 400–5, 5 Elizabeth, c. 1.

duced the bill in Commons with much milder provisions. They wanted stronger legal weapons to use against Roman Catholic intrigues, but no domestic crusade. Cecil wrote to Sir Thomas Smith in France that 'a law is passed for sharpening lawes agaynst Papists, wherein some difficulties hath bene because they be made very penall; but such be the humours of the commons house, as they thynk nothing sharp ynough ageynst Papists'. In replying, Smith expressed his own dislike 'that our howse is still so extreme in making more penal laws'. An M.P. opposing the bill exhorted the house to follow 'the example of the queen's majesty' who 'hath with such clemency ruled us, and so tempered her justice with mercy, as I ween never prince since the conquest'. However, the militants controlled the Lower House. When Parliament was prorogued on 10 April, they may have envisaged popish episcopal heads soon rolling from the executioner's block, for Elizabeth assented to the bill and, through the Lord Keeper, commended their efforts 'for the abolishing of the Romish power, the Common Enemy of this realm'. Late in February, de Quadra had been equally convinced that executions would follow, for he reported that 1 April had already been set as the date on which the bishops in prison would be offered the Oath of Supremacy for the second time.[1]

The legislators forgot that although they passed the laws, they did not administer them. They could not force Queen Elizabeth to execute the severe provisions of the law. On 26 April the oath was administered to Bishops Bonner and Watson, to Dr Cole, and to John Storey, and after their refusals, a commission was drawn up to bring them to trial. The bishops who administered the oaths had acted on the authority which the bill had assigned to them, but the implementation required the queen's approval. On 9 May de Quadra reported, 'The commission has not yet been signed by the Queen, so when they took it to her she said she would sign it another day at her convenience.' It never became convenient for Elizabeth to

[1] J. E. Neale, *Elizabeth and her Parliaments*, I, 117–20; Wright, *Queen Elizabeth*, I, 126, Cecil to Smith, 27 February 1563; Forbes, *A Full View*, II, 362, Smith to Cecil, 7 March 1563; Strype, *Annals*, I, part I, 452–3; Mr Atkinson's speech, quoted at length by Neale; D'Ewes, *Journals*, p. 75; *CSP, Sp.* I, 303, de Quadra to Philip, 20 February 1563.

sign that commission. Once again Elizabeth had frustrated the hopes of the militant reformers—and in this case, of many of the not-so-militant reformers as well.[1]

Elizabeth could hardly block executions by allowing unsigned commissions to collect in her files. Possibly it was the beginning of May when she instructed Parker to order the bishops not to offer the oath the second—and deadly—time.[2] Reluctantly Parker obeyed, although he issued the order in his own name rather than

recite the Queen's Majesty's name, which I would not have rehearsed to the discouragement of the honest Protestant, nor known too easy, to the rejoice too much of the adversaries, *her* adversaries indeed. I had rather bear the burthen myself.[3]

Cecil wanted even Parker's order to remain secret so that the clemency might appear to come from the bishops' common pastoral concern rather than from a command specifically designed to thwart the will of the Commons.[4] Parker feared he might later be held in contempt of Parliament 'having no warrant in writing' for the action, and it was perhaps to ease his fears that the queen shortly assured him plenary pardon of 'all and every trespass, act or acts of retainer heretofore had, or any contempt, violation, or forfeiture' since 1 January.[5] At the same time, possibly in gratitude for his services and cooperation, she granted the archbishop the right to keep forty liveried servants. Together, Elizabeth and Parker, assisted by the advice of Cecil, vitiated the sanguinary plans of the precisians.

Archbishop Parker in one case permitted the oath to be offered to a Marian prelate—again to the 'bloody butcher' Edmund Bonner. In the spring of 1564 Bonner refused to swear the oath when Bishop Horn demanded it. Parker, Grindal, and Horn acted without the

[1] *CSP*, *Sp.* I, 322 and 323–4; de Quadra to Philip, 24 April and 9 May 1563.
[2] *Parker Corr.*, pp. 173–5, Parker to Cecil and to the bishops, both undated, but in the light of de Quadra's report, these are later than the editor of the correspondence or Neale suggests (*Parliaments*, I, 121).
[3] *Parker Corr.*, pp. 173–4; Parker to Cecil. V. J. K. Brook believes the action was a congenial task for the archbishop (*Parker*, p. 129). Possibly, but Parker expresses nothing but regret at taking the action.
[4] *Parker Corr.*, p. 175n.
[5] *Parker Corr.*, pp. 173 and 176, Parker to Cecil and Elizabeth to Parker.

knowledge of Cecil, and therefore almost surely without the knowledge of the queen.[1]

At the subsequent trial Bonner, an able canonist, challenged the
legality of the Ordinal by which Horn had been consecrated, for
the Ordinal had not been specifically mentioned in the Uniformity
bill reviving the 1552 Prayer Book. Although Parliament in 1566
did specifically authorize the Ordinal to preclude any such legal
ambiguities, if the government had wished to push the law against
Bonner in 1564, it could have done so without serious opposition.
In November de Silva, the new Spanish ambassador, reported the
case suspended. The order for suspension may have come from the
queen, but there is no evidence to show that it did. In October 1564,
de Silva reported that Cecil had admonished the bishops not to per-
secute 'those of the old faith'. The covert attempt of Parker, Grindal,
and Horn to act on their own against Bonner was no more effective
against the queen's determination than earlier attempts to execute
the Marian prelates.[2]

The precisians who had called for the Marian bishops' heads early in
1563 must have been galled in September when the council ordered
that the Tower prisoners be removed to the custody of various
clerics around the kingdom. Stowe reported that the greater freedom
so offended the people that preachers at Paul's Cross and elsewhere
were preaching 'verie sedyssyowsly'.[3] Thirlby, Turberville, Watson,
Bourne, Feckenham, and possibly Heath were farmed out in custody
of some of the men who had succeeded them in the leadership of the
English Church.[4] Undoubtedly living conditions were more comfortable for the former prelates in their successors' palaces, but the constant
efforts to bring them to a 'better mind' may have proved more irk-
some to some of them than the stricter imprisonment in the Tower.

[1] *CSP, Sp.* I, 360, Luis Roman to de Granvelle, 29 April 1564; Dixon, *History*, VI,
29, from S.P.Dom., Eliz., XXXIV, 1, Grindal to Cecil, 2 May; see pp. 29–35.
[2] *Statutes of the Realm*, IV, 484–6; 8° Eliz., c. 1; *CSP, Sp.* I, 387, 392 and 396,
de Silva to Philip, 9 October and 13 and 27 November 1564.
[3] *Stowe's Memoranda*, p. 126.
[4] *Parker Corr.*, pp. 192–4, council to Parker, 15 September 1563; Thirlby to Parker,
16 September; Parker to Thirlby, 20 September; p. 253, Parker to Cecil, 4 January
1566; Grindal, *Remains*, pp. 281–2, Grindal to Cecil, 15 October 1563; Dasent,
Privy Council, VII, 190.

Bonner and Scot, imprisoned by order of the Ecclesiastical Commission, were not affected by the council's order, although it may have been about this time that Scot was released from the Fleet and allowed to remain at liberty within twenty miles of Finchingfield, Essex. Before June 1564, Scot had broken his bond and fled overseas.[1] Bonner remained in the Marshalsea to the end of his life in 1569.[2]

The danger of the plague was the immediate occasion for the mitigation of the bishops' imprisonment, but the underlying reason was undoubtedly the easing of international tensions. The government had not yet concluded a treaty with France, but the war itself was over. Henry Gee mistakenly credited Emperor Ferdinand's intercession on behalf of the bishops with the easing of the Romanists' lot. The emperor had written to Elizabeth in April to plead for the bishops' lives. When in September he wrote again to thank her for her clemency, he undoubtedly referred to her staying the hand of the expected executioner rather than to this rather minor change of conditions of imprisonment.[3] Elizabeth, in this case, was perfectly willing to let Ferdinand think that she had indeed acceded to his request in saving the lives of the bishops when, in fact, she had merely followed her consistent policy.[4] The lightening of the former bishops' imprisonment in September 1563 was an additional reminder to the militant reformers that the queen and her advisers had no intention of accepting their dictation in policies towards English Roman Catholics.

Fifteen months later, in January 1565, the Privy Council changed the conditions of three of the bishops—one for the worse and two for the better. They ordered Watson back to the Tower, and they granted Turberville and Pate the liberty of London.[5] Pate, like Scot the previous year, broke his bond and fled overseas some time in

---

[1] *CSP, Dom., 1547–80*, p. 247 (xxxv, 38), *Parker Corr.*, pp. 217–18, Privy Council to Parker, 23 June 1564.

[2] *CSP, Sp.* I, 533, 18 March 1566, de Silva to Philip; Grindal, *Remains*, p. 307, Grindal to Cecil, 9 September 1569; Godwin, *De Praesulibus*, p. 251.

[3] Gee, *Elizabethan Clergy*, p. 193; Bayne, *Anglo-Roman Relations*, pp. 198–9 and 301–4, Ferdinand to Elizabeth, 12 April 1563; *CSP, Rome*, I, 149, 24 September; *CSP, Sp.* I, 333, Philip to de Quadra, 15 June 1563.

[4] *CSP, Rome*, I, 154–5, Elizabeth to Ferdinand, 3 November 1563.

[5] Dasent, *Privy Council*, vii, 183 and 190.

1565 as he had done once before in Henry's reign.[1] Turberville, like David Pole who had never been imprisoned, seems to have lived quietly until his death five years later.[2] Watson remained in trouble with the authorities for the rest of his life. After enjoying three years of freedom from 1574 to 1577, he, together with Feckenham, was ordered back to episcopal custody for abusing 'the liberty granted unto them'. They had convinced other Englishmen 'by their secret persuasions' not to attend church any longer. Watson then remained in custody until his death in 1584.[3]

When the Privy Council met in June 1565 to consider the threat of the marriage of Mary Stuart to Lord Darnley, they recommended that Elizabeth return the released bishops to the Tower 'where they might not have such liberty to seduce her subjects as they daily do'. The advice was ignored, and the bishops remained in their various conditions. Bourne and Thirlby continued as the enforced guests of the new bishops until their deaths in 1569 and 1570. At some time soon after the end of Nicholas Heath's Tower imprisonment, he was permitted to retire to his own country house, Chobham Park, in Surrey. There he lived, as he himself once wrote, 'in great quietness of mind' until his death in 1579.[4]

Before 1565 was out, the pattern of the government's policy toward the former Marian bishops had been established: of the nine living bishops, certainly four and probably five had been granted mildly circumscribed freedom (David Pole, Scot, Turberville, Pate and probably Heath), two were in the custody of diocesan bishops (Thirlby and Bourne), and two suffered the stiffer imprisonment of

---

[1] T. E. Bridgett and T. F. Knox, *Catholic Hierarchy*, p. 77.

[2] Pole died in 1568 and Turberville in 1570 (Gee, *Elizabethan Clergy*, pp. 195–6).

[3] Grindal, *Remains*, p. 351, Grindal to Burghley, 13 November 1574; instruction to the bishops, 1577, reprinted by Philip Hughes (*Reformation*, III, appendix IV, 115–16, from S.P.Dom. Eliz. CXIV, 69); Strype, *Annals*, II, part II, 660; Godwin, *De Praesulibus*, p. 361; *CSP, Dom., 1547–80*, p. 250 (XXXVI, 23), Feckenham to Cecil, 14 March 1563.

[4] *CSP, For.* VII, 386, minutes of Privy Council meeting; *CSP, Sp.* I, 682, de Silva to Philip, 1 November 1567; *Parker Corr.*, pp. 253 and 369, Parker to Cecil, 4 January 1566 and 25 August 1570; Wright, *Queen Elizabeth*, I, 374, 31 August 1570; *ZL*, II, 181, Hilles to Bullinger, 8 March 1571; Gee, *Elizabethan Clergy*, p. 196; Strype, *Annals*, I, part I, 213; Godwin, *De Praesulibus*, p. 44; *CSP, Dom., 1547–80*, p. 467 (XCII, 28); Birt, *Elizabethan Settlement*, p. 422.

21-2

Marshalsea and the Tower (Bonner and Watson). The different treatments accorded them seem to be directly related to the government's suspicion of their involvement in foreign intrigues and of their propensity to encourage others to emulate their non-conformity. They were finally free to stay away from church themselves, but they were not free to try to persuade fellow-Englishmen of the rightness of their cause. The government failed completely in their attempt to win some measure of outward conformity from the Marian bishops, but they successfully protected them from the self-righteous vindictiveness of the militant reformers.

THE QUEEN'S POLICY

Emperor Ferdinand, in his letter to Elizabeth of 24 September 1563, not only thanked her for saving the bishops but, on behalf of English Roman Catholics, he also bid for toleration. At the suggestion of the papal legates at Trent, Ferdinand proposed that the English queen grant 'the Catholics' the use of at least one church in every city of her realm. Elizabeth's reply is noteworthy:

We and our people—thanks be to God—follow no novel and strange religions, but that very religion which is ordained by Christ, sanctioned by the primitive and Catholic Church and approved by the consentient mind and voice of the most early Fathers. But to found churches expressly for diverse rites, besides being openly repugnant to the enactments of our supreme Parliament, would be but to graft religion upon religion, to the distraction of good men's minds, the fostering of the zeal of the factious, the sorry blending of the functions of church and state, and the utter confounding of all things human and divine in this our now peaceful state: a thing evil in itself, of the worst example, pernicious to our people, and to those themselves, in whose interest it is craved, neither advantageous nor indeed without peril.

Like Jewel's apology, the royal letter rings with confidence that the English Church rests solidly on the foundations of Scriptures and the traditions of the patristic church.[1]

---

[1] *CSP, Rome*, I, 149, Ferdinand to legates, 24 September 1563; I, 154–5; Strype, *Annals*, I, part II, 574–5. The copy in Strype described the English religion as that

It sounds curious to twentieth-century ears to hear Elizabeth argue *in favour of* uniformity on the grounds that toleration would confuse 'the functions of church and state'. Yet this remained a cardinal principle of Elizabeth's convictions and ecclesiastical policies. She kept the estates temporal and spiritual carefully distinct. To grant to Roman Catholics the right of public worship would be a civil act of the state which would violate the church's proper domain. In religion, the country was to be governed by its rightful bishops, and the imposition of ministers not under their jurisdiction would have been an intolerable civil interference with their episcopal rights and duties. Throughout her reign, Elizabeth protected her royal prerogative in church matters. Far from a dictatorial whim, this was the very means by which she kept the lines of church government distinct from those of civil government. Her refusal of the emperor's request was of a piece with her repeated refusal to allow the church to be governed by Parliament or Privy Council. She could grant non-conforming worship a legal standing only by allowing the state to intrude into the affairs of the church.

The national government had taken only occasional action against recusant worship in 1564 and 1565, but by the beginning of 1567 Roman Catholic activities had become so prevalent in Lancashire that Queen Elizabeth wrote to the bishop of Chester and to the special diocesan Ecclesiastical Commission, insisting that they move against the 'seditious persons' who 'under colour of religion' were encouraging disobedience and disloyalty.[1] The English exiles had begun a concerted effort to provide a more regular ministry to Roman Catholics in England and to discourage them from outward conformity to the established church. A letter has survived from 1566 in which a recusant priest, Lawrence Vaux, authoritatively disabused his correspondent of the notion that he might attend his parish church without incurring sin:

'approved by the consentient mind and voice of the most illustrious fathers', but the copy which reached the Vatican—and whose translation is quoted here—is almost certainly the final version approved by Elizabeth and sent to Ferdinand.

[1] Dasent, *Privy Council*, VII, 142, 151, 242, and 247; Leatherbarrow, *Lancashire Recusants*, p. 28; from S.P. Dom. Eliz. XLVI, 19–20 and 32–3.

The Pope cannot dispense any of the laity to entangle themselves with the schism...concerning sacraments and service: that we may not be present among them. If ye associate yourselves at sacraments or service that is contrary to the unity of Christ His Church, ye fall into schism, ...and...although you lead never so good a life in the sight of the world, the wrath of God hangeth over you, and dying in that state shall lose the everlasting life of Heaven.[1]

Although both the Vatican Holy Office and the committee of theologians at Trent had forbidden the faithful to attend Prayer Book rites, the decisions do not seem to have been known, much less obeyed, in England. Rishton wrote that some Romanists not only conformed but were on the same day 'partakers of the table of our Lord and of the table of devils, that is, of the blessed Eucharist and the Calvinistic supper'. As late as 1580 William Allen wrote that 'many priests said Mass privately and celebrated the heretical offices and supper in public'.[2] Vaux in 1566 was beginning the campaign to end such practices. His letter carried authority and, linked to his secret ministries in Lancashire, it discloses the organized campaign of English Roman Catholics to stiffen the consciences and wills of their sympathetic brethren.

It was against such activity that Elizabeth sent her orders to arrest Roman Catholic leaders in Lancashire. She believed that the campaign had been largely regional, for she told the bishop that these disorders in his diocese were such 'as we hear not of the like in any other parts of the realm'.[3] Elizabeth's clemency did not allow Roman Catholics to mount organized efforts to persuade her subjects to disobey her ecclesiastical laws. After Pius V in 1570 declared Elizabeth rightfully deposed and her subjects released from their obligations of obedience, all such activities took on a much more sinister appearance, but even in these earlier years the queen expected her ecclesiastical and lay officials to check them.

[1] The letter is largely reprinted by both Dixon (*History*, VI, 217–20n.) and Hughes (*Reformation*, III, 249–50) from S.P. Dom. Eliz. XLI, I.
[2] Sander, *Anglican Schism*, p. 267, in Rishton's section of the book; a letter of Allen to Vendeville of 16 September 1580, quoted by Leatherbarrow (p. 23) from Martin Haile, *An Elizabethan Cardinal* (London, 1914, p. 44).
[3] Leatherbarrow, *Lancashire Recusants*, p. 28.

The queen's policy

Elizabeth's policy in these early years forms a consistent pattern. No public dissenting worship was to be legally permitted, nor were clerics or laymen of papal loyalties to be permitted to speak openly in the attempt to win others to their convictions. Papal propagandists were imprisoned when their activities became known, and the government's vigilance was redoubled when such activities were linked with continental Roman Catholic powers. At the same time, the queen refused to countenance the severe penalties which were demanded by the militant reformers.

The record of Elizabeth's first decade of policy towards Roman Catholics does reveal 'extraordinary leniency' and tends to support the claim she made in 1591 on the punishment of Jesuits:

They have been impeached by direct execution of laws against such traitors, for mere treason, and not for any points of religion, as their fautors would colour falsely their actions, which are most manifestly seen and heard at their arraignment, where they are neither executed, condemned, or indicted, but for high treason: affirming, among other things, that they will take part with any army sent by the pope against us and our realm. And of this, that none do suffer for matter of religion, there is manifest proof, in that a number of men of wealth in our realm, confessing contrary religion, are known not to be impeached for the same, either in their lives, lands, or goods, or in their liberties, but only by payment of a pecuniary sum, as a penalty for the time that they do refuse to come to church.[1]

The one clear invasion of private conscience which she permitted in the latter part of her reign was the 'bloody question' asked of seminary priests: 'If England were attacked, would they support Elizabeth or a foreign army bearing the Pope's approbation?' To Elizabeth this was a political question; to the seminary priests, a complicated problem of conscience with no simple response.

In determining the dynamics of Elizabethan ecclesiastical policies, we would probably not be far from the mark if we assumed that Elizabeth herself would have treated Roman Catholic and protestant non-conformists alike. Foreign politics and internal attitudes forced

[1] Strype, *Annals*, IV, 80, 18 October 1591.

her to distinguish in practice. She had to goad the bishops into action against protestant non-conformists and to hold them back from too severe action against the papists. The recurring evidence of Roman Catholic attempts against her crown forced her to accept the judgment of her chief advisers that stricter measures against Roman Catholics were required. As late as 1591 zealous reformers such as Francis Knollys still did not understand the queen's position:

I do marvell how her Majestie can be persuaded that she is in as much danger of such as are called Purytanes as she is of the Papysts, and yet her Majestie cannot be ignorant that the Purytanes are not able to change the government of the clergie, but only by petition of her Majestie's handes.[1]

Knollys made the mistake of thinking that Elizabeth acted only out of political expediency. It is characteristic of religious zealots to imagine that those who oppose them inevitably do so in order to secure their own temporal advantage. Elizabeth recognized political necessities, but many of the struggles over policies can be better understood on the assumption that, in so far as she was able, she sought to treat all non-conformists alike: with forbearance, but without legal toleration.

By 1566 the Roman Catholic authorities actively began to persuade their English adherents not to compromise with the independent national church. Their task was formidable, for it was not, by and large, respect for papal *authority* which led men and women to reject the national church and her new ways. Rather, they loved the familiar pattern of church life: the Latin Mass, the regular shriving, the invocation of favourite saints, the anointing on the death-bed, the liturgical petitions for family and friends who had died. To them, these things, with the teachings that underlay them, belonged to the heart of the Christian faith, and they would not give them up. The English exile community launched a campaign to persuade these lay people at home that obedience to papal orders to avoid schismatic worship was a necessary consequence of such devotion. Some Englishmen gave themselves to this campaign in a spirit of self-sacrificing determination. Their increasingly voluminous literary productions

---

[1] Wright, *Queen Elizabeth*, II, 417, 9 January 1591.

provide a measure of their industry.[1] Their conscientious zeal to return England to the papal fold inevitably challenged Elizabeth's medieval concept of a unitary society, just as much as the non-conformity of the precisians. The zeal of some English Roman Catholics to achieve the same goals through political and military means aroused the self-protective instincts of the government. Most Roman Catholics remained fully English in their politics, and the queen undoubtedly knew that this was true. Yet all the papal recusants were compromised by the misplaced zeal of a few. The remarkable characteristic of the Elizabethan government is that in the life-and-death struggle of succeeding decades, the queen was able to preserve as much of the lenient spirit of the first decade as she did. Contemporary events in the Spanish Netherlands and in France remind us of the rarity of such policies in the sixteenth century.

On this issue as on so many others, Queen Elizabeth and the precisians were the chief protagonists of conflicting policies towards English Roman Catholics. Francis Bacon described the queen's policies in these terms:

I find her Majesty's proceedings generally to have been grounded upon two principles: the one, That consciences are not to be forced, but to be won and reduced by force of truth, by the aid of time, and the use of all good means of instruction or persuasion: the other, That causes of conscience when they exceed their bounds, and prove to be matter of faction, lose their nature; and that sovereign princes ought distinctly to punish the practice or contempt though coloured with the pretences of conscience and religion....Although, as a prince of great wisdom and magnanimity, she suffered by the exercise of one religion, yet her proceedings towards the papists were with great lenity, expecting the good effects which time might work in them....Her majesty not liking to make windows into men's hearts and secret thoughts, except the abundance of them did overflow into overt express acts and affirmations, tempered her law so, as it

[1] A valuable study of the character and the impact of the literary campaign is found in the as yet unpublished doctoral thesis of Richard M. Spielmann at the General Theological Seminary: 'Elizabethan Exiles: A Discussion of the Content and Influence of English Writings of Seven Elizabethan Exiles.' On the problem of church attendance, see especially pp. 89 f.

restraineth only manifest disobedience in impugning and impeaching advisedly and ambitiously her majesty's supreme power, and maintaining and extolling a foreign jurisdiction.

Alongside this accurate but none the less admiring description of Elizabeth's policies, Dean Nowell's sermon at the opening of the 1563 Parliament stands in contrast:

The Queen's majesty of her own nature is wholly given to clemency and mercy, as full well appeareth hitherto. For in this realm was never seen a change so quiet; or so long reigning without blood (God be praised for it). Howbeit those which hitherto will not be reformed, but obstinate... ought otherwise to be used. But now will some say, Oh bloody man! that calleth this the house of right, and now would have it made a house of blood. But the Scripture teacheth us that divers faults ought to be punished by death: and therefore following God's precepts it cannot be accounted cruel. And it is not against this house, but the part thereof, to see justice ministered to them who would abuse clemency. Therefore the goodness of the Queen's majesty's clemency may well and ought now therefore to be changed to justice seeing it will not help. But now to explicate myself, I say if any man keeping his opinion, will, and mind close within himself, and so not open the same, then he ought not to be punished. But when he openeth abroad, then it hurteth, and ought to be cut off. And specially if in any thing it touch the Queen's majesty. For such errors of heresy ought not, as well for God's quarrel as the realm's, to be unlooked into. For clemency ought not to be given to the wolves to kill and devour, as they do the lambs. For which cause it ought to be foreseen; for that the prince shall answer for all that so perish, it lying in her power to redress it. For by the scriptures, murderers, breakers of the holy day, and maintainers of false religion ought to die by the sword.

It is difficult for modern men to sympathize with the opinions of a zealot who would execute sabbath-breakers, but the learned pro-locutor of Convocation can teach us much about the attitude of the precisians towards Roman Catholics. The queen and the dean agree on certain principles: public laws are not to touch completely un-expressed internal convictions, and yet violations of religious statutes must be punished. They disagree in the all-important practical applications of those principles: what kinds of violations are to be punished? how severe ought punishments to be? what results can be expected from the enforcement of legislation against Roman Catholics?[1]

Dean Nowell implied that any expression whatsoever of pro-papal opinions 'abroad' renders its perpetrators worthy of punishment. Bacon wrote that Elizabeth wanted to punish only 'overt express acts and affirmations' which lead to attacks on the royal supremacy 'advisedly and ambitiously' carried out.

Nowell explicitly called for the death penalty for 'maintainers of false religion', in spite of the knowledge that many would accuse him of being a 'bloody man'. Bacon could describe Elizabeth's application of the laws in terms of her 'great lenity'. However one may judge the cruel executions of Roman Catholics in the latter part of Elizabeth's reign, it is abundantly clear that they were not carried out on the grounds that their victims were 'maintainers of false religion'.

Nowell would have had penal laws so that promoters of 'errors or heresy' might be 'cut off' before they infected the orthodox Christian society of England. He found clear scriptural grounds for his position just like so many inquisitors before him. Nowell acknowledged the possible value of clemency to bring a Roman heretic to his right mind, but he clearly believed that four years was stretching the legitimate limits of justice, and that it was now time for firm action. In contrast, Bacon wrote that Elizabeth did not wish to force consciences, but that she believed that the gentle insistence of mild legal pressures provided a better means of allowing truth to instruct and orthodoxy to persuade. Elizabeth encouraged a pragmatic, socially realistic policy grounded not in express words of scripture, but in common sense and human experience. Modern Christians might perhaps agree that it was also a policy closer to the *spirit* of scripture than that of Nowell.

Both Elizabeth and Nowell upheld the medieval tradition of one religion in one society; but whereas Nowell and his fellow-precisians sought to enforce religion through the severest penalties inflicted by the state, Elizabeth preferred patiently to await the slow attrition of

[1] Bacon, *Works*, v, 428–9; see also III, 470–5; Nowell, *Catechism*, appendix, pp. 225–6.

recusants due to the complementary effects of the teaching of the established church and the financial penalties of the Uniformity bill. She reserved capital punishment for offenders whose disobedience to religious statutes posed a threat to the peace and stability of the realm and its government.

English Roman Catholics today have every reason to honour the memory of the martyred seminary priests who sought to save souls in spite of the inevitable political reactions which their ministries aroused, but they might say an occasional *Ave* in thanksgiving that the missionaries' chief protagonist was Elizabeth Tudor and not a ruler such as a doctrinaire but indecisive Philip II, or an unprincipled Catherine de Medici, or a pious cipher willing to follow the spiritual advice of such clerics as Alexander Nowell.

Epilogue

WHEN the first reforming synod of Elizabeth's reign gathered in St Paul's in 1563, the Church of England stood at an ecclesiastical crossroads. The queen wished to continue on the same route. From her standpoint, religion had been settled in 1559. The exigencies of the political forces in the Commons and the scruples of the Marian hierarchy had forced Elizabeth to concede more to militant reformers than she had wished, and she was determined to maintain the settlement as it was delineated in the Acts of Supremacy and Uniformity and in the Royal Injunctions. The precisians wished to make a left turn which would finally set the English Church in a truly reformed direction. From their standpoint, the successive changes of direction in the reign of Edward VI had all led to a godlier path, and the concessions which they had made to the conservative queen in 1559 had been temporary setbacks. The time had come to complete the Reformation.

The precisians came to Convocation with carefully designed written plans to implement their reforming goals. They achieved a notable victory in the Lower House. There, they failed only in ceremonial reform when the 'Seven articles' won only thirty-four signatures, and even their toned-down 'Six articles' failed by one vote to win a majority of the house. The Lower House codified the militants' administrative, financial, and minor ceremonial reforms in the 'Articles for government'. They proposed to the bishops a programme of thorough doctrinal reform in the 'Twenty-one articles'. In the concurrent Parliament their lay supporters won approval of strong measures against Roman Catholics. The precisians had failed, however, to reckon with the power structure of the synod, and they misjudged the collective temper of the bishops. Real power in Convocation lay with the bishops, and they stopped the militant programme by the simple expedient of refusing to act on the proposals. The queen effectively nullified the anti-Roman Catholic measures by refusing to allow the bishops to execute the law.

The convinced precisians were a minority in the Lower House but, like their lay allies in the House of Commons in 1559, they possessed the organized and disciplined zeal to carry the greater part of their programme against scattered and poorly marshalled opposition. It did them no good. Elizabeth had picked out her bishops with care. Although she had failed to carry more than a token representation from her sister's episcopate, the queen had refused to nominate clerics with a record of too vigorous militancy in reform. From among the Marian exiles and from among clerics who had remained in England during the Roman Catholic restoration, Elizabeth selected a group of convinced, but moderate reformers. To win their support, she made more concessions than she intended, and more than once she was to be disappointed with their failures to enforce conformity with more vigour. Above all, in the subsequent struggle over vestments and images, Elizabeth barely maintained, in legal theory, the standards of 1559, and she permitted the bishops, in practice, to enforce a lower standard. Yet on the whole she had chosen well for her purposes. In this Convocation of 1563, they bore the brunt of the defeat of the precisians' programme, and subsequently, by their obedient inaction, they frustrated the anti-Roman Catholic legislation. Many, perhaps most of them, were unhappy with both these roles, but they reckoned obedience to the Supreme Governor a part of their religious responsibilities. Some of them had drawn the line when the queen ordered them to restore images to churches, for this touched their consciences, but in general they reckoned ceremonies and vestments among the adiaphora, and most of them were eventually willing to enforce even what they did not believe to be expedient. In their secret sessions under Parker's patient and effective leadership at Convocation, they adopted their Articles of Religion and new book of Homilies and pressed the queen to approve them. Either from conviction or from a fear of losing the queen's assent to these fruits of their deliberations, the bishops blocked the proposals of the precisians in the Lower House.

The Convocation decisions propelled the Church of England well past the fateful crossroads. It continued on the route chosen by the queen instead of turning to that proposed by the militant reformers.

Had the queen been indifferent to these ecclesiastical decisions, the bishops might well have followed the lead of the Lower House. Some important milestones in securing the religious settlement still lay in the future. Although the bishops had blocked the full militant programme in Convocation, they had, in Parker's words, so far done little in their 'own cause'. The vestiarian controversy had not yet reached its height, and the pragmatic compromise of the Advertisements was three years ahead. Not until 1571 were the bishops to adopt a moderate doctrinal discipline for the clergy and to secure royal assent for the full Thirty-nine Articles. Thirteen years of Elizabeth's rule were required to tie up the loose ends of the settlement, but the handwriting was clearly on the wall by the end of Convocation in 1563. Elizabeth won the confirmation of her settlement of 1559.

The protagonists of the struggle in Convocation were the presiding officers of the two houses: Archbishop Parker and Prolocutor Nowell. Yet Nowell was Parker's own choice. Why? Many reasons could have guided Parker to make the choice. First, Parker and Nowell seem to have been on the best of personal terms. Parker invited Nowell for dinner to reassure him after the queen interrupted his sermon at court, and the archbishop encouraged and authorized the publication of Nowell's *Catechism*. Second, the differences between the theological convictions of Parker and Nowell undoubtedly did not loom as large at the time as they now seem to us who are aware of four hundred years of subsequent anglican development. In many instances, Parker may have sympathized with some of the positions of the precisians which his loyalty to the queen required him to oppose. Third, Parker was not an inept leader, in spite of his own protestations to the contrary. He must have known the temper of the militant clerics who were to take the lead in the Lower House. It would have been foolhardy and perhaps disastrous to try to force on the Lower House a prolocutor whom the precisians would not easily accept. Far better to urge them to take a man of their own stripe with whom Parker could, in fact, work.

Nowell served the established church until his death in 1602 as dean of St Paul's and a member of the queen's Ecclesiastical Commission. Parker had taken right measure of the man. Even though

335

Epilogue

his notions of reform were well in advance of Parker's, he remained loyal to the settlement. From this standpoint, Parker's choice of Nowell to be prolocutor was a master-stroke: the dean would vigorously press the precisians' cause, but he could be counted upon to accept defeat with resignation, if not with grace.

The defeat of the precisians in 1563 led to the metamorphosis of the most zealous among them into the full presbyterian movement of Thomas Cartwright and John Field. As the bitter puritan letter of 1566 reveals, after the bishops snatched victory out of the precisians' hands, many began to wonder if episcopal government could be tolerated in a church rightly reformed. Bishops were defending a 'mingle-mangle' of popery and the gospel, and some precisians were ready to demand the pure biblical patterns which John Calvin had established at Geneva and which their religious brethren in neighbouring Scotland and France were adapting to their countries with such effectiveness. They saw that the episcopal office seduced former comrades-in-exile into compromises with popery and with Mammon. No wonder they were ready to be convinced that only the disciplined presbytery met the test of the New Testament.

The defeat of the precisians in 1563 also led to their alliance with the parliamentarians in the Commons who were beginning to seek to limit the power of the Crown. The work of the House of Commons in 1559 foreshadowed that alliance, but the results of Convocation in 1563 made it a practical necessity. Undoubtedly elements of puritan religion fitted well with the ideals and the interests of the rising moneyed men who comprised the mainstay of the parliamentarians. Christopher Hill has pointed out that a morality which supported disciplined lives, a sabbatarianism which discouraged wasteful weekday holy days, and a pattern of church government which offered key positions to local laymen of substance, were elements of puritanism congenial to the new bourgeoisie.[1] Yet there is, at the same time, a fortuitous element in the alliance. Had the precisians gained the solid support of the bishops in 1563, the queen would herself probably have blocked much of the programme for the moment. But the precisians could then have returned to sub-

[1] Christopher Hill, *Society and Puritanism in Pre-Revolutionary England* (London, 1964).

sequent Convocations to press for their reforms instead of concentrating all of their efforts in Parliament. Queen and bishops were increasingly close allies, but it need not have been so. Elizabeth chose bishops both for their inherent integrity and for their potential loyalty to the fundamentals of her ecclesiastical convictions and policies. It was a gamble, but she won. James I could quip 'No bishop, no king', only because he had inherited the workings of Elizabeth's rule. By the end of Elizabeth's reign, no question could arise concerning the bishops' loyalty to her and to the settlement, but in the opening years of her rule, it had been touch and go.

The first years of the Elizabethan settlement established the basic conditions for the future development of anglicanism. The parliamentary legislation of 1559 gained for the Church of England independence from foreign rule. Rome hoped to restore the English jurisdiction through the submission of Queen Elizabeth, but these hopes were based only on some popular Roman Catholic sentiment, a small but influential number of Roman Catholic families among the nobility and gentry, and a large dose of wishful thinking. Elizabeth attempted to be lenient towards practisers of Roman Catholic religion, and she opposed the kind of fanaticism that labelled Roman Catholics as 'Antichrist'. Yet, as a convinced supporter of the Reformation, she never showed the slightest inclination to compromise England's ecclesiastical independence.

The 1552 Book of Common Prayer, modified by the few conservative touches which Elizabeth demanded, proved to be the greatest single influence in the settlement. This book, with its many provisions for vernacular scriptural readings and its retention of traditional liturgical structures, shaped the religion of England. A. L. Rowse has commented,

By the end of the reign several generations had been brought up in its formularies, had found consolation in its rites and services as their fathers had done in those of the old religion before them: to them it was the catholic church; the language, the very rhythms of the prayer-book services had become a habit, had entered deeply into the subconscious life of the people.[1]

[1] A. L. Rowse, *Tudor Cornwall* (London, 1957), p. 341.

Epilogue

In spite of the precisians' desire to remove its 'imperfections', or better still, to replace it with a liturgy more akin to the book of Geneva, the Elizabethan Prayer Book remained unchanged.

The physical setting and the accessories of worship kept a remarkably traditional appearance. If churches were to lose much of their statuary and paintings, they were to retain much of their stained glass and their rood screens. If stone altars were to be replaced by wooden tables in the midst of chancel or nave for holy communion, the holy table was restored to the east wall out of service and made to look something like an altar. If the queen was not able to enforce eucharistic vestments, she did maintain their technical legality and insist on copes in cathedrals and the surplice in parish churches. If she could not restore crucifixes to the churches after they had been destroyed, she stubbornly insisted upon their legitimacy and exemplified it by the cross in her own chapel.

The government of the Church of England retained its medieval structure. The antiquated system of courts and the grossly unjust system of clerical finances remained unreformed. A parish discipline to enforce morality, administered by ministers and local laymen, was beloved of the Reformed churches, but it was never successfully foisted on the English Church. Basing her rule upon the medieval distinction between the temporal and spiritual estates, Elizabeth used her royal prerogative to keep the church free from the interference of Parliament and Privy Council. She employed no lay vicar, expecting that metropolitans and bishops would properly administer ecclesiastical affairs. She never granted any legal standing to nonconforming worship of either protestant or catholic varieties.

In the first years of Elizabeth's reign the attempt to make the Church of England a 'confessional' church was decisively repudiated. The Articles of Religion were never accorded the same legal protection as the Prayer Book, and they remained tests of doctrinal conformity for the clergy alone. Laymen had only to eschew open opposition to them. The Articles themselves generally agreed with the doctrine of the Lutheran and Reformed churches of the continent, although they preserved distinctive English emphases and reflected a restrained temper which resisted unnecessary theological circumscription. Except on the crucial matter of the eucharistic presence of Christ, the Articles reveal closer parallels with Lutheran than with Reformed confessions. The distinctly Calvinistic catechism of Dean Nowell became a school textbook authorized by the bishops, but it failed its original purpose of providing a firm doctrinal stand for the Church of England. The doctrine of the Articles and the place they held in the church's life left room for the development by Hooker and his successors of what McAdoo recently called 'the authentic note of Anglicanism, ... its aim being one of interpretation by means of a theological method which combined the use of Scripture, antiquity, and reason'. He found this admirably expressed in a passage from the seventeenth-century Robert Sanderson:

> There is ... much reverence to be given to the writings of the godly ancient Fathers, more to the canons and decrees of general and provincial councils, and not a little to the judgment of learned, sober, and godly divines of later and present times, both in our own and other reformed churches. But we may not 'jurare in verba', build our faith upon them as upon a sure foundation, nor pin our belief upon their sleeves, so as to receive for undoubted truth whatsoever they hold, and to reject as a gross error whatsoever they disallow, without further examination.[1]

Richard Hooker, who first clearly expressed the spirit of anglican theology, did not write in a theological vacuum. He wrote to explain and to defend the Elizabethan church in which he had experienced the Christian religion and learned Christian theology. Due to the events in the early years of Elizabeth's reign, he did not defend a confessional Christianity.

Recently A. G. Dickens and Patrick Collinson have suggested that the religious position of those who opposed the militant reformers in early Elizabethan years was too unformed, too accidental, and too politically motivated to be dignified by the later label 'anglicanism'.[2] Indeed the first defenders of the settlement never presented a comprehensive rationale of their own position. The majority who held the fort never had to demonstrate the

[1] H. R. McAdoo, *The Spirit of Anglicanism* (London, 1965), p. 49; from Sanderson, *Works* (Library of Anglo-Catholic Theology), III, 288.
[2] Dickens, *English Reformation*, p. 313; Collinson, *Puritan Movement*, pp. 13, 26, 55.

cohesion of the organized band of besiegers. Yet we have, I am convinced, been right to discern in these years a struggle between incipient forms of anglicanism as well as of puritanism. 'Anglicanism' can justly be used to describe the established religion even in this period when its rationale lagged behind its sturdy existence.

Of course the militant reformers contributed to the heritage of the Church of England. The more moderate puritans, whose story has now been so judiciously told by Dr Collinson, found themselves increasingly pressed between the bishops' erratic pressures for conformity and the zealots' logical demands for the presbytery. The results of the 1563 Convocation channelled their considerable zeal into their pastoral charges and into the largely para-canonical organizational structures which were to provide instruments of puritan evangelism and discipline. Anglicans they were, dedicated to the ideal of a national church, but it was their opponents who foreshadowed the character of the established church of later centuries. The programme which the militant reformers had so well delineated as early as 1563 was expressly designed to destroy those characteristics of the English Church which have marked it off as a distinctive Christian tradition for four centuries. Even had the English Church retained its episcopal government as the early precisians presumed, the Church of England patterned after the militant proposals would have become an exotic variety of the Reformed tradition. It would have stood among Reformed churches rather like the Church of Sweden among Lutheran churches. Convinced as I am that 'anglicanism' through the succeeding centuries has been characterized not only by its liturgy and polity, but by its decisive repudiation of confessionalism, I find in the queen, her bishops, and their supporters of these early years the forgers and the first defenders of the distinctive anglican tradition. The frontal attack of the precisians brought together in alliance the heirs of Henrician conservatism and the moderate reformers, and it was largely their convictions and practices that pointed the way to the future development of anglicanism. Few anglicans of later generations would agree with the puritan judgment that, taken as a whole, the things suppressed by the bishops in 1563 were truly 'of greatest advantage' to the church.

Queen Elizabeth was the real enemy of the puritans and the precisians before them. On this, all recent interpreters agree. The effective governorship of the church by a monarch is distasteful to the twentieth century, but the consequences of Elizabeth's role are much more congenial to modern tastes and values.

She introduced a lay voice into the rule of the church and, by her determined but restrained use of authority, she endowed the church with a significant degree of independence from English legislators and other government officials.[1] Many churches since the Reformation have struggled with the problem of integrating lay authority with that of the ordained clergy. Elizabeth's solution depended heavily on the ability and commitment of the sovereign but, in her hands, the church fared well. She refused to allow the clergy to become the sole arbiters of moral, political, and religious questions as both papist and presbyterian would have had it. She insisted that an outward liturgical and clerical discipline be maintained to protect congregations from dissident clerics. She reminded the highest councils of the church that ecclesiastical decisions must take account not only of 'principle' but also of human reality measured in political and social terms. At its worst, this could mean a Christianity captive to worldliness and political expediency. At its best, it could ensure the recognition, sometimes absent in religious circles, that the so-called 'secular' orders of human life possess an integrity of their own. A church which ignores that integrity either retreats into irrelevant pious sentimentality or attempts to impose a demoniacal clerical tyranny.

The future Church of England turned out to be in the design of Queen Elizabeth rather than in that pattern which the militant reformers proposed in Convocation in 1563. If the leaders of the sixteenth century were to be arranged according to their influence on the eventual character of anglicanism, the first rank would include only two figures: the martyred cleric, Thomas Cranmer, and the royal laywoman, Elizabeth Tudor.

[1] Dawley, *Whitgift*, p. 57.

Appendix I

The records of the Convocation

The full records of the 1563 Convocation of the province of Canterbury have not survived, but enough remains to allow us to reconstruct a great portion of the events which took place there. Most important for the course of events is a transcript of the proceedings of the Upper House taken from a MS. volume once belonging to Archbishop Parker. The volume has disappeared, but Bishop Edmund Gibson printed them in his *Synodus Anglicana*, first published in 1702. Gibson also reproduced a brief treatise prepared for Archbishop Parker's use outlining the proper procedures for opening Convocation.[1] The records of the Lower House are completely lost except for the brief account attached to the so-called 'Six articles' discussed below.

Ten working papers from the Convocation survive in the libraries of the Inner Temple and of Corpus Christi College, Cambridge and have been partially transcribed in standard works of Strype, Burnet, Hardwick, and Cardwell. Five of these appear to have been prepared before Convocation opened or during its very first sessions:

1 Bishop Sandys' liturgical and canonical proposals (Petyt MSS. of the Inner Temple and transcribed by Strype).
2 Bishop Sandys' proposed orders (Petyt MSS. and Strype).
3 Bishop Alley's proposals (Petyt MSS. and Strype).
4 'Certain articles in substance desired to be granted by the queen's majesty'—hereafter called 'Certain articles' (Petyt MSS. and Strype).
5 'General notes of matters to be moved by the clergy in the next parliament and synod'—hereafter called 'General notes' (Petyt MSS. and Strype).

Five other working papers seem to have been produced in the Lower House during the course of Convocation:

[1] Edward Cardwell produced a modern edition in 1854 (Oxford); Parker's paper appears on pp. 164–6, the acts on pp. 145–63. Cardwell also reprinted the acts in his *Synodalia* (II, 495–527), and part of them appear in Wilkins' *Concilia* (IV, 232 f.). For the description of the volume, see Cardwell, *Synodalia*, II, 516n.

6 The working copy of the Thirty-nine Articles, subscribed by the bishops and Lower House (Corpus Christi College and Strype and Lamb).

7 The 'Seven articles', subscribed by thirty-four members of the Lower House (Petyt MSS. and Strype).

8 The 'Six articles' with a brief extract from the acts of the Lower House describing their introduction, the debate, and the division which defeated them by one vote (Petyt MSS. and Burnet and Strype).

9 'Articles drawn out by some certain, and were exhibited to be admitted by authority; but not so allowed'—entitled by Strype 'Articles for government and order in the church', and hereafter called 'Articles for government' (Corpus Christi College and Strype)

10 Twenty-one articles, entitled 'The requests and petitions of the clergy in the Lower House of Convocation'—hereafter called 'Twenty-one articles' (Petyt MSS. and Strype).

John Strype, who transcribed most of these documents, was accurate enough to give a true general impression of their contents, but he occasionally omitted sections and erred in certain details which do alter the significance. In the brief considerations below of each of these papers, I have noted such errors and omissions, but I have not included those minor changes which leave the meaning unaltered. Since Strype generally used spelling of his own day in his transcriptions, I have used modern spelling and punctuation in transcribing the documents. The 'Articles for government' occupy almost one hundred manuscript pages, and although I quote in the course of this book from my own transcription of them, I have not attempted to include them at length.

I. BISHOP SANDYS' LITURGICAL AND CANONICAL PROPOSALS[1]

Since the paper refers to 'this present session of parliament', it was presumably prepared on the eve of the opening of Convocation and Parliament or during the first few days. Together with the two following papers, it may have been presented in response to the archbishop's invitation to the bishops to suggest those matters needing reformation.[2] The original directly requests the queen to make changes in the Prayer Book, and

---

[1] Inner Temple Library, Petyt MSS. 538.47, fo. 531; Strype, *Annals*, I, part I, 500; Wilkins took them from Strype (*Concilia*, IV, 239).

[2] 16 January 1562; Cardwell, *Synodalia*, II, 505.

Appendix I

Strype's version weakens this sense by changing the verb to the passive voice; the original begins: 'First, that *by* her majesty's authority, with the assistance of the archbishop of Canterbury, according to the limitation of the act provided in that behalf, *she would take* out of the Book of Common Prayer'... (italics indicate differences from Strype's version).

The marginal Latin note, that this 'can be done in synod', identified by Strype as in Grindal's hand, appears beside this first item as Strype indicates.

2. BISHOPS SANDYS' PROPOSED ORDERS[1]

This paper begins just below the previous one and continues overleaf; it is entitled: 'Orders to be observed of the bishops and other ecclesiastical persons, by their consents and subscriptions in this present synod.' No subscription appears, and a Latin marginal note states that consent was not given. Strype conflated items 6 and 7 of the eight articles of the paper, in effect leaving item 7 out entirely. These two articles should be as follows: 'Item. That no bishop, dean, or chapter shall bestow their benefices, whereof they be patrons, but upon such as are learned and fit to serve in that office. Item. That none be admitted to be a public preacher but such as for learning, life, and discretion is fit for that office, and such as will subscribe to sound religion now by authority set down.'

3. BISHOP ALLEY'S PROPOSALS[2]

The form of Alley's paper on doctrine and discipline is more of a speech than of articles presented for legislative action. From such addresses as 'my honourable good lords', it clearly was designed to be delivered in the Upper House alone. Strype misleads in adding a heading 'Matters Ecclesiastical' to the final paragraph of the first part of Alley's two-part paper. This first part treats of doctrine, and he intends that the squabbles over vestments and clerical clothes should be considered a doctrinal issue. In the second part Alley proceeds to 'discipline'—administrative and legal matters.

[1] Inner Temple Library, Petyt MSS. 538.47, fo. 531; Strype, *Annals*, I, part I, 506–7; Wilkins, *Concilia*, IV, 240.

[2] Inner Temple Library, Petyt MSS. 538.47, fos. 448–9; Strype, *Annals*, I, part I, 518–22.

4. 'CERTAIN ARTICLES'[1]

The authors of this paper proposed reforms on a variety of matters including doctrine, liturgy, clerical dress, discipline, and finances. They once refer to themselves as 'we', but give no further clue to their identity. Strype presumably used his familiarity with handwritings as his basis for his statement that the articles were composed 'by a secretary of the archbishop's, and were mended and added to in some places by the archbishop's own hand, and in some places by Bishop Grindal's'. The paper is neatly written; the clear interlinear additions suggest thoughtful revision after this copy was made. Strype, of course, transcribes the copy as corrected. Strype concludes too much about the composition of the paper. The secretary of the archbishop may well simply have copied the articles after the paper was submitted for the metropolitan's perusal. Grindal, as the dean of the province, was an officer of Convocation who could well have gone over such proposals as a matter of course. Strype identified as Grindal's one marginal modification, the cancellation of one article, and an actual textual addition. These interested comments and modifications suggest that Grindal, on the whole, approved and supported its proposals, even if he had little to do with their composition. The few alterations that might be identified as Parker's prove nothing more than his official interest in matters under consideration in the synod. V. J. K. Brook, Parker's recent biographer, wrote that these articles may have been 'suggestions for reform made to the bishops by Parker and Grindal'.[2] This seems highly unlikely. Given the picture of Parker painted by Dr Brook himself, it is difficult to imagine Parker urging that Prayer Book rites and ceremonies 'be reduced to edification, as nigh as may be to the godly purity and simplicity of the primitive church'. These were loaded phrases in the early years of Elizabeth's reign. It also may be questioned whether Parker would have proposed that doctrinal articles be drawn out of Jewel's *Apology*, for he himself seems to have prepared the articles for Convocation by working on a revision of the Forty-two Articles of 1553.

'Certain articles' was probably drawn up before the next paper, 'General notes', for it refers to Nowell's catechism as 'well nigh finished', whereas the latter stated that the work was 'already done'. In item 7, 'divers patronages' is the correct reading rather than Strype's 'divers parsonages'.

---

[1] Inner Temple Library, Petyt MSS. 538.47, fos. 450–3; Strype, *Annals*, I, part I, 522–5.   [2] Brook, *Parker*, p. 136.

Appendix I

5. 'GENERAL NOTES'[1]

This is the most important and influential of these preliminary synodical papers. Its title referring to 'the next parliament and synod' indicates that it was prepared before the opening of Convocation. It is a lengthy paper, carefully divided into four main sections. Strype obscured this division by the dislocation of some sections, and he also omitted items of importance.

There are two contemporary manuscripts of the document in the Petyt collection. One of these is a draft of the proposals, which was written either by several hands or by the same hand under varying conditions (fos. 435-46). The other manuscript is the fair copy of the draft, and it was this which Strype used as his model; he gives no indication that he knew of the draft (fos. 419-32).

The draft has many words crossed out and replaced by interlinear and, occasionally, by marginal additions. It was a working copy, but a copy good enough to be presented for the consideration of the officials of Convocation. Other than the additions of its writer, it has only six marginal comments, one of which is: 'Addantur annotationes D. Cantuar. ad dom. secretarium', suggesting that Archbishop Parker may have dictated the comments after the document had been given to him for his perusal.

The fair copy reproduces the final version of the draft, and it also includes the six later marginal comments. In addition, the fair copy has twelve additional marginal comments. Seven of these are 'deliberatur' or 'expendatur' (one more than Strype reproduced), indicating that the commentator thought these suitable for further consideration—presumably in contrast to the others. The other five new comments are modifications of the proposed regulations, and Strype identifies two of these as being in the hand of the archbishop himself. The fair copy may have been made for the archbishop before the draft was returned. Parker himself, and his officials, would then have added these further comments. However, the evidence is too scant to make any firm conclusions beyond these: (1) the draft preceded the fair copy which includes its interlinear corrections; and (2) Parker, Grindal, and others saw one or probably both of these manuscripts and added marginal comments.

As both manuscripts are bound, extraneous material has been included

---

[1] Inner Temple Library, Petyt MSS. 538.47, fos. 419-46. An error in numbering has left two consecutive folios with number '420'; blank pages include 425b, 432b, 443b, and 446b. Strype, *Annals*, I, part I, 473-84. Cardwell has taken the document from Strype and included it in *Synodalia*, II, 495-516, footnotes.

in each manuscript and between them (fos. 426–9, 433–4, and 436). Just possibly, one of these leaves in the draft MS. may have belonged to it at some stage, for it contains appropriate regulations for the increase of benefices of small value (fo. 436, both sides).

Fortunately, the introductory page of the document lists the four topics to be considered (fos. 419a and 435a). These clearly prove that the leaves, as they are bound, are out of order. Strype partly corrected the order. However, he left at the end a section dealing with discipline of the laity, which clearly forms the second half of part III, 'Ecclesiastical laws and discipline to be drawn, concerning both the clergy and laity'. The first half of part III in the manuscripts has, as a heading, 'First, concerning the clergy'; Strype misleadingly reprints this as part of the succeeding item. Similarly, in the manuscripts, the section dealing with the laity has a similar heading, 'Touching the discipline of the laity'; Strype omits 'Touching the'. Strype deliberately omits a large section of regulations dealing with the discipline of the clergy, and wrote that he had done so. More seriously, he omits a set of regulations dealing with doctrinal discipline which he may simply have overlooked (fos. 421a and 439a).

The document can be reconstructed then as follows:

	Fair copy MS.	Draft MS.	Strype (1824 ed.)
Introduction	fo. 419a	fo. 435a	pp. 473–4
I 'A Certain form of doctrine' Included by Strype Omitted by Strype	fo. 419b fo. 421a	fo. 435b fo. 439a	pp. 474–5 —
II 'Concerning Certain Rites, etc.'	fo. 421b	fo. 439b	pp. 475
III 'Ecclesiastical Laws and Discipline' A 'Concerning the Clergy' Included by Strype (Items 1–19) Omitted by Strype (Items 20–34, except no. 30 which he does include) B 'Touching the Discipline of the Laity'	fos. 422a–423b fos. 423b–425a fos. 430a–432a	fos. 440a–441b fos. 441b–443a fos. 444a–446a	pp. 475–8 (Item 30 on p. 479) pp. 481–4
IV 'The Supply of...small benefices'	fos. 420a and b; 420x, a and b.	fos. 437a–438b	pp. 479–81

Appendix I

Significant errors in Strype's transcription of particular articles are the following:

Part I. Doctrine

3. Strype added the comment that the Apology was that 'writ by bishop Jewell'.

The sentence describing the gathering of the books should read: 'These *three* to be joined *together* in one book, and by common *authority* to be...' (italics indicate differences from Strype's transcription).

Part III. Ecclesiastical Laws and discipline

A. *Clergy*. These are all numbered in the MS.

11. 'That none *now having* any deanery, provostship, archdeaconry,...'

13. Strype omits the following from the end of this article: 'And no longer unless they be made priests within one year after, that they shall give over the exercise of such spiritual jurisdiction.'

B. *Laity* (last section of Strype's transcription). There is a chasm in both MSS. as Strype reports, but Strype apparently added the words 'parents and masters of', for the MSS. begin after the break with the words 'householders having children...'. In this same sentence the MS. word is 'convicted' where Strype has 'convinced'. The time of the examination of laity in the Creed, Lord's Prayer, and Ten Commandments is specified in the MSS.; after the words 'offer himself once a year' comes the phrase: 'between Christmas and the 4th Sunday in Lent'. The final words of that same paragraph are 'any faults or *negligences* in them'. The title, as Strype has it, beginning 'That execution of penalties...' is no title in the MSS., but simply the opening lines of the article. It also ought to be noted that in both MSS. the final sections, 'De juramentis' and 'De matrimoniis' which end this session begin on new sheets.

Part IV. Finances

The comment that 'here occur four evils' is an explanatory note added by Strype. 'Remedies' is not a title, but is in the text, and the succeeding such titles are not in the MSS. In the third section concerning patronage, the word 'during' ought to be in the text: 'to lose his patronage during his life, and to be given *during* that term by the queen's...'

The sections omitted by Strype follow.

Additions to Part I 'A certain form of doctrine'
(fos. 421a and 439a)

6. If any ecclesiastical person having any benefice or promotion spiritual and being required by his ordinary to subscribe to the said articles, or to declare his open consent in any public place of assembly where, by his ordinary or other competent judge, he shall be appointed, do peremptorily refuse so to do; he shall *ipso facto* be deprived of all his ecclesiastical benefices and promotions.

7. And if any presented, nominated, or elected to any benefice or spiritual promotion, do refuse to subscribe or declare his consent to the said articles in form aforesaid: the same shall be judged disabled in the law to receive, take, or have any such benefice or spiritual promotion.

8. Likewise those that take degrees, or are to be admitted to any fellowships in the universities shall subscribe to the said articles and the recusants shall be disabled to take any degree or to receive any fellowship, and to be expelled [*sic*] both the universities; and such as have fellowships already, being required by the masters or heads of their colleges or houses to subscribe, if they refuse, shall *ipso facto* be deprived of their fellowships, and be expelled out of both the universities. For the better execution thereof, all masters and heads of colleges or houses shall within 4 months next after the publishing hereof demand all fellows of their colleges and houses to subscribe and give their consent to the said articles.

9. And if any master or head of any house or college do not require the said subscription within the said 4 months, or do admit to any fellowships without such subscription, or if any master or head do not himself subscribe and declare his consent to the said articles when any of them shall be required so to do, by the chancellor being present, and in his absence by the vice-chancellor or deputy in that behalf, that the said master or head refusing so to do shall *ipso facto* be deprived of his mastership or room and expelled out of the said university.

And if the vice-chancellor or his deputy do not within the said 4 months require the said subscription and consent of the said masters and heads of every college and house in their universities, or do suffer any to take degrees without such subscription, he shall, for every offence in that behalf, forfeit to the queen's majesty 100 marks.

Appendix I

Additions to Part IIIA: Discipline of the Clergy
(fos. 423 b–425 a and 441 b–443 a)

20. That every one that is admitted to any benefice, not being a preacher, be enjoined by the ordinary to study some part of the Scriptures, which if he refuse to do, then by the discretion of the ordinary, he may be deprived.

21. That every parson and vicar which giveth himself to hawking, hunting, drinking, dancing, swearing, playing at tables cards or dice, or other dissolute manners, or otherwise spendeth his time idlely or un-profitably, after peremptory monition once given him thereof by his ordinary, if he thereupon do not reform himself and give himself to the study and reading of the Scriptures, may be deprived from his benefice, and every curate so misusing himself removed and suspended from the ministry.

22. That every parson, vicar, or other having spiritual promotion or benefice and committing fornication, incest, or adultery and thereof law-fully convicted, shall be by the ordinary deprived of all his ecclesiastical livings and be suspended from his ministry for one whole year, and further be compelled to ecclesiastical satisfaction, and if any spiritual person having no benefice or promotion do commit fornication, incest, or adultery and be thereof lawfully convicted, then he shall be suspended from his ministry for one year and imprisoned without bail or mainprize for half a year, and to be compelled to make ecclesiastical satisfaction.

23. Item. It is to be wished that every nobleman would retain and keep a preacher in his house and have an ordinary sermon every Sunday either in his own house or at his parish church, and that the same preacher should teach the catechism to his servants, which preacher might be dispensed withall to have one benefice with cure if it were not past 12 ['ten' in draft MS.] miles from him besides a prebend and to be non-resident from his said benefice so that he have support that the cure be sufficiently served and that he preach himself there at diverse times.

24. Whosoever having any benefice with cure of souls doth not pro-vide that the same be served with a sufficient curate to be allowed by the ordinary by the space of 6 weeks in one year accounting the same jointly and severally, if he be absent himself, or doth not provide that 4 sermons be made quarterly by himself if he be a preacher, or by some other licensed to preach in his church, the same to be deprived of his benefice.

25. And likewise if one have 2 benefices with cure and they or one of them be not sufficiently served by himself, and a meet curate to be allowed

350

as afore, and provide quarterly sermons in form afore said, then as the default shall require, he to be deprived of both or the one of the said benefices.

26. That none be admitted to have any plurality for more benefices than one, unless he have first the consent of the bishop of the diocese, where the same benefices do lie, if they be within one diocese, and if they be in diverse dioceses, then to have the consent of every bishop in whose diocese any of the said benefices doth lie. For the which consent, if any such bishop shall take any thing, then the same bishop to forfeit to the queen's majesty 100 pounds.

27. That no dispensation be granted to give licence to any man to be non-resident from his benefice with cure continually, nor yet for a time, above the space of 6 months and that in case of sickness.

28. That the queen's majesty's chaplains (if they be preachers) be dispensed withall for non-residence, if they have but one benefice apiece not distant from London above 20 miles for so long time as they shall be occupied in her majesty's service.

29. That it may be lawful for every bishop to sequester in cases where sequestration is incident the yearly rent of any parsonage, vicarage, or other spiritual promotion in his jurisdiction; if the same be let by lease in which case the said lessor shall incur no forfeiture or damage for paying the same rent to the sequestrator notwithstanding any covenant, grant, or agreement made between the lessor and the said lessee.

30. On rural deans [see Strype, *Annals*, p. 479].

31. Every curate minding to go out of the diocese where he serveth into another shall first bring a testimonial from the rural dean, and other honest men, especially preachers, where he serveth unto the bishop of that diocese of his honest behaviour and conversation whilst he served there, and the bishop thereupon shall give him his testimonial under seal, which testimonial the said curate before he attempt to serve in any other diocese shall bring to the bishop of that diocese where he desireth to serve, or his officer appointed by him for that purpose, and so desire to be admitted to some cure. If the same bishop or officer shall think him meet, then to appoint him to some cure and signify such appointment to the churchwardens, whereupon the churchwardens shall receive him to serve there. Whoso offereth himself otherwise to serve in any cure, the churchwardens shall not permit him to serve there, and further, the said person attempting to serve without such licence shall be suspended for one whole year after from ministration.

32. Whosoever shall at any time hereafter say mass or procure mass to be said or willingly suffer it to be said in his house and thereof shall be lawfully convicted either before a spiritual or temporal judge within two years next after the fact done, shall be judged in law a felon and shall suffer the pains of death and forfeiture of goods as in case of felony.

33. Whoever shall hear mass and be thereof convicted before either spiritual or temporal judge within 2 years next after shall forfeit for every mass that they shall hear 100 marks if they be worth so much, and if they be not, then they shall forfeit all their goods and chattels and no forfeiture to be redeemed in this case with imprisonment.

34. What parson, vicar or curate soever shall attempt to marry any persons without the banns be lawfully asked thrice before, shall lose all his spiritual promotions if he hath any, and if he hath none, shall be deposed from the ministry.

6. THE THIRTY-NINE ARTICLES OF RELIGION[1]

This well-known manuscript consists of a revision of the 1553 Forty-two Articles of Religion in Latin with further changes indicated with red ink in Parker's hand. The subscriptions to the paper follow a careful description of the number of pages and lines on each page to preclude subsequent alteration. Dated 29 January, the subscriptions include all the living Elizabethan bishops of both provinces except Kitchin, Guest, Cheyney, and Best.[2] The signatures of the members of the Lower House appear on separate folios designed to be attached to the archbishop's copy. This manuscript is available in the beautifully printed study of this and other documents concerning the Thirty-nine Articles made by John Lamb, the nineteenth-century master of Corpus Christi College. Lamb gave careful attention to every detail.

[1] Library of Corpus Christi College, Cambridge, MS. 121, pp. 233–53. Strype only describes the paper and lists its subscribers (*Annals*, I, part I, 484–91). John Lamb presents it in detail among his unpaginated appendices (*Thirty-nine Articles*). Charles Hardwick included most of the variations in the MS. in his collation of various forms of the Articles (*Articles of Religion*, pp. 289–353; this MS. is 'C' among the Latin variants; see also Wilkins, *Concilia*, IV, 233–8).

[2] Thomas Stanley of Sodor and Man is also missing, but because of the peculiar status of the island, Stanley had no seat in the Lords and, although his diocese was part of the province of York, he held no seat in the Upper House of its Convocation. He had the right, rather, to preside over his own diocesan convocation. For comments on Lower House subscriptions, see appendix II.

7. THE 'SEVEN ARTICLES'[1]

The manuscript in the Petyt collection is a copy of the original since the subscriptions are all in the same hand. The title reads: 'The Request of them whose names are underwritten, concerning such things as yᵉ Lower House of Convocation have not agreed upon by common consent.' Strype has accurately transcribed the text of these proposals for reform in liturgy and clerical garb, except that in item three, the word 'oftentimes' is rather 'otherwise' in the manuscript. Strype was more careless with the signatures, stating that thirty-three signed and listing only thirty-two. In matter of fact, thirty-four names appear in the manuscript; the two names omitted by Strype are John Pedder, dean of Wigorn, following the name of Alexander Nowell, and Thomas Cole, archdeacon of Essex, following the name of Thomas Watts. The list also, incidentally, includes first names which Strype also omitted.

The request in the petition for the mitigation of article 33 on ceremonies of the Articles of Religion suggests that they were drawn up after 29 January when the bishops signed the completed Articles. Slightly more than half of the proposals made in the 'Seven Articles' may be found in 'General notes', but the authors went beyond this preliminary paper in ordering directions for the manner of using the psalms, for the omission of the cross in baptism, and for relaxing the rubric requiring kneeling at communion.

8. THE SIX ARTICLES[2]

These orders are remarkably similar to those in the preceding paper. They are more militant in their demand for the abrogation of all holy days except Sundays and feasts of Christ, but otherwise their requests were more moderate. They made no prohibition about the singing of psalms or other 'curious singing', no abrogation of lay baptism, no change in clerical street dress; they asked for no mitigation of article 33; and, instead of eliminating the surplice, they would have retained it as the clerical garb for all services.

[1] Inner Temple Library, Petyt MSS. 538.47, fos. 576–7; Strype, *Annals*, I, part I, 500–3; Wilkins, *Concilia*, IV, 239–40.
[2] Inner Temple Library, Petyt MSS. 538.47, fos. 574, 575, and 588; Strype, *Annals*, I, part I, 502–6; Burnet, *Reformation*, VI, 480–2; Wilkins, *Concilia*, IV, 240. Cardwell appears to have reprinted them from Burnet in *A History of the Conferences and Other Proceedings, Connected with the Revision of the Book of Common Prayer; from the Year 1558 to the Year 1690* (Oxford, 1849; pp. 40 and 119–20).

Appendix I

The transcriptions of the texts of the articles themselves are substantially accurate in both Burnet and Strype, although in two minor differences in item 1, Burnet shows himself more precise. Each of them leaves out certain other sections of the manuscript. Strype does not reproduce the Latin text of the acts of the Lower House for Saturday, 13 February, but merely summarizes their contents. Burnet, on the other hand, omits the list of names of members of the Convocation who were not represented at the voting division. These names are on a separate folio, now bound some thirteen leaves away from the rest of the document (fo. 588).

Both transcriptions give the correct voting totals: 43 persons and 58 votes, including proxies, in favour of the Articles; 35 persons and 59 votes against them. Neither is completely correct in reproducing the proxy votes assigned to each name, and so their columns of votes do not add up properly. Burnet is far more accurate, erring only in one particular: he credits Mr Tremayn with 2 votes where the manuscript assigns him only one. Strype also errs in a few titles of those who neither voted in person nor by proxy: in the manuscript, Norley is listed as a proctor of the chapter of Worcester (not Winchester); Weston is a proctor of the clergy rather than the cathedral church of Coventry and Lichfield; and although the handwriting makes it less certain, this would also seem to be true of Lowth and Fluydd from the dioceses of Gloucester and Peterborough.

9. 'ARTICLES FOR GOVERNMENT'[1]

Strype identifies the title in the hand of Archbishop Parker: 'Articles drawn out by some certain, and were exhibited to be admitted by authority: but not so allowed.' This manuscript, like that of the Articles of Religion, belongs to the 'Synodalia', part of that great collection of documents which Parker bequeathed to his college. The articles are written out in a fair hand, each with its own title. Clerical and lay administration, finances, discipline, and judicial matters form most of the content of the articles which are not organized into sections; in this respect they are like many sets of royal and episcopal injunctions. Strype has assigned numbers to the articles which are unnumbered in the manuscript. In contrast to the other documents, Strype gives only the titles of most of the articles, summarizing only a handful and leaving a few out entirely. Like Strype,

[1] Library of Corpus Christi College, Cambridge, MS. 121, pp. 267–355; the volume contains no leaf corresponding to pp. 277–8, but nothing seems to be missing; Strype, *Annals*, I, part I, 507 and I, part II, 562–8.

I do not include the full text of the articles, but I do wish to point out a few cases in which Strype's summaries are misleading; for convenience I retain Strype's numbers.

Two further articles follow article 2, entitled 'Concerning appeals in cases of correction'. One deals with the order in which appeals are to be made, and the other limits inhibitions in such cases (MS. pp. 269–71). The two titles Strype lists in articles 8 and 11 are actually, in each case, two distinct articles. After article 9 appears a distinct, and interesting, article on rural deans and their authority (p. 285). Article 30 which Strype summarizes, does include the curiously varied subjects of public fasts, music, and the ringing of bells (pp. 308–11). It is possible that this article was put together hastily and so not divided into the three titled articles which we would expect. After this article come five blank pages (pp. 312–16), and a new hand begins on article 31 (p. 317). Article 44 provides not only for punishment for those molesting clergy and asking counsel of witches, but also for the public absolution of the excommunicate, and it proposes that the 'penal statutes for sodomity, witchcraft, sorcery, and prophesying be revived' (pp. 336–7).

The wording of many of these articles closely resembles items in 'General notes'. Articles 25, 29, and the third part of 30 follow the liturgical proposals in part II of 'General notes'. The following articles show the influence of one or more items from the first half of part III on clerical discipline: 1, 2 (1st and 3rd items), 7, 9 (2nd part), 11 (1st part), 19, 21, 22, 23, 34, 35, 36, 37, 38, 39, 42, and 47. Articles 43 and 48–51 are all drawn from the second half of part III on discipline of the laity. Articles 17 and 18 partly follow the financial proposals in part IV of 'General notes'. Another part of article 7, the first half of article 8, and article 33 all resemble the less precise proposals in 'Certain articles'.

10. THE 'TWENTY-ONE ARTICLES'[1]

These articles treat primarily of the enforcement of doctrinal standards. Like the previous paper, these bear a strong resemblance to parts of 'General notes'. Articles 1, 2, 8, 10, 11, 14, 15, and 16 are all directly related to part I of 'General notes'. Articles 3 and 4 reproduce the proposals of part II for changes in the baptismal liturgy.

The manuscript is neatly written on four folios. Only one side is used,

---

[1] Inner Temple Library, Petyt MSS. 538.47, fos. 581–4; Strype, *Annals*, I, part I, 508–12; Wilkins, *Concilia*, IV, 240–2.

Appendix I

except for the final leaf which contains the sixty-three signatures on the obverse.[1] Eleven marginal titles indicate the sections of the document; these appear opposite specific articles as follows: I. Doctrines; III. Baptism; V. Mass openly renounced; VI. Communicants only present at the communion; VII. Images; VIII. Discipline for doctrine; X. Subscribing to doctrine; XVII. Beneficed students must preach in the universities; XVIII. Ordinary may cause any suspected to subscribe; XIX. Articles to be read by all ecclesiastical persons; XXI. The Book of Common Prayer and ordering ministers authorized. Strype has made his usual minor alterations in transcription, but only the following are significant: in article 4, it is the 'church of God', rather than the 'church of Christ'; in article 8, the word 'depraving' is to be added after 'derogation'; in 11, Strype's 'pretended' should be 'presented'; in 15, 'living' should be 'living place'; '&c' should be added to article 20; and article 21 should begin 'That some', rather than 'That the same'. In the signatures, Strype erroneously indicates that in Calfhill's first signature, the Christian name is 'Johannes'; it is clearly (and properly) 'Jacobus'. The 'Tho. Richley Peterb.' on inspection turns out to be 'Tho. Byckley' with a Latin note following taking exception to the article on private baptism. A similar note stands after John Kennall's name.

[1] James Calfhill signed twice, making sixty-four actual signatures for sixty-three persons.

Appendix II

The members of the Lower House and their careers in the reign of Queen Mary

The documents discussed in appendix I provide names for 104 clerics eligible to attend the Lower House; the multiple hats worn by these men bring the total number of known seats represented to 124 out of 144 seats in the House. Six of these known delegates left no evidence of their presence at Convocation, and three more, in all their recorded subscriptions, acted only through proxies; these nine may not have personally attended. I have accepted Lamb's analysis of the invalidity of a final set of names subscribed to the Thirty-nine Articles and included by Strype (Lamb, *Articles*, pp. 20–2). His reading of 'Wm. Leveson' is more accurate than Strype's 'Wm. Bucson'. I also identify 'Luson' who voted against the 'Six articles' with this Leveson. I have identified 'Edmund Meyrall' with 'Merick', archdeacon of Bangor (Foster, *Alumni Oxon.*). The 'Tho. Richley' whom Strype lists as a subscriber to the 'Twenty-one Articles' is actually in the manuscript 'Tho. Byckley'. 'Thomas Linnett, precentor of St. David's' is presumably 'Thomas Huet'. I have not been able to identify with certainty the offices held by three Convocation men, Burton, Richard Hughs [Huys], and Thomas Becon, although Becon probably represented the chapter of Canterbury. I cannot discover Burton's first name. Extra offices (or proxies held for an unnamed official) were held by the following: Thomas Bolt, John Calfhill, George Carew (2), John Cottrel, Gregory Dodds, Robert Grinsel (2), Anthony Hinton, John Kennall, William Latimer (2), Thomas Huet (2), Robert Lougher, John Mullins, Arthur Saul, Richard Walker, and Thomas Watts. One of the offices, the archdeaconry of Canterbury, was held by a man ineligible to attend the sessions of the Lower House: Bishop Guest of Rochester (certificate prepared by Parker, 9 July 1563, Strype, *Parker*, I, 257).

Those who apparently were not present include George Harvey, archdeacon of Cornwall; John Lowth, prolocutor of the clergy of Gloucester; Thomas Norley, prolocutor of the chapter of Worcester; William Turner, dean of Wells; Nicholas Wendon, archdeacon of Suffolk; and Nicholas Wotten, dean of Canterbury. Richard Barber, archdeacon of Leicester, subscribed the Thirty-nine Articles for Francis Mallet, dean of Lincoln; Robert Lougher subscribed them for Henry Squire, archdeacon of Barnstaple; and Gregory Dodds, dean of Exeter, subscribed for Mri. John Smith, archdeacon of Llandaff. Hugo Morgan, prolocutor of the clergy of Bangor, subscribed for Edmund Mayrick (Merril), archdeacon of Bangor, but Mayrick's own vote against the 'Six Articles' is recorded.

The careers of the members of the Lower House during the reign of Queen Mary can be partly discovered from a variety of biographical and sixteenth-century sources. Abbreviations after each name indicate the sources of information about the careers of these men: F, Foster, *Alumni Oxon.*; V, Venn, *Alumni Cantab.*; *DNB*, as usual; Fr., Frere, *Marian Reaction*, pp. 253–73, lists of ordinations during Mary's reign. These men were either ordained in Mary's years or received additional ecclesiastical preferment: John Bell (V), James Bond (F), William Bradbridge (F, *DNB*), George Carew (F, *DNB*), Stephen Cheston (V), John Cottrel (F), Gregory Garthe (V), Gabriel Goodman (V, *DNB*), George Harvey (Le Neve, I, 399), Richard Hughes (F), Walter Jones (F, Fr.), John Kennall (F), Justinian Lancaster (F, Fr.), William Latimer (V), John Lawrence (F), William Leveson (F), Francis Mallet (V, *DNB*), Andrew Perne (V, *DNB*), Robert Pound (F), John Pratt (F, Fr.), John Price (Fr., 'ApRice, John'), Nicholas Robinson (V, *DNB*), John Salisbury (V, *DNB*), Nicholas Smith (F), Henry Squire (F), Hugo Turnbull (F), John Warner (F, *DNB*), John Watson (F, *DNB*), Nicholas Wendon (V), Thomas White (V, Fr.), Nicholas Wotten (*DNB*). Men who received university degrees during Mary's reign include: John Bridgewater (V, *DNB*), John Calverley (F), William Constantine (F), Robert Hughes (F), Thomas Ithel (V), Robert Lougher (F, *DNB*), Edmund Mayrick (F), and Thomas Powell (F).

Twenty-nine men were either not listed in Venn, Foster, Frere's list of Marian ordinands, or the *DNB*, or else the records there included gave no definite indication of their ecclesiastical loyalties and services under Queen Mary: Robert Avis (V), Richard Barber (F), Thomas Bolt (F), Walter Bower (F), Burton, John Butler, Richard Chandler, Ralph Coccrel, Hugo Evans (F), William Flude (V), Robert Grinsel, Richard Guy, Thomas Huet (V), Anthony Hinton, David Kemp, John Lowth (V), Hugo Morgan (F), Thomas Norley, James Procter (F), Richard Reeve (F), Thomas Roberts, George Savage (F), John Smith (F, under 1539), William Todd, John Walker (V), Richard Walker (V), Edmund Weston, and Robert Weston. Arbitrarily estimating that half (15) of this group conformed to the Marian church, and adding the 39 known conformists of the previous paragraph, we may propose 54 as the number of estimated Marian conformists who sat in Elizabeth's Convocation.

The records of five suggest that they retired during Mary's reign: Gregory Dodds (V), John Ellis (V), Thomas Lancaster (*DNB*), John Longland (F), and Andrew Pierson (V, *DNB*). Five others seem to have held up their ordinations until Elizabeth's accession: James Calfhill (F, V, *DNB*), William Day (V, *DNB*), John Ebden (V), Thomas Godwin (F, *DNB*), and Stephen Nevinson (V, *DNB*).

The following 27 men of the 1563 Lower House had been émigrés in Mary's reign; their residences are indicated if evidence suggests that they spent the *major* part of their exile in the specified cities: John Aylmer, Robert Beaumont (Ge), Thomas Becon, Richard Beseley (Ft), Thomas Bickley (F and I), Thomas Cole, Robert Crowley (Ft), Guido Heton (St), John Hills (Ft), Thomas Lever (Arau), John Mullins (Ft), Alexander Nowell (Ft), Laurence Nowell (F and I), John Pedder (Ft), John Pullan (Ge), Michael Renyger (St), Richard Rogers (Ft), Thomas Sampson, Arthur Saul (Ft), Thomas Sorby (Ft), Thomas Spencer (Ge), Richard Tremaine (F and I), William Turner, Thomas Watts (Ft), Percival Wiburn (Ge), Thomas Wilson (Ft), and Robert Wisdom. Abbreviations for residences: Ft, Frankfort; Ge, Geneva; St, Strasburg; F and I, France and Italy.

In the controversy at Frankfort over the Prayer Book, the eight Convocation men who signed letters urging conformity included Lever, Mullins, Spencer, and Beaumont from Zurich, and Heton, Pedder, Renyger, and Saul from Strasburg (*Troubles at Frankfort*, pp. 16 and 22–3). The ten who signed the New Discipline were Beseley, Croweley, Mullins, Alexander Nowell, Pedder, Rogers, Saul, Sorby, Watts, and Wilson (pp. 133–5). I accept Miss Garrett's judgment that Laurence Nowell never came to Frankfort; if the second 'Alexander Nowell' was really Laurence, this would add an eleventh (*Marian Exiles*, pp. 238–9). She erred in stating that Mullins did not sign and overlooked the signature of 'Arthur Saule' on 21 December 1557 (pp. 234 and 284–5). Furthermore, as she notes, Richard Rogers joined the hard core of New Discipline supporters who refused reconciliation, yet his name does not appear as a subscriber (p. 273); I would therefore identify the enigmatic 'Richard Nagors' as a misprint for Rogers, solving Miss Garrett's 'puzzle' (p. 235). A similar mystery is solved if the name subscribed as 'Thomas Serbis' is identified with Thomas Sorby whose name in Latin was written as 'Sorebaeus' (pp. 287 and 291). The hard core included, in addition to Rogers, five other members of the Lower House: Beseley, Crowley, Pedder, Sorby, and Watts (*Troubles at Frankfort*, p. 174).

List of works cited

ADDLESHAW, G. W. O. AND ETCHELLS, F. *The Architectural Setting of Anglican Worship*. London, 1948.

ALESIUS SCOTUS, ALEXANDER (ALESS). *Ordinatio Ecclesiae seu Ministerii Ecclesiastici, in Florentissimo Regno Angliae*. Lipsiae, 1551. *STC* No. 16423.

ASHMOLE, ELIAS. *The Institution, Laws, and Ceremonies of the Most Noble Order of the Garter*. London, 1672.

AYLMER, JOHN. *An Harborowe for Faithful and Trew Subjectes Agaynst the Late Blowne Blaste, Concerning the Gouermēt of Women*. 'Strasburg', but probably London, 1559. *STC* No. 1005.

BACON, FRANCIS. *The Works of Francis Bacon, Lord Chancellor of England*, ed. Basil Montagu, 16 vols. London, 1825–34.

BARRY, J. C. 'The Convocation of 1562', *History Today*, XIII (1963), 490–501.

BATESON, MARY, ed., 'A Collection of Original Letters from the Bishops to the Privy Council, 1564', *Camden Miscellany*, IX, Camden Society, 2nd series, LIII. Westminster, 1895.

BAYNE, C[HARLES] G[EREWIN]. *Anglo-Roman Relations, 1558–1565*. Oxford, 1913.
  'The Coronation of Queen Elizabeth', *English Historical Review*, XXII (1907), 650–73.
  'The Visitation of the Province of Canterbury', *English Historical Review*, XXVIII (1913), 635–75.

BECON, THOMAS. *Works*, ed. John Eyre, 3 vols. Cambridge, 1842–4.

BICKNELL, E. J. *A Theological Introduction to the Thirty-nine Articles*, rev. ed. H. J. Carpenter. London, 1957.

BIRT, HENRY NORBERT, O.S.B. *The Elizabethan Religious Settlement*. London, 1907.

Book of Concord, ed. Theodore G. Tappert. Philadelphia, 1959.

A Booke of Certaine Canons concerning some parte of the discipline of the Churche of England. London, 1571. *STC* No. 10063.

BOOTY, JOHN E. *John Jewel as Apologist of the Church of England*. London, 1963.

BOUVIER, ANDRÉ. *Henri Bullinger, réformateur et conseiller œcuménique*. Paris, 1940.

BRETT, JOHN. 'The English Refugees in Germany', ed. I. S. Leadham, *Transactions of the Royal Historical Society*, N.S. XI (1897), 113–31.

BRIDGEMAN, GEORGE T. O. *The History of the Church and Manor of Wigan in the County of Lancaster*, Part I. Chetham Society, XV, Manchester, 1888.

BRIDGETT, THOMAS EDWARD AND KNOX, THOMAS FRANCIS. *The True Story of the Catholic Hierarchy Deposed by Queen Elizabeth*. New York, 1889.

A Brief Treatise Conteyning Many Proper Tables and Easie Rules...Newley sette foorth and alowed, according to the Queenes Majesties Injunctions. London, 1582. *STC* No. 12158.

BROOK, V. J. K. *A Life of Archbishop Parker*. Oxford, 1962.

BURNET, GILBERT. *The History of the Reformation of the Church of England*, ed. Nicholas Pocock, 7 vols. Oxford, 1865.

CPR. Calendar of the Patent Rolls preserved in the Public Record Office, Elizabeth, vols. I–IV. London, 1939–64.

CSP, Dom., 1547–80. Calendar of State Papers, Domestic Series, of the Reigns of Edward VI, Mary, Elizabeth, 1547–80; preserved in the State Paper Department of her Majesty's Public Record Office, ed. Robert Lemon. London, 1856.

CSP, Dom. Add., 1547–65. Calendar of State Papers, Domestic Series, of the Reign of Elizabeth, 1601–1603; with addenda, 1547–1565; preserved in her Majesty's Public Record Office, ed. Mary Anne Everett Green, pp. 320–576. London, 1870.

CSP, Dom. Add., 1566–79. Calendar of State Papers, Domestic Series, of the Reign of Elizabeth, Addenda, 1566–79, ed. Mary Anne Everett Green. London, 1871.

CSP, For. Calendar of State Papers, Foreign Series, of the Reign of Elizabeth, ...preserved in the State Paper Department of her Majesty's Public Record Office. Vols. I–VII, ed. Joseph Stevenson; vols. VIII–IX, ed. Allan James Crosby. London, 1863–74.

CSP, Rome. Calendar of State Papers, relating to English Affairs, preserved principally at Rome, in the Vatican Archives and Library. Vols. I and II, ed. J. M. Rigg. London, 1916–26.

CSP, Sp. Calendar of Letters and State Papers relating to English Affairs, preserved principally in the Archives of Simancas. Vol. I, ed. Martin A. S. Hume. London, 1892.

CSP, Ven. Calendar of State Papers and Manuscripts, relating to English Affairs, existing in the Archives and Collections of Venice and in other

Libraries of Northern Italy. Vols. V and VI, ed. Rawdon Brown; Vol. VII, ed. Rawdon Brown and G. Cavendish Bentinck; Vol. VIII, ed. Horatio F. Brown. London, 1873–94.

CALVIN, JOHN. *Institutes of the Christian Religion*. Best English edition: ed. John T. McNeill, tr. Ford Lewis Battles; The Library of Christian Classics, vols. XX and XXI. Philadelphia, 1960.

  CR. Corpus Reformatorum: Opera Quae Sunt Omnia, VI. Vol. XXXIV. Brunsvigae, 1867.

  Theological Treatises, ed. and tr. J. K. S. Reid; The Library of Christian Classics, vol. XXII. Philadephia, 1954.

CAMDEN, WILLIAM. *Annales, or the History of the Most Renowned and Victorious Princesse Elizabeth, Late Queen of England*. Tr. R[obert] N[aunton], 3rd ed. London, 1635. *STC* No. 4501.

CARDWELL, EDWARD. *Documentary Annals of the Reformed Church of England...from the Year 1546 to the Year 1716*. 2 vols. Oxford, 1839.

  A History of the Conferences and Other Proceedings, Connected with the Revision of the Book of Common Prayer; from the Year 1558 to the Year 1690. Oxford, 1849.

  Synodalia: A Collection of Articles of Religion, Canons, and Proceedings of Convocations in the Province of Canterbury, from the Year 1547 to the Year 1717. 2 vols. Oxford, 1842.

CRS. Catholic Record Society, *Miscellanea*, I, No. 1, 'Report to Cardinal Moroni on the Change of Religion in 1558–9', ed. J. H. Pollen. London, 1905.

  Miscellanea, II, No. 1, 'Testimonial by Bishop Goldwell and Others in Favour of Thomas Sackville', ed. H. D. Grissell; and three papers from the Vatican, ed. J. H. Pollen. London, 1906.

The Churchwardens' Accounts of Prescot, Lancashire, 1523–1607, ed. F. A. Bailey. Preston, 1953.

The Churchwardens' Accounts of S. Edmund and S. Thomas, Sarum, 1443–1702, ed. H. J. P. Swayne. Salisbury, 1896.

Churchwardens' Accounts of the Town of Ludlow in Shropshire from 1549 to the End of the Reign of Queen Elizabeth, ed. Thomas Wright. Camden Society, O.S. CII. Westminster, 1869.

CLARKE, W. K. LOWTHER AND HARRIS, CHARLES, ed., *Liturgy and Worship*. London, 1950.

CLAY, WILLIAM KEATINGE, ed., *Liturgies and Occasional Forms of Prayer Set Forth in the Reign of Queen Elizabeth*. Cambridge, 1847.

List of works cited

Private Prayers Put Forth by Authority during the Reign of Queen Elizabeth. Cambridge, 1851.

CLEBSCH, WILLIAM A. *England's Earliest Protestants.* New Haven, 1964.

CLIFFORD, ARTHUR. *The State Papers and Letters of Sir Ralph Sadler.* 2 vols. Edinburgh, 1809.

COLLIER, JEREMY. *An Ecclesiastical History of Great Britain.* 9 vols. ed. Thomas Lathbury. London, 1852.

COLLINSON, PATRICK. *The Elizabethan Puritan Movement.* London, 1967.

CRANMER, THOMAS. *Works.* 2 vols., ed. John E. Cox. Cambridge, 1844.

CURTIS, W. A. 'Confessions', in James Hastings' *Encyclopedia of Religion and Ethics.* Edinburgh, 1910.

DASENT, JOHN ROCHE, ed., *Acts of the Privy Council of England,* N.S. II–VII (1547–70). London, 1890–3.

DAVIS, E. J., ed., 'An Unpublished Manuscript of the Lords' Journal for April and May 1559', *EHR,* XXVIII (1913), 331–42.

DAWLEY, POWEL M. *John Whitgift and the English Reformation.* New York, 1964.

DE MAISSE. *A Journal of All that was Accomplished by Monsieur de Maisse Ambassador in England from Henri IV to Queen Elizabeth Anno Domini 1597,* tr. and ed. G. B. Harrison and R. A. Jones. London, 1931.

DEWAR, MARY. *Sir Thomas Smith.* London, 1964.

D'EWES, SIMONDS. *The Journals of All the Parliaments during the Reign of Queen Elizabeth, both of the House of Lords and House of Commons.* London, 1682.

DICKENS, A. G. *The English Reformation.* New York, 1964.

DNB. *The Dictionary of National Biography,* ed. Leslie Stephen and Sidney Lee. New York, 1885–99.

DIXON, RICHARD WATSON. *History of the Church of England from the Abolition of the Roman Jurisdiction.* 6 vols. Oxford, 1887–1902.

DOERNBURG, EDWIN. *Henry VIII and Luther.* Stanford, 1961.

DUGDALE, HENRY GEAST. *The Life and Character of Edmund Geste.* London, 1839.

DUGDALE, WILLIAM. *Monasticon Anglicanum: A History of the Abbies and Other Monasteries, Hospitals, Frieries, and Cathedral and Collegiate Churches, with their Dependencies, in England and Wales.* London, 1655–73.

Monasticon Anglicanum: The History of the Ancient Abbeys, Monasteries, Hospitals, Cathedral and Collegiate Churches, being the Additional

Volumes to Sir William Dugdale's Monasticon Anglicanum, ed. John Stevens, 2 vols. London, 1722–3.

DUGMORE, C[LIFFORD] W[ILLIAM]. *The Mass and the English Reformers*. London, 1958.

ELIZABETH TUDOR. *Queen Elizabeth's Defense of her Proceedings in Church and State*, ed. W. E. Collins. London, 1899.

ELLIS, HENRY. *Original Letters, Illustrative of English History*. 3rd series, 4 vols. London, 1846.

ERASMUS, DESIDERIUS. *Praise of Folly*, tr. Hoyt Hopewell Hudson. Princeton, 1941.

FORBES, P[ATRICK]. *A Full View of the Public Transactions in the Reign of Queen Elizabeth*. 2 vols. London, 1740–1.

FOSTER, JOSEPH. *Alumni Oxoniensis: The Members of the University of Oxford, 1500–1715*. 4 vols. Oxford, 1891.

FOXE, JOHN. *The Acts and Monuments of John Foxe*, ed. Stephen Reed Cattley, 8 vols. London, 1839.

FRAENKEL, PETER. *Testimonia Patrum: The Function of the Patristic Argument in the Theology of Philip Melanchthon*. Geneva, 1961.

FRERE, WALTER HOWARD. *The English Church in the Reigns of Elizabeth and James I*. London, 1924.

The Marian Reaction. London, 1896.

Visitation Articles and Injunctions of the Period of the Reformation. Vol. II, with the assistance of William McClure Kennedy; vol. III; Alcuin Club Collections XV and XVI. London, 1910.

GARRETT, CHRISTINA HOLLOWELL. *The Marian Exiles*. Cambridge, 1938.

GASQUET, FRANCIS AIDAN AND BISHOP, EDMUND. *Edward VI and the Book of Common Prayer*. 2nd ed. London, 1891.

GEE, HENRY. *The Elizabethan Clergy and the Settlement of Religion, 1558–1564*. Oxford, 1898.

The Elizabethan Prayer Book and Ornaments, with an Appendix of Documents. London, 1902.

GEE, HENRY AND HARDY, WILLIAM JOHN. *Documents Illustrative of English Church History*. London, 1896.

GERRISH, B. A. *The Faith of Christendom*. Cleveland, 1963.

GIBSON, EDGAR C. S. *The Thirty-nine Articles of the Church of England*. 2 vols. London, 1910.

GIBSON, EDMUND. *Synodus Anglicana, or the Constitution and Proceedings of an English Convocation, shown from the Acts and Registers thereof to be*

Agreeable to the Principles of an Episcopal Church, ed. Edward Cardwell. Oxford, 1854.

GODWIN, FRANCIS. *De Praesulibus Angliae*. London, 1616. *STC* No. 11941.

GRINDAL, EDMUND. *The Remains of Edmund Grindal*, ed. William Nicholson. Cambridge, 1843.

HARDWICK, CHARLES. *A History of the Articles of Religion*. 3rd ed. London, 1895.

HARDWICKE, PHILIP, EARL OF YORKE. *Miscellaneous State Papers from 1501 to 1726*, I (1501–1625). London, 1778.

HARINGTON, JOHN. *Nugae Antiquae*. Selected by Henry Harington, ed. by Thomas Park. 2 vols. London, 1804.

HAUGAARD, WILLIAM P. 'The Proposed Liturgy of Edmund Guest', *Anglican Theological Review*, XLVI (1964), 177–89.

'The Episcopal Pretensions of Thomas Sampson', *Historical Magazine of the Protestant Episcopal Church*, XXXVI (1967), 383–6.

HAYNES, SAMUEL. *A Collection of State Papers, relating to Affairs in the Reigns of King Henry VIII, Edward VI, Queen Mary, and Queen Elizabeth, from the Year 1542 to 1570. Transcribed from Original Letters and other Authentick Memorials, Never before Published, Left by William Cecil Lord Burghley, and now Remaining at Hatfield House, in the Library of the...Earl of Salisbury*. Vol. I. London, 1740.

HAYWARD, JOHN. *Annals of the First Four Years of the Reign of Queen Elizabeth*, ed. John Bruce. Camden Society, O.S. VII. London, 1840.

HEYLEN, PETER. *Ecclesia Restaurata: or the History of the Reformation of the Church of England*. London, 1661.

HILL, CHRISTOPHER. *Economic Problems of the Church from Archbishop Whitgift to the Long Parliament*. Oxford, 1956.

Society and Puritanism in Pre-Revolutionary England. London, 1964.

HOLINSHED, RAPHAEL. *The Laste Volume of the Chronicles of England, Scotland, and Irelande*. London, 1577.

Homilies. Certain Sermons or Homilies Appointed to be read in Churches in the Time of the Late Queen Elizabeth of Famous Memory and Now Thought to be reprinted...Anno MDCXXIII. Oxford, 1840.

See below, p. 369, *Certayne Sermons...*

The Seconde Tome of homelyes of such matters as were promised and Intituled in the former part of homelyes, set out by the aucthoritie of the Quenes Maiestie: And to be read in eyery paryshe Churche agreablye. London, 1563. *STC* No. 13663.

Also other editions: *STC* Nos. 13664–5 and 13668–74.

List of works cited

An Homilie Agaynst disobedience and Wylful rebellion. London, 1570. *STC* No. 13679.

HOSKYNS, EDGAR. *Horae Beatae Mariae Virginis or Sarum and York Primers with Kindred Books and Primers of the Reformed Roman Use.* London, 1901.

HOTSON, LESLIE. *The First Night of Twelfth Night.* New York, 1954.

HUGHES, PHILIP. *The Reformation in England.* 3 vols. New York, 1954.

JACOBS, HENRY EYSTER. *The Lutheran Movement in England during the Reigns of Henry VIII and Edward VI.* Philadelphia, 1890.

JEWEL, JOHN. *An Apology of the Church of England,* ed. John E. Booty. Ithaca, New York, 1963.

Works, ed. John Eyre. 4 vols. Cambridge, 1845–50.

JONES, WILLIAM. 'The Elizabethan Church Settlement in Wales', an unpublished S.T.B. thesis at the General Theological Seminary, New York. 1956.

JOURDAN, G[EORGE] V. *History of the Church of Ireland from the Earliest Times to the Present Day,* ed. W. A. Phillips. II, 169–579. London, 1934.

JHC. Journals of the House of Commons from November the 8th, 1547, in the First Year of the Reign of King Edward the Sixth, to March the 2nd, 1628, in the Fourth Year of King Charles the First. Vol. I. London, 1803.

JHL. Journals of the House of Lords: Beginning Anno Primo Henrici Octavi. Vol. I (to 1575).

KEMP, E. W. *Counsel and Consent.* London, 1961.

KENNEDY, WILLIAM PAUL MCCLURE. *Archbishop Parker.* London, 1908.

Elizabethan Episcopal Administration. 3 vols. Alcuin Club Collections XXV–XXVII. London, 1924.

Studies in Tudor History. London, 1916.

KETLEY, JOSEPH, ed., *The Two Liturgies, A.D. 1549 and A.D. 1552: with other Documents, set forth by Authority in the Reign of King Edward VI.* Cambridge, 1844.

KIDD, B[ERESTAND] J[AMES]. *Documents Illustrative of the Continental Reformation.* Oxford, 1911.

The Thirty-nine Articles, Their History and Explanation. 3rd ed. New York, 1906.

KNAPPEN, M[ARSHALL] M[ASON], *Tudor Puritanism: A Chapter in the History of Idealism.* Chicago, 1939.

KNOWLES, DAVID. *The Religious Orders in England.* 3 vols. Cambridge, 1959.

366

List of works cited

LAMB, JOHN. *An Historical Account of the Thirty-nine Articles from the First Promulgation of them in MDLIII to their Final Establishment in MDLXXI.* Cambridge, 1829.

LAUD, WILLIAM. *Works*, vol. VI, ed. James Bliss. Oxford, 1837.

LELAND, JOHN. *Joannis Lelandi Antiquarii de Rebus Britannicis Collectanea*, ed. Thomas Hearn. London, 1774.

LEATHERBARROW, J. STANLEY. *The Lancashire Elizabethan Recusants.* Chetham Society, N.S. CX. Manchester, 1947.

LEHINBERG, STANFORD E. 'Archbishop Grindal and the Prophesyings', *The Historical Magazine of the Protestant Episcopal Church*, XXXIX (1965).

LEITH, JOHN H. *Creeds of the Churches.* Garden City, New York, 1963.

LE NEVE, JOHN. *Fasti Ecclesiae Anglicanae*, ed. T. Duffus Hardy. 3 vols. Oxford, 1854.

Letters and Papers, Foreign and Domestic, of the Reign of Henry VIII, preserved in the Public Record Office, the British Museum, and Elsewhere in England, XIV, ed. James Gairdner. London, 1895.

LEVER, THOMAS. *Sermons, 1550*, ed. Edward Arber. London, 1871.

Liber Precum Publicarum, seu Ministerij Ecclesiasticae Administrationis Sacramentorum, Aliorumque Rituū & Ceremoniarum in Ecclesia Anglicana. London, 1560. *STC* No. 16424. Also revised edition of 1574, *STC* No. 16427.

LODGE, EDMUND. *Illustrations of British History, Biography, and Manners in the Reigns of Henry VIII, Edward VI, Mary, Elizabeth, and James I, Exhibited in a Series of Original Papers, Selected from the Manuscripts of the Noble Families of Howard, Talbot, and Cecil.* London, 1791.

LUTHER, MARTIN. *Three Treatises.* Philadelphia, 1947.

Works, vol. XXV, ed. E. T. Bachman and H. T. Lehmann. Philadelphia, 1960.

MCADOO, H. R. *The Spirit of Anglicanism.* London, 1965.

MACGREGOR, GEDDES. *Corpus Christi.* Philadelphia, 1958.

MCLELLAND, JOSEPH C. *The Visible Word of God.* Edinburgh, 1957.

MACHYN, HENRY. *The Diary of Henry Machyn*, ed. John Gough Nichols. Camden Society, O.S. XLII. London, 1848.

MAITLAND, FREDERIC WILLIAM. 'The Anglican Settlement and the Scottish Reformation', *Cambridge Modern History* (old edition), II (Cambridge, 1934), 550–98.

The Collected Papers of Frederic William Maitland, 3 vols., ed. H. A. L. Fisher. Cambridge, 1911.

MARSHALL, EDWARD. *Oxford.* S.P.C.K. diocesan history. London, 1882.

MARTIN, CHARLES. *Les Protestants Anglais Réfugiés à Genève*. Geneva, 1915.

MELANCHTHON, PHILIP. *Corpus Reformatorum. Opera Quae Supersunt Omnia*, XXI, ed. Henry Ernest Bindseil. Brunsvigae, 1854.

MEYER, ARNOLD OSKAR. *England and the Catholic Church under Queen Elizabeth*, tr. J. R. McKee. London, 1916.

MEYER, CARL S. *Elizabeth I and the Religious Settlement of 1559*. St Louis, 1960.

MOLLAND, EINAR. *Christendom*. 2nd English ed. London, 1961.

MOORE, A[RTHUR] W[ILLIAM]. *Sodor and Man*. S.P.C.K. diocesan history. London, 1893.

NEALE, JOHN E. *Elizabeth I and her Parliaments*. 2 vols. London, 1953–7.
'The Elizabethan Acts of Supremacy and Uniformity', *EHR*, LXV (1950), 304–32.
'Parliament and the Articles of Religion', *EHR*, LXVII (1952), 510–21.
Queen Elizabeth I. Garden City, New York, 1957.
'The Sayings of Queen Elizabeth', *History*, IX (1925), 212–33.

NOWELL, ALEXANDER. *A Catechism Written in Latin by Alexander Nowell, Dean of St. Paul's: together with the Same Catechism translated into English by Thomas Norton*, ed. G. E. Corrie. Cambridge, 1853.

OL. *Original Letters relative to the English Reformation, Written during the Reigns of King Henry VIII, King Edward VI, and Queen Mary: Chiefly from the Archives of Zurich*. 2 vols. Cambridge, 1846–7.

The Ornaments of the Church and its Ministers, 1908 report to the Upper House of the Convocation of Canterbury by a sub-committee appointed February 1907, No. 416.

PARKER, MATTHEW. *Correspondence of Matthew Parker, D.D., Archbishop of Canterbury*, ed. John Bruce and Thomas Thomason Perowne. Cambridge, 1853.
De Antiquitate Britannicae Ecclesiae. Hanoviae, 1603.

PECK, FRANCIS, *Desiderata Curiosa: or, a Collection of Divers Scarce and Curious Pieces Relating Chiefly to Matters of English History*. London, 1779.

PEEL, ALBERT, ed., *The Seconde Parte of a Register; Being a Calendar of Manuscripts under that Title Intended for Publication by the Puritans about 1593, and Now in Dr. William's London Library*. Cambridge, 1915.

PILKINGTON, JAMES. *Works*, ed. James Schoenfield. Cambridge, 1842.

POLLANUS [POULLAIN], V[ALERAND]. *Vera Expositita Disputationis Institutae Mandato D. Mariae Reginae...in Synodo...Anno 1553*. 1554.

POLLEN, JOHN H. *The English Catholics in the Reign of Queen Elizabeth: A Study of their Politics and Government, 1558–1580.* London, 1920.

PORTER, H[ARRY] C[ULVERWELL]. *Reformation and Reaction in Tudor Cambridge.* Cambridge, 1958.

Prayer Books. The First and Second Prayer Books of Edward VI, ed. E. C. Ratcliff. London, 1949.

The Primer, in Englishe and Latyn, set foorth by the Kynges Maiestie and his Clergie to be taught, learned, and read: and none other to be used throughout all his dominions. London, 1545. *STC* No. 16040. Also the Elizabethan edition of 1559, *STC* No. 16087, English only.

PRIMUS, J[OHN] H[ENRY]. *The Vestments Controversy: An Historical Study of the Earliest Tensions within the Church of England in the Reigns of Edward VI and Elizabeth.* Kampen, 1960.

PROCTER, FRANCIS, AND FRERE, WALTER HOWARD. *A New History of the Book of Common Prayer.* London, 1958.

PROTHERO, G[EORGE] W[ALTER]. *Select Statutes and other Constitutional Documents Illustrative of the Reigns of Elizabeth and James I.* 4th ed. Oxford, 1913.

PRYCE, ARTHUR IVOR, ed., *The Diocese of Bangor in the Sixteenth Century: Being a Digest of the Registers of the Bishops, A.D. 1512–1646.* Bangor, 1923.

READ, CONYERS. *Mr. Secretary Cecil and Queen Elizabeth.* First volume of a 2-volume biography of William Cecil. London, 1955.

Registrum Matthei Parker, Diocesis Cantuariensis, A.D. 1559–1575, Register I, 3 vols., transcribed by E. Margaret Thompson, and edited by W. H. Frere. Oxford, 1928.

RICHARDSON, CYRIL C. *Zwingli and Cranmer on the Eucharist.* Evanston, Ill., 1949.

RONAN, MYLES V. *The Reformation in Ireland under Elizabeth, 1558–1580.* London, 1930.

ROWSE, A[LFRED] L[ESLIE]. *The England of Elizabeth.* New York, 1961.
The Expansion of Elizabethan England. London, 1955.
Tudor Cornwall. London, 1957.

RUPP, E[RNEST] G[ORDON]. *Studies in the Making of the English Protestant Tradition.* Cambridge, 1949.

RYMER, THOMAS. *Foedera, Conventiones, Literae, et cuiuscunque Generis.* 3rd ed., ed. George Holmes, vols. VI and VII. The Hague, 1741.

SANDER, NICHOLAS. *De Origine ac Progressa Schismatis Anglicani,* ed. Edward Rishton. Ingolstadt, 1587.
Rise and Growth of the Anglican Schism. Published A.D. 1585 with a

Continuation of the History, by the Rev. Edward Rishton, tr. and ed. David Lewis. London, 1877.

SCHAFF, PHILIP. *The Creeds of Christendom, with a History and Critical Notes.* 3 vols. New York, 1877.

Certayne Sermons appoynted by the Quenes Maiestie to be declared and read by all persones, vycars and curates, every Sonday and holy daye in theyr Churches. London, 1559. *STC* No. 13648. Also other editions: *STC* Nos. 13649–53 and 13655–8.

SHIRLEY, EVELYN PHILIP, ed., *Original Letters and Papers in Illustration of the History of the Church of Ireland, during the Reigns of Edward VI, Mary, and Elizabeth.* London, 1851.

STC. A Short Title Catalogue of Books Printed in England, Scotland, and Ireland, and of English Books Printed Abroad, 1475–1640, ed. A. W. Pollard and G. R. Redgrave. London, 1926.

SOUTHGATE, W. M. *John Jewel and the Problem of Doctrinal Authority.* Cambridge, Mass., 1962.

SPIELMANN, RICHARD M. 'Elizabethan Exiles: A Discussion of the Content and Influence of English Writings of Seven Elizabethan Exiles', an unpublished Th.D. thesis at the General Theological Seminary, 1964.

State Papers Published under the Authority of His Majesty's Commission, Henry VIII. 11 vols. 1830–52.

Statutes of the Realm, vol. IV, London, 1819.

STONE, DARWELL. *A History of the Doctrine of the Holy Eucharist.* 2 vols. London, 1909.

Stowe's Memoranda. Three Fifteenth-Century Chronicles with Historical Memoranda by John Stowe, the Antiquary, and Contemporary Notes of the Occurrences Written by him in the Reign of Queen Elizabeth, ed. James Gairdner. Camden Society, 2nd series, XXVIII. Westminster, 1880.

STREATFEILD, FRANK. *Latin Versions of the Book of Common Prayer.* Alcuin Club Pamphlet XIX. London, 1964.

STRYPE, JOHN. *Annals of the Reformation and Establishment of Religion, and Other Various Occurrences in the Church of England, during Queen Elizabeth's Happy Reign.* 4 vols., of which I–III have two parts each. Oxford, 1824.

Cranmer. Memorials of the Most Reverend Father in God Thomas Cranmer, Sometime Lord Archbishop of Canterbury. 3 vols. Oxford, 1840.

The life of Sir John Cheke, Kt.; First Instructor, afterwards Secretary of State, to King Edward VI. Oxford, 1821.

The History of the Life and Acts of the Most Reverend Father in God, Edmund Grindal, the First Bishop of London, and the Second Archbishop of York and Canterbury Successively, in the Reign of Queen Elizabeth. Oxford, 1821.

Memorials. Ecclesiastical Memorials Relating Chiefly to Religion and the Reformation of it, and the Emergencies of the Church of England, under King Henry VIII, King Edward VI, and Queen Mary I. 3 vols., each in 2 parts. Oxford, 1822.

The Life and Acts of Matthew Parker, the First Archbishop of Canterbury in the Reign of Queen Elizabeth. 3 vols. Oxford, 1821.

The Life and Acts of John Whitgift, D.D., the Third and Last Archbishop of Canterbury in the Reign of Queen Elizabeth. 3 vols. Oxford, 1832.

STUBBS, WILLIAM. *Registrum Sacrum Anglicanum: An Attempt to Exhibit the Course of Episcopal Succession in England from the Records and Chronicles of the Church.* Oxford, 1897.

STURGE, CHARLES. *Cuthbert Tunstall, Churchman, Scholar, Statesman, Administrator.* London, 1938.

SYKES, NORMAN. *From Sheldon to Secker.* Cambridge, 1959.

THOMAS, W[ILLIAM] H[ENRY] GRIFFITH. *The Principles of Theology: An Introduction to the Thirty-nine Articles.* London, 1951.

THOMPSON, J[AMES] V[INCENT] P[ERRONET]. *Supreme Governor: A Study of Elizabethan Ecclesiastical Policy and Circumstance.* London, 1940.

TILLYARD, E[USTACE] M[ANDEVILLE] W[ETENHALL]. *The Elizabethan World Picture.* New York, n.d.

TJERNAGEL, NEELAK SERAWLOOK. *Henry VIII and the Lutherans.* St Louis, 1965.

Troubles at Frankfort. A Brief Discourse of the Troubles Begun at Frankfort in the Year 1554, About the Book of Common Prayer and Ceremonies, reprinted from the black-letter edition of 1575, ed. 'J.P.'. London, 1846.

TYLER, PHILIP. 'The Ecclesiastical Commission within the Province of York, 1562–1640', an unpublished D. Phil. thesis at Oxford University.

USHER, ROLAND G[REENE]. *The Reconstruction of the English Church.* 2 vols. New York, 1910.

VAN DE POLL, C. J. *Martin Bucer's Liturgical Ideas.* Assen, 1954.

VENN, JOHN AND VENN, J. A. *Alumni Cantabrigienses: A Biographical List of all Known Students, Graduates, and Holders of Office at the University of Cambridge, from the Earliest Times to 1900.* Part I, to 1751, 4 vols. Cambridge, 1927.

VON KLARVILL, VICTOR, ed., *Queen Elizabeth and Some Foreigners, Being a Series of Hitherto Unpublished Letters from the Archives of the Hapsburg Family*, tr. T. H. Nash. New York, 1928.

WALLACE, RONALD S. *Calvin's Doctrine of the Word and Sacrament*. Grand Rapids, Michigan, 1957.

WENDEL, FRANÇOIS. *Calvin*. Paris, 1950.

WHITE, F[RANCIS] O[VEREND]. *Lives of the Elizabethan Bishops of the Anglican Church*. London, 1898.

WHITE, HELEN C[ONSTANCE]. *The Tudor Books of Private Devotion*. University of Wisconsin, 1951.

WILKINS, DAVID. *Concilia Magnae Britanniae et Hiberniae, a Synodo Verolamiensi, A.D. CCCCXLVI, ad Londinensem, A.D. MDCCXVII*. 4 vols., London, 1737.

WILLIAMS, GLANMOR. 'The Deprivation and Exile of Bishop Richard Davies', *Journal of the Historical Society of the Church in Wales*, I (1947), 81–90.

WILLIS, BROWNE. *Notitia Parliamentaria: Containing an Account of the First Returns and Incorporations of the Cities, Towns, and Boroughs in England and Wales, that Send Members to Parliament*. London, 1750.

WILSON, THOMAS. 'The State of England, Anno Domini 1600', ed. F. J. Fisher, *Camden Miscellany: XVI*. Camden Society, 3rd series, LII, London, 1936.

WORDSWORTH, CHRISTOPHER, ed., *Ecclesiastical Biography: or Lives of Eminent Men, connected with the History of Religion in England; from the Commencement of the Reformation to the Revolution*, 3rd ed., III. London, 1839.

WRIGHT, THOMAS, ed., *Queen Elizabeth and her Times: a Series of Original Letters, Selected from the Inedited Private Correspondence of the Lord Treasurer Burghley, the Earl of Leicester, the Secretaries Walsingham and Smith, Sir Christopher Hatton, and Most of the Distinguished Persons of the Period*. 2 vols. London, 1838.

WRIOTHESLEY, CHARLES. *A Chronicle of England during the Reigns of the Tudors from A.D. 1435 to 1559*, ed. W. D. Hamilton, 2 vols. Camden Society, 2nd series, XI and XXVI. London, 1875–7.

ZL. *The Zurich Letters, Comprising the Correspondence of Several English Bishops and others with some of the Helvetian Reformers, during...the Reign of Queen Elizabeth*. 2 vols., ed. Hastings Robinson. Cambridge, 1842–5.

Index

NOTE. Offices held by members of the Convocation of Canterbury in 1563 appear marked with an asterisk. A question mark indicates that the evidence concerning the office includes some conflicting reports. Abbreviations: a. archdeacon; d. dean; p. proctor; cl. clergy; cath. chapter of cathedral church.

Advertisements, see Parker's Advertisements
Albert, Elector of Brandenburg, 31
Aless, Alexander, 113–15, 144
Allen, Edmund, 43 n.
Allen, William, 314, 326
Alley, William (*bishop of Exeter), 26, 44, 56–7, 67, 137, 178, see also Bishop Alley's proposals, Convocation of 1563, Documents
Anabaptists, 201, 224, 245, 247
  doctrine of, 17, 235, 241, 249, 251–2, 259–60, 262–3, 265
Anglesey, archdeacon of, see Salisbury, John
Anglicanism, characteristics and formation, viii, 53, 78, 100, 111, 119, 143, 147, 181–2, 208, 228, 233–4, 247, 269, 270, 283, 288–90, 335, 337–41
Anthony of Bourbon, king-consort of Navarre, 296
Aquinas, Thomas, 235
Arau, 28, 31, 49
Armagh, diocese of, 29, 48
Articles, doctrinal
  Ten Articles (1536), 10
  Thirteen Articles (1538), 10, 17, 249, 263–4
  Forty-two Articles of Religion (1553), 17, 18, 62, 87–8, 235, 236, 239, 241, 247–54, 249 n., 259, 264, 266–7, 277, 284, 345, 352
  Eleven Articles (1561), 239–42, 241 n., 246, 249, 257, 257 n., 282, 289, 298, 356
  Principal heads of religion (1561), 240–2, 250 n., 264, 267

Thirty-nine Articles of Religion (1563–71), 54, 57, 62–7, 73, 78, 125, 127, 167 n., 206, 234, 239, 240–1, 241 n., 246, 247–72, 273, 276, 278, 280–4, 285–90, 334–5, 337–8, 352, 357–8
  see also Exiles, Marian, Declaration of Articles of Inquiry
  Cranmer's 1548 visitation, 138–9, 138 n., 139 n., 140, 141 n., 144 n.
  1559 royal visitation, 138–9, 138 n., 139 n.
  Parker's metropolitical visitation, 162
Augsburg Confession, 5, 30, 84 n., 108, 234–5, 249, 263, 265 n.
Augustinian doctrine, 261, 267, 268 n.
Avis (Avys), Robert (*p. cl.? Worcester), 358
Aylmer (Aelmer), John (*a. Lincoln), 20, 48–9, 102, 204 n., 359

Babington, Gervase, 159 n.
Bacon, Anne (Cooke), Lady, 244
Bacon, Francis, 129, 217, 329, 331
Bacon, Nicholas, Lord Keeper, 33, 73, 82, 84, 88, 102, 103, 133, 208–9, 218, 225, 225 n., 244, 299, 316, 319
Bale, John, 7, 8, 15, 28, 29, 47, 49, 50 n.
Bancroft, Richard, 242
Bangor, diocese of, 19, 23, 44, 155 n.
  archdeacon of, see Mayrick, Edmund
  bishops of, see Glynn, William; Merrick, Rowland
Baptism, 113, 113 n., 150–1, 163, 165, 214, 242, 356
  doctrine of, 241, 260, 263, 264
  proposed reforms of, 69, 121–2, 125, 353, 355

Barber, Richard (*a. Leicester), 357–8

Barlow, William (*bishop of Chichester), 6–8, 10–16, 19, 20, 43, 68, 196

Barnes, Richard, 124, 242 n.

Barnstaple, archdeacon of, *see* Squire, Henry

Barrett, William, 158 n.

Barry, J. C., 70 n.

Barthelot, John, 2, 60 n.

Basle, 28, 30

Bath and Wells, diocese of, 22, 37, 41, 44, 137, 157, 157 n.
  bishops of, *see* Barlow, William; Berkeley, Gilbert; Bourne, Gilbert
  dean of, *see* Turner, William

Bath, archdeacon of, *see* Bond, James

Bayne, Charles Gerewin, 299 n.

Bayne, Ralph, 37, 41, 102, 311 n.

Beaumont, Robert (*a. Huntingdon), 50 n., 359

Becon, Thomas (*no evidence, but probably p. cath. Canterbury), 8, 29, 31, 48–9, 50 n., 136–7, 137 n., 253 n., 357, 359

Bedford, archdeacon of, *see* Todd, William

Belgic Confession, 263 n.

Bell, John (*p. cl. Ely), 358

Bell ringing, 164, 165, 166, 167–8, 168 n., 355

Bentham, Thomas (*bishop of Coventry and Lichfield), 19, 26, 27, 28, 28 n., 30, 44, 68, 136–7, 137 n., 150

Berkeley, Gilbert (*bishop of Bath and Wells), 20, 27, 44

Berkshire, archdeacon of, *see* White, Thomas

Berwick, 211, 226

Besely (Beseley), Richard (*p. cl. Canterbury), 50 n., 359

Best, John (bishop of Carlisle), 19 n., 25, 46, 134, 248 n., 352

Beza, Theodore, 27

Bible, 164, 176, 192, 194, 206, 248, 269, 276, 289, 296–7, 314, 324, 330–1, 336, 350
  Apocrypha, 120, 249, 261, 261 n.

doctrine of, 105, 236, 241, 246, 248–9, 256, 259, 260–1, 276, 339
  English, 4, 8–9, 30, 74, 237
  use of, 12, 117–18, 118 n., 138, 142, 149, 246, 337
  Welsh, 74, 126

Bickley (Byckley), Thomas (*p. cl. Coventry and Lichfield), 65, 204 n., 356, 357, 359

Bicknell, E. J., 262 n.

Bill, William, 48, 95, 131, 134, 134 n., 138

Birt, Henry Norbert, 37 n., 92

Bishops
  English and Welsh, Edwardian, 47
    Marian, 3–4, 5, 6, 18–19, 22–3, 36–42, 49, 81, 83, 86, 87–8, 91, 95, 96, 96 n., 97, 101 n., 101–4, 105, 111, 127, 139, 291, 310–13, 321–4, 333–4; imprisonment of, 3–4, 103, 309–13, 315, 318, 321–4
    Elizabethan, 102, 120, 126–7, 128–9, 162–6, 180–1, 183, 189–200, 203–5, 207–8, 213–17, 218, 223, 228–32, 239–40, 242, 247, 257, 268–9, 272, 273, 273 n., 278, 280, 282–3, 285–8, 297–8, 300–1, 320–1, 328, 334–5, 337–8, 340, 352; characteristics of, 11, 11 n., 18–19, 21–6, 27, 29, 30, 31–2, 47, 50, 76–8; *see also* Convocation of 1563, Upper House; Elizabeth I, relations with the bishops; Interpretations of the bishops
    Seventeenth century, 119, 158–9, 159 n.
  Irish, 15, 28, 29, 46, 47 n., 48, 158 n.
  manner of nomination and election, 15, 43–4, 91 n.
  suffragan, 24, 47, 47–8 n.
  Welsh, 44, 74, 126

Bishops' Book, 10

Bodleian Library, Oxford, 88 n.

Boleyn, Anne, 5, 6, 35

Bolt, Thomas (*a. Salop, p. cath. Lichfield?), 7 n., 357–8

Bond, James (a. Bath), 358

Bonner, Edmund, 5, 10, 11, 12, 13, 14, 15, 16, 18, 20, 21, 22, 37, 41–2, 87–8, 238, 311–12, 319, 320–2, 324

Book of Common Prayer, 12, 26, 27, 85, 92–4, 97–8, 119, 146, 234, 251
  1549, 13, 14, 18, 55, 93, 101 n., 108–10, 112, 113–15, 127, 147, 181, 197 n.
  1552, 14, 18, 29, 31, 79, 85 n., 91, 91 n., 93, 106–7, 108–11, 112, 113–15, 118, 118 n., 120, 122, 126–7, 143, 147, 148, 184, 203, 321, 337–8, 343–5, 356
  1559, 67, 69, 74, 79–80, 104–11, 117, 118, 122, 126–7, 128, 135, 135–6 n., 139, 145, 162, 163, 166, 169, 174, 183–4, 186, 197, 203–4, 214, 236, 242, 246, 256, 257 n., 269, 274, 280, 283, 288, 294 n., 311–13, 314–15, 325
  reform of, 56, 64, 69–70, 112, 125
  later editions and revisions, 114, 119
  Catechism of, 142, 170–1, 236, 246, 289, 350
  Lectionary of, 106, 117–19
  Latin
    1551, 113–15, 144
    1559, 112, 113–17, 119, 124, 127
    1571, 116
  Welsh, 74, 126
  see also Baptism; Burials; Calendar, ecclesiastical; Confirmation; Holy Communion; Litany, English; Ordinal

Book of Concord and Formula of Concord, 235, 265, 266 n.

Booty, John E., 242, 243 n., 244, 245 n.

Borromeo, Charles, Cardinal, 220, 299 n., 307

Bourne, Gilbert, 13, 18, 20, 22, 37, 41, 311, 321, 323

Bower, Walter (*p. cl. Somerset), 358

Bradbridge, William (*p. cath. [chancellor] Chichester), 358

Brandon, Frances, duchess of Suffolk, 115

Brecon, archdeacon of, *see* Jones, Walter

Bretano, Gerone, 306–7

Bridgewater, John (*a. Rochester), 358

Bristol
  dean of, *see* Carew, George
  diocese of, 46, 137, 157

Brook, V. J. K., 70, 70 n., 71 n., 162, 190, 320 n., 345

Browne, Anthony, Viscount Montague, 83, 90

Bucer, Martin, 16–17, 107, 170, 221, 244, 266–7, 268, 268 n., 275

Buckingham, archdeacon of, *see* Longland, John

Bucson, William, *see* Leveson, William

Bullinger, Henry, 1, 27, 37, 60 n., 73, 78, 84 n., 89, 108, 169, 188, 223, 229, 230, 234, 243, 244, 252, 261, 266–7

Bullingham, Nicholas (*bishop of Lincoln), 1, 6, 13, 19, 20, 26 n., 27, 44, 67, 68, 162 n., 196, 213

Burials, 113 n., 114–17, 124, 226–7
  prayers for the dead, 9, 14, 114–16, 164, 328

Burnet, Gilbert, ix–x, 48, 342–3, 354

Burton, ? (*unknown), 357–8

Butler, John (*a. Cardigan), 358

Calendar ecclesiastical, 9, 118 n.
  in 1559 Latin Prayer Book, 114, 117, 127
  New (1561), 112, 117–19, 149
  proposed reforms of, 120–1, 336, 353

Calfhill (Calfhil), James (*p. cl. London; p. cath. Oxford), 356, 357, 359

Calverley, John (*p. cl. Rochester), 358

Calvin, John, 27, 28, 29, 107, 170, 175, 233, 235, 244, 245 n., 250, 252, 261–3, 265 n., 266–7, 268, 268 n., 276, 279, 280, 336
  Institutes of the Christian Religion, 235, 251, 262

Calvinism, *see* Discipline, Calvinist; Reformed Churches

Cambridge University, 23, 24, 158, 158 n., 221, 281 n.

Index

Camden, William, 80, 129, 294 n.
Canon law, 4–5, 164
  canons of 1575, 1585, and 1597, 217, 217 n.
  canons of 1604, 255–6, 278, 282 n.
  reform of, 17–18, 56–7, 70, 169–70
  see also Convocation of 1571, canons of; Reformatio Legum Ecclesiasticarum
Canterbury
  archbishops of, see Bancroft, Richard; Cranmer, Thomas; Grindal, Edmund; Laud, William; Parker, Matthew; Pole, Reginald; Whitgift, John
  archdeacons of, see Guest, Edmund; Harpsfield, Nicholas
  cathedral, 34, 168, 214 n., 357
  dean of, see Wotton, Nicholas
  diocese of, 21, 22, 32–6, 131, 137, 162
  province of, 158 n., 213, 225, 345
Cardigan, archdeacon of, see Butler, John
Cardwell, Edward, 88 n., 217 n., 342, 342 n., 346 n., 353 n.
Carew, George (*d. Windsor, d. Bristol, a. Exeter), 10, 11, 72, 253 n., 357–8
Carlisle
  bishops of, see Best, John; Oglethorpe, Owen
  cathedral, 167
  dean of, see Weston, Robert
  diocese of, 37, 44 n., 46, 155 n.
Carmarthen, archdeacon of, see Leveson, William
Cartwright, Thomas, 193, 279, 336
Cassander, George, 189 n., 195
Catechism, see Book of Common Prayer, catechism of; Geneva, Catechism of; Nowell, Alexander, catechism of; Poynet, John, catechism of
The Catechism, 67, 67 n.
Catherine of Aragon, queen of England, 5
Catherine of Medici, queen of France, 296, 303–4, 332
Cave, Ambrose, 133

Cave, Francis, 132–3, 134 n.
Cecil, William, Lord Burghley, 33, 37–41, 50, 56, 83, 84, 86, 111, 116, 133, 135, 144, 152, 156, 156 n., 159, 168, 180, 188, 193, 194, 201–2, 211–13, 211 n., 218–21, 218 n., 224–5, 225 n., 242, 244, 253 n., 254–5, 273, 277–8, 278 n., 286, 293, 295, 297–302, 306, 311, 313, 315, 316, 319–21
Challoner, Thomas, 293
Chancels, repair of, 123, 149–50, 155
Chandler (Chaundler), Richard (*a. Salisbury?), 358
Charles I Stuart, king of England, 159, 159 n.
Charles II Stuart, king of England, 159 n.
Charles V Hapsburg, emperor, 5, 258
Charles IX Valois, king of France, 297, 307
Charles Hapsburg, archduke of Austria, 187
Chester
  bishops of, see Downham, William; Scot, Cuthbert
  diocese of, 22, 37, 46, 155 n., 314, 325
Chester, William, 133, 133 n.
Cheston (Cheaton), Stephen (*a. Winchester), 23, 24, 358
Cheyney, Richard (*bishop of Gloucester with jurisdiction over Bristol), 19, 19 n., 23–4, 46, 204, 223, 250–1, 253, 253 n., 254, 254 n., 352
Chichester
  archdeacon of, see Spencer, Thomas
  bishops of, see Barlow, William; Scory, John
  dean of, see Turnbull, Hugo
  diocese of, 43, 137, 157, 157 n.
Cholmeley, Randall, 133, 134 n.
Christ Church, Oxford, 222; see also Sampson, Thomas
Christ's College, Cambridge, 22
Christ's descent into hell, 57, 252
Christopher, duke of Würtemberg, 243, 304
Church, doctrine of, 170, 232, 249, 252, 253–4, 262–3, 269–70, 275, 279

376

Index

Church buildings, care of, 122–3, 147–51, 181, 201, 338

Churching of women, 113, 113 n.

Churchwardens, 142, 147, 164, 171, 174–5, 237

Clement VII, Pope, 306

Clergy, 22–6, 31–2, 139, 165, 177–8, 215
  education of, 141–2, 164, 166, 175–6, 180–1
  street wear (cap and gown), 142, 143, 184, 205, 208–10, 211, 214–15, 220–2, 228–30, 345, 353
  subscription to doctrine, 240–1, 256–7, 282, 287, 289, 338, 349, 356
  see also Finances of the church, pluralities, parish benefices

Coccrel, Ralph (*p. cl. Surrey, d. of Winchester), 358

Colchester, archdeacon of, *see* Pullan, John

Cole, Henry, 102, 103, 310, 319

Cole, Thomas (*a. Essex), 29, 31, 50 n., 79, 221, 353, 359

Cole, William, 232

Coligny, Admiral, 303

Collinson, Patrick, 37 n., 339–40

Commination service, 113, 113 n.

Commission
  diocesan for Chester, 314, 325
  ecclesiastical at York, 134
  permanent ecclesiastical at London, 116, 117–19, 121, 130–5, 138, 142, 149, 165, 181, 186, 199–200, 212–13, 216, 224, 226, 240, 322, 335

Confirmation, 113, 113 n., 264

Congregational polity, 29–30

Constantine, George, 136

Constantine, William (*p. cl. St David's), 358

Convocations, 97, 98, 163, 191, 200, 228, 232, 236

Convocation of Canterbury
  before 1558, 4–5, 10, 11, 16, 17, 23–4, 55, 58, 60, 63, 65
  of 1559, 62, 87–8, 90, 102, 238
  of 1563, vii–viii, 2, 32, 51, 76, 80, 127, 128, 184, 233–4, 267, 273, 284,

288, 291–2, 305, 309, 315, 333–6, 343
  Upper House, 43, 46, 47, 48–9, 55–63, 65–73, 76–8, 127, 209, 210, 247–54, 277, 280–4, 318, 333, 343–4; 'secret discussions', 56, 62, 67–8, 72, 334; *see* Bishops, Elizabethan, characteristics of
  Lower House, 1, 55–73, 76–8, 121, 126–7, 166, 169, 177–80, 205, 210, 248, 253, 277–8, 281–4, 317, 333–5, 342–3, 352; characteristics of members, 7, 11, 19, 21–6, 27, 28, 29, 30, 31–2, 42, 47–9, 50–1, 76–8, 152, 226, 354, 357–9; relation to Upper House, 57–61, 62, 64–5, 66, 77–8, 333; Prolocutor of, role of, 55, 57–8; *see* Nowell, Alexander
  documents of, ix–x, 247, 342–56; acts of the Upper House, x, 53–73, 342; acts of the Lower House (fragment), 64–5, 342, 354; Parker's preliminary procedural notes, 55, 58, 242; 'Articles for government', x, 68–72, 120, 124, 125, 127, 167–9, 167–8 n., 171–6, 178–80, 205, 317, 318 n., 333, 343, 354–5; Bishop Alley's proposal, 56–7, 171, 174, 177, 178, 179, 209, 247, 252, 342, 344; Bishop Sandys' proposals, 56–7, 121, 121 n., 122, 169, 170, 172, 176, 179, 342, 343–4; 'Certain articles', 60–1, 68–9, 79, 120, 122–3, 128, 172–4, 177, 209, 247, 277, 342, 345, 355; 'General notes', 60–1, 68–70, 120, 121, 167–8, 167–8 n., 169–74, 172 n., 176–80, 209–10, 247, 277, 280–2, 317, 318 n., 342, 345–53, 355; 'Seven articles', 64–5, 121, 122, 123, 124–5, 127, 168–9, 210, 226, 333, 343; signed MS of Articles of Religion, 62–3, 65, 248, 251, 251 n., 273, 273 n., 343, 352, 352 n., 354; 'Six articles', 64–5, 67, 71–2, 73, 121,

Convocation of Canterbury *(cont.)*
122, 123, 125, 127, 169, 210, 284,
333, 342, 343, 353–4; 'Twenty-
one articles', 68–72, 121, 123–4,
125, 127, 205–6, 277, 280–4, 286,
318, 333, 343
measures adopted
Book of Homilies, 273, 276;
clerical subsidy, 54, 62, 64, 65–6,
74, 78; Thirty-nine Articles, 62–4,
247–53, 272
measures proposed
for doctrinal discipline, 277, 280–
4; against images, 205–8; liturgical reforms, 64–5, 119–27, 166–9;
reform of clerical administration
and finance, 176–80; reform of
clerical education, 175–6; reform
of lay discipline, 169–75; reform
of vestments, 208–10; against
Roman Catholics, 317–18
proceedings, 1–4, 44, 52–78
of 1571, 254–7, 257 n., 276, 285, 286,
288
canons of, 146, 146 n., 217, 255–7,
278, 280, 282, 287
Convocation of York, 4, 16, 43, 63
Cooke, Anthony, 84–5, 132–3
Cooper, Thomas, 279
Cornwall, archdeacon of, *see* Harvey,
George
Corpus Christi College, Cambridge, 6,
116, 352
Library of, 53, 342–3
Cottrel (Cotterel), John (*a. Wells, a.
Dorset), 24–5, 65, 72, 357–8
Council, General, 105, 236, 239, 246,
263
definition of a 'free', 293–5, 297–8,
300, 303, 309
of Trent, 5, 234, 245, 249, 259, 292–
302, 302–5, 309, 315, 324, 325
decrees of, 235, 315
English participation in, 240, 292–
302, 302–5, 309, 314
Courts, ecclesiastical, 69, 75, 174, 338,
354–5

Coventry and Lichfield
bishops of, *see* Bayne, Ralph; Bentham, Thomas
cathedral of, 354
dean of, *see* Nowell, Lawrence
diocese of, 37, 44, 137
Coventry, archdeacon of, *see* Lever,
Thomas
Coverdale, Miles, 7, 8, 15, 28, 30, 31, 47,
49, 50, 223
Cox, Richard (*bishop of Ely), 6, 8, 10,
11, 13, 18, 20, 27, 29, 39, 43, 43 n.,
68, 82, 84, 89, 90 n., 95, 131, 134–5,
150, 157, 184, 189 n., 190, 192,
194–6, 194–5 n., 198–9, 202, 204,
207, 213, 228, 230, 273–4
Cranmer, Thomas, 6, 8–9, 10, 13, 14, 16,
20, 21, 29, 138–9, 140, 237–8, 245,
262, 341; *see also* Articles of Inquiry,
Cranmer's 1548 visitation
Creed, Lord's Prayer, and Decalogue, to
be taught and learned, 9, 170–1,
246, 348
Cromwell, Oliver, 148
Cromwell, Thomas, and office of Vicar-
general for ecclesiastical affairs, 6–7,
16, 130, 181, 338
Crowley (Croweley, Croley), Robert
(*a. Hereford), 50 n., 65 n., 226–7,
359
Crucifix, *see* Images and iconoclasm;
Elizabeth, chapel cross
Curwen, Hugh (archbishop of Dublin),
46

Daniel, Edmund, 310
Darnley, Henry, Lord, 218, 323
Davies, Richard (*bishop of St David's),
20, 30, 30 n., 44, 46, 47 n., 67, 126,
136, 137 n.
Davies, Thomas (*bishop of St Asaph's),
19, 23, 46, 47
Day, John, 21
Day, William (*provost of Eton Col-
lege), 54–5, 68, 359
De excommunicato capiendo, writ of, 75,
174

De Maisse, French ambassador to England, 160

Decalogue, to be set up in churches, 149, 150; *see also* Creed, Lord's Prayer, and Decalogue

Derby, archdeacon of, *see* Walker, Richard

'Device for the alteration of religion', 80

Dickens, A. G., 4 n., 339–40

Discipline, 67, 129, 138–9, 141, 169, 212, 260, 341, 347–8, 354
  Calvinist, 27, 170, 174, 180, 233, 279, 336, 338
  for laity, 164, 166, 169–75, 256, 279, 288, 347, 354–5
  reform of, 57, 61, 68–73, 77, 85, 85 n., 162, 228, 344–5, 350–2, 355
  see also Doctrine, discipline for

Dixon, Richard Watson, 17 n., 38 n., 70 n., 71, 159

Doctrine, 100, 170, 185, 214, 233–90, 333, 338–40
  discipline for, 170–2, 255–7, 280–9, 317, 335, 338–9, 349, 355–6
  reform of, 4, 9–11, 12, 16–18, 57, 61, 69–70, 72, 77, 97, 228, 344–5, 347–9
  subscription to, clergy, *see* Clergy, subscription to doctrine; diocesan officials, 256; laity, 282–3, 288
  see also Anabaptists, doctrine of; Lutheran churches, doctrine of; Reformed churches, doctrine of; Roman Catholic Church, doctrine of

Dodds, Gregory (*d. Exeter, p. cath. Exeter), 7 n., 357–9

Dorset, archdeacon of, *see* Cottrel, John

Downham, William (bishop of Chester), 23, 46, 248 n., 325

Dudley, John, duke of Northumberland, 15–16, 20, 23

Dudley, Robert, earl of Leicester, 188, 211, 218, 220, 298, 306

Dugmore, Charles William, 84, 93 n., 244, 267–9

Durham
  bishops of, *see* Barnes, Richard; Pilkington, James; Tunstall, Cuthbert

cathedral, 19, 22

deans of, *see* Horn, Robert; Watson, Thomas; Whittingham, William

diocese of, 15, 22, 37, 40–1, 45, 156, 156 n., 161, 242 n.

Ebden, John (*p. cl.? Winchester), 359

Edification, 122, 233

Edward VI Tudor, and church policies of his reign, 4, 12–19, 31, 45, 53, 57, 81, 92–4, 95, 105, 130, 132, 143, 147, 153, 161, 169, 184, 191, 196, 201, 227–8, 234, 236, 237–8, 270, 333
  royal visitation of, 12, 138; *see also* Injunctions, royal, of Edward VI

Election, *see* predestination

Elizabeth I Tudor, 1, 32, 33, 81, 200, 211, 220, 224, 273, 285, 298, 324, 333
  accession and early intentions for church, 31, 81, 85, 90, 91, 94–5, 98–100, 144
  proposed interim policy, 94–5, 97, 98, 100, 111, 127
  chapel royal of, 25, 81, 82, 89, 91, 93–4, 95, 95 n., 106, 107, 129–30, 130 n., 168, 185–9, 190, 192–4, 197–8, 231, 338
    cross in, 183, 185–9, 189 n., 190, 192–4, 203, 206, 210, 231, 338
  chaplains, 23, 48, 177–8, 351
  church policies, 80, 93, 104, 108, 126, 139, 160–1, 166–7, 181–2, 187, 190–2, 195–6, 198–200, 200–1, 207–8, 208–9, 211–13, 215–17, 218–20, 222, 228–32, 253–5, 254 n., 273–5, 278, 285, 287 n., 300–2, 325, 337–41
  finances, 45, 152–61
  government through hierarchy, 130, 131, 134–5, 181, 202, 204, 218–19, 222–3, 224–5, 227–8, 232, 286–7, 338
  Injunctions, *see* Injunctions, royal, of Elizabeth
  leaders, choice of, 33–6, 41–2, 43–50, 129, 131–4, 204, 236, 334, 337
  proclamations and other royal orders, December 1558, 81, 88,

Index

Elizabeth I Tudor, proclamations (*cont.*)
138; March 1559, 92–4; September 1560, 148–9; August 1561, 201–5; October 1561, 149–50, 201
  patronage, use of, 51, 51 n., 154, 156–8
  representation at Council of Trent, 294–6, 298, 300–2, 303–5, 309
  Roman Catholics, 291–2, 311–13, 319–21, 322–4, 326–32, 337–8
  supremacy, use of, 69, 81, 94, 105, 112, 115, 116–17, 119, 128–30, 143, 166, 181–2, 211, 213, 215–17, 217 n., 218–19, 225, 227–8, 236, 253–4, 255, 270–1, 285, 287, 335–8, 341
  visitation, 112, 135–9, 141, 144, 163, 181, 184–5, 187, 197–8, 203
illegitimacy, 52, 306
princess, 6, 23, 97
progresses, 187, 198, 201, 204
relations with bishops, 166, 181, 183, 200, 204–5, 210–11, 227–8, 228–32, 285–8, 300–1, 337
religious convictions, viii–ix, 25, 52, 82, 105, 107–11, 129–30, 147, 182, 187, 189, 198–200, 200–5, 208, 217, 220, 224, 229, 231–2, 236–7, 254–5, 270–1, 271 n., 275, 285–7, 300–2, 325, 328, 329–32, 333–5, 337–41
Elizabethan settlement of religion, vii, 3, 32, 52, 78, 97, 99–100, 119, 126–7, 135, 139, 142, 166, 181–2, 183, 198–9, 210–11, 216–17, 228, 231–2, 235–6, 258–9, 280, 288–90, 300, 309, 333–4
Ellis, John (*d. Hereford), 253 n., 359
Ely
  archdeacon of, *see* Wisdom, Robert
  bishops of, *see* Cox, Richard; Heton, Matthew; Thirlby, Thomas
  cathedral, 17, 202
  dean of, *see* Perne, Andrew
  diocese of, 22, 37–40, 43, 136, 157–8, 157–8 n., 161
Emden, 26–7
Epiphanius, 191–2

Episcopacy, 176, 200, 225, 227, 228, 240, 251, 257, 272, 279, 297, 325, 336, 340; *see also* Ministry, doctrine of
Erasmus, Desiderius, 152, 252
Essex, 201, 322
  archdeacon of, *see* Cole, Thomas
Este, Ippolito de, Cardinal de Ferrara, 303–4
Eton College, provost of, *see* Day, William
Eucharist, *see* Holy Communion
Evans, Hugo (*d. St Asaph's), 358
Exeter
  archdeacon of, *see* Carew, George
  bishops of, *see* Alley, William; Coverdale, Miles; Turberville, James
  cathedral, 167
  dean of, *see* Dodds, Gregory
  diocese of, 22, 37, 40, 44, 137
Exiles (émigrés), Henrician and Edwardian, 8, 18, 26
  Marian, 21, 26–32, 34, 43, 48–9, 50, 64, 77, 84, 89, 95, 96, 105, 107–9, 126, 132 n., 133, 136–8, 183–4, 196, 203–4, 208–9, 209 n., 223, 229–32, 238–9, 283, 334, 359
  'Declaration of doctrine', 238–9, 249, 267
  Elizabethan, 200, 305, 307, 322–3, 325, 328, 329 n.

Faith and justification by faith, doctrine of, 121, 238–9, 241, 245, 249, 262, 262 n.
Feckenham, John, 7, 21, 33–5, 48, 81, 103–4, 321, 323
Ferdinand I, emperor, 115, 185, 293, 297, 305–6, 307, 322, 324–5
Feria, count of, Gomez Suarez de Figueroa, 39, 82, 89, 92, 95, 96, 100–1, 105
Field, John, 336
Finances of the church, 6–7, 15, 66, 69, 151–61, 166, 180–1, 229, 333, 338, 345, 354–5
  episcopal incomes, 7, 15, 45, 46–7, 76, 152–61, 193

Index

Finances of the church (*cont.*)
 leases of church property, 154–6, 161, 179, 351
 parish benefices, 61, 75, 151, 154, 161, 165, 167, 167 n., 176, 179–80, 181, 338, 344, 347
 pluralities and non-residence, 47, 47 n., 157, 167, 167 n., 176–8, 350–1
 tithes, impropriated, 123, 153–6, 161, 167, 178–9
 personal, 179
 transfer of income from Rome to Crown, 4, 82–3, 151, 153
Fitzalan, Henry, earl of Arundel, 95, 136
Fleetwood, William, 137 n.
Fletcher, Richard, 159 n.
Flude (Fluyde, Fluydd), William (*p. cl.? Peterborough), 354, 358
Foxe, John, 21, 30, 133, 170
France, 30, 65, 99, 168, 242–3, 258, 291, 293, 294, 296, 303–5, 309, 310–12, 313, 314, 322, 329, 336
 French embassy in London, 310, 316
 Huguenots, 243, 304, 313, 316
Frankfort, 29, 31, 196, 397
 'New Discipline', 29–30, 49, 74, 133, 226, 279, 359
 Prayer Book dispute, 29, 84, 85 n., 359
Frederick III, elector Palatine, 243
Freke, Edmund, 159 n.
Frere, Walter Howard, 70, 70 n., 71 n., 115, 358
Frith, John, 8

Gallican Confession, 235, 263 n.
Gardiner, Stephen, 5, 10, 12, 15, 20
Garrett, Christine Hollowell, 26, 132 n., 359
Garthe (Garth), Gregory (*p. cath. Ely), 358
Gee, Henry, 38 n., 51 n., 135, 186–7, 322
Geneva, 18, 27–8, 29, 30, 31, 49, 132 n., 148, 175, 260, 280, 281, 336, 359
 Catechism of, 29, 235, 279
 Confession of, 235
 Consensus Genevensis, 235
 Service book of, 79, 85 n., 168, 338

Gerard, Gilbert, 133, 134 n.
German princes, *see* Lutheran princes
Gibson, Edgar C. S., 262 n.
Gibson, Edmund, x, 53, 55, 58–9, 60, 63, 66, 342
Gilpin, Bernard, 44 n., 204 n.
Gloucester
 archdeacon of, *see* Heton, Guido
 bishops of, *see* Cheyney, Richard; Hooper, John
 cathedral, 24
 deans of, *see* Man, John; Saul, Arthur, who acted as proctor for at 1563 Convocation
 diocese of, 15, 46, 137, 155 n., 157, 157 n., 354
Glynn, William, 23, 24
Godwin (Godwyn), Thomas (*p. cl. Lincoln), 359
Goldwell, Thomas, 5, 7, 18, 22, 37, 41
Gonville Hall, Cambridge, 116
Goodman, Christopher, 30, 184, 311
Goodman, Gabriel (*d. Westminster), 56, 134, 224, 358
Goodrich, Richard, 81, 132–3, 134 n.
Government by women, 31, 239, 241–2
Granvelle, Cardinal de, 306
Grey, Lady Jane, 20, 49
Grindal, Edmund (*bishop of London), 17, 19, 27, 29, 43, 54–5, 57, 59, 60, 63, 67, 68, 87, 89, 99, 102, 115 n., 121 n., 131, 134–5, 159 n., 190, 192, 196, 199, 204, 205, 206–8, 209, 213, 219, 221, 224–5, 225 n., 228–30, 253 n., 273 n., 320–1, 344–5
Grinsel, Robert (*a. Shropshire, p. cl. Hereford, p. cath. Hereford), 357–8
Gualter, Rodolph, 2 n., 60 n., 232
Guest, Edmund (*bishop of Rochester), 19, 25, 44, 45, 97–8, 102, 123, 124 n., 131, 134–5, 196, 211 n., 213, 214 n., 248, 250–1, 252–3, 253 n., 254, 254 n., 254–5 n., 256 n., 267, 352, 357
Guy, Richard (*p. cl. Bristol), 358

Index

Haddon, Walter, 116, 116 n., 132, 134 n., 226
Halford, 19 n.
Harding, Thomas, 243-4, 246 n.
Hardwick, Charles, 342, 352 n.
Harington, John, 156, 157, 200
Harpsfield, Nicholas, 87, 102
Harvey, George (*a. Cornwall), 357-8
Harvey, Henry, 137
Heath, Nicholas, 5, 6, 9, 10, 11, 13, 14, 15, 16, 18, 19 n., 20, 22, 36-9, 42, 311, 313, 321, 323
Heidelberg Catechism, 235, 263 n.
Helvetic Confession
first, 235, 238
second, 84 n., 235
Henry II, king of France, 115
Henry VIII Tudor and church policies of his reign, 4, 5-12, 15, 16, 17, 40, 49, 53, 57, 83, 89, 92, 95, 105, 129-30, 145-6, 147, 152, 155, 161, 164, 178, 196, 234, 235-6, 258, 271, 323, 340
Hereford
archdeacon of, 226; see also Cheyney, Richard; Crowley, Robert
bishop of, see Scory, John
dean of, see Ellis, John
diocese of, 43, 74, 136
Heresy, 9-10, 21, 49, 88, 95, 105, 130, 133, 172, 174, 236, 271, 280-4, 288, 302, 307, 308, 330-1
Heton (Eaton, Etton), Guido (*a. Glou-cester), 359
Heton, Matthew, 158 n.
Heylen, Peter, 116 n.
Hill, Christopher, 152, 154, 154 n., 155, 336
Hill, Rowland, 133, 134 n.
Hills (Hylls), John (p. cl. Oxford), 359
Hills, Richard, 84, 84 n., 89, 108
Hinton, Anthony (*p. cl. Peterborough; also p. for unnamed a. Northamp-ton), 357-8
Hodgekin, John, 48 n.
Holy Communion, 12-13, 14, 55, 64, 70, 74, 92-5, 106, 113, 172, 197-8, 215, 225, 263, 264, 276, 313, 315, 326, 356

bread to be used, 112, 113, 119, 120, 125, 143, 163, 165, 197, 221
Christ's presence in, doctrine of, 13, 14, 24, 62, 87, 106-7, 108-9, 238-9, 241, 249, 250-1, 252, 254-5, 259, 264, 265-9, 272, 276, 279, 287, 289, 339
'black rubric', 14, 206-7
elevations at consecration, 81, 95
kneeling for communion, 14, 123, 125, 221, 353
frequency of, 214, 214 n.
holy table and stone altars, 112, 147, 189, 338
cloth covering for, 112, 150
position of holy table, 112, 113, 119, 120, 122, 125, 143, 148, 163, 165, 188, 338
requiem celebration of, 115-17, 115 n., 124, 125
reservation of, 114, 116-17, 186, 263
sacrifice in, doctrine of, 96, 238, 241, 262, 292
taken in two kinds, 12, 84, 92-5, 242, 294 n.
see also Latin Mass
Holy days, see Calendar, ecclesiastical
Holy Week, 1559, 92-100, 199
Homilies, book of, 167, 175, 214, 278, 289
first volume of, 16, 206, 236, 237-8, 246, 251, 252, 262, 270, 273
second volume of, 54, 206, 248, 264, 270, 273-6, 334
Homily
against peril of idolatry, 206-8, 210, 275
against rebellion, 276
Hooker, Richard, 339
Hooper, John, 13, 184, 221
Horn, Robert (*bishop of Winchester), 15, 17, 20, 22, 27, 28, 28 n., 29-30, 45, 59, 67, 67 n., 68, 95, 102, 136, 136 n., 137 n., 204 n., 206, 213, 222, 224, 228, 229, 231, 256 n., 298, 320-1
Howard, Thomas, duke of Norfolk, 76
Howard, William, 299

382

Index

Hubert, Conrad, 99

Huet (Hewitt, Hewit), Thomas (*precentor St David's, p. cl. St David's, p. cath. St David's), 7 n., 65 n., 357–8

Hughes, Philip, 310

Hughes (Hughs, Huys), Richard (*unknown), 357–8

Hughes (Hues), Robert (*p. cath. St Asaph's), 358

Huick, Thomas, 132, 132 n., 134 n., 136, 136 n.

Humphrey, Lawrence, 78, 211, 211 n., 218, 218 n., 221–2, 229, 266

Huntingdon, archdeacon of, see Beaumont, Robert

Images and iconoclasm, 12, 40, 70–1, 122, 138, 140–1, 143, 147–9, 183–200, 203, 205–8, 210, 220, 222, 228–31, 242, 262, 273, 334, 338, 356

  crucifix, 141, 189 n., 189–200, 204, 206, 216, 222, 228, 231–2, 275, 338
  see also Elizabeth, chapel royal of, cross in

  inexpedient, but not forbidden, 192, 207–8

  violation of second commandment, 191, 194, 206, 222, 275
  see also Homily, against peril of idolatry

Incent, John, 162

Injunctions, episcopal, see Visitations, episcopal

Injunctions, royal
  of Henry VIII, 9
  of Edward VI, 12, 16, 139 n., 139–41, 140 n., 141, 143, 205
  of Elizabeth I, 112, 113, 120, 127, 128, 135, 135–6 n., 138, 139–44, 146, 162–5, 166, 167, 168, 169, 170–1, 176–8, 181, 183–5, 186, 197, 200, 205, 205 n., 212, 215, 221, 236, 237, 251, 273, 333

Inner Temple Library (Petyt MSS), 53, 194, 28 4 n., 342–3, 346, 346 n., 353

Interpretations of the bishops, 120, 122, 163–5, 165 n., 197–200, 214–15, 240, 273, 273 n., 298

Ipswich, 201

Ireland, 29, 48, 113 n.

Italy, 5, 30, 359

Ithel, Thomas (*p. cl. Ely), 358

James I (VI) Stuart, 158, 159 n., 242, 281 n., 288, 337

Jesus, bowing at name of, 142, 143

Jewel, John (*bishop of Salisbury), 17, 19, 27, 29, 43, 67, 73, 94 n., 96, 96 n., 97, 99 n., 102, 105, 107–8, 136–7, 137 n., 184–5, 189–90, 192, 194–5, 196, 207, 208, 222, 229, 230, 238–9, 242–6, 243 n., 245 n., 246 n., 268 n., 303, 311

  Apologia Ecclesiae Anglicanae, 242–6, 247, 277, 289, 324, 345, 348

Jones, Walter (*a. Brecon), 358

Jones, William, 44 n.

Justification, see Faith

Katherine Bertie, duchess of Suffolk, 30, 86

Kemp, David (*a. St Albans), 358

Kemp, E. W., 59

Kennall (Kenal), John (*a. Oxford, p. cl. Oxford), 356, 357–8

Kennedy, William Paul McClure, 199 n.

King's Book, 11, 16

Kingsmill, Richard, 137 n.

Kitchin, Anthony (*bishop of Llandaff), 1 n., 7, 10, 11, 13, 14, 18, 22, 23, 36–8, 42, 47, 273 n., 352

Knollys, Francis, 73–4, 84–5, 132–3, 186, 192, 194, 218, 328

Knollys, Henry, 243

Knowles, David, 34

Knox, John, 27–8, 29, 30, 79, 84, 123, 184, 221

Lamb, John, 38 n., 352, 352 n., 357

Lambeth articles (1561), 134, 165, 297

Lancashire, 237, 314, 325–6

Index

Lancaster, Justinian (*a. Taunton), 358
Lancaster, Thomas (*treasurer, cath. Salisbury, thus probably p. cath.), 15, 47–8, 359
Latimer, Hugh, 21
Latimer (Latymer), William (*d. Peterborough, p. cath. Peterborough, a.? Westminster?), 24, 357–8
Latin Mass and other liturgies, 12, 81, 85, 87, 91, 93–5, 94 n., 123–5, 130, 185, 291, 313, 328
  illegal use of, 23, 301–2, 310, 313, 316, 317–18, 325–7, 352
  rejection of, 14, 31, 81, 84, 86, 107, 123–5, 165, 188, 318, 356
Laud, William, 131, 148, 253 n.
Lawrence (Lawrance), John (*a. Wiltshire), 7 n., 358
Lay readers, 164–5
Leicester, archdeacon of, see Barber, Richard
Lever, Thomas (*a. Coventry), 28, 29, 31, 48–9, 50 n., 65, 72, 105, 137, 153, 169, 188, 359
Leveson (Luson, Bucson), William (*a. Carmarthen), 357–8
Lewes, archdeacon of, see Weston, Edmund
Lincoln
  archdeacon of, see Aylmer, John
  bishops of, see Bullingham, Nicholas; Cooper, Thomas; Watson, Thomas
  cathedral, 23
  dean of, see Mallet, Francis
  diocese of, 22, 24, 37, 44, 47, 137, 155 n., 257
Linnett, Thomas, see Huet, Thomas
Litany, reformed
  Latin, 55
  English, 9, 54, 81, 82, 94–5, 106, 124, 138, 142, 145, 145 n., 163
Liturgy, 4, 12–15, 18, 27, 29, 61, 64–5, 69, 79–127, 162, 166–9, 180–1, 214, 228, 233–4, 269–70, 271, 276, 337–8, 344–5, 347, 353, 355
  vernacular, 9, 12–14, 93–5, 96, 102, 242, 249, 262, 333

Llandaff
  archdeacon of, see Smith, John
  bishop of, see Kitchin, Anthony
  diocese of, 37–8, 157, 157 n.
London, 184, 219, 226, 312, 322
  archdeacon of, see Mullins, John
  bishops of, see Aylmer, John; Bonner, Edmund; Grindal, Edmund; Ridley, Nicholas
  cathedral, see St Paul's
  diocese of, 15, 22, 37, 43, 131, 136, 219, 224–5, 228
Longland (Longlond), John (*a. Buckingham), 359
Lougher, Robert (*a. Totnes, p. cl. Exeter), 357–8
Lovelace, William, 137 n.
Lowth, John (*p. cl.? Gloucester), 354, 357–8
Luther, Martin, 5, 7, 10, 90, 233, 244, 254 n., 258, 261–3, 261 n., 262 n., 264 n., 266
Lutheran churches, 89, 107, 108, 223, 234–5, 245, 249, 258–9, 283
  attitudes towards English Church, 28, 30, 243, 258
  doctrine of, 10, 17, 78, 251, 254, 254 n., 258–72, 259 n., 284 n., 289, 338–40
Lutheran princes, 5, 10, 30, 258, 295–6, 297, 303–4, 305, 306, 309
Lylly, Peter, 137 n.

McAdoo, H. R., 339
MacGregor, Geddes, 263
Machyn, Henry, 89, 90 n., 115, 184–5, 188, 202, 310
Magdalen College, Oxford, 222
Maitland, Frederick William, 83, 187
Mallet, Francis (*d. Lincoln), 23, 24, 31, 358
Man, John, 161
Marburg, Colloquy of, 258
Margaret, Duchess of Parma, 294
Marprelate, Martin, 279
Marriage, 113, 113 n., 164, 172–3, 172 n., 241–2, 264, 276, 352

Index

Marriage, clerical, 16, 20, 24, 25, 35, 142–3, 151, 200–5, 232, 241, 249–50, 262

Martinengo, Abbot, 295–6, 299, 301–2, 313, 315

Mary Tudor and church policies of her reign, 3, 4, 7, 18, 20–6, 31, 32, 41, 43, 50, 52–3, 76, 81, 82, 92, 99, 100, 107, 124, 132, 133, 137, 153, 230, 280, 283, 291, 313
persecutions under, 21, 37, 124, 133, 139 n., 142, 291, 311

Mary Stuart, queen of Scotland, 188, 218, 291, 308–9, 316, 323

Mason, John, 39, 116, 144

Mass, see Holy Communion; Latin Mass

Masters, William, 137, 137 n.

May, William, 44–5, 45 n., 131, 134 n., 134, 138

Mayrick (Meyrall, Merril, Merick, Myrall), Edmund (*a. Bangor), 357–8

Melanchthon, Philip, 10, 30, 97, 234, 244, 245 n., 264–5 n., 266–7, 266 n., 268, 271

Merioneth, archdeacon of, see Robinson, Nicholas

Merrick, Rowland (*bishop of Bangor), 19, 20, 25, 44, 47 n., 136–7, 196

Meyer, Carl, 259 n., 262

Middlesex, archdeacon of, see Watts, Thomas

Militant reformers, see precisians

Ministry, doctrine of, 241, 251, 260, 273, 292; see also Congregational polity; Episcopacy; Presbyterianism

Molland, Einar, 259 n., 270

Monastic communities, 4, 6–8, 21, 81–2, 151, 153, 175, 178, 262

Morgan, Henry, 37, 40–1, 311 n.

Morgan, Hugo (*p. cl. Bangor), 358

Morice, Ralph, 137 n.

Morning and Evening Prayer (daily offices), 14, 106, 113, 117–18, 119, 129–30, 145, 214, 314–15
proposed reforms of, 122–3, 125

Moroni, Giovanni de, Cardinal, 296, 301–2, 307, 312

Mullins (Mullyns), John (*a. London, p. cl. London), 50 n., 357, 359

Mundt, Christopher, 243, 295–6, 304

Music, church, 143, 166, 168–9, 353, 355

Nagors, Richard, see Rogers, Richard

Neale, John E., vii, 73 n., 77, 80, 82, 84, 85, 85 n., 91, 93 n., 95, 96, 97, 98–101, 110, 154, 155 n., 160, 284, 286, 287–8, 287 n., 318–19, 320 n.

Neile, Richard, 159, 159 n.

Netherlands, 329
protestants in, 258

Nevinson (Nevynson), Stephen (*p. cl. Canterbury), 65 n., 137, 359

New College, Oxford, 23, 256 n.

Newman, John Henry, 259, 259 n.

Non-residence, see Finances of the church, pluralities and

Norley, Thomas (*p. cath. Worcester), 354, 357–8

Norwich
bishops of, see Parkhurst, John; Thirlby, Thomas
cathedral, 7, 241
dean of, see Salisbury, John
diocese of, 15, 39, 43 n., 44, 48, 137, 158 n.

Nowel, Robert, 137 n.

Nowell (Nowel), Alexander (*d. St Paul's), 54, 73, 134, 137, 220–1, 278–80, 309, 318, 330–2, 335–6, 353
Catechism of, 67, 68, 71, 73, 164, 176, 277–83, 278 n., 288–9, 335, 339, 345
English translation of, 278, 278 n.
'Middle Catechism', 278
in exile, 30, 31, 48–9, 50 n., 359
prolocutor of 1563 Convocation, 55–8, 60, 62, 72, 253 n., 277–8

Nowell (Nowel), Lawrence (*d. Lichfield), 65, 359

Obedience to civil authority as religious duty, 25, 30–1, 230, 239, 263, 270–1, 334

Index

'offendicle', 193-4
Oglethorpe, Owen, 6, 36-7, 42, 81, 102, 311 n.
Orarium, 147, 147 n.
'Order of Communion', 12, 13 n., 93-5
Ordinal and rites of ordination, 13, 75-6, 176, 251, 252, 256, 265, 272, 321
Ornaments rubric, 79, 106, 183-4, 197, 203, 208-9, 216-17, 225, 231
Orthodox (Eastern) churches, 259
Oxford
    archdeacon of, *see* Kennall, John
    bishop of, *see* Curwen, Hugh
    dean of, *see* Sampson, Thomas
    diocese of, 46-7, 46 n., 137, 155 n., 157-8, 158 n.
Oxford University, 17, 132, 222, 281 n.

Paget, William, 86
Papal obedience, *see* Rome, English obedience to
Papists, *see* Roman Catholic Church
Parish registers, 76
Parker, Matthew (*archbishop of Canterbury)
    before 1559, 6, 8, 11, 13, 16, 17, 20, 25
    archbishop-elect and nomination of, 33-6, 40-1, 43, 45, 89, 131, 184, 186, 209 n.
    archbishop, 1, 44, 46, 47 n., 50, 53-72, 110, 112, 116, 134-5, 144, 162, 164, 168, 190, 192-4, 195-6, 198-9, 200-4, 207-8, 211-30, 211 n., 213 n., 218 n., 225 n., 239-40, 244, 248, 251, 255, 273, 275, 278, 286, 312, 320, 320 n., 334-6, 342-6, 354
Parker, Mrs Matthew, 200
Parker's Advertisements, 135, 151, 213-17, 225-6, 229, 231, 232, 241 n., 255, 257, 335
Parker's *Correspondence*, 190, 193, 320 n.
Parker's Eleven Articles, *see* Articles, doctrinal, Eleven Articles
Parkhurst, John (*bishop of Norwich), 1, 2, 13, 27, 37, 44, 57, 78, 150, 162, 184, 188, 201, 204, 204 n., 206, 228, 230, 234

Parliaments, 236, 281, 318, 324, 325, 332, 336-8
    of Henry VIII, 9, 11
    of Edward VI, 12, 14, 16, 101, 101 n., 133
    of Mary I, 20-1, 133
    of Elizabeth I, 1559, 36, 40, 54, 77, 80, 81-111, 126, 129, 153-4, 170, 183-4, 186, 201, 203, 238, 284, 333-4, 336-7
    1563, 73-6, 126, 174, 179-80, 180 n., 208-9, 284, 291, 309, 316, 318-19, 330, 333, 343, 346
    1566, 285-6, 321
    1571, 167, 167 n., 170, 257, 257 n., 286-8
Parpaglia, abbot of San Saluto, 293-4, 294 n.
Parr, William, marquess of Northampton, 225
Parry, Thomas, 86
Parrye, Henry, 137, 137 n.
Pate (Pates), Richard, 5, 11, 18, 22, 37, 41, 311, 322-3
Pate, Richard (lawyer), 137 n.
Patristic age, as authority for sixteenth century, 11-12, 191-2, 206, 236, 239, 243, 244-6, 245 n., 246 n., 252, 256, 269, 289, 296-7, 324, 339
Paulet, William, Lord treasurer and marquess of Winchester, 76, 110
Peace negotiations at Cateau-Cambrésis, 35, 39, 99-100
Peculiar jurisdictions, 76, 178, 204
Pedder, John (*d. Worcester), 30, 48-9, 50 n., 65, 72, 353, 359
Penance
    private (auricular confession), 174
    public, 173-4, 355
Percy, Thomas, earl of Northumberland, 136
Perne, Andrew (*d. Ely), 17, 65, 358
Peter Martyr Vermigli, 16-17, 27, 85, 94, 96, 97, 99 n., 107, 140, 185, 189, 190, 194-6, 221, 230, 238, 243, 244, 263-4, 266-7, 268, 268 n., 303

Peterborough
  bishops of, *see* Pole, David; Scambler, Edmund
  dean of, *see* Latimer, William
  diocese of, 22, 37, 41, 46, 137, 354
Petre, William, 134 n.
Philip II Hapsburg, king of Spain, 20, 37, 39, 96, 110, 129, 220, 240, 258, 285, 294, 297, 298, 306–9, 314–15, 332
Piers, John, 159 n.
Pierson (Peerson), Andrew (*p. cl. Llandaff), 359
Pilkington, James (bishop of Durham), 19, 22, 27, 28, 28 n., 31, 44, 45, 45 n., 104, 134, 204 n., 211, 221, 226, 230, 248 n.
Pius IV, Pope, 293–300, 304, 305–7, 314
Pius V, Pope, 292, 307, 308
  bull of excommunication of Elizabeth, 291, 307, 326
Pluralism, *see* Finances of the church, pluralties and non-residence
Poland, 30, 86
Pole, David, 6, 10, 11, 13, 18, 21, 22, 37, 41, 312, 323, 323 n.
Pole, Reginald, 5, 20, 22, 32
Pound (Pownde), Robert (*p. cl. Berkshire, diocese of Salisbury), 358
Powell (Powel), Thomas (*p. cl. St Asaph's), 358
Poynet, John, 15, 17, 30
  Catechism of, 17, 18, 236, 279
Pratt, John (*a. St David's), 358
Prayers for the dead, *see* Burials; Holy Communion, requiem celebrations of
Preaching, 9, 16, 49, 136, 163, 166–7, 175, 177, 203, 207, 210, 220, 237, 246, 255, 256, 270, 276, 350–1, 356
  at court, 33, 34, 87, 88–90, 188, 209 n., 224
  licences for, 163, 165, 214, 256, 344
  required in parishes, 9, 140, 143, 143 n.
  at St Paul's Cross, 20, 95–6, 152, 221, 246, 321
  other sermons, 5–6, 54–5, 82, 95–6, 298, 335

Preces Privatae (1564), 147, 147 n.
Precisians, use of term, viii, 50
Precisians (militant reformers), 2, 50–1, 53, 61, 64–5, 67, 71–3, 76–8, 79–80, 105, 114, 119–27, 128–9, 133, 137, 147, 148, 150, 162, 165, 166, 168–9, 172–3, 175–7, 181, 183–5, 196, 198–200, 205–6, 210–11, 228–32, 247–8, 272, 277, 280–5, 286–8, 311, 317–22, 324, 327–31, 333–41
Predestination and election, 239, 250, 252, 261–2, 263, 263 n., 279, 283–4, 284 n.; *see also* Geneva, *Consensus Genevensis*
Presbyterianism, 176, 280, 336, 340
Price (ApRice), John (*p. cler. St Asaph's), 358
Primers, Medieval, 9
  Reformed, traditional type
    Henrician editions, 9, 144
    Edwardian editions, 14, 145
    Elizabethan editions, 144–7, 181, 280
  Reformed, drastically revised type
    Edwardian edition, 14–15, 145–6, 146 n.
    Elizabethan editions, 145–7
Primus, John Henry, 212, 215–16
Privy Council
  under Edward VI, 12, 14, 15–16, 22, 130, 141, 221, 227–8
  under Elizabeth I, 37, 39, 81, 87, 88, 89, 96, 101, 103, 110, 133, 142, 154 n., 180, 186, 215–16, 218–19, 221–2, 224–5, 226–8, 232, 299, 302–3, 306, 313, 315–16, 321–3, 325, 338
Processions, 140, 143, 143 n., 163, 165, 214
Procter, James (*p. cl. Salisbury?), 7 n., 358
Prophesyings, 219
Puckering, John, 157 n., 158, 158 n.
Pullan, John (*a. Colchester), 28, 31, 48–9, 50 n., 65, 359
Purgatory, doctrine of, 241, 242, 262; *see also* Burials; Holy Communion, requiem celebrations of

Index

Puritans, 50, 53, 59–60, 85, 118–19, 121, 122, 123, 154, 175, 204, 216, 217, 228, 257, 261, 263, 279–80, 286–8, 328, 336, 339–41

Quadra, Bishop Alvaro de, 37, 39, 40, 185–6, 189, 197, 240, 293, 294, 297–300, 299 n., 309–12, 314–17, 318–19, 320 n.

Read, Conyers, 187, 299 n.
Reeve (Reve), Richard (*p. chapter of Westminster), 358
Reformatio Legum Ecclesiasticarum ('bill for 32 persons'), 18, 70, 91 n., 169–70, 170 n.
Reformed churches, 78, 245, 269, 338–40
    abroad, 27–9, 85, 108, 127, 175, 230–1, 243, 272
    doctrine of, 233, 250, 251, 258–72, 289, 338–9
    see also Discipline, Calvinist; Calvin, John; France, Huguenots; Netherlands, protestants; Zwinglians
Reformers, continental, 11, 26, 124, 169, 230–1, 233, 245–6, 262, 265 n., 268, 280, 288–9; *see also* Bucer, Martin; Bullinger, Henry; Calvin, John; Cassander, George; Gualter, Rodolph; Luther, Martin; Lutheran churches; Melanchthon, Philip; Peter Martyr Vermigli; Reformed churches; Zwinglians
Reformers, militant, *see* Precisians
Reformers, moderate, 53, 71, 77, 79–80, 135, 137, 147, 175, 183–5, 195–6, 198–200, 210–11, 232, 243, 334, 340
Reforming party in the 1559 House of Commons, 77, 83, 84, 86, 88, 91, 95, 97, 98–100, 104, 107–11, 126–7, 183–5, 195–6, 211, 232, 288
Renaissance, 152, 291
Renyger, Michael (*p. cath. Winchester), 359
Requiem Masses, *see* Holy Communion, requiem celebrations of
Richley, Thomas, *see* Bickley, Thomas

Ridley, Nicholas, 15, 21
Rishton, Edward, 293–4, 326
Roberts, Thomas (*p. cl. Norwich), 358
Robinson, Nicholas (*a. Merioneth), 24, 358
Rochester
    archdeacon of, *see* Bridgewater, John
    bishops of, *see* Guest, Edmund; Scory, John
    cathedral, 214 n., 156 n.
    diocese of, 43 n., 44, 45, 137, 155 n., 162
Rogers (Nagors), Richard (*a. St Asaph's), 50 n., 158 n., 359
Roman Catholic Church and English Roman Catholics, 20–3, 50, 51, 53, 76, 78, 80, 81, 95, 100, 104, 105, 107, 187, 194, 200, 202, 218, 223, 238, 243, 246, 247, 248, 258–60, 285, 287, 291–332, 337
    conformity to Elizabethan settlement, 314–15, 325–6, 328–9
    doctrine of, 17, 234–5, 241–2, 245, 249–50, 263, 265–6
    English obedience to Rome, 4–5, 11–12, 20, 22–3, 32–3, 52, 62, 82–3, 138, 258, 294, 299, 301, 311, 318, 328, 337
    papal authority, defence of, 20, 87–8, 90, 102, 103, 127, 238, 291, 294, 295, 314, 323, 328
    sedition alleged against English government, 299, 301–2, 310–12, 316, 324–5, 327–8
    threat of coalition against England, 294, 308–9
    anti-Roman Catholic proposals and actions, 70, 73–4, 76, 83, 106, 123–4, 139, 139 n., 145, 145 n., 153, 172, 205, 228–9, 246, 251, 252, 262–3, 265, 275, 283, 289, 299, 300–1, 309–17, 317–24, 325–7, 329–31, 333–4, 352
    see also Council of Trent; Latin Mass and other liturgies; Vatican
Rood beams with crucifix, Mary, and John, 149–50, 185, 190, 195, 203, 205–6, 216, 222, 338
Rowse, A. L., 126, 159, 187, 292, 337

Index

Royal supremacy, 88, 91, 103, 135, 139, 236
doctrine and definition of, 143, 236–7, 241, 251, 252, 270–1
exercise of, 15–16, 20, 22, 130, 181
title for, 4, 83, 105, 143, 251
see also Elizabeth, government through hierarchy, supremacy, use of; Supremacy Act; Supremacy oath
Russell, Francis, earl of Bedford, 211, 218, 226, 296

Sackford, Thomas, 133, 134 n.
Sackville, Thomas, 306–7
Sacraments, doctrine of, 170, 239, 249, 250–1, 252–3, 254, 263–9, 279; *see also* Baptism, doctrine of; Holy Communion, doctrine of Christ's presence in
St Albans, archdeacon of, *see* Kemp, David
St Asaph's
archdeacon of, *see* Rogers, Richard
bishops of, *see* Davies, Richard; Davies, Thomas; Goldwell, Thomas
dean of, *see* Evans, Hugo
diocese of, 38, 44, 46, 155 n.
St David's
archdeacon of, *see* Pratt, John
bishops of, *see* Davies, Richard; Morgan, Henry; Young, Thomas
cathedral, 19
diocese of, 37, 40, 44, 45, 46, 155 n.
precentors of, *see* Huet, Thomas; Young, Thomas
St John's College, Cambridge, 22
St Patrick's deanery, Dublin, 161
St Paul's Cathedral, London, 43, 45, 54–5, 186, 197, 218 n., 226, 333, 335, *passim*
deans of, *see* Cole, Henry; May, William; Nowell, Alexander
Saints, cult of, 9, 118–19, 220, 241, 242, 262, 314, 328
Saints' days, *see* Calendar, ecclesiastical
Salisbury
archdeacon of, *see* Chandler, Richard
bishops of, *see* Jewel, John
cathedral, 48, 214 n.
diocese of, 43, 137, 157, 157 n.

Salisbury, John (*d. Norwich, a. Anglesey), 7, 7 n., 11, 24, 48 n., 358
Salop, archdeacon of, *see* Bolt, Thomas
Salvyn, John, 137 n.
Sampson, Thomas (*d. Oxford), 13, 27, 28, 29, 30–1, 48–9, 48 n., 50 n., 56, 68, 95, 111, 188–9, 193, 197, 211, 211 n., 218, 218 n., 221–3, 226, 229, 266, 359
Sander (Sanders), Nicholas, 34, 34 n., 39, 96 n., 312–13
Sanderson, Robert, 339
Sandys, Edwin (*bishop of Worcester), 19, 20, 27, 29, 44, 56–7, 67, 89, 102, 121–2, 136–7, 137 n., 159 n., 162, 184, 190, 192, 195, 196, 198, 201, 205, 206; *see also* Convocation of 1563, documents, Bishop Sandys' proposals
Saul (Saull), Arthur (*p. cath. Gloucester; also p. for unnamed d. Gloucester), 50 n., 357, 359
Savage, George (*p. cl. Gloucester), 358
Scambler, Edmund (*bishop of Peterborough), 19, 19 n., 26, 46
Schifanoya, Il, 33, 35, 38–9, 81–3, 89, 90–1, 92, 93–4, 94 n.
Schoolmasters (teachers), 142, 146, 146 n., 164, 278, 280, 289, 318
Scory, John (*bishop of Hereford), 6, 7, 13, 14, 15, 19, 20, 27, 27 n., 43, 67, 68, 89, 102
Scot, Cuthbert, 18, 21, 22, 36–7, 42, 90, 90 n., 102, 311–12, 322–3
Scotland, 65, 152, 184, 220, 234, 258, 307, 310, 312, 336
Scottish confession (1560), 234, 263 n.
Sexual morality, 72, 139, 173–4, 350
Seymour, Edward, duke of Somerset, 16
Shoreham, deanery of, 257 n.
Shropshire, archdeacon of, *see* Grinsel, Robert
Silva, Canon Guzman de, 110, 129, 188, 211, 218, 218 n., 220, 224, 285, 308, 321
Simony, 139, 165, 176–7
Six Articles Act, 11, 16, 130 n.

389

Index

Smith, John (*a. Llandaff), 358
Smith, Nicholas (*p. cl. Hereford), 358
Smith, Thomas, 81, 132, 132 n., 134 n.,
    161, 316, 319
Sodor and Man
    bishop of, see Stanley, Thomas
    diocese of, 22, 36, 42, 158–9 n., 352 n.
Sorby (Sorbaeus, Soreby, Serbis), Tho-
    mas (*p. cl. Chichester), 50 n., 359
Southcote, John, 133, 134 n.
Southgate, W. M., 189 n., 244, 245 n.
Spain, 294, 309, 310; see also Philip II
    Hapsburg
Spanish embassy in London, 316
Spanish Inquisition, 291, 316
Spencer, Thomas (*a. Chichester), 50 n.,
    359
Spielmann, Richard M., 329 n.
Squire, Henry (*a. Barnstaple), 358
Stafford, archdeacon of, see Walker,
    Richard
Stanley, Henry, earl of Derby, 23, 299
Stanley, Thomas (bishop of Sodor and
    Man), 22, 36, 36 n., 42, 352 n.
Staples, Edward, 47 n.
Stevens, John, 34, 34 n.
Stoke Clare, College of, 6
Storey, John, 317, 319
Stowe, John, 321
Strasbourg (Strasburg), 16, 18, 27, 28,
    29, 30, 133, 359
Strype, John, ix–xi, 33, 34, 37 n., 54, 60,
    61, 69, 70, 70 n., 115, 132, 154 n.,
    162, 180 n., 211 n., 213, 217 n., 239,
    253, 277, 284 n., 324–5 n., 342–8,
    353–6, 357
Suffolk, 201, 203
    archdeacon of, see Wendon, Nicholas
Supremacy acts, 4–5, 80, 83–92, 97, 103,
    104–5, 130, 236, 280, 289, 316, 333
Supremacy, oath of, 37, 38, 53, 74, 106 n.,
    135–6 n., 165, 215, 318–19
Surrey, 323
    archdeacon of, see Watson, John
Swearing, 173–4
Sweden, Church of, 340
Sykes, Norman, 59

Talbot, Francis, earl of Shrewsbury, 90,
    95, 115
Talbot, Thomas, 284 n.
Taunton, archdeacon of, see Lancaster,
    Justinian
Thetford, suffragan bishop of, see Salis-
    bury, John
Thirlby, Thomas, 5, 7, 11, 13, 14, 15, 16,
    18, 22, 37–41, 311, 321, 323
Throckmorton, Nicholas, 242–3, 293–6,
    300–2, 303–5, 311
Tiepolo, Venetian ambassador in France,
    294, 294 n.
Todd, William (*a. Bedford), 358
Totnes, archdeacon of, see Lougher,
    Robert
Tremaine (Tremayn), Richard (*p. cl.
    Exeter), 354, 359
Trinity and Christology, doctrine of, 205,
    206, 239, 241, 242, 248–9, 259
Tunstall, Cuthbert, 9, 15, 16, 18, 20, 22,
    37–8, 40–2, 311 n.
Turberville, James, 18, 22, 37, 40–1, 311,
    321–3, 323 n.
Turnbull, Hugo (*d. Chichester), 358
Turner, William (*d. Wells), 357, 359
Tyler, Philip, 130 n., 131 n., 134
Tyndale, William, 8

Uniformity acts, 13–14, 80, 84, 85, 97,
    104–11, 118 n., 130, 171–2, 184, 215,
    236, 280–1, 314, 316, 324, 332, 333
Universities and students, 88, 178, 281,
    349, 355
Usher, Roland, 152, 155

Valor Ecclesiasticus, 66, 155–6
Vatican, 220, 258, 292, 295, 304, 305,
    307–9, 314, 324–5 n., 326
    hopes of winning Elizabeth's al-
        legiance, 292–4, 296–8, 301, 302–3,
        307–8, 337
    military and political plans against
        English government, 305–6, 307,
        308, 329
    willingness to recognize Elizabeth's
        crown, 291, 293–4, 308

Vaux, Lawrence, 325–6
Vestiarian controversy
  under Edward VI, 13, 49, 228
  under Elizabeth I, 64, 77, 79, 163,
    183–5, 196–200, 208–10, 211–32,
    286, 334–5, 344
  see also Clergy, street wear; Vest-
    ments; Ornaments rubric
Vestments, 13–14, 93–4, 106, 108–9, 142,
    149, 183–5, 186, 196–200, 205, 208–
    10, 209 n., 211, 215, 222, 225, 228–
    32, 334
  cope, 106, 183, 196–8, 203, 208, 209,
    210, 215, 230, 231, 338
  eucharistic (mass), vestments, chasuble,
    'a vestment', 106, 184, 197–9, 208,
    209, 216, 230, 231–2, 338
  rochet and chimere, 230
  surplice, 106, 184, 197, 201, 203, 208,
    209, 210, 211, 215, 221, 226, 227,
    230, 338, 353
  tippet, 220, 224
Vicar-general for ecclesiastical affairs, *see*
  Cromwell, Thomas
Visitations and injunctions, episcopal,
    115, 124, 146, 150, 151, 162, 171,
    204, 206, 240, 273, 277, 277 n.
Visitation, royal, *see* Edward VI, royal
  visitation; Elizabeth I, visitation

Wales, 44, 47 n., 126, 135, 136, 316
  Welsh Bible and Prayer Book, 74,
    126
Walker, John (*p. cl. Suffolk, diocese
  of Norwich), 65 n., 358
Walker, Richard (*a. Stafford, a. Derby),
    72, 357–8
Warner, John (*d. Winchester), 358
Watson, John (*a. Surrey), 358
Watson, Thomas, 18, 22, 37, 41–2, 102,
    311, 319, 321–4
Watts, Thomas (*a. Middlesex, p. cath.
  London), 50 n., 134, 353, 357, 359
Wells, archdeacon of, *see* Cottrell, John
  dean of, *see* Turner, William
Wendon, Nicholas (*a. Suffolk), 357–8
Wesel, 28, 49

Westminster Abbey, 7, 19, 21, 48, 54,
    57, 73, 81, 82, 101, 101 n., 204
  abbot of, *see* Feckenham, John
  deans of, *see* Bill, William; Cox,
    Richard; Goodman, Gabriel
Westminster
  bishop of, *see* Thirlby, Thomas
  diocese of, 7, 15
Westminster disputation, 39, 96 n., 96–
    104, 107, 249
Weston, Edmund (*a. Lewes), 358
Weston, Robert (*p. cl. Coventry and
  Lichfield), 354, 358
Weston, Robert, 132–3, 132 n., 134 n.,
    137 n.; identical with preceding?,
    see 132 n.
White, John, 37, 41–2, 91 n., 102, 311 n.
White, Thomas (*a. Berkshire), 23, 358
Whitehead, David, 29, 30, 33–5, 48–9,
    50, 89, 102
Whitgift, John, 118, 156, 157–8, 158 n.,
    166, 217, 217 n., 257 n., 279
Whittingham, William, 211
Wiburn, Percival (*p. cath. Rochester),
    50 n., 359
Wickham, William, 257 n.
Wilkins, David, 70–1
Wilson, Thomas (*p. cl.? Worcester),
    50 n., 359
Wilson, Thomas, 156 n.
Wiltshire, archdeacon of, *see* Lawrence,
  John
Winchester
  archdeacon of, *see* Cheston, Stephen
  bishops of, *see* Gardiner, Stephen;
    Horn, Robert; Poynet, John; White
    John
  cathedral, 214 n.
  college, 67 n., 214 n.
  dean of, *see* Warner, John
  diocese of, 15, 37, 44, 45, 45 n., 137,
    156, 156 n., 161
Windsor
  collegiate chapel, 204
  dean of, *see* Carew, George
Wisdom, Robert (*a. Ely), 8, 48–9,
    50 n., 137, 359

Index

Withers, George, 2 n., 60 n., 221
Wittenberg, 258–9, 260
Wittenberg Concord, 266 n.
Wolsey, Thomas, Cardinal, 5
Worcester
    bishops of, see Heath, Nicholas; Hooper, John; Pate, Richard; Sandys, Edwin
    cathedral, 354
    dean of, see Pedder, John
    diocese of, 5, 13, 15, 22, 37, 44, 137, 196
    St Helen's, 19 n.
Wotton, Nicholas (*d. Canterbury), 10, 13, 33–5, 161, 357–8
Wren, Christopher, 148
Wrotham, 19 n.
Würtemberg
    Confession of, 249, 254 n.
    duke of, see Christopher, duke of Würtemberg
Wyllett, Thomas, 137

Yale, Thomas, 66, 134
York
    archbishops of, see Grindal, Edmund; Heath, Nicholas; Young, Thomas
    dean of, see Wotton, Nicholas
    diocese of, 22, 37–9, 44–5, 155 n.
    province of, 44–6, 134, 137, 226, 248, 352 n.
Young, Thomas (archbishop of York), 19, 27, 44, 45–6, 47 n., 134, 136–7, 196, 224, 226, 248, 248 n.

Zealous reformers, see Precisians
Zurich, 17, 27, 28, 29, 108, 188, 230, 238, 243, 359
    Consensus Tigurinus, 235, 239, 268 n.
    correspondence with England, 1, 2, 59, 85, 223, 229
Zwinglians, 17, 89, 107, 235, 245, 250, 251, 252, 258, 260, 263, 265–6, 265 n.